The History
of the 51st Highland Division

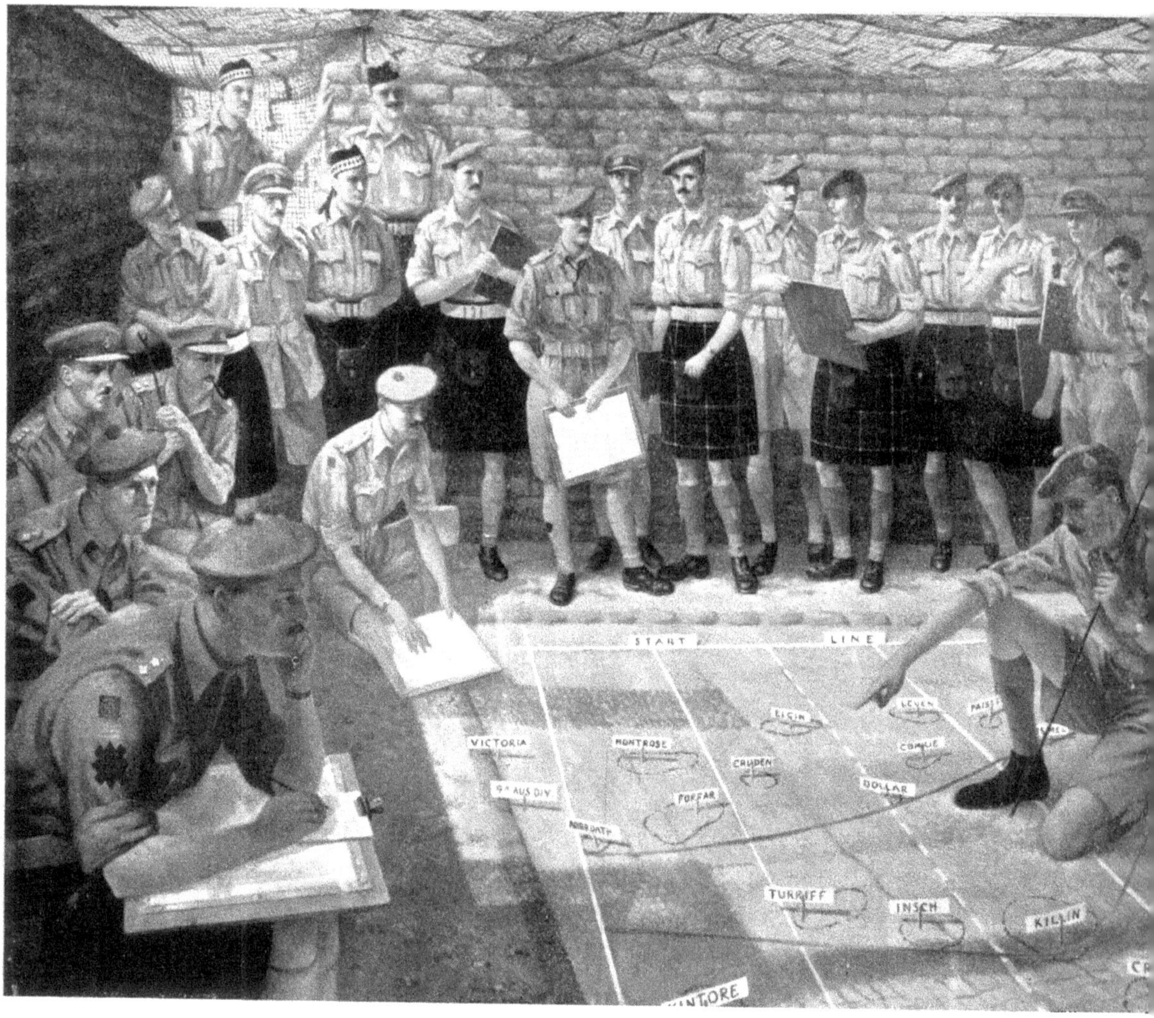

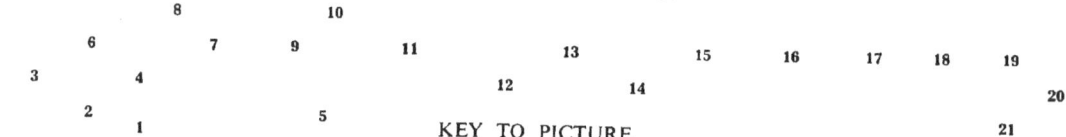

PLANNING FOR ALAMEIN

8 10

6 7 9 11 13 15 16 17 18 19

3 4 12 14 20

2 1 5 21

KEY TO PICTURE

1. Lt.-Col. J. A. Oliver, 7th Bn. Black Watch.
2. Lt.-Col. McKessack, 2nd Bn. Seaforth Highlanders.
3. Col. Galloway, A.D.M.S.
4. Lt.-Col. J. Colam, A.A. and Q.M.G.
5. Lt.-Col. R. Grant, Div. Recce. Regiment.
6. Lt.-Col. L. Campbell, 7th Bn. Argyll and Sutherland Highlanders.
7. Brig. G. Elliot, Commander Royal Artillery.
8. Lt.-Col. R. Saunders, 5/7th Bn. Gordon Highlanders.
9. Lt.-Col. H. Murray, 1st Bn. Gordon Highlanders.
10. Lt.-Col. R. D. M. C. Miers, 5th Bn. Cameron Highlanders.
11. Lt.-Col. T. G. Rennie, 5th Bn. Black Watch.
12. Brig. D. A. H. Graham, 153 Brigade Commander.
13. Lt.-Col. A. Thicknesse, 126 Field Regiment R.A.
14. Brig. H. W. Houldsworth, 154 Brigade Commander.
15. Lt.-Col. R. W. Urquhart, G.S.O.1.
16. Brig. H. Murray, 152 Brigade Commander.
17. Lt.-Col. R. Stirling, 5th Bn. Seaforth Highlanders.
18. Lt.-Col. W. N. Roper-Caldbeck, 1st Bn. Black Watch.
19. Lt.-Col. W. A. Shiel, 128 Field Regiment, R.A.
20. Lt.-Col. J. W. A. Stephenson, 7th Bn. Middlesex Regiment.
21. Maj.-Gen. D. N. Wimberley, Commanding 51st Division.

From the original painting by Ian G. M. Eadie

The History
of the 51st Highland Division
1939 - 1945

by

J. B. SALMOND

The Naval & Military Press Ltd

Published by

The Naval & Military Press Ltd
Unit 5 Riverside, Brambleside
Bellbrook Industrial Estate
Uckfield, East Sussex
TN22 1QQ England

Tel: +44 (0)1825 749494

www.naval-military-press.com
www.nmarchive.com

Cover image: Men of the 2nd Battalion, Seaforth Highlanders and Churchill tanks in the Reichswald forest, Germany, 10 February 1945.

In reprinting in facsimile from the original, any imperfections are inevitably reproduced and the quality may fall short of modern type and cartographic standards.

Dedicated

BY GRACIOUS PERMISSION

TO

HER MAJESTY QUEEN ELIZABETH, THE QUEEN MOTHER,

Colonel-in-Chief of The Black Watch,
the senior Highland Regiment,

a Scotswoman by birth, who, with His late Majesty, King George VI., throughout the weary years of the War, did her duty to the uttermost in the great position it was ordained that she should fill,

and

to all the Wives and Mothers of the men of the 51st Highland Division of Scotland.

" During the last War, I had the opportunity of seeing most of the British, Dominion and Indian Divisions, many American Divisions, and several French and Belgian Divisions, and I can assure you that, amongst all these, the 51st unquestionably takes its place alongside the very few which, through their valour and fighting record, stand in a category of their own."

> (From an Address to past and present members of the Highland Division, given after the War by Field Marshal the Viscount Alanbrooke, wartime Chief of the Imperial General Staff.)

" Of the many fine Divisions that served under me in the Second World War, none were finer than the Highland Division. . . .

" I have a very great affection for the Highland Division. It was the only Infantry Division in the armies of the British Empire that accompanied me during the whole of the long march from Alamein to Berlin."

> (From an Address to past and present members of the Highland Division, given after the War by Field Marshal the Viscount Montgomery, wartime Commander of the 8th Army and 21st Army Group.)

PREFACE

ONE day a professional military historian will prepare an account of the doings of the 51st Highland Division where the i's on all map-references will be dotted and the t's of each artillery barrage crossed. Such a record will be rightly demanded by and for students of the science of warfare. Meanwhile here is the tale of the Division told in affection for and in memory of comrades of long ago; as a pious tribute to the brave men of yesterday; in the belief in the continuance of a great tradition; and with a "Sir Toby" feeling that, though much may be demanded in the aridity of dead triplicate, we should still have something akin to living epic, for the father, the mother, the maid to read because someone near and dear to them played a part in that story; and that he who reads may cheer.

The complete story of any warfare could be only the story of one individual who took part in that warfare, because of the importance to himself of each smallest incident of that individual's record. In reconstructing the story of a Division, the writer is very well aware that he lays himself open to the criticism by the reader who was "there" that "there is not enough about my brigade, about my battalion, about my company, about my platoon." But a writer is under the necessity of selecting, and he courteously asks the reader to remember that his (the writer's) unit is the Division.

The writer would now express his gratitude to all who have assisted him with the written and the spoken word. Especially must he bear witness on this page to the time and help given by Major D. F. O. Russell, M.C.

Particular thanks are due to Lieutenant Eadie for the permission so freely given by him to reproduce his paintings, the most graphic form of illustration, and to Sergeant Martin Langlands for his expert professional help in reading proofs.

J. B. S.

ST ANDREWS,
St Andrew's Day, 1952.

CONTENTS

CHAPTER	PAGE
PREFACE	vii
LIST OF ILLUSTRATIONS	xi
LIST OF MAPS	xiii
I. THE SACRIFICE	1
II. THE PHŒNIX	19
III. THE PURSUIT	53
IV. ONE-WAY STREET	72
V. THE THIRTY-NINE DAYS	100
VI. THE ETERNAL TRIANGLE	135
VII. THE BREAK-OUT	150
VIII. THE RETURN	172
IX. GATEWAY TO THE FATHERLAND	182
X. THE LOWLANDS OF HOLLAND	194
XI. THE BARRING O' THE DOOR	205
XII. THE PATH THROUGH THE WOODS	213
XIII. ONE MORE RIVER	229
XIV. THE LAST LAP	245
XV. THE TOWEL COMES IN	253
XVI. THE AULD ALLIANCE	269
APPENDIX	274
INDEX	275

ILLUSTRATIONS

PLANNING FOR ALAMEIN	*Frontispiece*
	FACING PAGE
MAJOR-GENERAL VICTOR FORTUNE, DIVISIONAL COMMANDER 1939-40	16
HIS MAJESTY KING GEORGE VI. WITH LT.-COL. LORNE CAMPBELL, AND HER MAJESTY QUEEN ELIZABETH WITH BRIGADIER HOULDSWORTH, INSPECTING 7TH A. AND S. HIGHLANDERS AT ALDERSHOT. JUNE 1942	17
"THE BALMORALS" IN ACTION IN THE WESTERN DESERT	17
MAJOR-GENERAL DOUGLAS WIMBERLEY, DIVISIONAL COMMANDER, NORTH AFRICA AND SICILY	32
GENERALS IN THE DESERT (*l. to r.*), MORSHEAD (9TH AUSTRALIAN DIVISION), WIMBERLEY, LEESE (30TH CORPS), AND PIENAAR (SOUTH AFRICAN DIVISION)	32
VICTORY PARADE, TRIPOLI. 4TH FEBRUARY 1943	33
THE "HIGHWAY DECORATORS" IN TRIPOLI	80
ANTI-TANK DITCH AT GABES GAP. APRIL 1943	80
LT.-COL. LORNE CAMPBELL, V.C. APRIL 1943	81
GENERAL MONTGOMERY AND BRIGADIER GRAHAM AT SFAX. APRIL 1943	96
HIS MAJESTY KING GEORGE VI. INSPECTING DIVISIONAL DETACHMENT AT ALGIERS. JUNE 1943	96
LANDING IN SICILY. JULY 1943	97
HIGHWAY IN SICILY	97
SFERRO BRIDGE	112
GERBINI BATTLEFIELD	112
GERBINI POEM	113
DIVISIONAL MEMORIAL AT SFERRO, SICILY	128
HER MAJESTY QUEEN ELIZABETH WITH BRIGADIER OLIVER AT AMERSHAM	129

ILLUSTRATIONS

                                                                            FACING PAGE

MAJOR-GENERAL BULLEN SMITH, DIVISIONAL COMMANDER AT NORMANDY LANDING, WITH (*left*) BRIGADIER "NAP" MURRAY	176
NORMANDY BEACH-HEAD. JUNE 1944	176
MAJOR-GENERAL THOMAS RENNIE, DIVISIONAL COMMANDER FROM NORMANDY TO THE RHINE, WITH HIS A.D.C., LIEUT. DOUGLAS TWEEDIE	177
GENERAL RENNIE AND FRENCH DEPUTATION AT ST VALÉRY. SEPTEMBER 1944	177
BAILEY BRIDGE OVER THE MAASTRICHT–NORDER CANAL	192
MAJOR-GENERAL MACMILLAN, DIVISIONAL COMMANDER FROM THE RHINE TO BREMERHAVEN, WITH HIS A.D.C.	192
THE ROAD TO THE ARDENNES FRONT	193
A PATROL IN THE ARDENNES	193
THIS WAY FOR THE REICHSWALD!	224
5/7TH GORDONS MOVE UP TO THE REICHSWALD FOREST. FEBRUARY 1945	224
HEKKENS CORNER. FEBRUARY 1945	225
THE PRIME MINISTER WATCHES DIVISIONAL MASSED PIPE-BANDS. 5TH MARCH 1945	240
GERMAN MUD	240
JEEP AMBULANCES ON BUFFALOES MOVE UP TO CROSS THE RHINE	241
D.U.K.W.S CROSSING THE RHINE	241
GERMAN COMMANDERS SURRENDER AT BREMERVÖRDE. MAY 1945	256
VICTORY MARCH PAST AT BREMERHAVEN. GENERAL HORROCKS TAKES THE SALUTE. 12TH MAY 1945	256
UNVEILING OF DIVISIONAL MEMORIAL AT ST VALÉRY. JUNE 1950	257

MAPS

	PAGE
ABBEVILLE AND ST VALÉRY, 1940	11
PORT TEWFIK, 11TH AUGUST 1942. BATTLE OF ALAMEIN, 23RD OCTOBER-3RD NOVEMBER	28
BATTLE OF ALAMEIN—NIGHT, 23RD-24TH OCTOBER 1942	34
MAP COVERING OPERATIONS, DECEMBER 1942-23RD JANUARY 1943	59
THE BATTLE OF THE HILLS, 20TH-21ST JANUARY 1943	65
MAP COVERING OPERATIONS, FEBRUARY-MAY 1943	76
DIAGRAM TO ILLUSTRATE BATTLE OF WADI AKARIT, 6TH APRIL 1943	84
CAMPAIGN IN SICILY, 10TH JULY-20TH AUGUST 1943	114
NORMANDY, "D" DAY, 6TH JUNE 1944. ST SYLVAIN, 9TH AUGUST 1944	146
LA BÛ-SUR-ROUVRES, 15TH AUGUST. LISIEUX, 22ND AUGUST 1944	167
WILHELMINA CANAL, 3RD OCTOBER. VUGHT, 25TH OCTOBER. GEERTRUIDENBERG, 1ST NOVEMBER 1944	185
NEDERWEERT, 6TH NOVEMBER. BAARLO, 23RD NOVEMBER 1944.	198
THE ISLAND, 28TH NOVEMBER-19TH DECEMBER 1944.	203
THE ARDENNES. MARCHE, 7TH JANUARY; NISRAMONT, 13TH JANUARY 1945	211
THE REICHSWALD, 8TH-18TH FEBRUARY 1945	222
THE RHINE CROSSING, 23RD MARCH 1945	234
ENSCHEDE, 5TH APRIL. WESTERTIMKE, 27TH APRIL 1945	250
BREMERVÖRDE, 1ST MAY. THE SURRENDER, 5TH MAY 1945	259

ERRATA

Page 85. For "210 Guards Brigade" *read* "201 Guards Brigade."
Page 168. For "Major I. S. Douglas" *read* "Major P. S. Douglas."
Pages 195, 196, 198. For "Noorder" *read* "Norder."

The History of the 51st Highland Division 1939-1945

CHAPTER I.

THE SACRIFICE

" *Am fear nach gleidh na h-airm an àm na sìth, cha bhi iad aige an am a' chogaidh.*"
(He that keeps not his arms in time of peace will have none in time of war.)

" At the hour the Barbarian chose to disclose his pretences,
And raged against Man, they engaged, on the breasts that they bared for us,
The first felon-stroke of the sword he had long-time prepared for us—
Their bodies were all our defence while we wrought our defences."
From RUDYARD KIPLING'S " The Children " (' A Diversity of Creatures ').[1]

THIS is the tale of an infantryman whose weapon was essentially a sword, although that sword was fixed on the end of a rifle and designated a bayonet. It is the tale of a Scottish infantryman, who was essentially a clansman with all the glorious traditions, estimable prejudices, and fortunate relationships of a clansman. In this particular tale each clan was a regiment with its own chief and its own peculiar significance of territory. Clan jealousy and clan pride formed the separate strength of each unit, and, by their very divisions, made of all the clans that Unity known as the 51st Highland Division.

In the story of the Scottish Highlands you will read, time and again, of a family from another part of the country who settle in a clan territory and, while retaining their own quality, become part of the clan ; in time in their own name they are recognised as a sept of that clan. Such was the case with certain units of the Highland Division who

---

[1] By permission of Mrs George Bambridge and Messrs Macmillan & Co.

came into that Division from a far country, but who, in the retention of their own tradition and the acceptance of the adopted one, not only were held in honour in the clan, but were proud to belong.[1] Then there were other septs, with particular qualifications for the various toils of the long dusty day of war, without whose co-operation and comradeship that man with the bayonet would have been in ill-pass.

Of those particular septs of the clan a padre wrote home from Tunisia in 1943: " Pride of place must go to the gunners, as is their right; men in the Field, Anti-Tank, and Anti-Aircraft Regiments have been in no respect inferior to their brothers in the infantry, and have on all occasions performed their respective tasks in accordance with the highest traditions of the Royal Regiment, and of the Division. The same is equally true of the sappers, who, of all the units, have probably had the toughest time of any men in this campaign. There are also those, whose work is done more 'behind the scenes'—the R.A.S.C., the R.A.O.C., the R.E.M.E., the Royal Corps of Signals, the C.M.P., the R.A.M.C.—though it would be a mistake to imagine that any of these units remain in the background when a battle is in progress. In their own spheres, these units have done their allotted tasks no less creditably than the infantry battalions. The anti-aircraft gunners admire the courage of the infantryman, who advances at night across an enemy minefield; the infantryman in turn admires the courage of the anti-aircraft gunners who stand up in their gun-pits manning their guns during a Stuka raid. All unite in paying tribute to the particular brand of courage required by an R.A.M.C. stretcher-bearer seeking for the wounded under shell-fire. And so it goes on—each branch of the service recognises the help and support it receives from every other branch, for one of the reasons for the high morale of this Division is that it has learned to co-ordinate itself as a team; and the spirit of brotherhood in the Division is most marked."

The vague tradition of a Highland Division goes as far back as Mons Graupius. It was given definite shape just two hundred years before 1939, when the then Government resolved to form Wade's Highland Companies into a regiment of the line. Fifty years later General Stewart of Garth put the idea and ideal of that tradition on

[1] It is interesting to note here that the Middlesex were the first English Regiment to have a pipe band. The pipers were recruited from Glasgow, and one of them was killed with the 16th Battalion on the Somme on 1st July 1916. Further, away back in 1791, in the 57th Foot (Middlesex) nearly half the men and three-quarters of the officers were Scotsmen.

paper. He wrote [1]: "When, in a national or district corps, he [the Highland soldier] is surrounded by the companions of his youth, and the rivals of his early achievements, he feels the impulse of emulation strengthened by the consciousness that every proof, which he displays either of bravery or cowardice, will find its way to his native home. He thus learns to appreciate the value of a good name, and it is thus, that in a Highland regiment, consisting of men from the same country, whose kindred and connections are mutually known, every individual feels that his conduct is the subject of observation, and that, independently of his duty as a member of a systematic whole, he has to sustain a separate and individual reputation which will be reflected on his family and district or glen. Hence he requires no artificial excitements. He acts from motives within himself, his point is fixed, and his aim must terminate either in victory or death." [2]

The immediate tradition was created in the 1914-18 War when the Division, disheartened by their failure to take High Wood, christened themselves "Harper's Duds" [3]—a name to which, covered by the glory of Beaumont Hamel, in later days they were only too proud to answer. At Vimy, Roeux, the Steenbeck, Poelcappelle, Cambrai, on the Lys, in Champagne, and many another field they continued to win respect and honour, till they met the Armistice in the vicinity of Mons.

There is little pleasure or satisfaction in telling the story of the dispersal of a fighting force once its fighting days are over, so we need not follow home the cadres of the 1914-18 Highland Division. But we leave them with Haig's words in our ears [4]: "If it were possible for the General, who for three years commanded all the British Divisions in France, and was served with great gallantry, devotion, and success by each, to admit a predilection for any of them, my affection would naturally turn to the Division that drew so many of its recruits from the same part of Scotland where my boyhood was spent, and my own people lived. . . . The 51st Division does not need to boast of its prowess or its record. It can point to the story of its deeds, plainly and simply told, and leave the world to judge."

[1] 'Sketches of the Highlanders of Scotland,' Second Edition, 1822, pp. 235-236.
[2] Over a century later, when the African Campaign had ended, Montgomery was to state of the Highland soldier that "*esprit de corps* and tremendously high morale were very marked in the Highland Division, and I am sure it was largely due to the fact that it was composed of material from the same part of Britain."
[3] After their Divisional Commander, General Harper, of 1916-18.
[4] Bewsher's 'The History of the 51st (Highland) Division, 1914-1918.' (Blackwood, 1921.)

Shortly after his cadre had returned to this country in 1919 the commanding officer of a battalion, which had served throughout with the Division, was called upon to unveil a War Memorial. He made a strange and, some folks felt, a cruel speech, when he told his hearers that the best thing the young men of the district could do, in memory of the fallen, was to join a Territorial Unit at once, and spend any other leisure time they had at a miniature rifle-club range, for, he emphasised, the Germans had no idea they had been beaten; theirs was only a temporary set-back. As soon as they felt themselves strong enough, the Huns would come again.

Twenty years of British and French apathy, twenty years of neglect of our armed forces, and the time was ripe for the prophecy made at that War Memorial to be fulfilled. War was declared against a Germany strong in all things, and ready for the challenge. But the spirit of the 51st had remained, a shining flame. Despite lack of general interest in Britain, the units of the Highland Division were strong in personnel and enthusiasm, and it was a companionship of high heart which landed at Le Havre in January 1940 under the command of Major-General Victor M. Fortune. Fortune was a son of the Scottish Borders and had been commissioned to the Black Watch in 1903. He held the position of Adjutant to the 1st Battalion of that Regiment in 1914, and was given command of the 1st Battalion in September 1916. His fighting record in the First World War was quite outstanding. He was O.C. 1st Seaforth in 1927, and in 1930 took over command of the 5th Infantry Brigade. As Major-General he commanded the 52nd (Lowland) Division in 1935-36, and became Commander, Highland Division, in 1937. Fortune was essentially a fighting soldier. His idea was that every individual in the Division should have, as it were, a nodding acquaintance with the G.O.C., and when the 51st was training in England, previous to going overseas, Fortune on occasion would pop up from nowhere and chat with any squad of men in his vicinity. On active service, and especially in the Maginot Line, he was—almost embarrassingly—fond of the front area, keen to know what each platoon, what each section was doing, keen to take part in any action.

The three infantry Brigades of the Division were made up of two Black Watch, two Gordon, two Seaforth, two Argyll and Sutherland battalions, and one Cameron battalion. The Divisional Cavalry was a Fife and Forfar unit. There were three Field and one Anti-Tank Regiment of Royal Artillery, four Field Companies of Royal Engineers, Divisional Signals, and three Divisional R.A.M.C. Field Ambulances.

It is not proposed to give in detail in this account the history of the Division from Le Havre to St Valéry-en-Caux. That has already been done excellently by Eric Linklater in his 'The Highland Division.' The rapid survey which follows has for its purpose to preserve the continuity of the story.

The twenty years of peace were as if they had not been. The 51st was back in France, carrying on after the 51st of that earlier war. There was an unwritten and unspoken suggestion everywhere that the sons (in some cases the fathers with their sons) now took up the war from where the fathers had laid it down. That January of 1940 was as the January of 1917. The frost was iron-hard round Le Havre in 1940, as it had been iron-hard round Abbeville in 1917. Then came the thaw bringing the mud and the mist with all their memories, and the Division moved to the well-remembered rim of Belgium, where in many a village

> " Marie Prévost, that used to sing
> *Bel Chevalier* by the kitchen fire,
> Marie Prévost has a wedding ring,
> And her youngest of six is mucking the byre."

The Mademoiselles of yesterday stood, the Madames of to-day, with their children about them listening again as the pipes and drums of a Highland battalion played " Retreat " in their village, and they watched the troops march out of that village to a war that in general acceptance was to be as before—all trenches and pill-boxes. Earlier days were recalled when André Maurois (the creator of that Colonel Bramble of long ago) lectured to the troops in Béthune. So we find the Division, at the beginning of April 1940, in that part of France's defence line from Bailleul to Armentières where they had relieved the 21st French Division, and where they proceeded to strengthen what had been known as " The Small Maginot Line," and which had been re-named the Gort Line.

After the 1914-18 war the French military authorities had set about fortifying their frontiers in much the same manner as that which they had adopted after the 1870-71 trouble. The new defences were designated the Maginot Line, and they stretched for some 314 kilometres from Belfort near the Swiss border to the junction with the Belgian frontier. Northwards the Belgian defences ran roughly in a line from the Meuse to Antwerp. The French had decided to continue their Maginot Line westwards along the Belgium-France frontier. Those defences were known as "The Small Maginot Line." The Belgian Government, however, had objected very vigorously in the years of peace to such defences being developed, on the grounds that, should another war break out between Germany and France, such defences offered a definite invitation to the Germans to violate the neutrality of Belgium again. So the construction of "The Small Maginot Line" had been abandoned, and it was this abandoned Line on which the 51st Division were now working. Belgium still held aloof, although Belgium knew that the German plans for her invasion were fully prepared. The Highland Division and other British troops worked hard on the defences, building forts and anti-tank obstacles, and actually mixing the concrete. There was a suggestion of energy and expectancy about all their actions. It would seem, however, that certain French troops, on the other hand, had been allowed to go stale. It was remarked on by our men, when the Division was sent to take over from French troops on part of the Saar front, that little interest seemed to have been shown in improving defences even in the real Maginot Line.

The main defences in the Maginot Line were a series of underground concrete forts, which, throughout the Maginot's short and very unsatisfactory active life, were held by the French. Those forts functioned not at all when the crucial hour arrived. They were simply by-passed by the enemy. In front of them lay a large defensive area, the front line of which was up to seven miles from the fort system. That front line was known as the Ligne de Contact, and faced a No-Man's-Land, varying in depth from a few hundred yards to six miles, beyond which stretched the German Siegfried Line (in many ways of the same set-up as the Maginot), about which the most vapid of all war-songs was written. The support line was known as the Ligne de Soutien, which in its turn was supported by a Ligne de Recueil (a defensive position to fill the gaps between the forts), while behind the forts was an imaginary line, the Ligne d'Arrêt—a kind of "thus far and no farther" line.

Some British battalions had seen service in the Maginot Line, among them the 1st Black Watch, the fortunes of which were now united with those of the 51st Division; for some authority decided that a Territorial Division would be strengthened by including in it units of the Regular Army, which units, of course, had had a much longer period of training. So at the beginning of March the 6th Black Watch, 6th

THE SACRIFICE

Gordons, 6th Seaforth, 76th and 77th Field Regiments Royal Artillery were withdrawn from the Division and replaced by the 1st Black Watch, 1st Gordons, 2nd Seaforth, and the 17th and 23rd Field Regiments Royal Artillery. There was a Ceremonial March through Lille when the change-over took place. At an earlier date the Fife and Forfar Yeomanry had been transferred to an Armoured Brigade, and their place in the Division had been taken by the 1st Lothians and Border Horse. Certain other troops were attached at the beginning of April and the Division, together with the attached troops, was known as the Saar Force and was now composed as follows :—

Major-General V. M. Fortune (Commanding).
Lt.-Col. H. Swinburn, G.S.O.1.

1st The Lothians and Border Horse (Yeomanry).
152 Brigade : Brigadier H. W. V. Stewart (Seaforth).
    2nd Bn. The Seaforth Highlanders.
    4th Bn. The Seaforth Highlanders.
    4th Bn. The Queen's Own Cameron Highlanders.
153 Brigade : Brigadier G. T. Burney (Gordons).
    4th Bn. The Black Watch.
    1st Bn. The Gordon Highlanders.
    5th Bn. The Gordon Highlanders.
154 Brigade : Brigadier A. C. L. Stanley-Clarke (R.S.F.).
    1st Bn. The Black Watch.
    7th Bn. The Argyll and Sutherland Highlanders.
    8th Bn. The Argyll and Sutherland Highlanders.
The Royal Artillery : C.R.A., Brigadier H. C. H. Eden.
    17th Field Regiment Royal Artillery.
    23rd Field Regiment Royal Artillery.
    75th Field Regiment Royal Artillery.
    51st Anti-Tank Regiment Royal Artillery.
The Royal Engineers : C.R.E., Lt.-Col. H. M. Smail.
    26th Field Company Royal Engineers.
    236th Field Company Royal Engineers.
    237th Field Company Royal Engineers.
    239th Field Park Company Royal Engineers.
The Royal Corps of Signals : Lt.-Col. T. P. E. Murray.
    51st Divisional Signals Company.
The Royal Army Medical Corps : A.D.M.S., Lt.-Col. D. P. Levack.
    152nd Field Ambulance.
    153rd Field Ambulance.
    154th Field Ambulance.

The Royal Army Service Corps : Lt.-Col. T. Harris-Hunter.
Divisional Ammunition Company.
Divisional Petrol Company.
Divisional Supply Column.

Attached Troops :—

    51st Medium Regiment, Royal Artillery.
    1st Royal Horse Artillery (less one Battery).
    97th Field Regiment Royal Artillery (one Battery).
    213th Army Field Company, Royal Engineers.
    1st Bn. Princess Louise's Kensington Regiment (Machine-Gunners).
    7th Bn. The Royal Northumberland Fusiliers (Machine-Gunners).
    6th Bn. The Royal Scots Fusiliers (Pioneers).
    7th Bn. The Norfolk Regiment (Pioneers).
    Sections of the Royal Army Ordnance Corps and the Royal Army Service Corps.

Shortly afterwards the Division took over a sector of the Maginot Line, as supporting troops attached to a French Corps. East of Metz, the Moselle and the Nied (a tributary of the Saar) are only some ten miles apart, and it was in an area between those two rivers that the 51st found themselves at last in touch with the enemy. But still there was something "phoney" about it all. The Division had reached Metz by way of villages where the inhabitants seemed to be enjoying themselves as if war were a thousand miles and a thousand years away. In Metz, the sort of capital of the area, there was " a sound of revelry by night." But with the arrival of the Gort Force the temperature changed. "Now that the British are here, the war will commence," said the French civilians, and they began to evacuate the district.

The smile of May lay on the pleasant woods of the defensive area, where dwelt a silence like the silence of a Sleeping Beauty. The villages certainly were deserted, the houses shuttered, but they were undamaged and produced the general impression that the inhabitants had gone off all together on some holiday jaunt and had forgotten to come back.

On the first day of May the French handed over to the 51st a front-line of trenches and of sunken wooden huts, well wired in. Those the Division decided more or less to forget about, and proceeded to reconstruct the whole defensive position, in fact to

    " Rebuild it nearer to the heart's desire."

Soon the Division considered they were properly dug in, and ready for trouble.[1] And it came along. The Germans began to make detached night-attacks on selected posts. But the Division did not sit back and take it. Patrols—with faces blackened as in the old raiding days of 1914-18—set out nightly to look for Germans. The 7th Argylls made this patrolling somewhat of a speciality. Captain Ian C. Cameron tells in his 'History'[2] of that Battalion how "a battle patrol was organised, which consisted of twenty men under the command of 2nd Lieutenant Alan Orr Ewing, who later earned the M.C. for his work. This patrol, in conjunction with similar patrols from the other two battalions of the brigade, took its turn at deep nightly penetration into the enemy's positions. Every night a patrol, with blackened faces, rubber boots, and every type of infantry weapon from a tommy-gun to a hunting-knife, would sally forward into 'No-Man's Land.' There were frequent encounters with the enemy, and usually the enemy got the worst of it. The usefulness of these patrols was undoubted. The front-line troops were as a result allowed considerably more peace at night and freedom from enemy interference. Nevertheless, it was an eerie experience to set out for the first time knowing that an enemy patrol bent on the same purpose might be encountered at any moment. Once this happened there was little time to think—a flurry of flashes, tommy-gun shots, exploding grenades, and then all was over."

In this spasmodic fighting the Division took some prisoners, and had some of their own men captured by the enemy. And so things went on until the 10th of May, when the Germans invaded Belgium. Three days later the enemy put down a heavy barrage along the 51st Divisional front and some very stiff fighting took place. The Division proved themselves indeed. They held on grimly to their positions. Sometimes small units were cut off, but other units came to their assistance. Men were killed, men were wounded, but there was a sensation of elation in all ranks. They were now busy on the kind of job they had been sent out to do. It was admitted ungrudgingly by our French Allies that the Division had everything which that other 51st had had a quarter of a century before.

On 15th May orders came that the Division were to retire and take up a position in conformity with the French defence plan. The 51st

[1] It is generally the case that no formation is satisfied with the positions taken over from another formation.
[2] By permission of the author and Messrs Thomas Nelson & Sons. From 'The History of the Argyll and Sutherland Highlanders, 7th Battalion, 1939-45.'

had to make the "Ligne de Recueil," in front of the Maginot Forts, and it was up to the sappers to do all they could in the way of demolitions. That retiral was the beginning of the end. The Highlanders had set foot on the weary road that was to lead to St Valéry.

The Division was taken out of the line and moved by Metz to Étain and Varennes, where it was learned that the Germans had broken through the French defences and that a river of enemy armour was flowing between the 51st and the other B.E.F. troops; but no one guessed then that it was a river that would never be crossed. It was, however, realised that there was much indecision on the part of the French Higher Command. Now the Division was to move to the defence of Paris, now for some other purpose to some other place. Finally they divided the 51st into two parts, sent one by train far south of Paris, by Troyes, Orléans, and Le Mains north to Rouen and so to Neufchâtel, and moved the other by motor-transport north of Paris by Gizors to the Bresle River which enters the sea halfway between St Valéry-sur-Somme and St Valéry-en-Caux.

The Highland Division became one again in time to hear the news that Leopold of the Belgians had thrown in his hand, that the B.E.F. were retiring on Dunkirk, that they (the 51st) were to fight on a new line with the French 9th Army, and that their first job would be to hold a position from just north of Abbeville north-westwards to the sea. On this front the enemy had two bridgeheads, one in front of St Valéry-sur-Somme and the other just to the south of Abbeville. The Division began digging in and, by the time the last of the B.E.F. had been evacuated from Dunkirk, were in a position—along with the French—to make an attack on the Abbeville bridgehead. The French had already had a couple of goes at it. "A" Company of the 1st Black Watch had been attached to them and that Company took their objectives, but later, to conform with the action of the troops on their flank left otherwise in the air, the men of the 42nd had to come back.

The 154 Brigade was holding the line nearest the sea, 153 Brigade was in the centre, and 152 Brigade on the right, the whole line being some twenty-three miles in length. It can therefore be understood that there was no mobile reserve. The attack on the Abbeville bridgehead began on the morning of 4th June, with the 4th Camerons on the right, French troops with the 4th Seaforth in the centre, and the 1st Gordons and 2nd Seaforth on the left. Some considerable gains were made by 152 Brigade, but our forces were too thinly spread out to hold those

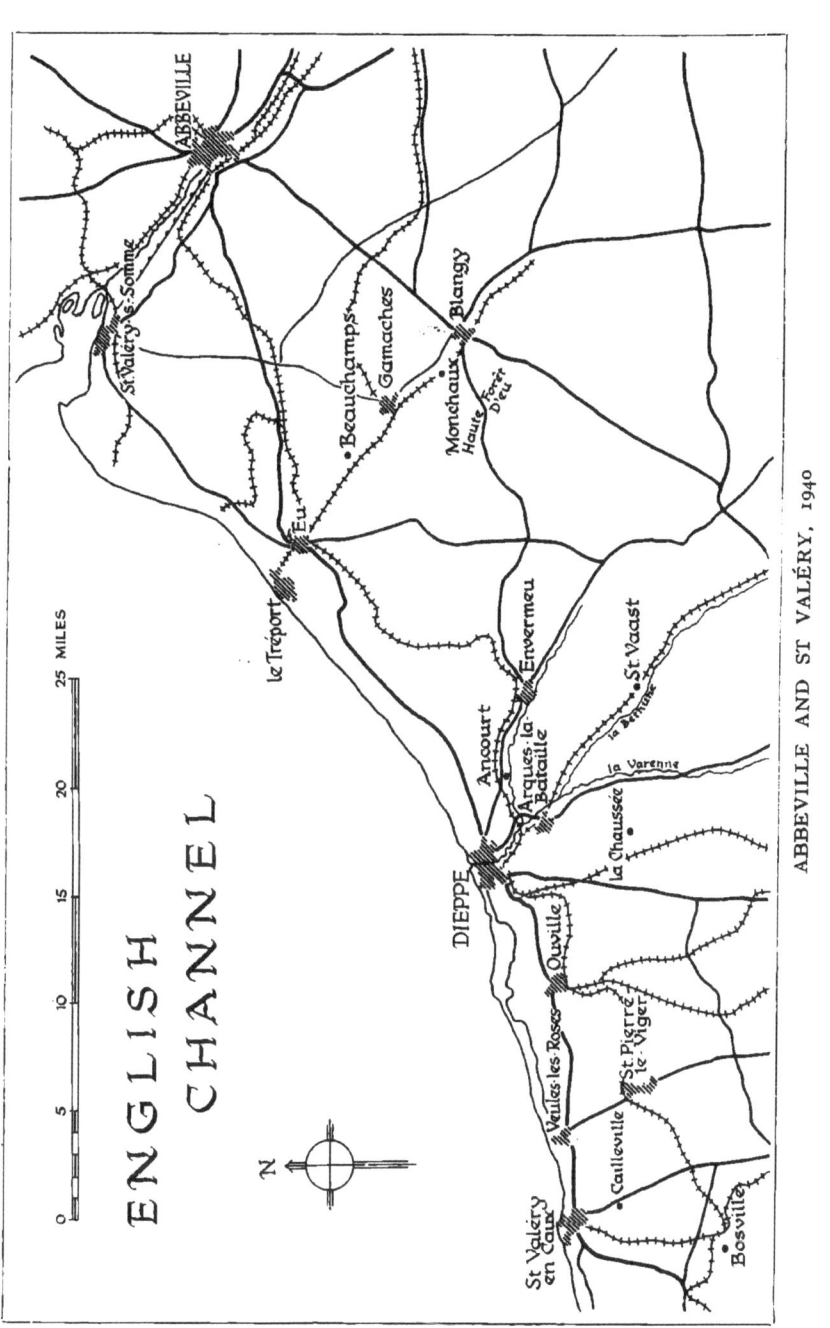

ABBEVILLE AND ST VALÉRY, 1940

gains and later had to retire to their original positions.¹ Next day the Germans attacked. The 7th and 8th Argylls holding the line nearest the sea had a very bad time, many of their posts being overrun. As a result the 1st Gordons on their right were enfiladed, and their withdrawal, as well as that of the 1st Black Watch on the Gordon right, became essential. On the extreme right, units of the Lothians and Border Horse put up a very good show, but they in turn had to retire.

The 7th Argylls had been reduced to 5 officers and 130 other ranks; in fact the whole 154 Brigade was down to 50 per cent of its strength. A composite body of troops known as " A " Brigade was now brought into the line. It consisted of the 4th Buffs, 4th Border Regiment, and 5th Sherwoods.

There is a road that runs in a straight line from the sea at Le Tréport west to Blangy, a distance of some fifteen miles. On the 6th day of June the Division had retired to that line from a line almost parallel and seven miles farther north. On the 7th our troops were positioned as follows :—

On the right 152 Brigade held the three miles from Blangy to Monchaux; from Monchaux to Gamaches (another three miles) was stationed 153 Brigade; 154 Brigade covered the next three miles to Beauchamps; " A " Brigade was responsible for the four miles from Beauchamps to Eu, and the 6th Royal Scots Fusiliers the two miles from Eu to the sea. The 152 Brigade retired to the Forêt d'Eu to cover the withdrawal of French troops on the right. At the east end of the line " A " Brigade attacked repeatedly with great gallantry, but our whole front was dive-bombed all day, and our only weapons against that form of attack were the gallant but few fighter planes who flew over from England. Fighting desperately, the Division retired to the line of the Béthune River, which runs south-eastwards from Dieppe to St Vaast. The 152 Brigade was in position from Dieppe to Arques, with 153 and " A " Brigades north-east of it between Ancourt and Envermeu, and 154 Brigade at the junction of the Béthune and the Varenne. General Fortune had his headquarters at La Chausée behind the Varenne, and to him there came British naval officers to discuss arrangements for the evacuation of the Division from Le Havre. Transports were there, Dieppe being useless for the purpose since blocking vessels were already in position in that port. The nearest

---

[1] The 152 Seaforth and Cameron Brigade lost 20 officers and 543 other ranks in this day's fighting.

THE SACRIFICE

embarkation point was St Valéry-en-Caux, but the Navy did not consider it suitable. So Le Havre it was to be.

Le Havre then must be defended, and the troops lying near Arques-la-Bataille were selected for that purpose. They were put under the command of Brigadier Stanley-Clarke, and became known as "Ark" Force. One reason for the designation of this Force has been given as that "they had two of everything, and knew that sooner or later they would be going to sea." Ark Force consisted of Headquarters of 154 Brigade with the remnants of the two Argyll and Sutherland Battalions, 4th Black Watch, 6th Battalion Royal Scots Fusiliers, "A" Brigade, and the following attached troops:—

1st Bn. Princess Louise's Kensington Regiment (less two Companies).
17th Field Regiment Royal Artillery.
75th Field Regiment Royal Artillery.
51st Anti-Tank Regiment Royal Artillery (one Battery).
236th Field Company Royal Engineers.
237th Field Company Royal Engineers.
239th Field Park Company Royal Engineers.
154th Field Ambulance.

Ark Force set out on the night of the 9th-10th June to take up a defensive position from Fécamp to Lillebonne. The French troops (with only horse transport) were however slow to move, and, although General Fortune could have got his Division away earlier, it would have meant leaving the French 31st Division's flank in the air. By the evening of 10th June the enemy had reached the sea between Fécamp and St Valéry-en-Caux. The result was that Ark Force alone escaped the German encirclement, and, owing to our Government's decision to cover the French flank, the Highland Division was sacrificed. Hence the title of this chapter.

By 8th June enemy troops had been passing through Neufchâtel on the Béthune. Till orders came to withdraw on the 10th, the 1st Black Watch held the Germans on the Varenne. The Highlanders then retired by Ouville to the railway line at St Piérre-le-Viger, some seven miles from St Valéry. General Fortune sent a signal to the Navy stating that it was his intention to hold a square round St Valéry, and requesting that the Division should be evacuated from that port. A special envoy, using a plane, was keeping the General in direct communication with the Prime Minister in London, and again British naval officers arrived at Fortune's headquarters to discuss the plans for evacuation. Those sailors were still with the Division when it was captured at St Valéry. The Navy did make preparations, however, to carry out the job, but, from their point of view, St Valéry became a kind of fireworks display against which signals could not be seen. A reconnaissance party was sent in to the beaches from the destroyer *Codrington*, and that party discovered that it might be possible to evacuate the troops from Veules-les-Roses. Some thousand men were actually taken off from that point at dawn the following morning.

By this time General Fortune had withdrawn his troops to what he hoped would be a St Valéry perimeter holding-line. Unfortunately that perimeter line was never completed. The Lothians and Border Horse held the west, the French were on the south-west at Bosville, the 4th Seaforth and 5th Gordons were on the south-east, with the 1st Black Watch to the east. On the morning of the 11th General Fortune informed officers commanding units that embarkation might begin that night. Meanwhile the Germans were pressing powerfully on the perimeter. The 1st Black Watch, whose defence had been strengthened by a hard-fighting squadron of French cavalry, held. But the Germans eventually broke through on the west. Seaforth, Camerons, and Norfolks did their best but had to retire, and a grim circle of tank-wolves surrounded the town.

It was hoped, however, that the Division could begin embarking at half-past ten. Major Rennie (later to command the second 51st which was to return victorious to St Valéry), who was G.S.O.2, went with a naval liaison officer to the beach to make the necessary arrangements, but no signal came from any ships.

Now the crazy, twisting streets of St Valéry were packed with men trying to find their way to the harbour and to the ships that could not get there. British vessels had been in the harbour on the night of the 10th, but left in the morning. Transports had lain off the beaches that same morning, but had been driven off by enemy gun-fire. One tug picked up some men near St Valéry. But that was all. The news was then received that no more ships were coming. But to the west the Seaforth fought practically to a finish, as did the 1st Gordons. The 1st Black Watch, the Camerons, and the other Gordon battalion still held out, but the French had surrendered.

And so Victor Fortune was called on to make his decision. The artillery ammunition was finished. His troops had done all that men could do. He gave the order to surrender.

THE SACRIFICE

Meanwhile Ark Force had reached Le Havre. "A" Brigade was evacuated on the night of 11th June, the remainder of the troops on the morning of the 13th, and the ships steamed into Cherbourg where the troops were disembarked. A certain amount of transport was sent by road across the Seine. On the 15th Ark Force re-embarked, and on 16th June landed at Southampton.

The Rt. Hon. Winston Churchill explains the position in his 'Second World War,' Vol. II., p. 134 [1]:—

"The 51st Division, with the remnants of the French IXth Corps, was cut off in the Rouen–Dieppe cul-de-sac.

"We had been intensely concerned lest this Division should be driven back to the Havre Peninsula, and thus be separated from the armies, and its commander, Major-General Fortune, had been told to fall back if necessary in the direction of Rouen. This movement was forbidden by the already disintegrating French Command. Repeated urgent representations were made by us, but they were of no avail. A dogged refusal to face facts led to the ruin of the French IXth Corps and our 51st Division. On 9th June, when Rouen was already in German hands, our men had but newly reached Dieppe, thirty-five miles to the north. Only then were they ordered to withdraw to Havre. A force was sent back to cover this movement, but before the main bodies could move the Germans interposed. Striking from the east, they reached the sea, and the greater part of the 51st Division, with many of the French, was cut off. It was a case of gross mismanagement, for this very danger was visible a full three days before. . . . The French force capitulated at eight o'clock (12th June), and the remains of the Highland Division were forced to do so at 10.30 A.M. . . . I was vexed that the French had not allowed our Division to retire on Rouen in good time, but had kept it waiting till it could neither reach Havre nor retreat southward, and thus forced it to surrender with their own troops. The fate of the Highland Division was hard, but in after years not unavenged by those Scots who filled their places, re-created the Division by merging it with the 9th Scottish, and marched across all the battlefields from Alamein to final victory beyond the Rhine."

The position of the 51st at St Valéry from the German point of view is well expressed in Mr Desmond Young's 'Rommel.' Mr Young writes [2]:

"St Valéry was the real prize, for here were the Headquarters of General Fortune, commanding the 51st Division, and it was here that the bulk of the Division was preparing to embark. During the night of 10th June and the morning of the 11th Rommel seized the high ground to the west, from which he could bring the port under artillery fire. At 3.30 P.M. he himself led

---

[1] By permission of the author and the publishers, Messrs Cassell & Co.
[2] By permission of the author and the publishers, Messrs Collins.

the 25th Panzer Regiment and part of the 6th Infantry Regiment into the attack, under cover of his guns. . . . A written demand from Rommel to General Fortune to surrender and march out the 51st Division under white flags to the west was refused and the Germans could see that barricades were being erected on the harbour moles and that guns and machine-guns were being brought into position.

"At 9 P.M. a heavy bombardment was opened. The concentrated fire of the whole of the Divisional heavy and light artillery was brought to bear on the northern part of St Valéry and the harbour and 2500 shells fell in this small area. At the same time the 25th Panzer Regiment was again put into the attack, with the 7th Infantry Regiment and the 37th Pioneer Battalion. The line was advanced nearer to St Valéry. But 'in spite of the heavy fire the tenacious British troops did not give up. They hoped to be embarked during the night but the enemy was prevented by heavy artillery fire from loading. In the early morning hours the British are busy trying to embark from the steep coast to the east of St Valéry, under cover of fire from warships. But the Divisional artillery first hinders this and later makes it impossible. There is a duel between a warship and the 88-mm. A.A. battery. . . . 8th Machine Gun Battalion attacks. . . . Parts of 6th and 7th Infantry Regiments attack and gain more ground near St Valéry. On the left Rommel, with the 25th Panzer Regiment under Colonel Rothenburg, and part of the 7th Infantry Regiment, pushes into St Valéry itself and compels capitulation as the enemy commander sees that further resistance is impossible.'

"Rommel never forgot General Fortune of the 51st Highland Division and often spoke of him to Frau Rommel and to his son Manfred as the gallant leader of a good Division who had had bad luck. While he was in a prison camp in Germany, General Fortune was given the chance by the Germans of being repatriated to England on the grounds of age and ill-health. Because he felt that he could still do something for the morale of the officers and men of his Division by sharing their captivity with them, he refused and remained a prisoner until the end of the war. Rommel came to hear of this and it increased his respect for his former opponent. It would appear that General Fortune also remembered and respected Rommel. Two years or more after the collapse of Germany a German prisoner of war, repatriated from a British prison camp in the Channel Islands, came to Herrlingen to see Frau Rommel. He had met General Fortune in the Channel Islands, he said, after the latter's return from Germany, and the General had asked him to visit her, if possible, when he himself returned home and to express his sympathy with her on her husband's death. I could not check this story with Major-General Fortune before he died, but it would appear to be true, since a German soldier could hardly have invented it or, for that matter, have heard of General Fortune. I hope so, for I am one of those old-fashioned persons who regret that chivalry should be among the casualties of total war."

There has been a tendency in some quarters to write and talk as if the 51st Highland Division had "lost its soul" at St Valéry, and that

MAJOR-GENERAL
VICTOR FORTUNE,
DIVISIONAL
COMMANDER
1939-40

*By courtesy of the
Imperial War
Museum*

By courtesy of the   WAR OFFICE

HIS MAJESTY KING GEORGE VI. WITH Lt.-Col. LORNE CAMPBELL, AND HER
MAJESTY QUEEN ELIZABETH WITH Brigadier HOULDSWORTH, INSPECTING
7TH A. AND S. HIGHLANDERS AT ALDERSHOT. JUNE 1942

"THE BALMORALS" IN ACTION IN THE WESTERN DESERT

By courtesy of the   IMPERIAL WAR MUSEUM

it " found its soul " again at Alamein. While it existed as a fighting formation, the Division never lost its soul. At no time in all its history did the 51st show more courage, more determination, than during those long and weary hours when it fought from the Bresle line to the streets of St Valéry. Nothing in all its history exceeds in gallantry the show it put up in those last days.

In fact, from the time of the attack on the Abbeville bridgehead, the Division's story is really a series of short stories about individuals or isolated groups. You will find many of those short stories detailed in the various battalion histories—a platoon of 4th Seaforth all gone in that Abbeville attack, one sergeant, and he, badly wounded, advancing alone on the enemy; the 7th Argylls' great defence of the village of Franleu, in which action twenty-three officers and half a thousand other ranks were dead, wounded or missing; the 1st Black Watch fighting for three hours after that surrender order, of which they knew nothing, had been given. Those incidents, taken at random, and a hundred others will live in history, a memorial to the brave men of yesterday, a beacon showing the way to those who shall follow them, when danger threatens on any of our to-morrows.

And even in captivity the lamp of Divisional tradition burned with a clear pure flame which neither starvation, nor ill-treatment, nor such indignities as hair clipped convict-short could quench. As in the field Major-General Fortune set an example of fortitude that was followed by all. As far as he could, he still commanded his Division and insisted on sharing any ill-treatment meted out to his men. In the words of Bernard Fergusson: " Those [prisoners] who never set eyes on him still drew self-respect and courage from his reputation and his example. His health declined steadily, but he refused repatriation and would not leave his men." Many of those men were sent to wretched prison camps in Poland, but even under the most demoralising conditions, morale never gave way. The men of the Highland Division made it always perfectly clear to their German guards that these guards were their inferiors, and cheerfully suffered detention and solitary confinement just to prove their point.

Escapes from German hands by members of the Division were legion and exciting. Many have been recorded elsewhere, as that of Major Thomas Rennie of the Black Watch and Major R. Macintosh-Walker of the Seaforth.[1]

[1] Bernard Fergusson, ' The Black Watch and the King's Enemies.' (Collins, 1950.)

The men who did not escape kept the flag of Scotland flying in the prisoner-of-war camps. In Stalag 383 they inaugurated a St Andrew's Society. As one prisoner wrote, that Society's activities represented "a complete, if miniature, cross-section of Scottish life, a spot of normality in an existence in so many ways abnormal." The men formed an An Comunn Gaidhealach, kept hives of bees, held Highland Gatherings, arranged classes in agriculture, and in all sorts of subjects dealing with occupations and professions. Many prisoners succeeded, through the help of the facilities placed at their disposal by the Red Cross and other organisations, in passing examinations in law, banking, and architecture. On Sunday nights speakers lectured on Scottish history. Scotland was still " for ever."

One little tale in conclusion, of a Scots village the inhabitants of which, after the war was all over, were celebrating a V Day anniversary. Flags were flying from the windows of the houses in the village, and the local police-sergeant began to be bombarded by telephone calls from agitated old ladies informing him that out of one window a Swastika flag was waving. He made investigations and found that the case was not over-stated. So he called at the house to find that the " culprit " was a Highland Division soldier who had spent five years in the worst of the German prisons in Poland. That soldier had suffered all sorts of punishments, but, though weak through illness when the day came that the prison doors were opened, he had climbed the flagpole, pulled down the Swastika flag and brought it home with him as a souvenir—and he thought that V Day was a good day to fly it. The village, when it heard the story, thought so too.

For a comprehensive account of the 51st Highland Division in this part of the war, see 'The Highland Division' by Eric Linklater, published by H.M. Stationery Office (1942).

CHAPTER II.

THE PHŒNIX

"Alba gu Brath."
(Scotland For Ever.)

"Oh yesterday our little troop was ridden through and through,
Our swaying, tattered pennons fled, a broken, beaten few,
And all a summer afternoon they hunted us and slew;
But to-morrow,
By the living God, we'll try the game again!"
From JOHN MASEFIELD'S "To-morrow." [1]

IN the 1914-18 struggle the 51st Highland Division had both a second and a third line. The third line was the immediate reserve, and first from Bridge of Earn, later from Ripon, and finally from various barracks in Scotland that line sent out reinforcements to the first line in France and Flanders. The second line was retained in Norfolk as a kind of anti-invasion force, but in time it also became a direct source of reinforcements. In 1939 the 9th (Scottish) Division, which was recruited from the same areas as, and was a duplicate of the 51st, was in a way a second line for the 51st. In World War I. the 9th had served with the 51st in the 17th Corps (1st Army) during the Battle of Arras in 1917. In 1940 it was commanded in turn by General Sir Alan Cunningham, who was instrumental in changing its name to the 51st, and then by General Neil Ritchie, and it was spread out thinly as an anti-invasion force along the beaches of the north-east coast of Scotland; thus in 1940 after St Valéry this re-named 9th Division became the reincarnation of the 51st. The regular battalions of the lost Division (1st Black Watch, 1st Gordons and 2nd Seaforth) were themselves re-raised. The Brigades were reconstituted under 51st numbering, and in August 1940 Brigadier Douglas Neil Wimberley was given command of 152 Brigade. He held that position for eight months when he was called away to take over the 46th Division. General Ritchie, however, was very soon afterwards ordered to the Middle East as Deputy-Chief of the General Staff, from which position he proceeded to the command of the

[1] By permission of The Society of Authors and Dr John Masefield, O.M.

8th Army, where he was later succeeded by Montgomery. Thanks, in no small degree, to General Ritchie, General Wimberley was thereupon recalled from the 46th Division in May 1941 to take over the 51st, a position he held till August 1943.

A fighting Division takes not a little of its colour from its commanding officer, and, since General Wimberley commanded the 51st all through the African and Sicilian Campaigns, it is essential that some idea should be given of his background and his personality. His paternal great-grandfather was an Englishman, but since then his forbears had been resident in Scotland, and had taken to themselves Aberdeenshire and Argyllshire wives. He was born in a Scottish town and so into a Highland regiment. That town was Inverness, that regiment was the Cameron Highlanders. His grandfather had been Captain and Adjutant of the 79th Highlanders during the Indian Mutiny. Wimberley was educated at Nairn, Wellington, Cambridge and Sandhurst, and was commissioned to the Camerons in 1915. He served with them and in the 51st in France, was awarded an M.C., and attained Major's rank at the age of twenty-one.

After hostilities ceased he was appointed Captain and Adjutant of the 2nd Battalion of the Camerons. He commanded the 1st Battalion in 1938 and took it to France in 1939. His army tradition was entirely Scottish and in the re-formation of the 51st Division, and especially when the battalions were being brought up to full strength at Aldershot in 1942, he steadfastly refused to accept all and sundry drafts that were sent to him. He insisted on having Scots whenever and wherever they could be found. He personally visited a large number of Divisions and battalions in England, extracted, by every means in his power, such Scots as were serving in these units and had them transferred to the 51st. He made himself exceedingly unpopular with certain members of the " A " Staff at the War Office, where he was considered as a kind of "importunate widow "; he was in many ways as irritating as the lady in Luke's Gospel. The weary " A " Branch gave way to Wimberley's enthusiasm for everything Scottish. " Tartan Tam," the Jocks named him. Wimberley's ardour never flagged. His was the ecclesiastical belief that " whatsoever thy hand findeth to do, do it with thy might." The point was emphasised in the training at home and on the transport going to Africa, where Wimberley exhibited this super-enthusiasm for any form of activity which had for its purpose the training or the amusement of his men. He took part in all those activities, with the result that every Jock on the ship felt he had a personal acquaintance with the General.

That personal relationship between Divisional Commander and men continued all through the African and Sicilian Campaigns, and can be demonstrated by an incident which occurred just after the Battle of Alamein, when the whole position was somewhat fluid and uncertain, and information of what was happening was rather vague. A certain battalion was in a reserve position when Wimberley drove through in his jeep. When the General was passing close to a Jocks' slit trench, one of the " tenants " called out to him, " Could you tell us what is happening, sir ? " Wimberley stopped his jeep, got down into the slit trench, stretched out his map, which covered the whole Corps plan, and explained the situation in considerable detail to his two inquirers. Much of the information was considerably above the heads of the two Jocks, but nevertheless they were able to pass on through their platoon officer some details which even Battalion Headquarters did not then possess.

When General Wimberley arrived at any particular point he always created the impression that he was there, not to criticise anything you might be doing wrong, but to help you put things right. Although on occasion individuals might come in for an exceedingly severe dressing-down, no one ever complained that he had been unjustly reproved by the General.

Wimberley was no Divisional Headquarters' General. Where there was something doing, there he was to be found. When riding in a jeep his knees seemed to be constantly on a level with his chin, and that jeep and these long legs were a very familiar sight to all men of the Division, particularly when and where there was any form of trouble going on.

On one occasion, when the Division was moving along the coast road from Homs, near Tripoli, the German withdrawal had exceeded the speed of our advance, due partly to the difficult country we had to cross. When our troops reached the main road, they found the Germans had left it in chaos. Every bridge, of which there were a considerable number, had gone. At the corners all banking had been blown. The vanguard of the Division—moving in transport vehicles—could not make any great progress. The tired men did what they could to fill in holes, and make the " crooked places straight." But their efforts were by no means enough for General Wimberley's liking. He arrived in his jeep right up with the leading troops, and even helped with his own two hands to fill in the holes, exhorting and emphasising the dire necessity for further effort.

One of the points on which General Wimberley always insisted was that every Jock should be kept as fully in the picture as possible, and invariably before going into full-scale planned attacks on a Divisional basis he would have a conference to explain the whole position on a large Divisional model with all officers, generally down to Company Commanders, and on occasions down to Platoon Commanders. He then insisted that each Battalion Commander make his own scale model of the operation and show and explain it to every single man in the unit. This had the effect of keeping morale extremely high. Before Alamein the troops had not merely viewed the attack on models, but an area of ground had been laid out in full scale, and the whole operation rehearsed to such an extent that every man, before the actual operation began, knew absolutely in detail what he was expected to do, with the result that morale was so high that the personnel of the Division were not even conscious of what morale meant.

General Wimberley maintained that one of the essentials of good morale was the soldier's pride in his own unit. He insisted on the wearing of regimental tartan whenever possible, and he was fanatically enthusiastic about unit sign-posts. The enthusiasm and competition between units in the Division in the construction of their road sign-posts was intense, and resulted in the Division being named, when in North Africa, " The Highway Decorators." However, apart from the psychological effect, which was considerable, that sign-posting also had its practical effect in that units in the Highland Division were always easily found.

Such was the man who a second time acted the part of " the importunate widow." He held that the real place for the Highland Division and Highland regiments was in the fighting line, and it was due not a little to his insistence that in 1942 the scruples of certain authorities, who were somewhat chary, at a time when so small a part of Britain's army was engaged overseas, of pushing out another Highland Division into the front line of the war, were overcome. Those authorities were apparently not sure how the thinly populated North of Scotland would stand up once again to heavy casualties. General Wimberley, who knew the true spirit of the North, disabused their minds of that doubt.

Wimberley was a firm believer in spit-and-polish as an aid to morale. Just as when the 7th Black Watch came back from the Shetlands in September 1941 to Fochabers Castle and paraded before him in much worn battle-dress, he had the whole battalion at once reclothed, so, all through the campaigns in Africa and Sicily, he saw to it that, whenever out of battle, his men paraded as well turned out as circumstances permitted. When the Division arrived in Africa he discovered that the idea among many of the troops already there was to go about rather like wild men of the woods. This was supposed to be the proper thing to do in the Desert Army. General Wimberley would have none of it. His Division was to have " a guid conceit o' themsel's " on all occasions. They were the " Highway Decorators " in more ways than that of plastering the Divisional sign wherever they went, that " the world might behold and know." Whenever and wherever possible, guards and pipe-bands had to be turned out spick and span and, when kilts were available, kilts were worn.[1]

Further, Wimberley believed that a high sense of duty had a far better effect than an inculcation of hate in making a Scottish battalion an efficient fighting unit. When the Division moved down into England in 1942 in their final preparation for going overseas, they found in force there a new system of battle-training, in which the underlying psychological idea was this inculcation of hate. In some Divisional Battle Schools instructors went about shouting " Hate ! Hate ! Hate ! "; dummies on bayonet-fighting courses were even smeared with pigs' blood to stimulate realism. It was thought a good thing that the men in training should also be smeared with blood. The G.O.C. Highland Division would have absolutely none of it. He believed—and rightly—that the strong religious background of his Scots, with their national and traditional sense of freedom and justice, with their immense pride of regiment and their inherent belief in a worthy cause, made such things as the inculcation of synthetic " hate " entirely unnecessary.

---

[1] That this policy paid a dividend was later obvious from a letter from General Leese sent to the Divisional Commander soon after Montgomery arrived. It stated : " The Army Commander was most impressed with the training, discipline, and general bearing and turn-out of your troops. You have magnificent material and you have brought it up to a high state of discipline and morale." Again, the author of ' The History of the Rifle Brigade, 1939-45,' writing of the North African Campaign, states : " As the war went on, various loyalties outside the regiment arose. There was a genuine Divisional spirit. The 50th Division were quite sure they were better than the 51st, and no one in the Highland Division imagined that any other formation could approach the smartness or performance of his own."

Moreover, the G.O.C. entirely disapproved of any form of entertainment where concert parties put on turns which, to say the least of it, were low. His disapproval was seconded by the men, who simply stayed away from shows of that kind, and the " Balmorals "—that Divisional concert party with a tradition back to 1915—found always full and appreciative " houses " for their straight clean entertainment.

There had been a " Balmorals " concert party captured with the Division at St Valéry. The tradition was continued in the reconstituted Division and a new " Balmorals," sponsored by General Neil Ritchie, had its first rehearsal in Dufftown Town Hall in October 1940 and gave its first performance in His Majesty's Theatre in Aberdeen a month later. Sergeant Barker (Gordons), who was " O.C." of the party, has recorded in his diary Wimberley's influence on the " Show."[1] " One evening in June (1941)," writes Barker, " when the curtain went up in the village hall in Kemnay we saw the drain-pipe Cameron ' trews ' stretched out towards the footlights. The following morning I was summoned to Kemnay House, the lovely thirteenth-century castle which was 152 Brigade H.Q. and where Wimberley was staying overnight. The interview lasted an hour and was memorable. Wimberley started by saying that he believed that in peace-time I had been a dramatic critic. He, of course, was not a dramatic critic: he was just a plain regular soldier who knew very little about the theatre. Now he had enjoyed last night's show immensely, really very clever and amusing, but (if I as a dramatic critic would not mind a few remarks from a plain regular soldier) he had just one or two comments. He then produced a number of suggestions, all designed to give the revue what perhaps it lacked—a quite unmistakable Scottish flavour.

" ' You people are a link between all the battalions and the units in the Division,' he told me. ' At the moment there isn't a 51st Highland Division, just a series of battalions—the Black Watch, the Seaforth, the Argylls, the Camerons and all the rest. You can be a unifying force. Travelling as you do from one to the other it is up to you to convey the general tone and spirit of the Division as a whole. I want to build up an *esprit de corps*—the tradition of the old Highland Brigade. I want you to help me get over the idea.' "

From the beginning General Wimberley inculcated into his Division the conception of " Here's tae us! Wha's like us ? " That made for brotherhood in a Division, where even senior officers addressed each

[1] By permission of Mr Felix Barker.

other by their first names. There was no question of cheap familiarity. It was a matter of a deep sense of that "family" relationship which was not the least of the qualities that helped the Division to victory.

So with Divisional Headquarters at Aberlour in Banffshire, and Brigade Headquarters at Dingwall, Elgin and Banchory, the new 51st went into hard training.[1]

In April 1942 the Division was relieved in north-eastern Scotland by the 52nd (Lowland) Division and moved to Aldershot, where six weeks were spent in the final training and outfitting. Billets were bad, the weather was good, training was intensive. Everyone had more than his fill of P.T. and route-marching, so that the diversion of combined action with tank units was very welcome, even if being "run over" by a tank—the experience every infantryman had to undergo—was not accepted with universal enthusiasm. The issue of tropical kit was a direct indication that the Division was for the East—but, Middle or Far, no one knew. The Medical Officers did their bit by purging units of the unfit and got busy with the inoculating needles. Other needles were kept at it sewing on new Divisional and regimental marks on uniforms, and, when all was spick and span and ready, their Majesties the King and Queen arrived on the 1st of June to inspect the Division. And then—such is the way of the Intelligence Branch of the War Office —instructions were received to remove all the new distinguishing marks from the uniforms—for security reasons. Still, the Division had the satisfaction of knowing that their Majesties had appreciated the turnout; for General Wimberley received a letter from the Royal Secretary congratulating him " on the outstanding success of the visit of the King and Queen to your Division. It is impossible to imagine a better-run show and I hope, if you have not already done so, you will let the troops know how delighted their Majesties were with everything they saw. You must indeed feel proud of your splendid Command."

In the third week of June the Division left by train, some units for the Mersey, some for the Severn, some for the Clyde, and embarked on transports for active service for a destination and a fate unknown. It was to travel far, to earn great renown, and to suffer almost 16,000 casualties before its task was done. On 21st June, in dense fog, one contingent steamed down the Clyde, foghorns, not pipes, playing them

[1] They had trained for two and a half years, most of that time under the supervision of General Thorne, C.-in-C. Scotland. How different from the conditions in the First World War, when the 9th Division went into battle at Loos one year after being embodied.

out, and not till Islay lay astern did the sun shine on the armada of transport vessels with the escort of destroyers and corvettes. Six days out the defence was strengthened by the battleship *Malaya*.

At the end of the week the fleet passed the Azores, and three days later the Cape Verde Islands. Then, perhaps, came the most unhappy period of the voyage, when the ships lay off Freetown to refuel. The threat of malaria made shore-leave impossible, and from the crowded decks the troops in the sweltering heat gazed at the greenery of Sierra Leone. It is not the least of the Division's credits that the men, though grumbling luxuriously at their cramped quarters and the appalling atmospheric conditions, never lost their sense of humour. Up to this time black-out regulations had been enforced rigorously, and smoking on deck in the dark was treated as a major offence. Natives in their canoes hovered round the ships, and men who disregarded the warning not to purchase fruit paid the penalty in what is described as "gripes."

A few days after leaving Freetown the convoy crossed the Line, and Father Neptune replicated himself the necessary number of times. The battle against boredom was fought with considerable success. In some ships the troops went back, as it were, to school. There were departments in all sorts of military subjects, and officers and men moved in small classes from one to the other "school" in periodic rotation. B.B.C. methods of intelligence competitions were adopted, and there were all sorts of athletic contests. By day the various denizens of the deep kept interest going, and by night the stars and planets "did their stuff."

Then one morning (18th July) the troops set eyes on that hill, three feet higher than Schiehallion. Table Mountain had kept on her table-cloth of mist for the Division's benefit, and beneath the hill lay in the peace and contentment of the sunshine the white houses of Cape Town. The convoy dropped anchor here. The officers and men went ashore that evening to a city that knew no black-out, to a welcome that knew no limits. In their march through the town they underwent their first bombardment, but the ammunition of the "enemy" consisted of oranges. The visit was all too short, for the fleet had to be off Durban by the 26th. The ships lay off that city, but only the troops on board the *Stratheden* were allowed ashore, and were given quarters on the Greynell race-course where their particular hosts were Colonel Lloyd Rennie (a Black Watch man of the 1914-18 war) and Major Neville Blair (of the 2nd Battalion of the same regiment) who was responsible for movement control in the city. Major Blair had been severely wounded at Tobruk, torpedoed when being evacuated, and was convalescing in Durban. The pipes and drums of the 7th Black Watch played " Retreat " in the city square.

It was at this point that General Wimberley, his G.S.O.1, Colonel Roy Urquhart, and his A.Q.M.G., Colonel J. A. Colam, set out on a private adventure. They were to fly to Cairo. Since such a flight necessitated a landing in neutral territory, General Wimberley had to take upon himself some civilian designation. He selected that of a traveller in Scotch whisky while his G.S.O.1 posed as a piano-tuner! The flight was without incident, except that the G.S.O.1 was not then " air-bodied." [1] He did, however, fall asleep at one point, only to be awakened by the whisky traveller who thought he had spotted some hippopotami. The piano-tuner showed no interest in the wild life.

Meanwhile the convoy set sail from Durban on 26th July.[2] All this time less and less happy news was filtering through from North Africa. The Division learned that Tobruk had fallen. Our troops had failed to hold Mersa Matruh and had to retire to a place called El Alamein. But the New Zealand Division had stemmed the enemy rush. A crack German Division, the " 90th Light," had attacked time and again on the coastal road, but had been held. But the German guns could be heard in Alexandria, and our navy had had to abandon that port as a base. Alamein, the New Zealand Division, the 9th Australian Division, the 90th Light—they had not much meaning for the 51st then! But they were to mean very much to the Highland Division in the not so distant future. The convoy crossed back over the Equator on 3rd August. By this time all were aware that it was to be Egypt and Rommel, and three days later the fleet reached the hot barrenness of the rocks made famous in a pipe-tune so well known to all the Division— " The Barren Rocks of Aden." Good-bye was said to that part of the convoy which was carrying troops to the Far East, and in their eight ships the Highland Division hung about in the horror of the Red Sea until such time as berths became vacant at Suez. The nine weeks' voyage was over.

The majority of the troops disembarked at Port Tewfik and Geneffa, and finally the Division concentrated around Quassassin. Undoubtedly this was a good area in which to break the men into the miseries of

[1] Later Urquhart commanded with distinction an Airborne Division.
[2] Temporarily under the command of Brigadier Douglas Graham (Cameronians), who had commanded 153 Brigade since 1940.

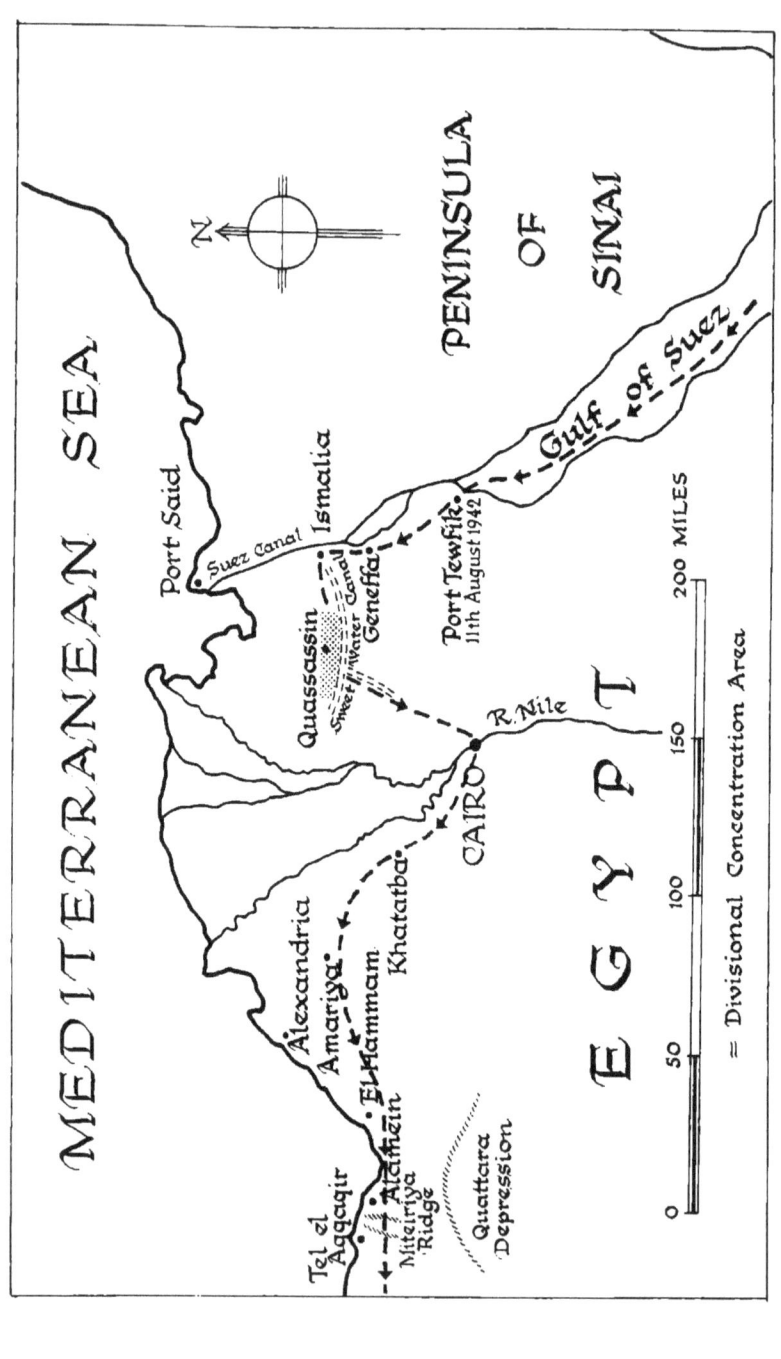

PORT TEWFIK, 11TH AUGUST 1942. BATTLE OF ALAMEIN, 23RD OCTOBER-3RD NOVEMBER

Egypt. One tarmac road, with nothing about it to suggest whence it came or whither it was going, ran across a bleak stony desert. Of wild or other life there was none, except for flies which expressed their resentment of the invasion of the Scots by biting them night and day. The sun also took a hand in the baptism. At fifty camps—each 1000 yards long by 500 yards broad, and marked by huge water-towers—the Division lived in tents dug well into the sand, and everyone down to Company Commanders listened to lectures, while the people of lower rank did physical training and route-marching by the sun by day and by the compass by night. The transport practised driving over the desert. Most of the troops had a certain amount of time off, spent in the agonies of dysentery. Many fought their battle against this "gyppy tummy" while carrying on the breaking-in training, but there was a large percentage of hospital cases. The one tonic was a visit from Mr Winston Churchill complete with his cigar. He was accompanied by General Alan Brooke, the Chief of the Imperial General Staff, and he personally addressed the officers of each battalion. Mr Churchill wrote: "The 51st Highland Division was not yet regarded as 'desert worthy,' but these magnificent troops were now ordered to man the Nile front."

How thankful all were when Rommel's threat of an invasion of the Nile Delta got the Highland Division going again! In the fourth week of August the Division moved into the Delta area by way of Khatatba. Their job was to defend the approaches to Cairo from the west and the south-west. The 152 Brigade took up positions across the Mena–Cairo road, the 153 Brigade was deployed in the desert south of Mena, and the 154 Brigade covered the Nile Barrage area west of Cairo. General Wimberley had his headquarters at Ghizira Island, and the Divisional artillery were in battle positions along the Nile Valley from Mena to Cairo. The troops in the vicinity of Cairo had, if anything, the more uncomfortable time. The flies continued their ravages, and the irritation they caused to the body was equalled only by the irritation caused to the mind by certain Egyptians who, under their standard of neutrality, seemed to take pleasure in interfering on every possible occasion with our precautionary defence plans. The local inhabitants were continually arguing about the rights of private property and the destruction of crops. In the region of the Delta Barrage the Arabs were equally disagreeable about the digging-up of their pea-nuts. The further trouble was the filth in which sections of the local population were content to live and thrive, but which did not suit Western habits.

There the Division waited for full moon and the Bosche attack. He was only fifty miles away, on a line that stretched from El Alamein in the north to the Quattara Depression some forty miles to the south. The sea, and this Depression—a great salt waste—limited the area of the attack. In the majority of the descriptions of the fighting in North Africa, the language of the technique of the boxing-ring has been used. Our High Command did not seem to be worried by the possibilities of Rommel's straight lefts or straight rights, but the possibility of this right hook—or rather right swing for it was so far out—did trouble them. Montgomery had taken over command of the 8th Army on 13th August, and he had immediately ordered that there would be no withdrawals under any circumstances from what was known as the Alamein Line. He stopped all breaking-up of Divisions,[1] introduced a very powerful reserve line, and he was ready for Rommel, his full moon, and what the German leader had stated to be the " final annihilation of the enemy." The attack began on the night of the 30th-31st August. The straight left in the north was taken on their gloves by the Australians ; the straight right in the centre caught the 5th Indian Division, shook them, but their counter was effective. The real punch was perhaps more of a right hook than, as some had expected, a swing, and it hit Montgomery's forces in the Ragil Depression. It was a severe punch, but the mobile troops used the ring well. Still the enemy pressed, and it was obvious he was aiming at the Alam El Halfa Ridge almost halfway between the sea and the Quattara Depression. But our guard was too good, our counter-punches too hard, the enemy backed away and by 7th September the Battle of Alam Halfa was over, and all we had lost was the western edge of our minefields. Round one was completed. It would be the Commonwealth Army's business to carry the fight to the enemy in round two.

Unlike conditions in an ordinary boxing-match, it was left to Montgomery to say how long the rest was to be between rounds. Meanwhile the Highland Division moved out into the " real " desert. It should be understood that this " desert " did not consist entirely of deep sand. In many areas it had a bottoming of hard rock with a thin layer of sand like a carpet on top of it. The main difficulty, as far as movement (especially of vehicles) was concerned, was that in areas, often several square miles in extent, there was very deep sand which

[1] Over a smaller matter Montgomery also at once showed his wisdom. He encouraged the use of Divisional " flashes " on the arm. This was fortunate for the 51st, who had brought out many thousand HD flashes from home, but, till General Montgomery's arrival, had been told that flashes were not to be worn in the 8th Army.

THE PHŒNIX

completely held up transport. Vehicles were regularly " bogged " in this sand. The rock areas also presented a problem, because digging-in there was practically impossible. The whole terrain was comparatively flat and the result was that, as the vehicles carrying the troops bumped along, the grains of sand, ground to even smaller particles by the wheels and caterpillars, rose in dense clouds and not only reduced visibility to a matter of yards, but powdered all the troops and, mixing with the perspiration, coloured them like cinema actors with a " make-up " very difficult to get rid of.

The Division went to an area some twenty-five miles east of El Alamein in front of El Hammam, where they proceeded to occupy what were known as " Boxes." Those " Boxes " were really reserve defensive areas, each capable of holding a complete Brigade, and were closed in on all sides by minefields. From them the 51st functioned in two ways. In the first place it was affiliated to the friendly and very efficient 9th Australian Division, and batches of officers and men were sent up to the front line to be educated in the economy of the warfare of the desert. In fact each Brigade in turn did a tour of one week's duty with the Australians, who helped them in every possible way. At the Battle of Alamein that part of the line visited during those tours was the actual frontage of the Highland Division's attack.

The Australians had a different type of discipline from ours, but in the line our men learned very valuable lessons from those fine troops. The Aussies kept their weapons scrupulously clean and always free from sand. Their slit trenches were prepared with the utmost care, and each trench was completely equipped with such things as grenades. Before a party left on patrol each member of it was searched thoroughly for any identification marks. By night silence was enforced and no lights were allowed. When a patrol returned from its job a complete account of its investigation and acquired information was recorded on a map, and such maps combined with air-pictures gave the most detailed information of the enemy's minefields and other defences.[1]

General Wimberley spent a great deal of time in the line, and, from the excellent maps and his own personal observation, there was constructed about ten miles to the south of our " Boxes " area a full-scale

[1] General Morshead, the distinguished Commander of the 9th Australian Division, after his return to Australia was most generous in his praise of the 51st, singling the Division out for special comment. He also paid tribute to the efficiency of the British Artillery in the battle of Alamein. He described the Highlanders as the Australians' staunch friends. This was much appreciated by the 51st, as the Jocks knew that the 9th Australians had had fiercer fighting during the battle than any other Division in the whole 8th Army.

dummy of the German position which the Division were to attack in the coming offensive. Wire and minefields had been laid down at the correct distances and of the correct depth. The dummy no-man's-land was exactly the same width as the actual area. Our own guns fired barrages with live ammunition and advances were made on facsimiles of the actual positions, and, as far as could be accomplished, under the actual conditions. The troops would advance in those sham attacks as much as 8000 yards, take their objectives, re-organise for counter-attacks, lay new minefields, and dig new slit trenches. The front each battalion had to take extended to some six hundred yards, and Wimberley, to increase interest and *esprit de corps*, named the parts of the trench system to be attacked by the various battalions after the home-towns of those battalions.[1]

Slowly operation orders were built up to the very last detail, and, by the time the Division departed to take over the actual line from the Australians, the officers and men had completed their apprenticeship and felt themselves qualified as journeymen. So they waited for the full moon on the night of 23rd-24th October.

To understand what the Division had to accomplish in the Battle of El Alamein it is necessary to have a general idea of Montgomery's plan. In short, that plan consisted of a reverse of the up to then accepted desert procedure. Instead of first sending in armour against the enemy to do the breaking-up and then following up with infantry, the G.O.C.-in-C. decided to have his infantry first force a gap through which the armour could later pour, flood out, and, to continue the metaphor, drown the enemy completely. The second idea was to cheat the enemy into believing that Montgomery intended to force a gap in the weak defence in the south, while in actual fact the attack was to be made on the enemy's strongest positions in the north. Montgomery accordingly made a concentration of dummy tanks, etc., on his southern rear, and moved 13th Corps into that area.

The main thrust was to be made by 30th Corps (General Leese) on a four-Divisional front, from which two gaps were to be driven through the enemy's minefields. The 9th Australian Division was to attack on the right, the 51st Highland Division on the right centre, the 2nd New Zealand Division on the left centre, and the 1st South African Division on the left. Thus the Highland Division was placed, as part of General

---

[1] So realistic were those practice attacks that a certain price had to be paid. Sir Arthur Wilmot, Second-in-Command of the 42nd, along with several others, was killed.

Major-General DOUGLAS WIMBERLEY, DIVISIONAL COMMANDER, NORTH AFRICA AND SICILY

GENERALS IN THE DESERT (*Left to Right*), MORSHEAD (9TH AUSTRALIAN DIVISION), WIMBERLEY, LEESE (30TH CORPS), AND PIENAAR (SOUTH AFRICAN DIVISION)

By courtesy of the   IMPERIAL WAR MUSEUM

VICTORY PARADE, TRIPOLI. 4TH FEBRUARY 1943

By courtesy of MAJOR D. F. O. RUSSELL

Montgomery's plan and greatly to its benefit, between two most experienced fighting Divisions. When the gap was made, the 1st Armoured Division was to pass through the 51st, who had attached to them for the duration of the battle the 50th Battalion of the Royal Tank Corps and a detachment of the 30th Corps Royal Engineers. The 2nd Seaforth (Lt.-Col. MacKessack) were initially sent to Corps Reserve.

There were four positional enemy lines which it was the Division's business to capture. But it should be clearly understood that those lines were not definite enemy strong-points. They were really lines laid down by the artillery barrage, which lifted from one line to another as the attack developed. Groups of the enemy were to be met before the first of those barrage lines was reached. The 153 Brigade was on the right, the 154 on the left, and the 152 in reserve.[1] The first four lines (Green, Red, Black, and Blue) were to be taken in three attacks, with reorganising periods in between, by—from right to left—the 5th Black Watch (Lt.-Col. Rennie), 5/7th Gordons (Lt.-Col. Saunders), 1st Black Watch (Lt.-Col. Roper Caldbeck), 7th Argylls (Lt.-Col. L. Campbell), and two Companies of the 5th Camerons (Major Davey). The 5th Black Watch and the Cameron detachment, however, were to halt at the Red Line, and their places were to be taken by the 1st Gordons (Lt.-Col. Murray) and the 7th Black Watch (Lt.-Col. Oliver). The 1st Black Watch and 5/7th Gordons were to halt at the Black Line, and the final assault on the Blue Line was to be made by the remaining battalions in conjunction with elements of the Reconnaissance Regiment (Colonel Grant) and the 50th Battalion of the Royal Tank Corps. On capturing the Blue Line, fighting patrols were to be sent forward to do their best to destroy enemy gun-positions and to assist the advance of the 1st Armoured Division, while the detachment from the 5th Camerons was then to rejoin its unit in 152 Brigade, whose business was to act as moppers-up of the captured area. The advance up to the forward enemy minefield was to be at the rate of one hundred yards in two minutes and afterwards one hundred yards in three minutes.

Before the attack began it was the job of 152 Brigade to make eleven gaps through our own minefields to the assembly positions. Three of these gaps had already been made and were named (north to south) Sun, Moon, and Star. The 5th Seaforth (Lt.-Col. Stirling) were given the

[1] The Brigadiers were George Murray (152), Douglas Graham (153), and Harry Houldsworth (154).

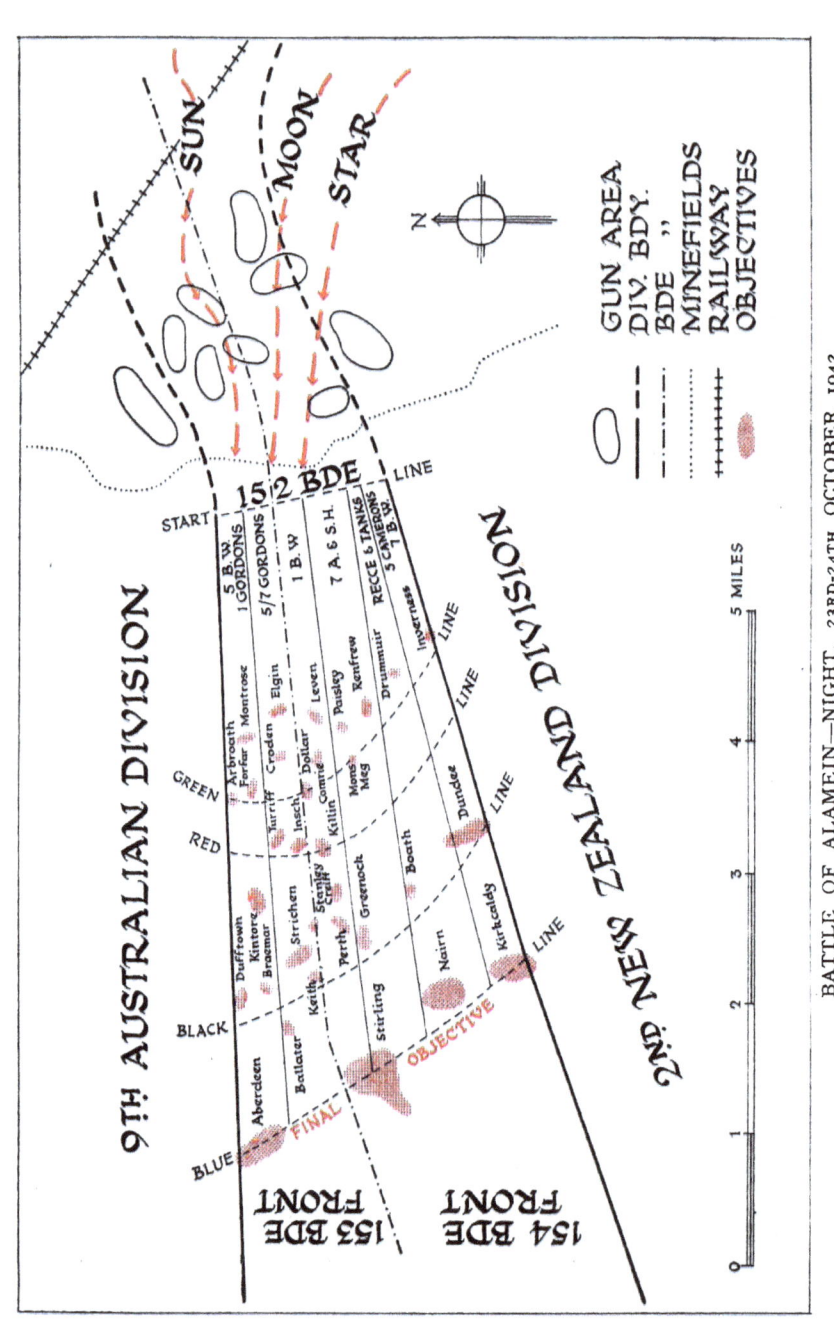

BATTLE OF ALAMEIN—NIGHT, 23RD-24TH OCTOBER 1942

particular job of laying tapes along the whole 2500 yards of the Divisional start-line, and nine lines backwards from that tape along which the various formations could advance. Alastair Borthwick describes how this work was done in his 'Sans Peur.'[1] He writes :—

"It was not an easy task. If we laid all the tape—and there were nine miles of it—on the night before the attack, any German patrol stumbling on it would know what we were up to. If we waited until the night of the attack before laying it and then spent too much time over the job, the assaulting troops would be caught by daylight before they had dug in on their objectives. However, by planning and much practice, a solution had been found. We and the rest of the Division had already fought the battle three times in 'M' Training Area behind our lines and after a good deal of trial and error a drill had been evolved.

"We began work on the night of 19th-20th October. The first difficulty was to pinpoint the ends of the start-line. If they were wrongly placed the whole layout would be wrong; and the only way to fix them in surroundings as featureless as the ocean was to have several officers start with compasses in their hands from known points behind our trenches and pace carefully along on bearings until they converged. Once these key points had been fixed, a drum of signal cable, invisible in the dark, was unrolled along the start-line and tied to short metal pickets which we hammered in every fifty yards. It was unlikely that the Boche would find the cable, and if they did it would not tell them much.

"Sixty men finished this part of the job in one night. On the night of 21st-22nd October we were out again; and by dawn the nine routes had been plotted, the nine cables laid, and the pickets driven in. We still had a night in hand before the attack; and Colonel Stirling, who had practically lived in no-man's-land since the taping began, spent it in guiding representatives of the other battalions along the cable to show them the layout and allow them to mark their own boundaries and centre-points. It was found by pacing that the routes delivered units on to the start-line very accurately throughout its length.

"The spade-work was now complete. On the night of the battle, parties went out at dusk with drums of white tape, unrolled them, fixed the tape to the cable at intervals so that it could not be blown or dragged away, and ninety minutes later the nine miles of start-line and routes were clearly marked."

One Company of the Middlesex Regiment (Lt.-Col. Stephenson) was attached to 153 Brigade and another to 154 Brigade, and each Brigade had Tank Squadrons under command. In the Divisional operation order one paragraph is headed "Morale," and states: "There will be no surrender for unwounded men. Any troops of the Highland Division

---

[1] By permission of the author.

cut off will continue to fight. The vital parts which such pockets of resistance will play in attaining victory must be impressed on all ranks before battle." On the map for the attack the names of Scottish towns, intimately connected with the attacking regiments, were used to designate objectives, and this kind of game was continued in the success code-words which were "porridge, haggis, whisky, brandy, tea, coffee, plum and apple." A memory of 1916 was held in the passwords. On D Day and till midday on D-plus-1 Day the word was to be "Uncle." After midday on D-plus-1 Day and on D-plus-2 Day it was to be "Harper."[1]

We may be permitted at this point in our story to listen to the words of Montgomery months afterwards in Tripoli, for they explain the position of the untried Highland Division in its relationship to the other Divisions taking part in the battle. In his address to all officers of 30th Corps in Tripoli on 9th February 1943, the Army Commander said: " I well remember that night on 23rd October when the Highland Division went into battle with its bagpipes for the first time. I don't suppose anyone will forget that night. I know that the Highland Division was anxious to do its stuff well, to wipe out and avenge the debt passed on to them by that other Highland Division that fought at St Valéry. I put the Highland Division in between two veteran Divisions, the 9th Australian Division on their right and the New Zealand Division on their left, so that they need not worry about their flanks. There is no doubt that the Highland Division did its first battle right well. I had to leave it behind in the pursuit battle, but so long as I command this Army I shall never leave it behind again. I don't suppose that anyone who saw the parade on 4th February would ever forget that Division marching past in the square of Tripoli. I would say to the Highland Division that the debt you had to pay has been well and truly paid, and you have well and truly avenged that other Division who fought in France. I don't say you won't pay a few more debts before you are finished."

On the night of 22nd-23rd October the Division moved into positions consisting of slit trenches dug just behind the jumping-off line. Then came dawn of the 23rd, one of the most trying days that the men were called upon to endure. There must be no movement whatever during all that long day. So each slit trench had to suffice for all purposes—even that of a latrine. In all the high-tension expectancy the passing

[1] After General "Uncle" Harper of 1916-18.

of time seemed to slow down, till each leaden-footed second appeared to be an hour, and how welcome were the setting of the sun and the coming of the dark! With that dark came hot food and visits from senior officers, last orders and last " good-lucks," and then cramped limbs were dragged from the slits and the troops moved to the starting tape—it was in fact a tape. The whole desert lay quiet, lit up by the brilliance of the light of a full moon, and then at 9.40 P.M. came the starter's pistol—the firing of a single round from a single gun. There was scarcely time to appreciate it, when hell broke out behind our men in the roar of guns, hell shrieked over the top of them as the shells passed above their heads, and hell blazed into hideous noise and light in front of them where those shells exploded on the enemy's rear battery positions. Then those explosions moved towards them as our artillery shortened their range and concentrated on the enemy's front lines. But by that time enemy mortars and machine-guns got busy and were giving the Scots their baptism of fire.

And here tribute must be paid to the remarkable work of the Divisional artillery and of its Commander, Brigadier George Elliot. Not only had our gunners to carry out one of the most elaborate barrage bombardments ever known in warfare, but they had innumerable individual targets on which to concentrate, and they tackled their whole job in its wider aspects and in its details magnificently. Not a little of the efficiency of the Highland Divisional artillery throughout the battle, and indeed the whole North African Campaign, was due to Elliot. He was the most thorough and conscientious of Brigadiers. He took endless pains and often wore himself out in the process, to ensure that the Jocks going into the attack should have the best artillery support it was possible to give. As a result, as with the 51st Artillery in 1916-18, the infantry of the Division particularly liked having its own artillery behind them and had good reason to trust in that artillery's accuracy. A soldier might have described that mighty barrage passing over his head as the noise of many wings, and the couplet from the old poem might have come back to his memory :—

> " The Angel of Death spread his wings on the blast,
> And breathed in the face of the foe as he passed."

The success gained by the gunners was only the outcome of very hard practice. They had had four training exercises designed to produce similar conditions to those foreseen. Three weeks before D Day they had to begin digging their pit emplacements. That work had to be done at night, and all of it concealed before morning light. It was necessary even to hide the bootmarks of the working parties, who bivouacked on the seashore during the day. All ammunition had to be brought up by night and similarly concealed. Sometimes rocks made digging-drills difficult, and then the sappers with their compressors came to the aid of the gunners. Finally the guns were brought up, and two days before the battle began everything was in position. An F.O.O. complete with wireless was attached to each of the infantry battalions.

At 9.40 P.M. the guns opened up. The whole sky was lit by leaping flashes that seared the dark. For a split second each flash illuminated a few square yards of surrounding desert. In that moment of time every detail stood out pin sharp like a revelation—patches of desert scrub, the harsh outline of the gun, huddling figures of soldiers, the corner of a camouflage net, a petrol tin lying in the sand. The noise was like a physical blow. The men on the guns were deafened by the first shot. They never heard the other shells.

Every hour each gun rested for ten minutes to allow the barrel to cool. When they stopped firing, the crew cleared the pit of empty shell-boxes and the artificer quickly checked various parts of the gun mechanism. All that night the 800 guns of the 8th Army pounded the Afrika Korps. Next morning exhausted gunners slept in the pits. Empty green metal ammunition boxes lay in heaps all round. Each gun had fired over 600 shells.

At each pit one gunner was awake in case fire orders came through. Each gun was loaded and laid on a likely target. Eyes red-rimmed, faces caked with dust, the guards stood in steel helmets and with greatcoats buttoned over their shirts and shorts (for at dawn the desert is asleep and cold).[1]

Not only was the initial strafing a success, but shortly after midday on the first day of the battle some artillery units began an advance to forward positions through gaps in the minefields made by the Royal Engineers.

And no praise can be too great in considering the gapping-work of the sappers. Their coolness in their activities, the most productive of anxiety in the whole attack, was equalled only by the thoroughness with which they carried out the job. Observing the first of them

---

[1] In this battle two of the Artillery Lieutenant-Colonels were killed—Lt.-Col. Fraser-Mackenzie of Allangrange and Lt.-Col. J. H. B. Evatt.

moving up, with their mine-detectors, followed by mine-markers and mine-lifters, one might have found a verse from " Alice " keeping repeating in his mind :—

> " If seven maids with seven mops
> Swept it for half a year,
> Do you suppose," the Walrus said,
> " That they could get it clear ? "

So the reincarnated 51st Highland Division moved forward to its first battle, and in front of each battalion marched its pipers playing.[1] The value of the courage and music of those pipers can never be fully estimated. And in recording the bravery of one individual we pay homage to all.

Private Duncan McIntyre of the 5th Black Watch led his Company playing his pipes. Fearlessly he moved forward, men falling all around him in the intense concentration of enemy artillery, mortar, and small-arms fire. Then, as they came to the moment of the assault, McIntyre broke into the regimental march, and " by his complete disregard of personal danger and by his fine example he inspired his comrades to advance to the objective, which was captured." He died on that objective, hit by a mortar bomb, his pipes still clasped in his arms.

And all that sharp, thin, warlike music, which rang clear along the line in the lulls and played Scotland's honour in front of the advancing Highlanders at Alamein, was taken into that everlasting glory of sound that shrilled at Waterloo, at Sevastopol, by the walls of Lucknow and on the Dargai hills ; that music that the 1st Black Watch pipers made on 9th May 1915 at Richebourg-Festubert, when, as was written of them then : " With their characteristic fury they vanished into the smoke, and the only evidence that remained was the sound of the pipes " ; that music which the 4th Camerons played in the murderous attack at swampy Festubert ; that music which the 1st Gordons played at Longueval, when it was told of them : " They were out of sight right over the parapet, but we could hear at intervals the shouts of ' Scotland for Ever ' and the faint strain of the pipes." In all those old fights, as Philip Gibbs wrote : " Over the open battlefields came the music of the Scottish pipes, shrill above the noise of gunfire." So at Alamein the

[1] Kippenberger, the New Zealander, in his book 'Infantry Brigadier,' writes: " Far away on our right I could hear clearly the skirling of the Highland pipes, warlike stirring music."

tradition was maintained by Wimberley's battle message of "Scotland for Ever, and Second to None!"

But let us see how the various battalions fared.

The 7th Argylls attacked with "C" and "D" Companies leading, their pipers playing "Monymusk." Their enemies in the first advance were not so much Germans and Italians as anti-personnel mines and booby-traps. But by eleven o'clock these Companies had taken all their first objectives, and, after re-forming, set out half an hour later for the Red Line. Midnight saw them victors there, and then things began to get a bit more difficult. The enemy artillery had found the range, and some of our shells were falling short. So the Argylls dug themselves in and waited till one o'clock, when they advanced on *Greenock*, where the Italians played every dirty trick they knew—holding up their hands in token of surrender and then slinging across a grenade. But Argyll bayonets "won the night," and by two o'clock every Italian was dead or rendered incapable of further interest in the battle. The two leading Argyll Companies had suffered heavily—only some sixty effective men being left—and the commanding officer, Lt.-Col. Lorne Campbell, called off a further advance and set himself to prepare a position to meet a counter-offensive. The enemy, however, did nothing about it, and on Sunday night the reinforced Argylls proceeded to attack a ridge, *Nairn* in the battle nomenclature. Again magnificent work with the bayonet resulted in the capture of the position. On the night of 30th October the Argylls were relieved by the Royal Botha Regiment of the 1st South African Division, but three days later were sent in again to relieve a battalion of the 2nd New Zealand Division and attack a strong-point named Tel El Aqqaqir. This attack will be described later.

Among members of the battalion who particularly distinguished themselves were Sergeant Bauld, who led his men against machine-gun posts with extraordinary dash and determination, and was personally responsible for putting an end to ten of the enemy; Lance-Corporal Lake, who displayed great courage and initiative in collecting men temporarily "lost" owing to their officers having become casualties, and leading them on to their objectives; the Medical Sergeant Smith, whose work not only saved a great deal of suffering, but gave an example of the highest devotion to duty; Captain John Meiklejohn, who with a composite force captured and, though surrounded, held *Nairn*; Major Lindsay Macdougall of Lunga who, with complete disregard for danger, kept giving his men orders through a megaphone.

The job of the 7th Black Watch, who were on the left flank of the Division and who had the New Zealand Division on their left flank, was to pass through the Companies of 5th Camerons when those Companies had taken their objectives on the Red Line, and then to capture "The Ben," a prominent feature on the north-west end of the Miteirya Ridge. This ridge was the only real bit of high ground on the enemy's front. It rose some thirty feet above the desert, and, for the very reason of its unique nature, was all the more prominent, and all the more difficult an objective. "C" and "B" Companies led, and were a little more fortunate than "A" and "D," who suffered many casualties from enemy shelling. So two composite Companies were formed. "B" and "D" pushed ahead to the final objective, while "A" and "C" reorganised on the Black Line. "B" and "D" (under Captain Cathcart) did finally take the Miteirya position.[1] Up to 31st October the Battalion's business was to hold that position, to clean up any groups of the enemy left behind this new front line, and to make proper junction with the 7th Argylls on the right. All those things were done, and on 31st October the Cape Town Highlanders relieved the Black Watch. After a short rest the 7th also was sent to relieve a New Zealand Battalion nearer the coast.

The 7th Black Watch record in this action teems with stories of brave men who reorganised parties which had suffered severely from shelling. Captain Cathcart's and Lieutenant Gillies'[2] work in this line was very conspicuous, as was that of Captain Russell, the Adjutant, who though twice wounded insisted on remaining at his post of duty until a relief could be provided two days later. Private J. Smith also distinguished himself when a runner bringing a message from the 21st New Zealand Battalion was killed by a sniper. Without being instructed to do so, Smith set out and although shot in the shoulder and temporarily knocked out reached the dead man, found the message and brought it back to the officer commanding his Company—and then offered to take a reply back to the New Zealanders.

"B" and "C" Companies of the Camerons advanced to the tune of

---

[1] Kippenberger, the New Zealander, in 'Infantry Brigadier,' writes as follows: "I went across to see if there was a proper tie-up in the inter-Brigade boundary. Our neighbours on the right were a very depleted Black Watch Company in good touch with us. Their casualties were very heavy but they had all their objectives. I returned by the right-hand route seeing an extraordinary number of dead Highlanders who must have strayed into our area. In front of one post there was a whole section, corporal and seven men, lying in line, all on their faces."

[2] Son of the well-known Highland minister and Gaelic scholar of Kenmore.

"The Inverness Gathering" played by their pipers, one of them, Pipe-Corporal Campbell, bearded like the pipers of old.

> " Then wild and high the ' Camerons' Gathering ' rose!
> The war-note of Lochiel which Albyn's hills
> Have heard, . . .
> . . . But with the breath which fills
> Their mountain pipe, so fill the mountaineers
> With the fierce native daring which instils
> The shining memory of a thousand years." [1]

Move back then to Wimberley, still a Cameron, waiting at Tactical Divisional Headquarters. "It is arduous work," he was to say later, "waiting, waiting for the news that always seems to take so long ever to come through. At last a staff officer brings me the very first report of success to arrive. We had named our objectives, so that each regiment was set the task of capturing an enemy strong-point bearing the name of one of their county towns. The report reads: 'Camerons, Inverness.' From this it is clear that Lochiel's Battalion, under Major Ian Davey of Spean Bridge, have captured their objective and am I not the proud man!"

At the same time "A" and "D" Companies advanced with the R.E. and completed the vehicles gaps. On the morning of the 24th the Companies were reunited and the whole Cameron Battalion with the 5th Seaforth moved up in reserve to 154 Brigade. On the 27th the Battalion took over part of the Australian line, and three nights later advanced with the "Supercharge" Force.

The 1st Black Watch moved so closely under the artillery barrage that several times they had actually to wait for it to lift. As he was leading man in the Battalion, it is but right to mention Captain David Johnstone, who was navigating officer. And here is provided an opportunity to note the great work done by all the navigating officers.

This closeness of touch with the barrage meant that the men of the 1st Black Watch were in with the bayonet among the enemy's infantry and machine-gunners in record time and made short work of them. They reached their first objective exactly on time. The second wave moved on and took their objective. Officers as well as men used the bayonet, as in the case of Lieutenant Michael Allen. Allen, whose work in the "dog-fight" well exemplifies the actions of his comrades, though wounded continued to fight on, eliminating several of the enemy

---

[1] It was fitting that Lochiel's son, Capt. C. A. Cameron, went into action with them. He was wounded.

with his own bayonet, and refusing to be sent back until his physical powers absolutely gave way and he could carry on no longer. Private George McCulloch, when his Company after capturing the second objective, *Killin*, came under very heavy and devastating machine-gun fire, ran forward alone and attacked a machine-gun post, rendering it ineffective until his platoon arrived and wiped it out.

It was on a visit to the 42nd that the Divisional General had a very narrow escape. His jeep struck a mine, his driver and orderly were killed and Wimberley was blown some twenty yards across the desert; but, like all his officers and men, he carried on.[1] In fact it must always be remembered as one of the outstanding qualities of the Division at Alamein that wounds were incidents to which the victims paid no attention. They carried on, and carried on until nature itself gave the undisobeyable command: "No further!" After eleven days of fighting the 1st Black Watch was moved out for a rest.

The 5th Battalion of the Black Watch in 153 Brigade moved forward with Captain East as their leading navigating officer, who, compass in hand, proceeded to step out his distance with complete disregard for shells, bullets and mines. They also reached their objectives on time and the 1st Gordons, their commanding officer Lt.-Col. "Nap" Murray soon to be hit, passed through them. "A" Company suffered very heavy casualties and as a result became somewhat dispersed, but Lieutenant Alexander Davey gathered them together, and great credit must go to that officer for the fact that all reached the final objective and proper cover was given for the passing through of the 1st Gordons. On 2nd November the Battalion was withdrawn into the rear area.

The 1st Gordons were on the heels of the 5th Black Watch at the start-line, and followed some twenty minutes behind them. Major J. M. Hay acted as liaison with the Black Watch. The Gordons reached the Red Line without mishap, and thence Captain Keogh advanced with a party to lay tapes to the Black Line, the Battalion's final objective. "C" Company ran into trouble and had many casualties, including Captain Thomson and Lieutenant Williamson, both of whom later died of wounds. "D" Company now came forward on tanks, and joined up with "B" Company. They, however, had the misfortune to run into an unlocated minefield and five tanks were blown up. The Companies dug in and waited for daylight, when a long-range four-hour

---

[1] In the Peninsular War and wars of that period it was common enough for British Generals to have horses shot under them; now it was jeeps.

battle developed between our tanks (the Bays) and enemy tanks some three thousand yards away. At 1000 hours details were received of the doings of " A " and " C " Companies, who together had stormed the objective known as *Braemar*. During the final assault Captain Skivington led " C " Company through an inferno of bursting shells. Sixty-one of the Company fell, either killed or wounded, in the barrage, but even amidst the terrific carnage Skivington remained cool, and " his magnificent example inspired the remnants to maintain a steady and ordered advance until the objective was reached. It was when leading a bayonet charge against the last enemy strong-point that he fell, mortally wounded. He never wavered from his first resolution, as his last order to the twenty-two that remained was : ' " C " Company—advance ! ' " [1]

Captain McNeill was very severely wounded. But the junior officers of the two Companies (which had been reduced to some sixty men) put up what has been termed " a truly magnificent performance." Lt.-Col. H. Murray went forward to examine the general position and was caught in the middle of a tank battle, during which he was wounded. Major Hay took over command of the Battalion and, as soon as it was dark, relieved " A " and " C " Companies. Two platoons of " D " Company then advanced on the Battalion's final objective, *Aberdeen*. The following night the C.O. was ordered to make a full battalion attack on *Aberdeen*; but during a reconnaissance his carrier was blown up, he himself was wounded, and Major ("Scrappy") Hay took over command. Major Du Boulay led up the remainder of " A " Company and the whole of " B " to join the two platoons of " D," already in the vicinity of *Aberdeen* under the command of Major Paton. But direction was not too good, and " B " Company had to come back to their original positions.

On the night of Monday, 26th October, " B " Company advanced again, and this time made contact with " D " Company, and on the Tuesday morning a battery of 6-pounders on armed chassis (Deacons)

---

[1] In the early stages of the battle there appears to have been 1000 yards divergence of opinion between the Infantry and the Armour as to the position of a ridge on the Highland Division front known as " the Kidney feature." It took some time for this matter to be cleared up. By midday on 24th October the Armour knew that two Companies of the 1st Gordons (though isolated) were actually on that ridge, but it was not till night-time that the position of the ridge was agreed on, and it was not till the morning of the 26th that, after a further night attack by the Highlanders, the Armour actually reached " the Kidney feature." The difficulties experienced by the Armour are explained in ' The 10th Royal Hussars in the Second World War,' pp. 75-81.

moved through "D" Company and the enemy surrendered. That night Major Fausset-Farquhar took over command of the Battalion. There was one most extraordinary incident on the night of the 29th. The 4th Battalion The Royal Sussex attacked on the Gordons' left. By some error of direction they moved into the Gordon area, mistook the Highlanders for the enemy, and a battle broke out during which Corporal McGowan of the carrier platoon was killed. The next two nights were spent by the Gordons in improving their position, and on the night of 1st November they were relieved by a South African unit.

Among the incidents that flash out in the 1st Gordons' Alamein story are the actions of Lance-Corporal Beacham, who advanced on his own and bayoneted the occupant of a machine-gun post, thus saving many lives; of Sergeant Stephenson, who dealt with an enemy sniper in a most courageous way; of Lieutenant Fraser, who crawled forward alone and forced an enemy post of seven men to surrender; of Corporal John Niven's work with his bayonet; of Sergeant Dunlop and two men capturing an enemy machine-gun post and holding it alone for twenty-four hours; and of Lieutenant Bruce Rae's remarkable and valuable patrolling.

Up by Sun Track to the Start Line came the 5/7th Gordons (Lt.-Col. H. W. B. Saunders) with "A" and "B" Companies leading. They got forward a bit too quickly and found themselves practically on their first objective before our barrage had lifted. They therefore lay down behind the barrage. When it lifted they went in at once through the first minefield, and had a comparatively easy time when taking the first objectives. They had the misfortune to lose Lieutenant Stuart, who was killed while leading a mopping-up party against some enemy Spandaus. The Green Line was then occupied, Gordon casualties being chiefly due to enemy artillery and mortar-fire. The attached R.E.s advanced in most gallant fashion to cut the wire in front of the Battalion and lost their officer and several other ranks. But on went the Gordons for the Red Line. At this point a Company of 5th Black Watch, who had advanced too far to the left, were mistaken for a party of the enemy, but fortunately proper recognition was made before any damage was done. The Red Line was reached (4500 yards from the Start Line) and here sixty minutes were allowed for reorganisation. "A" and "B" Companies then proceeded to dig slit trenches, while "C" and "D" advanced some 2500 yards to the Black Line. "C" and "D" Companies, after a slight retiral to get out of the way of some of our shells which were falling short, advanced again. "D" Company (Captain Sharp) ran into very serious machine-gun fire, and it was not till next day that the Company Commander, Lieutenant Jackson, and many of the men were found dead in an enemy minefield. "C" Company dug in, when they were joined by mortars and machine-guns which had been brought forward by Captain Irvine. At dawn the 2nd Armoured Brigade came forward and passed between the two Gordon Battalions into the extensive system of enemy minefields just ahead. A vicious battle of armour was joined, which continued for several days. "C" Company's position was greatly improved by an excellent attack put in by the 2nd Seaforth who were assisted by tanks.

The 5/7th Gordons now became the rear battalion of the Brigade. On 2nd November the Battalion suffered somewhat from a plethora of conflicting orders, but finally on the 3rd were ordered to attack a position at the Mirbat–Kamli crossroads. Before they reached that point, however, news came that the enemy had gone. "A" and "B" Companies were getting into tanks to be taken forward to occupy the supposedly abandoned positions, when the situation can be expressed fittingly only by the phrase: "All hell was let loose." 88-mm. guns opened up from left and right on the tanks, Spandaus spattered the infantry. In "B" Company Captain Jardyne and Lieutenant Hardy were killed, and the two other subalterns were casualties. Six tanks were burned out. During the night of 3rd-4th November, however, the enemy withdrew and the Battalion advanced towards Daba Aerodrome, where they found no enemy.

During that unfortunate day at the Mirbat–Kamli crossroads Lieutenant Ritchie, although wounded, acted with great courage and foresight in reorganisation. To him was due the successful evacuation of many badly wounded officers and men. 2nd Lieutenant Robertson, who had only been five days with the Battalion, displayed remarkable coolness and kept perfect control of his platoon under the unexpected and very heavy fire of the enemy. Colonel Saunders on foot led his Battalion all through that very difficult period, and reorganised his forward Companies in the very best tradition of a Gordon officer. His example ran right through the Battalion down to many a private man, who, with his officers and N.C.O.s casualties, proceeded to reorganise and lead forward small commands.

The 2nd Seaforth (Lt.-Col. K. MacKessack) had been held in 30th Corps Reserve, but in the forenoon of 24th October they were returned to Wimberley, and in the afternoon were sent up through the 1st Black Watch to try to form a bridgehead through a minefield which was holding up the 2nd Armoured Brigade. The Seaforth held that bridgehead for thirty-six hours and suffered some hundred casualties. Two of the Companies, under command of Major A. M. Gilmour, held an isolated position during the whole of those thirty-six hours with great gallantry.

Three Companies of the Middlesex were sent forward with various infantry units of the Division, " D " Company being detached to the Australians. " A " Company was with the 7th Black Watch, while platoons were working in the forward area with the 1st Gordons, 7th Argylls, 1st Black Watch and 5th Black Watch, and others were in depth reserve. The Middlesex, under their ever-cheerful Colonel Stephenson, played also a very full part in " Supercharge." Outstanding in the battle was the devotion to duty of Lance-Corporal Herbert Sleeth. In the original advance Sleeth was hit in the back by a piece of shell-casing which knocked him off his feet. At the time he was carrying four belts of ammunition and a box of spare parts. Despite his wound he continued to advance another two miles and delivered his load to the gun crew, with whom he carried on although hit a second time. He advanced with the 5/7th Gordons (Lt.-Col. Saunders) to their final objective, and was wounded a third time. Next day, when the platoon was cut off without food, water, or wireless and very little ammunition, Sleeth offered to go back over the shell-swept ground for help. He reached Company H.Q. and insisted on returning with the supports bringing all necessary supplies. He only gave in when wounded for the fourth time.

Later in the battle the task allotted to the 152 Seaforth and Cameron Brigade was something different from what was being done by the rest of the Division. The 152 Brigade, along with 151 from the 50th Division, were attached to the New Zealand Division and were to make the final infantry punch on the north of our line, a punch which was to be followed up by the knockout blow from our armour. The New Zealand Division had taken part in the first Alamein attack, and had achieved their objectives.

On the night of 27th-28th October the infantry handed over to the 1st South African Division. All units (except the Divisional artillery) were moved into a back area. There the plans for the action " Supercharge " were put in motion. Under orders from the New Zealand

Commander, Lieutenant-General Freyberg,[1] the two British Infantry Brigades were to attack on a 4000-yard front and were to attempt to advance 4000 yards on a sector immediately to the south of the 9th Australian Division. When those Infantry Brigades had made the assault with the assistance of New Zealand Armoured Brigades, the 1st Armoured Division was to break through the gap which it was hoped would be made.

On the night of 31st October General Freyberg described the proposed tactics to officers of 152 Brigade. The rate of advance was to be 100 yards in two and a half minutes, with a half-hour pause for mopping-up purposes and reorganisation on the first objective. The infantry were to by-pass tank resistance pockets, but, should the pace become too fast, the New Zealand Tank Brigades were to press on in front of the infantry, which was to leave the start-line at 0055 hours on 2nd November.

As Freyberg reported, everything went like clockwork on the left of the attack, which was the position held by our 152 Brigade. The reports from his headquarters read as follows :—

"At 0105 hours on the morning of 2nd November every gun on the Corps front which could reach, opened fire. 15,000 rounds were to be fired on the 4000 yards front during the next $4\frac{1}{2}$ hours.

"The attack provided an interesting comparison, as on the left everything went like clockwork while on the right resistance was stronger and the situation remained obscure for hours. On the left 152 Brigade Headquarters were in contact throughout with forward battalions, and encouraging progress reports were received at Divisional Headquarters from this Brigade :—

"'0148 hours : We are in touch with both battalions and everything appears to be going smoothly.'

"'0218 hours : There is light shelling and moderate machine-gun fire on our front. We have taken some prisoners, a mixture of Italians and Germans. Everything appears to be going according to plan.'

"'0235 hours : Newly laid minefield discovered.'

"'0359 hours : On left flank our tanks are engaging enemy tanks between our Forward Defended Localities and first objective.'

"'0417 hours : Both battalions have reached objective and are in action with enemy tanks. (Previously arranged artillery concentration, "Roxborough," was called for and fired.)'

"'0525 hours : Enemy tanks are melting away and battalions are getting supporting arms up. One Italian tank captured intact.'

[1] Earlier, when training for the battle, Freyberg had done all he could to help the 51st, and had had attached to it some veteran New Zealanders.

"'0535 hours: Reorganisation of final objective is proceeding and battalions are linking up. Right gap is through and left will be as soon as small minefield is cleared. Our casualties will not exceed 40 per battalion.'

"The attack had gone like a drill, both objectives being taken according to schedule. It was a very fine performance."

It was a strange battle for an infantryman. In a general sense he was "lost" all the time. Now he was bombing Italians out of their slit trenches. Now he was digging a trench for himself. Now he was getting out of the way of an enemy tank. Now he was getting out of the way of one of our own. But always he was moving forward.

By 0600 hours 151 Brigade reported that they were on their final objective. All the time the armour was slowly advancing up a lane swept clear of mines by the New Zealand engineers. The tanks had a rough passage and " it may be argued that it was a costly and incorrect method of using armour ; but if one is to believe General Von Thoma it may well prove to have been the deciding factor in breaking the German line, though advantage was not taken of the breach until later."

The enemy counter-attacked on the 2nd in the early afternoon, but not successfully. In the evening 152 Brigade, which had returned to the Highland Division, made a further attack. They advanced 1500 yards in just over twenty minutes, suffered no casualties, and took some 100 Italian prisoners. By the morning of the 3rd November it was obvious that the enemy were making a general withdrawal, and on the morning of the 4th the pursuit began—and then the rains came.

In a letter to General Wimberley, dated 3rd November 1942, General Freyberg wrote :—

"After a very short but very distinguished attachment to our Division your 152 Brigade returned to your command last night. I cannot let them go without expressing to you the admiration of the Division for the way in which 152 Brigade carried out its part in the operation. I was very much impressed by the training and efficiency of all ranks, and everyone who came in contact with ' the Jocks ' formed the highest opinion of them. No one could have carried out the job more efficiently than Murray and his Brigade. Will you give him our congratulations also on the most successful attack on Skinflint. We shall always be proud of having one of your Highland Brigades serving with the Division. . . . I really did admire the business-like way Brigadier Murray did his job." [1]

So much for the general success of the 152 Brigade, but there were highlights in the actions of all the units. Lance-Corporal D. Macbeath of the 5th Seaforth, when all the senior N.O.C.s of his platoon had been killed, and though he himself was severely wounded early in the attack, took command of his platoon and led them on to their final objective, where he handed his men over to an officer and then collapsed. The Medical Officer of the same battalion, Lieutenant F. A. MacRae, displayed remarkable coolness in evacuating many severely wounded officers and men. Many, who were too badly hit to be moved, he treated in the field. He and his medical sergeant, Sergeant H. MacKay, were both captured, but took the first chance to escape and rejoin their unit. Private Samuel Hightens of the 5th Camerons (Lt.-Col. Miers) tackled a tank all on his own and killed the commander, who was looking out of the turret. Here, as in all the other battles fought by the Division, the actions of wounded men were of the highest order. If it were physically possible to carry on, a wound was never made the passport to the back area. Sir Andrew Barton's spirit was still alive.

> " Fight on, my men, says Andrew Barton.
> I am hurt, but I am not slaine;
> I'll lie me down and bleed awhile,
> And then I'll rise and fight again."

The padre of the 2nd Seaforth (Captain Donald MacRae) throughout that whole weary day of 2nd November remained in the open looking after the mortally wounded men of the battalion. All this he did in full view of the enemy, whose snipers were particularly active in that particular area. The 2nd Seaforth, after their part in the " Supercharge " affair on 1st-2nd November, made a battalion attack at dusk on the 2nd with the 50th R.T.R. to widen the salient formed by 152 Brigade.

Since units of the 51st had begun the Battle of Alamein, it was right and proper that a unit of the Division should finish it. That unit was the 7th Argylls of 154 Brigade, which, on 3rd November, was ordered to attack the strong-point Tel El Aqqaqir.

This attack was organised at very short notice by Brigadier Houlds-

---

[1] Murray, a Caithnessian, had had a good record as a fighting Seaforth in the First World War, and from those experiences had learnt many useful and practical lessons for the set-piece attack. A disciplinarian, and a fine soldier, he was most meticulous and thorough in all his planning.

worth and his staff. Like George Murray, Houldsworth was a Seaforth and had already distinguished himself, not only as a regimental officer in the 1914-18 War, but in command of the 4th Seaforth in 1940. Of this attack Montgomery wrote [1] :—

"On the night 3/4 November 51 Division and a brigade from 4 Indian Division launched a very speedily mounted thrust. . . . Very great credit is due to the formations which organised this attack in an extremely short time and carried it through successfully. . . ."

The author of 'The History of the 4th Indian Division' states of the 5th Indian Brigade's attack under orders of the 51st :—

"By 0100 hours it was apparent that the 5th Brigade would not be deployed in time, whereupon Brigadier Russell asked that the artillery programme be delayed for an hour. This last-minute request was arranged without delay—a tribute to the excellence of the staff work."

Seven regiments of artillery provided the barrage for this attack which roared over the Argylls' heads from 5.30 on the morning of the 4th. In fact, the noise of our bursting shells was the best, perhaps the only, guide the Battalion had to the enemy strong-point. In some ways, too, the occasional shell falling short was the most dangerous opposition met with, for when the strong-point was reached no enemy was to be found. As Captain Ian C. Cameron writes in his 'History' of the Battalion [2] :—

"Our objective was a former Divisional Headquarters, and after we consolidated we made a reconnaissance of the area and found masses of signal equipment of great value, a complete Orderly Room, Intelligence Office, and Regimental Aid Post, and a store full of valuable equipment. Documents which we captured were considered of such great importance as to merit sending them off by special plane to General Headquarters at Cairo. In addition to this, bottles of chianti, champagne, &c., were found in large quantities. A headline which appeared in one of our home newspapers, referring to the attack on the Tel El Aqqaqir, read : 'The Boche got the wind up and the Argylls got the wine.' A number of Iron Crosses and Afrika Korps badges were also among the newly discovered treasures which we found in a store. In the afternoon we held a mock investiture at which we invested our commanding officer with the Iron Cross, and eventually a number of 'Jocks' were seen wandering about with Iron Crosses pinned on their chests." [3]

[1] From 'Alamein to the River Sangro,' by Field-Marshal Viscount Montgomery, by permission of Messrs Hutchinson & Co. (Publishers) Ltd., London.
[2] See footnote p. 9.
[3] General Alexander reported to Prime Minister, 1st November 1942, after Alamein : "Formations with most casualties are the 51st Highland Division and the 9th Australian Division, each about 2000 ; 10th Armoured Division, 1350."

No praise can be excessive when considering the work done by the non-infantry units in the Battle of Alamein. The Royal Artillery's forward observers' devotion to duty was well exemplified in the action of Bombardier Dodds of the 128th Field Regiment. Dodds was acting as wireless operator at a forward observation post in support of the 1st Black Watch. His armoured post was put out of action by shell-fire, so Dodds carried on his job from an open truck. The infantry had to give way before an enemy tank attack, but Dodds continued to pass his fire orders although exposed to heavy direct fire from the approaching tanks. Result—a successful concentration from his guns and the arrest of the enemy advance. The work of the Field Companies may be epitomised in the action of Major Russell from Aberdeen and his men of the 274th who located and gapped undetected minefields with complete disregard for personal safety; the work of the Division Signals (under Lt.-Col. Denholm Young [1]) in the gallantry of 2nd Lieutenant John Carruth and his men who kept in serviceable order 130 miles of field telephone cables which they had previously laid to connect the Headquarters of Division, Brigades and Field Regiments—all that first night and day of the battle Carruth and his men kept on repairing breaks in that network of cables, many of which ran through minefields; the work of the Reconnaissance Regiment in that of Lieutenant Gall who early in the battle had his carrier knocked out and himself wounded by an 88-mm. shell—he transferred to another carrier which in turn was knocked out; finally, all his carriers were disabled, but he rallied his men and, placing them on the backs of tanks, continued to attack. The same devotion to duty was shown by the personnel of the R.A.M.C. and of all other units. As one man said : " They should just have given the Division a decoration for Alamein and not bothered about individual cases." [2]

Alamein will undoubtedly take its place in history alongside such great battles as Waterloo and Loos, as one in which Highland soldiers added to the honours of Highland regiments and to the honour of Scotland.

[1] Author of ' Men of Alamein.'

[2] Nor must we forget the unspectacular but indispensable staff work which planned and arranged the co-ordination between the various supporting arms—Artillery, Engineers, Tanks and Signals—which together enabled the individual fighting Jock with his bayonet, tommy-gun and bomb to take and hold the objectives given him to capture. In the Highland Division there was a real feeling of friendship and comradeship between the regimental officers and the staff officers at Brigade and Divisional Headquarters. This was helped, no doubt, by the fact that almost all the Infantry officers employed on these formation staffs themselves belonged to Highland regiments.

CHAPTER III.

THE PURSUIT

"*Slainte na Gaidheil !* "
(Here's to the Highlanders !)

" This time we shall not come back."
(MONTGOMERY.)

COURAGE in battle is of a different type from courage in pursuit. Hard and demanding as the Battle of Alamein had been, it had nothing of a heartbreaking influence. But in pursuing the retreating enemy the Highland Division was asked to display another type of hardihood. That retreating enemy moved over relatively cleared ground, while the pursuers had to make their way through a maze of minefields, on a road horrid with demolitions, over an anti-tank ditch where nothing was available but shifting sand to fill up a small portion and make a bridge. All the time the enemy shelled and sniped, and the advancing troops could afford themselves no respite. Transport could not be got forward, so they must use their feet ; food could not be got forward, so they must go hungry. There was no time for sleep. Follow, follow, follow ! And follow they did ! Wounded men kept going forward as long as they could move. The Divisional General himself wielded a spade in demolition filling. The Highland Division won their second great battle—this time against weariness and heartbreak, and lack of sleep and tired bodies.

In that desert warfare forces in retreat had always a certain strategical advantage. The farther they retreated, the shorter did they make their lines of communication. Moreover, they were always retiring on a new and fully prepared defensive position. A General in command of a pursuit must therefore do his best to race the retreating infantry with his motorised columns and so cut them off. That was what Montgomery hoped to do after Alamein—but Rommel found an unexpected ally in the rain of 6th and 7th November.

Not that much destruction of enemy forces had not been done, for as Montgomery himself stated, " Four crack German Divisions and eight Italian Divisions had ceased to exist as effective fighting formations." Thirty thousand prisoners, including nine Generals, had been taken. A great number of enemy tanks had been destroyed, and the quantity of guns, transport, aircraft and stores of all kind captured or destroyed was immense. But our cutting-off troops were bogged in the desert on 7th November, and the twenty-four hours' grace accorded the enemy allowed him to collect what was left of his battered forces, who made very good time along the coast road to their prepared positions at El Agheila. Our chase was resumed, however, on 9th November. Some small resistance was met at various points, but the New Zealanders and the 7th Armoured Division cleared Halfaya Pass, Capuzzo, Solum and Bardia, and by 11th November the only Axis troops in Egypt were prisoners.

Tobruk was taken on 13th November. Two days later the Martuba airfields were ours, so that we now possessed a forward harbour and forward runway. So on to Benghazi, which was entered on 20th November, and all was set for the Battle of El Agheila.

At El Alamein the Highland Division in twelve days had counted its advance in hundreds of yards. For a period after the battle it was to count its advance in hundreds of miles. And it was to realise why the camel has been described as the "ship of the desert." For the advance it was now to make was over a terrain where navigation was as navigation on the sea. The Mediterranean was the edge of this sea, the tarmac coast road a kind of high-water mark. Otherwise the desert was a weary ocean, where the convoys of vehicles moved like convoys of ships, steering well apart from each other during the day and drawing close at nightfall, when they lay at anchor until they moved forward again with the first light of the new day.[1]

"Escarpment" is a word which has a considerable place in descriptions of the Libyan adventure. It means the abrupt fall of cliff from a ridge. The escarpment was quite low at the beginning of the trek, but it heightened towards Sollum, where it became a very formidable obstacle, over which the "hell-fire" battles had taken place in the earlier phases of the North African Campaign. From Sollum across Cyrenaica to Adjedabya the country was practically a featureless dead flat, with certain depressions which had very little right to the title

---

[1] Nevertheless, across this "sea," and behind it, for hundreds of miles lay the Division's main axis, clearly marked by HD signs, cut out of petrol tins, and erected by the indefatigable efforts of Major Angus Ferguson (Camerons) and his devoted military policemen.

"valleys" that has often been applied to them. The coastal area from Benghazi to about Bardia is a well-cultivated belt bordered by a high escarpment dividing it from the above-mentioned featureless plain. Having cut across that plain to Adjedabya the Division reached the coastal belt, but at that particular period of the year there were no signs of cultivation and the terrain was much the same as that between Alamein and Sollum.

At Wadi Matratin, where the Division spent New Year's Day 1943, the troops came on the first spring flowers, and one soldier gathered more than forty different kinds in that one wadi on that New Year's Day. This was the first time the troops had seen any natural wild growth.

From Matratin to Ghedahia the country was much more broken up by fair-sized wadis coming down to the coast. None of these contained water but were obviously damper than the rest of the countryside. They were mostly sand, but firm enough to cross in vehicles, and, although the country was still largely completely barren, there were considerable areas of rocky ground covered by a small prickly scrub. There was some grass and other vegetation growing in the wadis between the large areas of bare sand or rock. Generally speaking the country was still flat.

The same applied to the country between Ghedahia and the edge of the escarpment which overlooked the valleys of Garibaldi and Zliten. This piece of country was the most rolling and smooth that the Division had so far encountered, and it was possible to travel in any direction unimpeded by obstacles.

It was a kind of "Cortez on his silent peak in Darien" experience for the Division to gaze on Garibaldi and Zliten from the top of the escarpment. For the first time in the long journey our men beheld green trees, green fields, ditches, walls and houses.

This coastal stretch was interrupted by a considerable range of hills running down to the coast just to the west of Homs. These hills were very steep and rocky and quite impassable for vehicles, a condition now met for the first time. As a result, in this area the Division carried out its encircling movement of the German positions on foot. At Tripoli itself the coastal belt widened and there was a large expanse of cultivated ground.

So much for the vast area of ground that had to be covered in this next stretch of the advance. Now, what about Montgomery's plan?

First there must be no delay; the enemy must be given no respite. Air bases must be established in Cyrenaica. Tobruk must be taken.[1]

Tobruk, as noted above, was taken on 13th November, the Martuba airfields on the 15th, Benghazi on the 20th, and the first real problem was how to turn the enemy out of the Agheila position, where on two earlier occasions our North African forces had been held up. What Montgomery wanted to do was to occupy the El Agheila position,[2] *facing west* this time, and since—as has been shown above—from the point of view of terrain the frontal attack was to be very difficult, the Army Commander determined to outflank the enemy defences by sending those splendid soldiers, the 2nd New Zealand Division, away out into the desert and round by the south—the left hook. The Highland Division was to attack astride the road. But Rommel went back, leaving units of his 90th Light Division to cover his withdrawal, and most of his troops escaped the New Zealand outflanking movement, although some twenty tanks and five hundred prisoners were taken.

Speedy follow-up became all the more important to Montgomery. Rommel's next line was back near Buerat. Contact with the enemy was kept by armoured-car patrols. The Commander of the 8th Army could not afford to stop again before Tripoli, or he might have to withdraw, and this he was determined not to do. A gale in January made frightful havoc of shipping in Benghazi harbour, thus adding to Montgomery's worries, but he was prepared to put everything on one throw. He decided again on the Highland Division attacking along the coast road, while the New Zealanders and the 7th Armoured Division delivered another left hook. Tripoli had to be reached ten days from the start of the battle.

When we follow the attack of the Highland Division, to understand

---

[1] And so was it accomplished. The actual pursuit was carried out in the first instance by 30 Corps (Leese) and only two Divisions—the experienced and battle-tried 7th Armoured, under their efficient General, John Harding, and Freyberg with his New Zealanders. The 51st Highlanders came up later to the front at MERSA BREGA, and again at BUERAT where set-piece attacks were considered necessary. The 50th Division was to have joined those three Divisions for the final advance on Tripoli, but for lack of supplies had to be left behind; they did not accordingly catch up till after the battle of Medenine, where they arrived just after the 201 Guards Brigade. As will be seen later from this story, the 4th Indian Division next moved up to join the Divisions committed to battle, and in time to take a distinguished part in the battles of MARETH and AKARIT. Thus, throughout the whole 8th Army's long and victorious campaign in Africa after Alamein, that Army consisted of only five fighting Divisions, and of these only three— New Zealanders, 7th Armoured, and 51st—were engaged until after the capture of Tripoli.

[2] At this period water was short in supply and brackish, and many a Jock shaved with the dregs of his tea.

how important was their job, we must remember that, as Montgomery himself puts it [1]:—

"I was experiencing the first real anxiety I had suffered since assuming command of the 8th Army. If I did not reach Tripoli within the ten days' time limit imposed by the administrative situation, I might have to face a most difficult decision : I would have to stop the advance and probably fall back to Buerat or even farther, in order to maintain the supply of the Army. I was determined, therefore, to accelerate the pace of operations, and to give battle by night as well as by day, in order to break through the Homs–Tarhuna position and secure my objective. I ordered attacks on both axes to be put in by moonlight. I issued very strong instructions regarding the quickening of our efforts, and made clear what I expected of commanders and the troops. On 19th January progress greatly improved ; pressure was being developed on Tarhuna and the 51st Division entered Homs. I had the 22nd Armoured Brigade at Zliten, still under my command, waiting for the right moment to release it. The Desert Air Force had a most successful day, and indeed it took a constant and heavy toll of the enemy throughout this action."

From the Highland Division's point of view this anxiety on the part of the Army Commander is emphasised by the fact that one night, when the Division was fighting round Misurata, Wimberley was summoned to report to Montgomery who was moving with the central column. The Divisional Commander had to make a long nerve-racking cross-country journey over the desert by night, guided by Lieutenant Chavasse of the Middlesex, and, when Wimberley reached his destination, Montgomery told him in no uncertain terms that, unless everybody got a much greater move on, the whole advance to Tripoli would have to be called off and the 8th Army might have to fall back once more on Buerat or Benghazi. In describing this situation later on, Montgomery referred to having "used the whip." When Wimberley returned to the Division he also in no uncertain terms made all commanders fully aware of the urgency of the situation—and he did it by personal visits not only to the Brigadiers, but to each of the leading regimental commanders as well.

So now that we know something of the country and the plan, we can retrace our steps and set out from Alamein to Tripoli with the Highland Division.

After Alamein most of the units of the Division had been relieved by South African troops and moved back to a rest area. Later they took over from the New Zealanders and then advanced to positions

[1] See footnote, p. 51.

near the sea, where reorganisation took place. Gaps resulting from the El Alamein fighting were filled by reinforcements. And here the Jocks licked their wounds and refurbished their weapons. Each day congratulatory messages from all over Scotland poured in—from Lord Provosts of big cities and Provosts of small towns, from Lord Lieutenants of Counties, Clan Chiefs, and shipyard and factory-workers. Best of all came one to Wimberley from Leese, their own trusted and popular Corps Commander, which read : " Now that we have finished the first phase of our fighting, I want to congratulate you on the magnificent fighting carried out by your Division. You have had a tremendous reputation to live up to, and you have fought side by side with highly experienced and trained Divisions. It speaks volumes to the credit of your Division that they have held their own magnificently with these Divisions and on all occasions achieved their objectives. The spirit of your men has been magnificent and I hope you will convey to them my intense appreciation and admiration of what they have done."

In sending this inspiring message round the Division, Wimberley added : " In the last fourteen days we have, I am sure, reminded Scotland that we, too, are chipped off just the same block of northern granite that provided the best fighting Division of the last Great War."

When troop-carriers finally became available the Division concentrated on Adjedabja, which had been captured by the armoured columns. Thence 152 Brigade was moved forward to hold a position across the main road opposite Mersa Brega, taking over from the Rifle Brigade Battalion of the 7th Armoured Division which was forming an outpost screen, while 153 Brigade were filling the gap to the salt marshes at Abu Suivera. The 154 Brigade relieved 152, and by 8th December the Division was once again in the front line, and 152 was preparing to attack. This village of Mersa Brega was reported as having been developed by the enemy into a very strong position. It was a kind of bottleneck with high ground all round which dominated the whole area. No-man's-land was some 5000 yards in width and the enemy had sewn it with thousands of mines, both anti-tank and anti-personnel. Owing to the fact that forward landing-grounds were not yet complete, the Division had no fighter-cover, so that the German planes were much more troublesome than usual.

On 13th December, shortly before a set-piece attack by the 51st was due to be launched, signs were not lacking that the enemy was, once more, about to withdraw. Accordingly the 1st Black Watch received

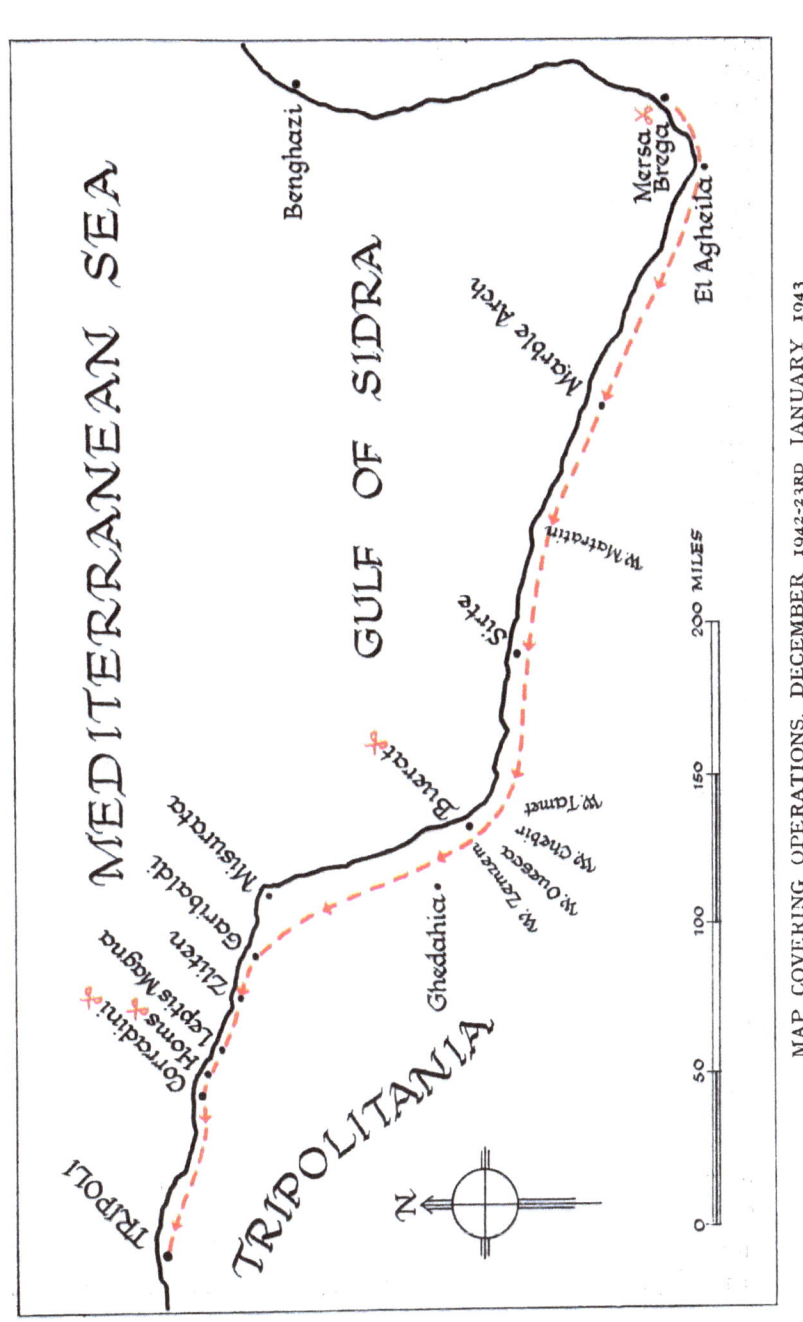

MAP COVERING OPERATIONS, DECEMBER 1942-23RD JANUARY 1943

orders to advance round the sea side of Mersa Brega and cut the road behind it at a point where they would be met by the 7th Battalion of the regiment, who were to make a similar move round the south side of the village. The night was pitch dark with no moon, the distance to be covered some four and a half miles. Everything worked out according to plan as far as the 7th Battalion was concerned, and casualties resulted mainly from contact with mines. The 1st Black Watch were not so fortunate. The ground over which they had to pass made very heavy going indeed, and was very thickly strewn with mines. It was now known that the enemy had finally evacuated Mersa Brega, so the 7th Argylls were moved up to fill the gap between the two Black Watch battalions. On the morning of 13th December "C" Company of the Argylls found Mersa Brega held by dead men only, but those dead men were still active in as much as booby-traps had been laid beneath them, and when the bodies were removed for burial the Argylls suffered considerable casualties. Another enemy was a violent sandstorm in the form of a wall of dust some hundred feet in height which hit our troops with extreme violence. It was followed by a torrential rainstorm.

After the Division had followed the enemy retreating from Mersa Brega a dozen or so miles, heavily strewn with mines, the 7th Armoured Division again took up the pursuit, and the 51st was placed in Corps Reserve. At this point Brigadier Houldsworth left [1] for the United Kingdom, specially selected by Montgomery to be the first commander of the newly formed Infantry School in England. Houldsworth was respected by all as a man of sterling character. He had been brought up in the 1914-18 tradition of the officers of the Highland Brigade, that it was the duty of senior officers to show themselves to their men, in the din and smoke of battle, cool, calm and unflurried. With troops new to battle, as were the 51st, Houldsworth appreciated that such action was all the more important, and he took many an opportunity to act accordingly. In this general area the Division celebrated Christmas 1942. Inter-battalion football matches were played; and then forward again some hundred miles to the region of the Wadi Matratin, where New Year's Day was spent.

Some interesting points were passed *en route*. Men stared openmouthed at that most flamboyant of all Mussolini's extravagances—Marble Arch. It had been built by the Duce for his own glory, but with a traditional story in its foundation. Above its capitals stood two

[1] His son, Captain Houldsworth, remained with the 5th Seaforth till wounded.

bronze figures representing those legendary brothers, the Phileni, who, somewhere about the year 350 B.C., played the leading parts in a debate between the Cyreneans and the Carthaginians concerning the frontier line separating those two nations' possessions in Africa. It was decided that two runners should set out from Carthage making for the west and two from Cyrene making for the east, and that the boundary line should be fixed at the point where they met. The Phileni represented Carthage and far outstripped in speed their rivals. It was at the point where Mussolini later raised his arch that they met. The Cyreneans wished the Phileni to go back a bit, but the brothers refused, and were buried alive in the desert sands. The Carthaginians raised two altars on the graves, and these altars became the boundaries of the Carthaginian Dominion which stretched some two thousand miles west to the Pillars of Hercules.

So to special exercises preparing for a frontal daylight attack against the enemy entrenched at Buerat and the Wadi Zemzem, while the New Zealanders delivered a left hook on the enemy's right flank.

On 5th January, 154 Brigade moved some 170 miles to Wadi El Chebir, in front of which, at Wadi Ouesca, two days later they relieved outposts of the 7th Armoured Division.[1] There each battalion of the Brigade established a strong-point (most efficiently covered by Lt.-Col. Thicknesse's guns of the 126th Field Regiment), from which patrols were sent out to make contact with the enemy some mile and a half away. Meanwhile 153 Brigade moved to a position eight miles behind in Wadi Mira, while 152 Brigade was positioned in the Wadi El Chebir.[2]

On 19th January Montgomery explained at an officers' conference his plans for the final attack at Buerat and the subsequent hoped-for advance on Tripoli. The rôle of the Highland Division was first to storm the enemy's position at Buerat, and thereafter to form a "coastal column" advancing on Tripoli along the road by the sea which was to be cleared and opened for supplies. The other (south) flank line of advance was to be followed by 30th Corps Headquarters with the 2nd New Zealanders and the 7th Armoured Division who were designated

---

[1] Brigadier Thomas Rennie was wounded when his jeep was blown up by a mine. Brigadier Stirling (Seaforth) took over the Brigade.

[2] The period was one of the few occasions in the advance across Africa in which 51st forward troops were in contact with the enemy beyond an "umbrella" provided by the R.A.F. The absence of this "umbrella" brought home to all the great value of air-cover.

the "inland column," and, filling in the wide gap between, was the 22nd Armoured Brigade, with which Montgomery himself would go. Montgomery issued the following message to all troops :—

"The leading units of the 8th Army are now only two hundred miles from Tripoli. The enemy is between us and that port hoping to hold us off. The 8th Army is going to Tripoli. Tripoli is the only town in the Italian Empire overseas still remaining in their possession. Therefore we will take it from them ; they will then have no overseas Empire. The enemy will try to stop us. Nothing has stopped us since the battle of Egypt began on the 23rd of October 1942. Nothing will stop us now."

The first stage of the 51st advance by the coast road was on Misurata. The nomenclature of the Operation Order was as usual correlative and amusing. There were four phases. The first (Silk) covered the action of 154 Brigade in getting in touch with the enemy ; the second (Satin) dealt with the capture and exploitation of the enemy's position at Buerat ; the third (Cotton) related to the advance itself ; the fourth (Rags) was to be the action by the engineers making the coast road behind the fighting troops fit for the use of wheeled transport. Among the additional troops placed under Wimberley's command was a detachment of the Sudan Defence Force, who were to act as police when Misurata was reached. The whole proposed action was described and explained by General Wimberley at a sand-model conference among the dunes at Tamet. Incidentally this particular conference was temporarily dispersed by certain enemy planes who chose the time to put in a low flying attack which, however, did little if any damage.

Phase "Silk" was set in motion by 154 Brigade on the night of 14th January, and twenty-four hours later 153 put the attack termed "Satin" in action. The 1st Gordons with Scorpions and the 40th R.T.R. with machine-guns, and with Companies of the 1/7th Middlesex covering the flanks, moved to the attack. There was a certain amount of shelling, and casualties were suffered as a result of mines, seven Scorpions being knocked out, but the hole was successfully punched in the enemy line, the enemy quickly withdrawing, and the 5/7th Gordons passed through their senior battalion and fanned out south-westwards. Then the 5th Black Watch, aided by tanks, Middlesex, sappers, and anti-tank battery units, passed through the 1st Gordons and fanned out to the north-west.

Much of the accuracy of the attack of the 1st Gordons was due to the Intelligence Officer, Captain L. W. Miller, who though under observation from the enemy marked out the starting-positions in no-man's-land with stone cairns and, after darkness had fallen, laid out tapes. As a result the battalion was able to form up in perfect order.

And so, on 16th January, 152 Brigade came in on " Cotton." Things were held up a little by the lateness of a delivery of petrol, and since, hard as the engineers were working, the gap through the minefields was still a very narrow one. Just after midday the news came through from Corps that the enemy were holding a line across the road at a place called Churgia forty miles on, and some third of the way to Misurata, and the Division were ordered to take it that night. The 152 Brigade advanced by motor transport, and the 5th Camerons (the leading battalion) were not too lucky. Colonel Miers was wounded, many trucks were put out of action, and the men inside them killed and wounded by the enemy rearguard long-range artillery. But after a temporary stoppage the advance was continued and, although direction was slightly lost, the Camerons with the 5th Seaforth found themselves on the high ground to the south-east of Misurata on the 19th. They by-passed the town and continued on beyond and south of Zliten.

On the 18th Brigadier Murray (152 Brigade) with " C " Company of the 2nd Seaforth entered Misurata, round which a cordon had been thrown. Our Sudanese police had had a bit of bad luck. They had moved in to the village of Crispe, east of Misurata, which had not been cleared of the enemy and accordingly suffered several casualties from a rear party of stout fighting Germans of the 90th Light Division.

General Wimberley ordered 154 Brigade, now commanded by Brigadier Stirling, who had already proved himself an efficient and energetic commanding officer of the 5th Seaforth, to by-pass Misurata and to make as fast time as possible for Homs. The 1st Black Watch led on the south flank and the 7th Battalion of the same regiment moved astride the road. Conditions, owing to demolitions, especially at Leptis Magna,[1] were as bad as bad could be, with the result that the 1st Black Watch had to leave the open country and come in on the road behind the 7th, who, with the help of local Senussi labour, were making a

---

[1] At Leptis Magna in A.D. 146 was born Lucius Septimius Severus, who became Emperor of Rome in A.D. 193, and who advanced farther into Caledonia than any other Roman General. He reached the Moray Firth somewhere about the year A.D. 209.

way for vehicles round the demolitions and themselves lifting mines. In the darkness the two Black Watch battalions were on the western edge of Homs and across the road fighting the rearguard of the enemy.

Daylight discovered the enemy holding in strength a line based on a fort four miles west of Homs to which the Division gave the name of "Edinburgh Castle." That fort had full control over the main road, and the enemy line extended from it to the sea on the north side, and to a deep wadi (Zenadi) on the south. The 1st Black Watch found themselves in difficulties here. They came under very accurate artillery and rifle fire. They were pinned to the ground, as were their forward patrols, who took cover some two hundred yards from the enemy, and here young Fortune, General Victor's son, among others, was wounded. In the afternoon of 20th January it appeared as if the enemy were withdrawing, and by five o'clock "A" Company of the 42nd had occupied Edinburgh Castle. The enemy's withdrawal was no doubt due to an outflanking movement on the sea side, to accomplish which General Wimberley had ordered forward first the 7th Argyll and Sutherland Highlanders, 7th Black Watch and later 2nd Seaforth, with part of the 40th Royal Tanks and a battery of the 126th Field Regiment, all under Brigadier Stirling of 154 Brigade. This column was instructed to cut the enemy off by getting astride the road near Corradini some fourteen miles ahead.

This engagement was to be known as the Battle of the Hills, and a very troublesome affair it proved for the forces moving on the right flank. It had been discovered that a very deep and wide anti-tank ditch had been dug across the road in front of Edinburgh Castle and right down to the sea. "A" Company of the 7th Black Watch was first moved forward to make crossings over that ditch. They did the job well and the troops following up were able to cross. The other Companies of the 7th led the way on foot, and marched some sixteen miles by the coast, where they were to cut the main road beyond the Wadi Genima. (Conditions were such that they had to leave all their vehicles and heavy weapons behind.) By a mischance a wadi half a mile short of it was mistaken for Genima. The 7th advanced across it and from a crest beyond it saw transport moving along the road. The Black Watch opened small-arms fire on this transport, when it was suddenly discovered that the vehicles were British. The firing ceased—and then a further discovery was made. The vehicles were British all

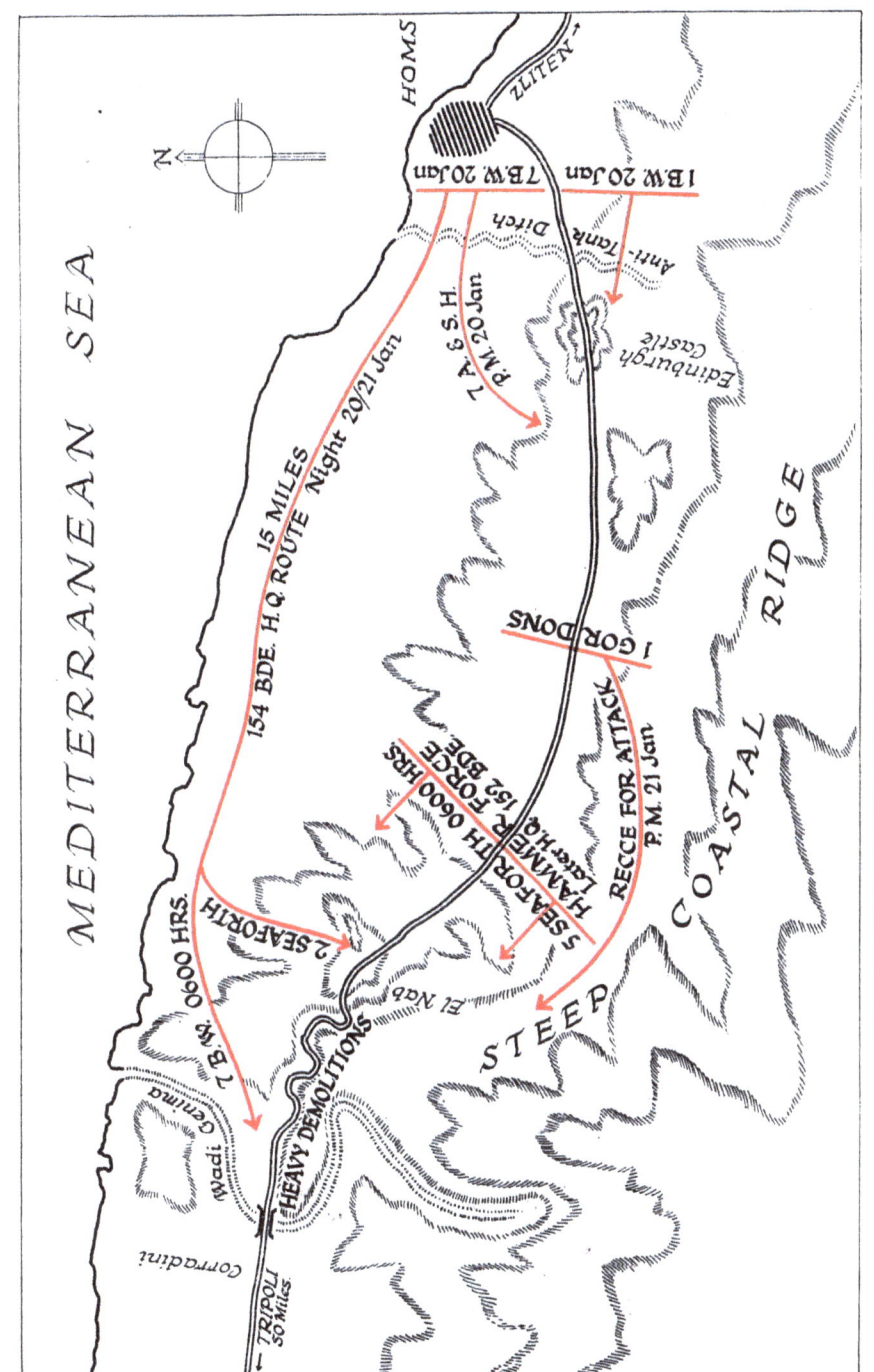

THE BATTLE OF THE HILLS. 20TH-21ST JANUARY 1943.

right, but they had been captured at some earlier date and were being used by the enemy, who opened fire on the 7th and especially on " A " Company who were in a very exposed position on a forward slope. The enemy were reinforced by a tank and several anti-tank guns, and overran the forward elements of " A " Company; but later heavy machine-gun fire from the left sent them retreating westwards.

The 2nd Seaforth (Lt.-Col. R. D. Horne) had preceded the 7th Black Watch up the wadi (mistaken for Genima), whence they attacked a piece of high ground, known as El Nab, which the enemy were holding in force. They in turn were to co-operate with their Territorial battalion, for the 5th Seaforth were assaulting El Nab from the front. But since they had come upon their objective from a wrong angle, and had to move over country which was very hilly and very difficult, the attack became a matter for small individual groups and sometimes even for individuals acting entirely on their own. When a Seaforth spotted an enemy then he set about stalking him and getting him. After twenty-two hours of continuous marching and fighting the 2nd Battalion did gain its objective. Meanwhile the 5th Battalion moving along the main coast road had made a great show in their frontal attack, despite snipers, hand-grenades, and dug-in machine-guns. They had to fight very hard, especially with the bayonet. The Germans made several vicious counter-attacks, and " B " Company had a particularly hefty time. Then the enemy put down a smoke-screen, and a further counter-attack was expected. But the Hun had had enough and his smoke had been released to help him in his get-away.

The Divisional Commander had personally detailed Brigadier Richards (23rd Armoured Brigade)[1] to command a separate advanced-guard moving down the main road. This advanced-guard was known as "Hammerforce." Its infantry consisted of one Company of the 2nd Seaforth, with " A " Company of the 1/7th Middlesex as machine-gunners. A squadron of tanks, two troops of the 61st Anti-Tank Regiment, a battery of field artillery and some sappers completed the

[1] This Armoured Brigade in whole or in part, and armed with its Valentine tanks, fought so much in company with the Highland Division that the Jocks came to regard it almost as a part of the Division, and in quite a different category to all the other Corps and Army units who were from time to time attached for various battles as Leese decided was necessary. Its experienced Commander, Brigadier Richards, was deservedly popular with the 51st, and time and again units of the Division acted under his direct command. It was Hammerforce that thumped the enemy rearguard at Corradini, and it was through the position gained by that force that Brigadier G. Murray ordered the 5th Seaforth at once into the attack.

THE PURSUIT

fighting men, and there was also an ambulance unit. The task of this force was to go full out down the main road as soon as the enemy had been ejected from his positions. Later a Company from the 1st Gordons was attached. On 21st January this force passed through the 5th Seaforth and made full speed for Castleverde, but exhaustive enemy demolitions held it up.

General Wimberley then proceeded to reorganise the whole Divisional forward movement. Because of lack of transport (or petrol) the 5/7th Gordons, 1st and 7th Black Watch, 2nd Seaforth, 5th Camerons, and some of the 1/7th Middlesex had all perforce to be left behind, along with one gunner battery.[1]

On the morning of the 22nd Hammerforce made Castleverde. There were no enemy there. So our tired men settled down to the hard work of filling up the craters on the roads, while the 22nd Armoured Brigade passed through them. But that Brigade could make little advance owing to further demolitions, so again Hammerforce went forward as a pick-and-shovel squad. The 22nd Armoured Brigade then found movement possible to the left, and Hammerforce advanced straight forward.

At 5.30 on the morning of the 23rd January the tanks of the 40th Royal Tank Regiment, acting as taxis for the 1st Gordons, with a Company of 2nd Seaforth in motor transport, entered the main square of Tripoli, the General and a small Tactical Headquarters moving just behind them. The Germans had all gone.[2] Headquarters of the Division moved into Tripoli Stadium just before midday, and by the 26th 153 Brigade were garrison troops and the whole Division was quartered in the Tripoli area. A war-time Divisional printed record states:—

" From Buerat to Tripoli the distance by road, by which axis the Division was ordered to advance, is approximately 253 miles. The Division, with the 23rd Armoured Brigade and the non-Divisional troops attached, covered this distance in 7 days, an average of 35 miles a day.

" In the course of this advance it gapped and moved itself through a

---

[1] There was troop-carrying transport for only a fraction of the Division, and petrol was perforce very severely rationed by Army Headquarters. Originally it had been the Army Commander's intention that the 51st should move, without undue speed, to clear the coast road, while the inland column seized Tripoli. This plan changed, as is so often the case in battle, and the 51st were urged to make Tripoli their goal. Unfortunately the " Q " staff at Army took some time to appreciate the change in plan, and could not, for a day or two, understand the large and urgent demands for petrol made by the 51st, demands which they naturally arbitrarily reduced.

[2] The Highlanders were the first troops of the 8th Army into Tripoli, except for some armoured cars of the 11th Hussars who had moved by the desert route.

wide and deep minefield held by the enemy, it crossed 6 anti-tank ditches, it dealt with no less than 117 road craters and 10 blown bridges, the deviations round some of which were mined.

"Apart from inflicting casualties on the enemy in a number of small rearguard actions and in the Battle of the Hills, it captured a total of 260 prisoners and 10 guns. In doing so the Division suffered 32 officers and 307 other ranks casualties, and a further 46 during the time contact was being made with the enemy at Buerat.

"It dislodged the enemy rearguard, apparently ahead of their timetable, from three prepared positions.

"This task was accomplished because the whole Division worked continuously by day and night as a team, a team wishing to reach only one goal— TRIPOLI."[1]

This bald military statement covers a week's operations which, in the opinion of some experienced observers, was perhaps the finest feat of arms which the 51st achieved as a Division in the whole long campaign. In a Divisional History there is not the space to detail the day-to-day happenings, but unit history after unit history, already published, bears witness to the speed and determination of the pursuit —a pursuit which lack of sleep, shortage of transport and shortage of petrol, not to mention the enemy rearguards, could do nothing to stop.

A selection from the catalogue of gallant deeds performed in the Battle of the Hills is given, first of all to emphasise the importance of the individual in that particular type of warfare, and secondly to emphasise the excellence of the morale of the whole Division. Initiative is epitomised in the action of Sergeant Charles Hunter of the 7th Black Watch, who, on 21st January when the leading Companies of his Battalion came under very heavy mortar and machine-gun fire, noticed that a bridge over the main road was shored up with scaffolding. Hunter, immediately realising that the bridge had obviously been prepared for demolition and that it was impossible for the Companies to advance in force against it, on his own initiative crawled along a wadi and reached the bridge. He got underneath it and succeeded in disconnecting the leads into the junction-boxes for several of the charges. He discovered, however, that to complete the job he must have wire-

---

[1] The 1st Gordons have a good story about General Wimberley. On his arrival in Tripoli the General asked the Gordons where they intended to paint the HD sign. The Gordons, a trifle put out, said they had no paint. "Oh, I've got the paint," said Wimberley, producing a pot from the back of his jeep. "We'll have it up there." He indicated the façade of one of the public buildings, and in no time one of the largest HDs ever seen by the Division—and others—was gleaming red from the wall.

cutters. So he came back, provided himself with the implements and returned to the bridge. He was busy on the job when the enemy, screened from our troops by the scaffolding, advanced on the bridge. Hunter hid in a conduit for some three-quarters of an hour and then decided to withdraw and report the situation to his unit. He was spotted and made his way back under very heavy machine-gun fire. It is to be regretted that his very gallant action did not meet with success, for in the end the enemy did succeed in blowing the bridge.

Then there was Sergeant John Jeffrey of the 2nd Seaforth who, during the advance on El Nab, with two comrades armed like himself with rifles only, worked his way into the enemy position, held up an enemy transport vehicle and forced the twenty men occupying it to come out and surrender. He passed his prisoners back, and then continued the good work.

The story of Private Charles Jones of the 1st Black Watch is the story of many a Company runner. At Homs, on 19th January, Jones' Company was close up with the enemy rearguard: the headquarters and all the platoons were in very exposed positions, but Jones, under heavy fire, carried messages to and from forward platoons with complete disregard for his personal safety.

During the advance-guard actions between 19th and 22nd January, Lieutenant Chavasse (1/7th Middlesex) had to make many journeys by day and by night in his jeep over roads and tracks which had not been cleared of mines. He had to travel alone and over a long period. He witnessed other jeeps being blown to pieces, but such experiences did not deter Chavasse from volunteering time and again for those particularly arduous and hazardous duties.

But the incidents are legion. At Corradini, on 20th-21st January, Gunner George Reynolds of 127th Highland Field Regiment, R.A., acting as observation post signaller to his Major, established his W/T set in an exposed position under heavy mortar and automatic fire. For five hours he sat on a rocky ridge ahead of our foremost infantry under that same fire, making it possible for his battery to bring effective retribution on the enemy. Corporal John Johnston of the 274th Field Company Royal Engineers, on 13th December at Mersa Brega, when one of the forward Companies of the 1st Black Watch found itself hemmed in by an up-to-then undetected anti-personnel minefield, and when several of his own men as well as infantry had been wounded, although he had no detectors, proceeded to organise the clearing of paths through the field so that the infantry might advance and the wounded be evacuated. He and his section lifted a great number of mines, and later in the day they removed no less than three hundred teller mines.

Those few examples of gallantry among the various fighting arms of the Division must stand for the gallantry of all, and this chapter can fittingly close with the message sent by Montgomery to all troops of the 8th Army :—

"To-day, 23rd January, exactly three months after we began the Battle of Egypt, the 8th Army has captured Tripoli and has driven the enemy away to the west towards Tunisia. By skilful withdrawal tactics the enemy has eluded us, though we have taken heavy toll of his army and air forces. The defeat of the enemy in the Battle of El Alamein, the pursuit of his beaten army and the final capture of Tripoli, a distance of some fourteen hundred miles from Alamein, has all been accomplished in three months. This achievement is probably without parallel in history. It could not have been done unless every soldier in the army had pulled his weight all the time. I congratulate the whole army and send my personal thanks to each one of you for the wonderful support you have given me. On your behalf I have sent a special message to the Allied Air Forces that have co-operated with us. I do not suppose that any army has ever been supported by such a magnificent air striking force. I have always maintained that the 8th Army and the R.A.F. in the Western Desert together constitute one fighting machine, and therein lies our great strength. In the hour of success we must not forget the splendid work that has been done by those soldiers working day and night in back areas and on the lines of communication. There are many soldiers quietly doing their duty in rear areas who are unable to take part in the triumphal entry into captured cities, but they are a vital part of our fighting machine, and we should gain no successes if they failed to pull their full weight. I refer especially to stevedores at our bases, to fitters in the workshops, to clerks in rear offices, and so on. I would like to make a special mention of our R.A.S.C. drivers. These men drive long distances by day and night for long periods, and they always deliver the goods. The R.A.S.C. has risen to great heights during the operations we have undertaken, and as a Corps it deserves the grateful thanks of every soldier in the army."

And here at the entrance to Tripoli the fighting infantryman particularly salutes the Field Company sapper.[1] In those three months since Alamein, across those fourteen hundred miles, the sapper had fought an unending battle, the kind of battle " where wounds are not infrequently grey hairs "—the battle against mines and booby-traps. There was the teller mine. There was the anti-personnel mine. There was the trip wire that exploded a mine nearby. There was the dead enemy—move him and a mine went up; the abandoned car—switch on and you were switched off; the pair of jettisoned field-glasses—pick them up and your friends had to pick you up in pieces. It was the sapper's business to render them all neutral. So he moved forward ever in the valley of death, ever waging war with an unseen enemy across a battlefield fourteen hundred miles wide.[2]

If the average Jock of any one of the leading battalions had been asked what he best remembered of all that hectic week, except the exciting moments when actually in action, he would probably have replied lack of sleep. If the men got little, the officers got even less. Bernard Fergusson, in his 'History of the Black Watch,' writes of the Jocks of the 1st and 7th Battalions being somnambulists to a man by the time they reached Tripoli. He was not exaggerating. There can be few examples in all military history when an infantry division with limited troop-carrying transport has moved so far and so fast on the tail of an enemy fighting rearguard.

[1] We must not forget that the Royal Engineers' morale was largely sustained by their most efficient C.R.E.—Lt.-Col. Sugden—himself soon to be badly wounded supervising a crossing on the Wadi Zigzaou at the Battle of Mareth.

[2] For a deserved tribute to the 8th Army sappers, and for fuller details of enemy mines and booby-traps, see Major P. W. Rainer's 'Pipeline to Battle,' pp. 177-179.

CHAPTER IV.

ONE-WAY STREET

"Cuimhnich gaisge agus treuntas ar sinnsear."
(Remember the valour and brave deeds of our forefathers.)

"I marched and fought with the Desert Army."
—THE PRIME MINISTER, in Tripoli.

SOME forty-eight hours after the city's capture a truck with a trailer was driven slowly through the orange-groves which fringe the town of Tripoli; past the white-walled red-roofed houses with their flower-filled gardens it went, then alongside tram-lines fringed by factories and cinemas, down a tree-lined avenue, over a railway crossing, past a palace, past blocks of flats, past shuttered shops, along the Via Roma, and so into the main square, the Piazza Italia, on which the old Moorish fort looks down. Here Mussolini had erected two pillars, on the top of one of which were the bronze figures of Romulus and Remus and their bronze foster-mother, and on the top of the other a Roman galley. Then the occupants of the truck drove round a corner where General Wimberley was impatiently waiting them—Sergeant Felix Barker (Gordons) and the other members of "The Balmorals."[1] Round that corner was the "Miramare Theatre," and above the door was painted in letters of red, "H.D. Theatre." Now let Sergeant Barker tell the story from his diary [2]:—

"Five minutes later Bunny Playfair and I were standing in the Miramare Theatre and General Wimberley was saying, 'Well, what do you think of it?'

"I looked round the auditorium of one of the most beautiful modern theatres I have ever seen.

"'Wonderful, sir,' I said inadequately.

"'Told you I'd do it all right, didn't I?' he smiled.

"He was just like a conjurer who'd produced a very large rabbit out of a very small hat and was enjoying to the full the effect he had created.

"'I think you might have shown up sooner though.'

---

[1] "The Balmorals" were late because someone on the "Q" side at Divisional Headquarters had ordered them to guard some captured tins of drinking water in the desert outside Crispe, one hundred and fifty miles from Tripoli. On 24th January they were allowed to abandon the water, but they required three days to reach Tripoli.

[2] See footnote, p. 24.

"Inwardly cursing, because obviously no one had explained the real reason why we were late, I could only say :

"'The roads were pretty badly congested, sir.'

"'Well, anyway, there you are. Come along, Gray.' And with that he strode away, followed by his A.D.C.

"I sat down in the nearest seat. I was suddenly quite faint with excitement. After all those months of living in the open and seeing nothing but desert sand in every direction, to find oneself suddenly in a magnificent theatre seating about two thousand, with a Royal Box and tiers of smaller boxes like an Opera House, was overpowering. Literally and physically there's only one way to convey the extraordinary sensation I experienced during those first few moments. It was exactly like stepping out into the cold air after having had rather too much to drink. I could hardly speak coherently. Even now this evening, when the full blast of the contrast has died away, it is still a little difficult to believe that this is quite true. The story, as I pieced it together, was as follows. The Division had got into Tripoli on the 23rd, in the early morning and, close behind the tanks, were the first infantry there. Before the day was out, Wimberley had found the Miramare. He immediately ordered an H.D. to be painted over the entrance—I like to think he actually held the tin of red paint while the signwriter was at work. Next he stationed a sentry with a fixed bayonet at the entrance. Then he'd asked Archie Angus (one of his liaison officers and generally responsible for 'The Balmorals') where we were. Wimberley wanted us performing the night the city fell. He has a proper sense of the dramatic. The Division which captures a city and affords itself the luxury of court players has the right to see them performing the same night."

And on 28th January "The Balmorals" played to eighteen hundred men in that theatre, and Montgomery was one of the audience who watched members of the pipe band of the 1st Gordons dance an eightsome reel.

Two days later a Memorial Service was held on the Piazza, at which the Assistant Chaplain-General took the service and Montgomery read Binyon's "For the Fallen." Then Churchill arrived on the 4th of February, when a Victory Parade was held on the same Piazza, and about a thousand representatives of the Highland Division with transport, and to the music of the massed pipes and drums, marched past as spick-and-span as if they had been at home and had never had a grain of desert sand on them.[1] The parade was led by the G.O.C. Division

[1] Brigadier Kippenberger, in his 'Infantry Brigadier,' writes : "The previous afternoon the Highlanders had marched past General Alexander in Tripoli. They had brought their kilts with them—where they found room in their transport I cannot imagine. The battalions moved along the Corniche and passed the saluting base in the little square under the Citadel. As they turned into the square they caught the skirl of the pipes, every man braced himself up, put on a swagger, and they went past superbly. I had climbed on to a tank to watch and for an hour was almost intoxicated by the spectacle."

in a Bren gun carrier bearing the Divisional flag, embroidered with the six tartans of the Highland regiments, and named " Beaumont Hamel " after the 51st's first great victory in 1916. Alan Brooke was there and Alexander, Montgomery and Leese—and they all heard the Prime Minister say : " You have altered the face of the war in a most remarkable way. The fame of the Desert Army has spread throughout the world. When a man is asked after the war what he did, it will be sufficient to say, ' I marched and fought with the Desert Army.' " [1]

It was the job of the Highland regiments to garrison the city and to provide guards for the many gates in the wall that surrounded it, for factories, power and water works, and the wireless and railway stations. In addition they had to act as stevedores. Store-ships were arriving in the harbour and the various battalions had to supply the dock-labour. All went well as long as arrangements were made by the Division, the dock-engineers and the navy, but something called Area Command took over and the confusion of orders resulted in much irritation and bad language. An order would come to a battalion headquarters at midnight to supply so many men for work at the docks at 6 A.M. That meant disturbance for all ranks, special breakfasts served generally in pouring rain, an hour's march to the docks where no one was awake, and where another party would be met from another battalion detailed for the same job. The men would have to kick their heels till probably 9 or 10 A.M.

But there were many happy gatherings, including a special dinner given by the senior officers of the 51st to their comrades in arms of the New Zealand Division, for whom they had a particular regard.

Considerable training was also carried out and a Divisional Battle School formed. Senior officers of the 51st together with those of the New Zealand and 7th Armoured Divisions, under General Montgomery's personal supervision, gave demonstrations of tactical lessons learned in the recent fighting. To attend those a distinguished company of British Generals was flown out from the United Kingdom, and also

---

[1] Later, Churchill reported on his tour to the House of Commons in the following words : " I had the honour, as your servant, to review two (51st and New Zealanders) of our forward Divisions. I should like to say this—I have never in my life, which from my youth up has been connected with military matters, seen troops march with the style or air of the Desert Army. Talk about spit and polish. The Highland and New Zealand Divisions paraded after their immense ordeal as if they had come out of Wellington Barracks." He further, in his message to the troops, wrote after the parade : " The parade smartness which they showed after 1400 miles of battle and pursuit was a miracle of discipline and organisation."

some high-ranking American General Officers, amongst them General Patton.

The Highland Division issued a pamphlet giving a narrative of the recent operations. To that pamphlet General Montgomery himself wrote a Foreword in which he stated, in reference to the Battle of Alamein : " In the fighting which followed, the Highland Division made a name for itself that will never die. The debt it owed (for St Valéry) was well and truly paid. The Division was splendidly led and fought magnificently. The Highland Division is now a veteran Division, skilled in battle, and with a morale that is right on the top line."

A general feeling of regret was experienced when on 18th February the Division said good-bye to that strange city on the beaches of which the keels of Phœnician traders had grounded, Roman legionnaires had sprung ashore from their galleys to conquer Africa, Vandals, Arabs, Turks, Genoese and Spaniards had arrived to fight and plunder, Italians had come to build a grotesque empire.

West from Tripoli the country became bare and with no natural features, but away in the distance could be seen the Matmata range. Those hills, fifty miles from the sea at their eastmost point, run inwards towards it with the result that at Mareth the coastal belt with its cultivated fields, its grass and its olive-groves, narrows away to some fifteen miles where the hills practically meet the coast. At Mareth the French had constructed a sort of Maginot Line in those days when Mussolini had been talking pompously of the development of his African Empire. They had heavily fortified the ground at the point where the hills ran closest to the sea, and the area between Tripoli and Mareth had been left as a kind of no-man's-land separating Italian and French possessions. In that no-man's-land were all sorts of wadis which provided excellent terrain for rearguard actions.

It must be noted that at this time a unification of the Allied Forces in North Africa had been taking place. Eisenhower had become Supreme Allied Commander, with Alexander as his Deputy.

In Tunisia our 1st Army were holding a line some fifty miles from Tunis. South of that the Americans had advanced through Morocco and Algeria to positions some sixty miles from the sea. If they could push on, they would cut through the enemy and divide Rommel's command in the south from Von Arnim's in the north. So Rommel went all out against the Americans and with his veteran Panzer Divisions drove them back some hundred and fifty kilometres, thus to a certain

MAP COVERING OPERATIONS, FEBRUARY-MAY 1943

extent exposing the right flank of our 1st Army. It was then that Alexander called upon Montgomery to do all he could to smash the Mareth Line. Now the harbour of Tripoli was in use, forward airfields had been cleared, and we had also improved our supply lines and our air support. So the job of the 8th Army was to press forward as far as possible and get into the wide plain beyond Mareth towards Sfax and Sousse.

A certain number of rearguard actions had been fought at the end of January and the beginning of February against units of the German 90th Light and 164th Divisions by the 51st's comrades, the 7th Armoured Division. By 4th February the last of the Italian Empire was in Allied hands.[1] The 15th Panzer Division made a determined stand in the area of the fortified village of Ben Gardane and heavy rain joined them as an ally, so that it was not until 15th February that Ben Gardane was cleared of the enemy. The next strong-point was Medenine, which was captured by the 7th Armoured Division.

On foot and by transport the Highland Division was moved to the north of the 8th Army line, with the 7th Armoured Division on their south flank. First contact with the Mareth Line outposts by the 51st was unwittingly made by the C.R.E., Sugden, in a solitary jeep. Out on a reconnaissance with the Divisional Commander he inadvertently went too far forward and ran into a large Italian working party mining a wadi-crossing. He had to beat a very hasty retreat but was quite unscathed despite considerable enemy fire. On the very eve of Rommel's attack the 2nd New Zealand Division also arrived and took position still farther to the south covering Medenine. The enemy were some two miles away, when 153 Brigade took up its original position on the extreme right with 152 on its left. The 154 Brigade was covering the eastern approaches to Medenine. Montgomery was running a very considerable amount of risk at this time, but he felt it was justified in order that some relief could be given to the hard-pressed American

---

[1] Just before the 5/7th Gordons crossed the frontier on 13th February they had a bit of bad luck. Major Barlow was moving up the main road when one of his men stepped on a mine. Barlow was wounded in the chest, a machine-gun officer was killed, and Lieutenant McAndrew wounded. About the same time the C.O. and Major Cochrane of 127th Field Regiment were moving up when Cochrane stepped on a mine. He was killed and the C.O. wounded. Comedy followed on the heels of tragedy. The Gordons marching across the frontier (on the building on which the Pioneers had painted " First across, HD 92nd. BYDAND ") were being filmed by an enterprising cameraman. They were suddenly stopped. The cameraman had forgotten to put any film in his camera. So the Gordons obligingly went back and did it over again.

troops. By his immediate threat to the Mareth Line, the G.O.C. 8th Army had forced Rommel (as Alexander hoped) to withdraw several crack Divisions from what might be termed the northern battle.

The Highland Division had to hold a very wide front and could therefore not be strong at every point. So it was decided to defend certain areas, as all-round keeps, in strength, astride a wide and deep wadi which covered the whole front, and to cover the gaps by anti-tank and machine-gun concentrations. Montgomery knew that Rommel would attack, and he issued the following personal message :—

" 1. The enemy is now advancing to attack us. This is because he is caught like a rat in a trap and he is hitting out in every direction trying to gain time to stave off the day of final defeat in North Africa.
2. This is the very opportunity we want. Not only are we well equipped with everything we need, but in addition the soldiers of the 8th Army have a fighting spirit and a morale which is right on the top line.
3. We will stand and fight the enemy in our present positions. There must be no withdrawal anywhere, and, of course, ' No Surrender.'
    The enemy has never yet succeeded in any attack against a co-ordinated defensive layout, and he will not do so now.
    We have plenty of tanks, and provided the defended localities hold firm then we will smash the enemy attack and cause him such casualties that it will cripple him ; we will in fact give him a very ' bloody nose.'
4. It will then be our turn to attack him. And having been crippled himself, he will be unable to stand up to our attack and we will smash right through him.
5. This attack of the enemy therefore really helps us, and is one more step forward towards the end of the war in North Africa."

One method of defence adopted by the Highland Division was to put out covering screens mainly composed of armoured carriers well in advance of our strong-point line. The idea—which proved very successful—was to delude the enemy into thinking that those forward screens formed our main defensive positions : as a result, his attacks and shells would be wasted on something that wasn't really there. He would then have to re-form in order to make a fresh assault on our actual defensive positions. The enemy would be rather like a boxer who, in delivering what he hopes to be a decisive blow, hits only the air, wastes considerable force, and takes some time to recover his balance. Rommel made such an attack on 3rd March on the Highland Divisional front with infantry and some tanks, but the attack was not pressed and was easily dealt with.

On the morning of 6th March the Afrika Korps Commander made his real attack. In most cases his infantry were bunched up, with the result that our artillery and Middlesex machine-gunners were presented with good targets, on which they exhibited the excellence of their marksmanship. There was a certain amount of dive-bombing by enemy aircraft. Here and there he made slight penetrations into our defences, but was driven back by vigorous counter-attacks.

The 1st Black Watch of Stirling's 154 Brigade had about as tough a time as any. They were on the left flank of the Divisional front, and the right-hand lorried infantry battalion of the 7th Armoured Division had been forced back, so that that flank was exposed. A Company of the 42nd immediately wheeled left and attacked, the infantry battalion of the 7th Armoured Division re-filled the gap, and the position was completely restored. The 7th Argylls also had a fairly heavy time and had to launch a counter-attack, but gave away nothing. In fact the main attack was to the south, where the Guards Brigade, on some high ground (termed by the 8th Army " The Wellington Hills "), took all that was coming to them, destroyed fifty of Rommel's tanks and forced the German Commander (by this time a very sick man in more ways than one) to withdraw his forces into the hills and behind his outpost line in front of the Wadi Zigzaou.

When the 50th Division came forward the Highland Division's wide front was considerably shortened. The 50th Division was moved into the area nearest the sea which had been held by 153 Brigade, and the 7th Armoured Division took over the area on the south held by 154 Brigade. A certain amount of rest was given to the troops, and on 15th March General Wimberley delivered a lecture to all officers of the Division down to Company Commanders as to what the next operation was to be. As a preliminary to the battle the Division's job was to advance northwards against strong German fort positions named Ksibia and Zarat, while the 201 Guards Brigade were to attack a ring of small hills at the south-west of the Mareth defences designated the " Horseshoe." [1] The 50th Division were then to make the main assault

---

[1] The 51st's task turned out to be a comparatively easy one, with little opposition, but the Guards Brigade met intensive minefields, suffered heavy casualties, and were withdrawn, after a night attack, at daylight on 17th March.

and form a bridgehead. Through them were to move the 4th Indian Division. Meanwhile General Freyberg with both the New Zealand and 7th Armoured Division was to deliver another left hook, by way of the Matmata Hills, on the Gabes Gap, which hook would outflank Rommel's position in the Mareth Line.

Let us take a look at the area from the Wadi Zessar from which a fairly complete view of the Mareth position could be had. The general terrain was a plain covered by sandhills and scrub. In the centre of that plain ran the Wadi Melah, and halfway between it and the Mareth Line lay the Wadi Zeuss. The main obstacle before Rommel's position was the Wadi Zigzaou, cutting into which was an artificial anti-tank ditch consisting of a six-foot vertical wall on the German side with a parapet. On our side the ditch simply sloped down at an angle of some forty-five degrees without any bottom level. The only means of defending this ditch, as far as our troops were concerned, was for men to make a defensive position on the top of the wall.

The Army Commander had sent out the following message to be read to all troops :—

"On the 5th of March Rommel addressed his troops in the mountains overlooking our positions, and said that if they did not take Medenine by the 6th of March and force the 8th Army to withdraw, the days of the Axis forces in North Africa were numbered. The next day he attacked the 8th Army. He should have known that the 8th Army never withdraws, therefore his attack could only end in failure, which it did. We will now show Rommel that he was correct in his statement which he made to his troops. The days of the Axis forces in North Africa are numbered. The 8th Army and the Western Desert Air Force, together constituting one fighting machine, are ready to advance. We all know what that means, and so does the enemy.

"In the battle that is now to start the 8th Army

(a) will destroy the enemy now facing us in the Mareth position ;
(b) will burst through the Gabes Gap ;
(c) will then drive northwards on Sfax, Sousse, and finally Tunis. We will not stop or let up till Tunis has been captured and the enemy has either given up the struggle or been pushed into the sea. The operations now about to begin will mark the close of the campaign in North Africa."

In the active patrolling before the actual attack on the Mareth Line the Gordon Battalions acquired much merit. For complete coolness under fire the action of Private George Stewart of the 5/7th Battalion takes some beating. The Battalion were attacking certain

THE "HIGHWAY DECORATORS" IN TRIPOLI

ANTI-TANK DITCH AT GABES GAP. APRIL 1943

Lt.-Col.
LORNE
CAMPBELL,
V.C.
APRIL 1943

By courtesy of the
IMPERIAL WAR
MUSEUM

enemy outposts in the Mareth Line, and Stewart was coming up behind the infantry driving his truck and its gun. The only gap in an extensive minefield was just wide enough to take Stewart's vehicle. He unhesitatingly drove along it, but the vehicle was hit by shell fragments and a tyre was burst. Stewart realised he must not block the only passage through the minefield and, although the shelling and mortaring were very heavy, he calmly proceeded to change his wheel and drove forward again. The result was that other vehicles carrying ammunition and guns were not held up and safely reached the Gordon infantry on their objectives. Another patrol at Mareth was led in full daylight on 28th March by 2nd Lieutenant Gibson, who was killed by enemy shelling. Without hesitation Sergeant Milton, who was in charge of the carriers, took over command, reorganised the patrol and brought them and the wounded safely back to our lines. Major Napier, also of the 5/7th Gordons, showed great determination in a night attack on a Mareth Line outpost, when he took " C " Company through two very large minefields and completed an excellent night's work by capturing the enemy position.

Sergeant A. Kemlo of the 1st Gordons was instructed with his section to occupy a feature opposite the Wadi Zeuss, south-east of the Mareth Line, known as Point 12. Through a concentration of mortar-bombs and machine-gun fire he led his men with great dash, occupied the position and held it until a Company of his Battalion were able to come forward and consolidate the position, which turned out to be most valuable during the preparation for the Mareth advance. Sergeant Wilson of the same Battalion made an equally gallant show in occupying Point 20. Lieutenant Reynold-Payne's patrolling in order to gain detailed information about an anti-tank ditch is also worthy of record.

Such work by the Gordon Battalions gives some idea of the amount of preparation that preceded the Mareth battle. As one Gordon soldier records [1] :—

" The Battle of the Mareth Line corresponded in tactics to most modern battles; it required an infinite amount of preparation and then a single, swift, all-powerful blow. It was five weeks after the Battalion arrived at Wadi Zesser before the enemy was again in retreat. But this was not five weeks of continuous struggle swaying one way and then the other until the stronger prevailed. As far as the 1st Gordons were concerned the actual ' battle ' lasted only a few hours—starting with the 1 A.M. attack on the

[1] ' Gordon Highlanders in North Africa and Sicily,' by Felix Barker (1944).

morning of 17th March across Wadi Zeuss, through the minefield to objectives some hundred yards forward. That was the job to be done (and extremely unpleasant during the short time it lasted) for which there had to be so many weeks of waiting. . . .

"The actual attack when it came was regarded by most of the Battalion as 'the next worst thing to Alamein.' In rehearsal two days earlier it had seemed as if it would conform in procedure with previous attacks. The Battalion would move on square formation; the taping party would be out in front putting down lights to mark the gap in the minefield cleared by the sappers; transport would follow when possible with ammunition and the anti-tank guns in case of counter-attack; all this was familiar. No one expected it to be easy, but it was thought that at least it would be straightforward. It turned out to be anything but straightforward. It was a perfect demonstration, if demonstration were necessary, of the unpredictability of even the best laid plan of battle. The soft sand of Wadi Zeuss in which transport churned so hopelessly and the difficulties of clearing a gap through the minefield all helped to make confusion's masterpiece. But through confusion the Battalion somehow achieved its purpose. It reached its objectives. Dawn found the Companies still in the minefield and three hours behind schedule, but by nine they were on the two hills they had to take. They were six hours late, but the all-important thing was that they were there."

If in this advance the 4th Indian Division were successful in their penetration, then the Highland Division was to act as part of a pursuit force.

In actual fact things did not work out according to plan, because the 50th Division, attacking on the night of the 20th March, did not succeed in forming a bridgehead. Torrential rain had turned the bottom of Wadi Zigzaou into a bog, impassable for any kind of armour. So, although those gallant men from Northern England had successfully crossed the wadi, they were left alone in an area where the enemy's strong pill-box defences were fairly intact, and where they had to suffer a merciless barrage. The Northumbrians fought on undaunted, and finally six tanks were got across the wadi. One enemy strong-point, known as "Jane," seemed impregnable, but all that weary March day the 50th Division held on, losing forty-seven of their fifty officers engaged in the action.

On the night of 21st March the 5th Seaforth (Lt.-Col. Walford) had gapped a minefield and reached the enemy anti-tank ditch, where they took over from the 7th Green Howards. The Seaforth were heavily shelled and for a time had both flanks in the air. But the following night the 5th Camerons also came up to occupy the vacant part of the ditch on the right, and, despite terrific enemy artillery fire and considerable casualties, advanced in the morning to positions in front of the ditch. A temporary retiral had to be made on 24th March.

Faced with the failure of the 50th Division's attack Montgomery, with his unerring tactical sense, did not hesitate. He called off the attack on the right. Leaving the Highland Division, Guards Brigade and 23rd Armoured Brigade to threaten the Mareth Line from the front, he rushed all other available troops to the support of his left hook, which was brilliantly successful. In the end and indirectly successful also was the very failure of the 50th Division to establish their bridgehead, inasmuch as, to meet their attack, Rommel had withdrawn his 21st Panzer Armoured Division from the defences on his right flank.

The 5th Black Watch were ordered to make a short subsidiary attack on 25th March and had the bad luck to be shelled in error by our own 8th Army artillery on the start-line. But they stuck it out and were warmly congratulated by the Corps Commander. General Leese wrote :—

" I am writing to congratulate all ranks of the 5th Battalion Black Watch on their magnificent bearing during the operations last night.

" It speaks worlds for their discipline and *esprit de corps* that the Battalion reached the objectives and captured 30 prisoners of war, after being shelled heavily by our own guns on the start-line.

"I am very proud of them and I send them my most hearty congratulations and my very sincere regret that they should have suffered casualties at the hands of their own guns. I know, however, that this will not impair their confidence in our artillery, which has so splendidly supported the infantry in all their attacks."

The 5/7th Gordons were successful in their part of this attack and took all their objectives, and the 1st Gordons relieved the 5th Black Watch.

On Leese's orders Wimberley moved up fresh units of the Highland Division to help the Northumbrians. The 7th Argylls took over from the East Yorks, who had lost very heavily, and had been forced to retire well behind the Wadi Zigzaou. The Argylls sent a fighting patrol into the wadi during the night of 25th March and their raid was very successful. By the 28th everything suggested that the enemy opposite the 51st were retiring, and Argyll patrols entered the Mareth Line and found it unoccupied. This news was confirmed by patrols from several battalions. The whole Battalion then moved across the Wadi Zigzaou

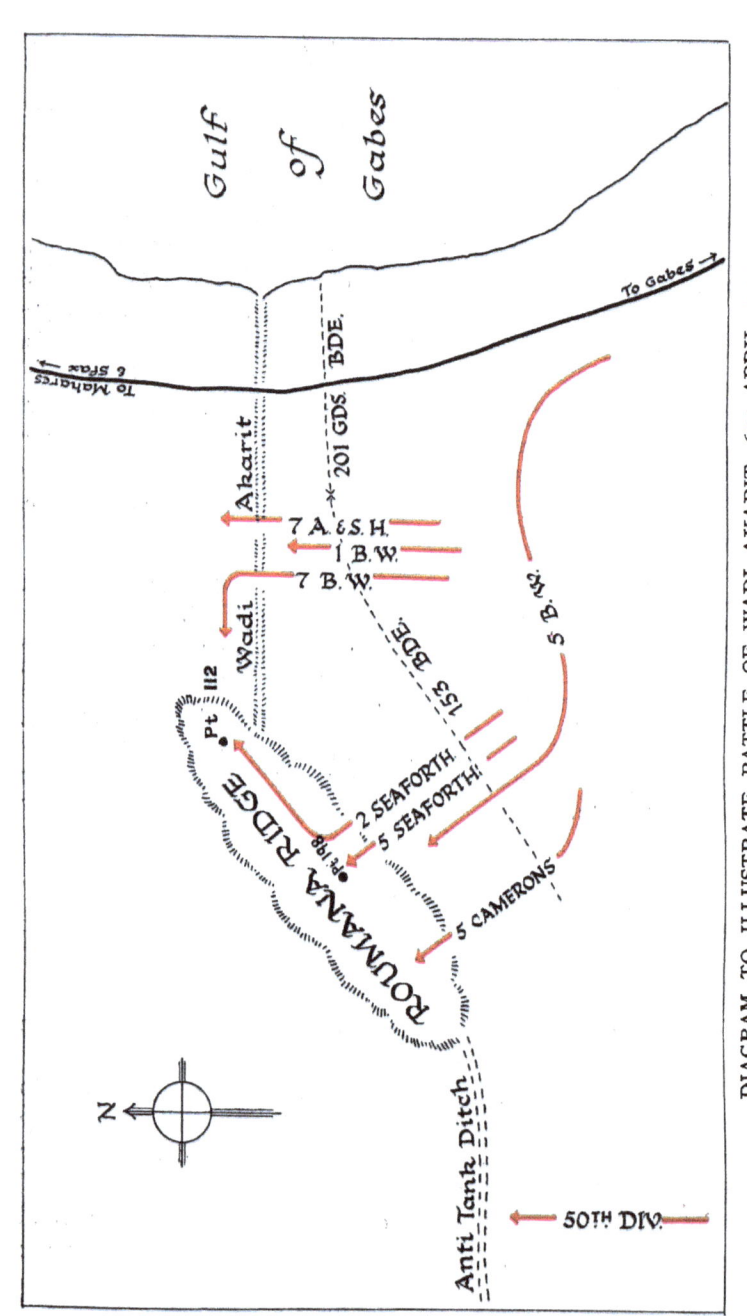

DIAGRAM TO ILLUSTRATE BATTLE OF WADI AKARIT, 6TH APRIL 1943

into the German positions and, after a night there, advanced on foot some sixteen miles to a point just east of Gabes.

The movement of the Division through the Mareth defences in its pursuit of the enemy was on the whole a very unpleasant experience. The dead of the 50th Northumbrian Division were scattered all over the area where they had fought so well and so bravely. Both in and in front of the anti-tank ditch lay many of the Seaforth and Camerons.[1] But the advance went on and men of the Highland Division arrived in Gabes from the south at the very same time as the New Zealanders entered it from the west.[2]

And so to another bottleneck. Just north of a line between the sea-coast town of Gabes and the inland settlement of El Hamma lay the narrow pass known as the Gabes Gap. El Hamma was situated at the south-eastern corner of an area of water-logged ground about fifteen miles from east to west and known as Shott el Jerid. The usual wadi presented a strong line of defence for the enemy. In this case the wadi was known as Akarit and it ran right across the Gap to the north of the narrowest point. Behind and to the left of the wadi on the Divisional front was a range of hill-ground, the Roumana Ridge (1600 feet at its highest point), which terminated, however, some distance from the coast and left the continuation of the Gap opening on a wide plain. There were a minefield and an anti-tank ditch between our troops and the Wadi Akarit. That anti-tank ditch was practically on the edge of the wadi, at some points actually cutting into it. The one road hugged the coast right on to Sfax.

Montgomery's plan of battle was as follows. The attack on the Wadi Akarit and the Roumana Ridge and the hills to the west of the Ridge was to be made by three Divisions—51st, 50th and 4th Indian, lined up in that order from the coast road westward—with the 210 Guards Brigade on the right and under command of the 51st, in a holding rôle from the coast road to the sea. Graham's 153 Brigade (less the 5th Black Watch in Divisional Reserve) first moved forward to gain contact with the enemy and consolidated on a line some 2000 yards from the Wadi Akarit. So far as the Highland Division's plan was concerned

---

[1] This ditch gave no protection, and the ground was like iron which made digging very hard. In the History of the 5th Seaforth, 'Sans Peur,' the statement is made: " It remains in the minds of those who were there as an experience worse than the battle of Alamein."

[2] The New Zealanders stated that, had the Jocks not stopped to put on their kilts for a ceremonial entry, they (the New Zealanders) would have been second in the race.

the attack was to be made on the Roumana feature by 152 Brigade and on the wadi by 154. To fit into this plan the Divisional Signals, under Lt.-Col. Cochrane, began without delay to ensure that communications both by line and by wireless, as is so vital in battle, were as good as it was possible for human ingenuity and determination to make them.

It should be realised that this attack could only gain satisfactory results provided the enemy were pushed far enough back to allow us to dominate the northern plain; for, once we were in that position, he would have to give up the whole of that plain leading to the valuable ports of Sfax and Sousse and retire right to Enfidaville, his last hope for a strong defensive line. The proposed action of the Highland Division was that on the 154 Brigade front the 7th Argylls were to push through the minefield, attack the anti-tank ditch and the Wadi Akarit and form a bridgehead. The 7th Black Watch were then to pass through the Argylls, turn west in the wadi and mop up right to the Roumana feature. The 1st Black Watch was to be in Brigade Reserve. Meanwhile on 152 Brigade front the 5th Camerons (left) and 5th Seaforth (right) were to capture the left end of the Ridge, and the 2nd Seaforth were then to mop up the top of the Roumana feature from south to north by turning to the right, by which means they would then eventually contact the 7th Black Watch below them in the plain. A few hours before the attack was due to begin a personal note arrived from Montgomery to Wimberley: " Good luck to you to-night. If you get your objectives the break-through should be a certainty."

Let us deal first with the attack of the 154 Brigade. At four in the morning of 6th April artillery laid down their opening barrage on the Indian Division's objective. A quarter of an hour later our own barrage opened, and under its protection (noise as well as damage) " Scorpions " moved forward through the holding Gordon Battalions of 153 Brigade to gap the minefield, followed later by units of the 40th Royal Tank Regiment, acting as transport for the guns of the 241 Anti-Tank Battery. Companies of Royal Engineers of the Division also advanced, and the greatest credit is due to them in that, despite furious enemy artillery and machine-gun fire, by midday not only had they gapped the minefield but they had also bridged the anti-tank ditch. At 5.15 the Argylls advanced. They successfully traversed the minefield; with the assistance of some obsequious Italian prisoners they crossed the ten-foot deep anti-tank ditch and achieved their first objectives with the help of most excellent support from the Middlesex machine-gunners. The enemy barrage was terrific and their fire down the wadi from the Roumana heights most deadly. Our own artillery fire, however, nullified the first German counter-attacks, but later the enemy got to close quarters and the Argylls put up a magnificent defence, the action of " No Surrender " Major John MacDougall of Lunga and five men being a good example of the many outstanding acts of gallantry.[1] To this Battalion and on this occasion there came later the honour of the award of a Victoria Cross to its Commanding Officer, and we quote the citation :—

" On the 6th of April 1943 in the attack upon the Wadi Akarit position (before the Gabes Gap), the task of breaking through the enemy minefield and anti-tank ditch to the east of the Roumana feature and of forming the initial bridgehead for a Brigade of the 51st Highland Division was allotted to the Battalion of the Argyll and Sutherland Highlanders commanded by Lt.-Col. Campbell.

" The attack had to form up in complete darkness and had to traverse the main offshoot of the Wadi Akarit at an angle to the line of advance.

" In spite of heavy machine-gun fire in the early stages of the attack, Lt.-Col. Campbell successfully accomplished this difficult operation, captured at least six hundred prisoners, and led his Battalion to its objective, having to cross an unswept portion of the enemy minefield in doing so.

" Later, upon reaching his objective, he found that a gap which had been blown by the Royal Engineers in the anti-tank ditch did not correspond with the vehicle lane which had been cleared in the minefield. Realising the vital necessity of quickly establishing a gap for the passage of anti-tank guns, he took personal charge of the operation.

" It was now broad daylight, and under very heavy machine-gun fire and shell-fire he succeeded in making a personal reconnaissance and in conducting operations which led to the establishing of a vehicle gap.

" Throughout the day Lt.-Col. Campbell held his position with his Battalion in the face of extremely heavy and constant shell-fire, which the enemy was able to bring to bear by direct observation.

" At about 1630 hours determined enemy counter-attacks began to develop, accompanied by tanks. In this phase of the fighting Lt.-Col. Campbell's personality dominated the battlefield by a display of valour and utter disregard for personal safety which could not have been excelled.

" Realising that it was imperative for the future success of the army plan to hold the bridgehead his Battalion had captured, he inspired his men by his presence in the forefront of the battle, cheering them on and rallying them as he moved to these points where the fighting was heaviest.

" When his left forward Company was forced to give ground, he went forward alone into a hail of fire and personally reorganised their position, remaining with the Company until the attack at this point was held.

" As reinforcements arrived upon the scene he was seen standing in the

[1] See ' History of 7th Argylls,' p. 93.

open directing the fight under close-range fire of enemy infantry, and he continued to do so although already painfully wounded in the neck by shell-fire. It was not until the battle died down that he allowed his wound to be dressed.

" Even then, although in great pain, he refused to be evacuated, remaining with his Battalion and continuing to inspire them by his presence on the field.

" Darkness fell with the Argylls still holding their positions, though many of its officers and men had become casualties.

" There is no doubt that but for Lt.-Col. Campbell's determination, splendid example of courage and disregard of pain, the bridgehead would have been lost.

" This officer's gallantry and magnificent leadership when his now tired men were charging the enemy with the bayonet and were fighting them at hand-grenade range are worthy of the highest honour and can seldom have been surpassed in the long history of the Highland Brigade."

The 7th Black Watch, under Lt.-Col. Oliver, moved forward at 0625 hours and had to pass through very heavy shelling in the minefield where the gap had been located by the enemy artillery. But that field and the anti-tank ditch were successfully passed, and the Battalion re-formed on the farther side, somewhat embarrassed by the large number of Italian prisoners thankfully crowding through to the southwards. Heavy machine-gun fire from the right caused many casualties, but by 0930 hours the 7th had gained its objectives. The difficulties which were by now being experienced by the 2nd Seaforth of 152 Brigade in the second phase of the Roumana attack, however, acted adversely on the 7th Black Watch, whose mopping-up in the wadi to the left was thereby rendered a well-nigh impossible task. They were under direct observation from the north point of the Roumana feature, and later in the day an attack by German infantry in strength supported by tanks overran some of the forward positions and got between the Battalion and the Argylls. Welcome reinforcements, however, were received from Lt.-Col. Roper Caldbeck's 1st Black Watch, but during the night the 7th were ordered to retire 1000 yards so as to close up with the Argylls. This manœuvre was successfully carried out.

Meanwhile at zero hour on the left of the 154 Brigade, Murray's 152 Brigade had made their attack on the Ridge proper. At 0330 hours the 5th Seaforth, with the 5th Camerons on their left, began their attack on the Ridge, the highest top of which was known as Point 198. The advance was through a wilderness of rocks on which our barrage roared and blazed. The 2nd Seaforth followed behind the 5th, and were to move to the right and capture the extreme east end of the Ridge where the vital position was Point 112. The 5th Seaforth's first encounter with the enemy was with half-dressed Italians, rubbing the sleep out of their eyes and very anxious to know their way to the prisoner-of-war cage. The 5th successfully captured their objective by 0545 hours, and a little later the 2nd, moving behind them and turning right-handed along the top of the Ridge, had also reached theirs. An hour later the counter-attacks began. There was no possibility of our men digging in among the rocks, and the enemy's mortars made sad havoc among the Seaforth. Meanwhile the Germans moved up machine-guns and added to the difficulties of holding the tops. Then came the full power of the counter-attack, which forced back the 2nd Seaforth off Point 112, and thus exposed both the flank of the 5th Seaforth and that of the 7th Black Watch in the wadi. Despite their setback the 2nd Seaforth's efforts were beyond all praise. The commanders of the leading Companies had both become casualties, and the Adjutant, Captain McHardy, took over, directed the initial attack on Point 112 and succeeded in capturing that feature. He then returned to report to his headquarters and have reinforcements sent up.

Lt.-Col. R. D. Horne went forward when his men had been forced back and led three desperate counter-attacks on the Ridge. Although Point 112 was not recaptured Colonel Horne formed a defensive line farther down the slope, and, despite heavy machine-gun and mortar fire, held that position all day long with the remnants of the other two Companies who had been fearlessly led by Major Gilmour of Rosehall.

As a sample of the many exhibitions of individual courage and leadership that of Private D. M. Bridges of the 5th Seaforth may be cited. For six hours this man was practically responsible for the security of the right flank of his Battalion. By the skilful use of his Bren gun he time and again prevented parties of the enemy from infiltrating to the rear of his Company's position, and, as the citation for his Military Medal reads, " thereby preventing the position from being overrun." That very gallant officer, Major J. H. Davidson, of the same Battalion, from Caithness, described his day on Point 198 in his ' Diary ' thus [1] :—

" I ordered a defensive position on Point 198, which was occupied

[1] See footnote, p. 35.

about 0930 by the remnants of the Company—about a dozen men in all, just enough to man the flanks and watch the front. Ian Mackenzie had disappeared. He was afterwards found well forward. He must have been cut off, but had fought to the last. There were three dead Germans lying near him.

"Shortly after occupying this position I became aware that the enemy had penetrated right forward and had at least two positions within forty yards of us, immediately above our heads. We tried to climb the last few yards of the crest to get at them, but were at once machine-gunned from the right. From then on it was a case of hanging on and being as offensive as possible. Magazine after magazine was fired from our Brens. Private Bridges was magnificent. Corporal Mitchell was wounded, but another gunner took his place. Corporals Thompson and Bain shot incessantly. Private Smith from Caithness and myself watched the crest above our heads. Sergeant Mackenzie moved about from place to place and was a tower of strength. About 1230 hours a determined German attempt was made to get round our left flank, and a party of nine was seen getting into position behind us. We gave them all we had and they withdrew in disorder, leaving three dead and assisting two wounded. We got one or two reinforcements from Battalion Headquarters who were immediately below and could see every move that both we and the Germans were making.

"About 1500 hours the situation was getting desperate. I could hear German voices above me, and I knew my right was vulnerable. Just then George Willock from Battalion Headquarters appeared with a Bren and helped a lot; but the Germans above had crawled forward silently and started to let us have a shower of stick grenades. I gradually moved the Company back about a hundred and fifty yards to another position and succeeded in re-establishing ourselves there, and managed to prevent the enemy getting Point 198. The 5th Black Watch arrived about 1800 hours and took over. We relaxed and heaved a sigh of relief. . . ."

It was as well for the course of the battle that General Wimberley had a good forward observation post and could see the ground for himself, quite apart from the R/T reports from Brigadier Murray that the Seaforth were meeting trouble as the day wore on. He had ordered Colonel "Chick" Thomson, O.C. the 5th Black Watch in the Divisional Reserve, to report to him in the morning, and later he gave him direct orders to move his Battalion to the top of the Ridge as reinforcements to 152 Brigade. The 5th Black Watch advanced in broad daylight, and having reported to Brigadier Murray, Colonel Thomson sent his two leading fresh Companies into the dog-fight on Point 198. This Battalion incurred some fifty casualties. The top was finally consolidated, but at nightfall German troops still barred the way to Point 112.

The 5th Camerons were on the extreme left of the Divisional attack and were the link with the right attacking infantry of the 50th Division. Under Lt.-Col. Ronnie Miers they crossed their start-line and began their attack at 0330 hours and made their way up over the lower end of the Roumana Ridge into the wadis running from its left-hand side, and began to consolidate on their first objective; unfortunately on their left troops of the 50th Division were for several hours unsuccessful in making their way forward as far as their own objective. There, later, the Camerons had to face the edge of the heavy counter-attack which the German 90th Light Division was making on the 5th Seaforth and had to watch their open left flank. All day long the Camerons held their ground and kept up a powerful defence. They were able in the afternoon to assist the 5th Black Watch as the latter advanced to the support of the Seaforth. Among the innumerable cases of individual bravery displayed in this Battle of a Day may be mentioned the action of C.S.M. Macrae of " D " Company of the Camerons. He personally led three bayonet charges and himself killed nine Germans. He simply had no concern at all for his own safety, and in the end was shot dead.

The detail of this action gives an opportunity of describing how the Middlesex machine-gunners played their part in all the Division's battles. They had necessarily to act in small units. On this day 15 Platoon advanced with the 5th Camerons and found an excellent field of fire across the plain, but later their position was made untenable by snipers still firing from the crest of Roumana, and they had to withdraw. 13 Platoon were attached to the 5th Seaforth. One section lost fifty per cent of its men in the advance on the summit, on reaching which it was discovered that the positions it was to occupy were held by the enemy. The section however took up position on open ground when it made an easy target for the enemy. The barrel-casings of both guns became punctured in several places, and to keep the weapons firing the men had to pour in water from their water-bottles. It was not until all the ammunition had been expended that the section commander ordered the locks to be removed and his men to withdraw. Only one man was unwounded. Before the other section could reach the top all but one man were casualties. 14 Platoon advanced with the 2nd Seaforth and fought all day in their desperate battle. 9 Platoon made a successful crossing of the anti-tank ditch with the Argylls, while 7 Platoon advanced from reserve with the 1st Black Watch. Two platoons of "C" Company fought alongside the Argylls and then with the 7th Black Watch.

And so all day long the battle went on backwards and forwards along that bloody Ridge and the wadis below it, a Divisional battle which, in the words of *The Times* newspaper correspondent, earned for the Highlanders a victory when they finally broke the German defence on the Ridge, described as "one of the greatest heroic achievements of the war." By nightfall the fighting died down. During darkness the G.O.C. had a conference with his Brigadiers at 153 Brigade Headquarters. It was clear that the Battalions of the 152 and 154 Brigades had lost heavily, the Divisional Reserve Battalion had been used up, and 153 Brigade's two Gordon Battalions were occupying wide fronts.

Would or would not the enemy again counter-attack at dawn was then the question. It was Brigadier Douglas Graham of 153 Brigade—"Old Lionheart" as some of the troops called him—who confidently asserted that the enemy were going. He seemed in all battles to share with Freyberg of the New Zealanders a cheerful spirit of optimism, so estimable a virtue in a battle commander. Sure enough, as dawn came, our infantry patrols from the Camerons on the left to the Argylls on the right, reported that the enemy had gone. It was a short sharp battle in which the Highlanders, ably supported by the artillery, played a distinguished part.[1]

As the Divisional Intelligence Summary No. 135 puts it :—

"There is no doubt that the day marked the fiercest fighting that the Division had experienced in this campaign. Our artillery and machine-gunners were in constant support on a very large number of targets throughout the day. Our infantry had a gruelling time and several units suffered very heavy casualties, but by nightfall our troops had succeeded in driving the enemy off some very difficult ground, holding most of it in the face of very fierce counter-attacks, causing the enemy severe casualties in dead and wounded, and taking over three thousand prisoners of war!"

Early in the morning of 7th April 8th Army armour had set out across the plain in pursuit of the retreating enemy, but we were considerably handicapped in this manœuvre by the nature of the bottleneck crossing of the anti-tank ditch and the Wadi Akarit. It was unlucky for us because the enemy commanded his rearguard very skilfully, and

---

[1] General Montgomery wrote in his ' El Alamein to the River Sangro ' : " My troops fought magnificently, particularly 51 and 4 Indian Divisions, and hung on to the key localities they had taken." See Note, p. 51.

he had time to place his guns and tanks in such strategic positions that many of his troops were enabled to get clear away. On the night of 8th-9th April it was discovered that the enemy had withdrawn his defensive screen, but not before he had blown a very large crater across the coast road. Some further resistance was offered here and there.

The 1st Gordons (Lt.-Col. Fausset-Farquhar) had led the advance on 9th April in company with the 23rd Armoured Brigade. They met a powerful German rearguard astride the Wadi Cheffar. Such was the nature of the ground and so devastating the enemy artillery that the tanks could not make much progress. The Gordons deployed and went into the attack, which was so vigorous that, before darkness fell, the enemy beat a hasty retreat, leaving behind them many prisoners and several guns. This attack laid open the road to Sfax.

An interesting incident which occurred during the Highland Division's advance on Sfax is described by Major Peter W. Rainer in his 'Pipeline to Battle.' Major Rainer had been responsible for the waterpipe across the desert and he had driven forward beyond Akarit in his car. He writes [1] :—

"By late afternoon I had reached the outskirts of Mahares, a village twenty miles short of Sfax. All day we had fought our way forward through dense traffic, all pushing forward in pursuit. Now we seemed to be among guns. There were rows of them by the roadside, while in a nearby barley field a wedge of tanks stood motionless, expectant, or moved restlessly about. At the edge of the village a tall officer was giving orders to a group around him. It occurred to me that I had worked my way farther forward than I had intended. I walked over to the tall officer to ask him ' the score.'

"Not till I was face to face with him did I notice the crossed swords on his shoulder strap. A General, by God! It was General Wimberley, Commander of the Highland Division.

"I saluted. 'Sorry, sir, but I didn't notice your badge of rank.'

"'That's all right. What can I do for you?'

"'I'm Royal Engineers. On water recce, sir.'

"'Good God, man!' His tone was still courteous. 'You can't recce water in the middle of a battle. The enemy is still holding the other end of this village. You are too far forward. Get back and get your vehicle off the road so that my guns can have a chance to come up.'

"I saluted again and turned back. I had always wanted to watch a General directing a battle. Now I had seen one. I admired his coolness. If I were a General busy with a battle and some damned fool came up to me looking for water, I am sure I wouldn't have been so courteous."

[1] By permission of Messrs John Farquharson and Messrs William Heinemann.

"A" Company of the 1st Gordons were the first 8th Army troops into Sfax and here a Free French liaison officer in immaculate uniform acquired a seat in General Wimberley's jeep and the two together entered Sfax, where the General addressed the inhabitants in French, to receive a somewhat mixed reception from the citizens. German occupation had been bad enough, but there was still a feeling abroad among certain of the French inhabitants of North Africa that, if we had thrown in our hand in 1940, it wouldn't have been any worse. Particularly since the 8th Army had advanced, it had in reality been worse, inasmuch as our bombing had destroyed much of the town. But things brightened up and Montgomery was given the freedom of the city of Sfax, at which ceremony a well turned-out Guard of Honour dressed in the kilt (supplied by the 1st Battalion) was provided by the 7th Black Watch.

Congratulatory messages had been many. On the 8th April Montgomery sent the following to be read out to all troops :—

"On 20th March, in a personal message before we began the battle of Mareth, I told you that the 8th Army would do three things :—

> Deal with the enemy in the Mareth position. That was done between 21st and 28th March and we took 8000 prisoners.
> Burst through the Gabes Gap. That was done on 6th April. The enemy was so unwise as to stand to fight us on the Akarit position. He received a tremendous hammering and we took another 7000 prisoners.
> Drive northwards on Sfax, Sousse, and finally Tunis. This is now in process of being done ; and if we collect in the prisoners at the present rate the enemy will soon have no infantry left to hold his position.
> I also told you that if each of us did his duty and pulled his full weight, then nothing could stop us. And nothing has stopped us.
> You have given our families at home, and in fact the whole world, good news, and plenty of it, every day.
> I want now to express to you, my soldiers, whatever may be your rank or employment, my grateful thanks for the way in which you have responded to my calls on you and my admiration for your wonderful fighting qualities.
> I doubt if our Empire has ever possessed such a magnificent fighting machine as the 8th Army ; you have made its name a household word all over the world.
> I thank each one of you for what you have done.
> I am very proud of my 8th Army.
> On your behalf I have sent a message of appreciation to the Western Desert Air Force. The brave and brilliant work of the squadrons and

the devotion to duty of all the pilots have made our victories possible in such a short time.

We are all one entity—the 8th Army and the Western Desert Air Force—together constituting one magnificent fighting machine.

And now let us get on with the third task. Let us make the enemy face up to, and endure, a first-class Dunkirk on the beaches of Tunis.

The triumphant cry now is :—

FORWARD TO TUNIS! DRIVE THE ENEMY INTO THE SEA!"

The Corps Commander, Leese,[1] wrote thus to General Wimberley on the 10th :—

" . . . I am writing to congratulate you and your Division on their magnificent fighting during the battle for the Akarit position.

" Your attack will be an outstanding epic in the annals of the Highland Brigade. When one looks at the ground from the enemy's positions one realises both their tremendous strength and the degree of achievement of your Division. I would like to congratulate you and your staff on the excellent organisation to form up the Division in complete darkness for two divergent attacks. It was a fine piece of staff work.

" Throughout the day you were ceaselessly counter-attacked. It was vital that the enemy should not penetrate the Roumana position until the armour had been able to break out into the open country. Your troops held the ground gained and thus played a vital part in the ultimate victory. You have fought unceasingly in 30th Corps since your first attack on 23rd October at Alamein. It is therefore a great source of pride to me to congratulate and thank you, both on your achievement in this battle of Akarit, and also on all the very excellent and arduous fighting which you have carried out during the long advance from Benghazi northwards."

And on the same day Wimberley sent this message to be read to all ranks of the 51st Highland Division :—

" As presently having the honour of commanding the famous Highland Division, it falls on me, at the end of this phase of the fighting, to thank one and all for the gallantry, uncomplaining cheerfulness, endurance and skill which have been shown in so great a measure during all the recent hard fighting. We can indeed proudly say that Scotland's troops have once again in North Africa shown the British Army that they are still ' Second to None.' "

The Division was kept in reserve round about Sfax, while other units

---

[1] While the generous praise given by General Oliver Leese was well deserved, the efficiency of the Corps arrangements should not be forgotten. Leese and his Brigadier, General Staff, Walsh, were held by all the senior officers of the 51st as true friends and mentors, and did much to make their Corps and the 8th Army the " band of brothers " which in effect it now was.

of the 30th Corps took Sousse on 12th April and advanced towards the anti-tank ditch in front of Enfidaville. The enemy were now holding a line roughly across the neck of the peninsula, the extreme point of which was Cap Bon. Our 1st Army were pressing in on Tunis from the west and the 8th Army's job was to go direct north for Enfidaville. General Alexander had made it clear that the heat and burden of this last day were to be borne by the 1st Army, since the direct approach north on Enfidaville was, in view of the nature of the country, very difficult indeed. But the Desert Air Force was now well forward on airfields near Sousse whence they could dominate the whole of Tunisia. On the night of 19th-20th April Montgomery sent in his attack on the Enfidaville position. Enfidaville itself was captured, but on the left the enemy offered very stiff resistance.

On the night of 21st-22nd April the Highland Division relieved the 4th Indian Division and the New Zealanders in the Enfidaville area. The three prominent positions on the front were the Garci Mountain, where Gurkha, Sikh and Punjabi dead told of the fierce fighting that had taken place before those hills had been cleared; the Snout; and the village of Takrouna, perched on a 300-foot-high pinnacle which had been scaled and gallantly captured by a Maori officer with eighteen of his men. It was an area of hills, and they were given code names from the children's "Tinker, tailor" right on to "thief," and from features as far apart as the Ganges and Snowdon. There was considerable shelling, some patrolling, but no aggressive attacking. There were Arab villages in the area and a certain amount of espionage went on. One day, for example, the enemy kept bombarding the Takrouna area. There was an Arab dwelling nearby from which a red flag was flying. The Arab owner of that dwelling had informed the previous troops in the line that the enemy had promised, as long as his red flag was flying, the area would not be shelled. Our observers noticed that when the flag was lowered the enemy shelling became both intense and accurate. The Arab was duly arrested. There is no record of his subsequent interests.

In the first week of May, Free French troops under General Le Clerc commenced taking over from the Division, who moved into a rest area near Monaster. The troops of the Highland Division did not then know it, but with the 50th Division they had already been selected for the initial assault being planned on Sicily, zero date for which was already fixed in the minds of the High Command.

By courtesy of Major D. F. O. Russell
GENERAL MONTGOMERY AND Brigadier GRAHAM AT SFAX. APRIL 1943

HIS MAJESTY KING GEORGE VI. INSPECTING DIVISIONAL DETACHMENT AT ALGIERS. JUNE 1943

By courtesy of the Ministry of Information

LANDING IN SICILY. JULY 1943
From the original painting by IAN G. M. EADIE

HIGHWAY IN SICILY
From the original painting by IAN G. M. EADIE

On 7th May General Wimberley left for an unknown destination [1] and temporarily handed over the Division to Douglas Graham, who a few days later, to the great regret of the whole Division, left on well-merited promotion to command the 56th Division. Graham, a staunch Cameronian and indeed the only infantry Brigadier in the Division throughout the campaign in Africa and Sicily who was not a Highlander, was a big loss. A great-hearted fighting soldier, a disciplinarian where necessary but with a real love for his units, both officers and men, and with a high sense of duty, he was sorely missed.[2]

It was now decided on the 8th Army front to hold what had been gained in this attack, while the Americans and our 1st Army pressed in from the west across the Tunisian plain. Many units and formations not being used for the coming assault on Sicily were then sent from 8th Army to reinforce 1st Army, and Montgomery held his line with what was left. On 6th May 1st Army made their big assault, Tunis fell. 8th Army's 7th Armoured Division were first into the city, a fact which pleased the 51st almost as much as the 7th Armoured themselves. The majority of the enemy were rounded up and the campaign was over. An Allied Victory March was held in Tunis in which the massed Pipes and Drums of the Division took part. Their turnout was very favourably commented on later by Air Chief Marshal Lord Tedder.

The Highland Division had travelled 1850 miles across the desert and, if they had now one regret, it was that, at the end of the day, their new " auld enemy," the German 90th Light Division, had not surrendered to them. They would have received such a surrender with honour, for the 90th Light (hard and skilled fighters as they were) had at the same time conducted their warfare with a sense of chivalry. They had treated wounded with consideration and prisoners with respect. The Division were soon to meet a different type of German among the Sicilian hills.

Wimberley returned about a week later with the information that the Division was to move to Algeria into areas round the coast towns of Djidjelli and Bougie. The infantry and some artillery were concentrated round the former, and artillery, R.A.S.C., some engineers and field ambulances round the latter, under the command of the C.R.A.

---

[1] Wimberley's destination was Cairo and his job to plan at 30th Corps Headquarters the invasion of Sicily and to meet Admiral McGrigor.

[2] General Graham has in the eyes of the 51st paid a compliment to the Division by retiring to live in the northern Highlands.

The Division was moved through country the scenery of which was of the "glorious technicolor variety," through fields of corn, by forests of cork trees, past ruins of the old Roman civilisation, over winding roads through mountain gorges, then down again to the Mediterranean, and so to a land that knew nothing of war; where you ate real bread, real margarine and, perhaps best of all, smoked real British cigarettes. The men of the Division kept a look-out for "the boat with the tartan funnels" which was to convey them home, but other ships were waiting to take them eastward once again. It was all hinted at in Montgomery's personal message issued on 14th May. That message read :—

"1. Now that the campaign in Africa is finished I want to tell you all, my soldiers, how intensely proud I am of what you have done.

2. Before we began the Battle of Egypt last October I said that together, you and I, we would hit Rommel and his Army 'for six' right out of North Africa.

   And it has now been done. All those well-known enemy Divisions that we have fought, and driven before us over hundreds of miles of African soil from Alamein to Tunis, have now surrendered.

   There was no Dunkirk on the beaches of Tunisia; the Royal Navy and the R.A.F. saw to it that the enemy should not get away, and so they were all forced to surrender. The campaign has ended in a major disaster for the enemy.

3. Your contribution to the complete and final removal of the enemy from Africa has been beyond all praise. As our Prime Minister said at Tripoli in February last, it will be a great honour to be able to say in years to come :—

   'I MARCHED AND FOUGHT WITH THE EIGHTH ARMY.'

4. And what of the future? Many of us are probably thinking of our families in the home country, and wondering when we shall be able to see them.

   But I would say to you that we can have to-day only one thought, and that is to see the thing through to the end; and then we will be able to return to our families, honourable men.

5. Therefore let us think of the future in this way. And whatever it may bring to us, I wish each one of you the very best of luck, and good hunting in the battles that are yet to come and which we will fight together.

6. TOGETHER, YOU AND I, WE WILL SEE THIS THING THROUGH TO THE END."

51ST HIGHLAND DIVISION—BATTLE CASUALTIES AFRICAN CAMPAIGN
From October 1942 to May 1943

Unit	Killed Offrs.	Killed O.R.s	Wounded Offrs.	Wounded O.R.s	Missing Offrs.	Missing O.R.s	Totals
H.Q. 51 Div.	1	4	4	3	..	..	12
H.Q. R.A.	..	1	..	..	..	..	1
126 Field Regiment	..	13	10	60	..	..	83
127 Field Regiment	2	9	6	25	1	11	54
128 Field Regiment	1	9	6	54	1	..	71
61 Anti-Tank Regiment	3	20	8	64	2	3	100
40 Light A.A. Regiment	1	9	1	25	..	9	45
H.Q. R.E.	..	..	3	..	..	..	3
239 Field Park Coy.	1	2	..	4	..	..	7
274 Field Coy.	1	11	2	62	..	3	79
275 Field Coy.	1	28	1	79	..	3	112
276 Field Coy.	4	20	2	66	..	1	93
Div. Signals	..	7	1	16	..	..	24
H.Q. 152 Inf. Bde.	..	..	2	11	..	..	13
2 Seaforth	8	100	27	306	2	40	483
5 Seaforth	12	105	18	273	1	63	472
5 Camerons	11	125	38	295	2	93	564
H.Q. 153 Inf. Bde.	1	..	2	5	..	..	8
1 Gordons	4	60	11	253	..	16	344
5/7 Gordons	9	58	28	244	..	54	393
5 Black Watch	4	85	22	347	..	52	510
H.Q. 154 Inf. Bde.	1	2	3	7	..	2	15
1 Black Watch	2	46	25	203	1	22	299
7 Black Watch	10	144	26	347	5	112	644
7 A. & S.H.	5	95	24	359	2	71	556
1/7 Middlesex	4	96	9	149	..	5	263
152 Inf. Bde. Coy. R.A.S.C.	..	1	1	2	..	..	4
153 Inf. Bde. Coy. R.A.S.C.	..	..	..	..	..	..	..
154 Inf. Bde. Coy. R.A.S.C.	..	1	..	13	..	..	14
51 Div. Tps. Coy. R.A.S.C.	..	3	..	7	..	..	10
174 Field Ambulance	..	2	1	8	..	..	11
175 Field Ambulance	..	6	..	12	..	..	18
176 Field Ambulance	..	3	..	15	..	1	19
29 Field Hygiene Sec.	..	..	..	1	..	..	1
Div. Tps. Ord. Field Park	..	..	..	1	..	..	1
152 Bde. Gp. W/Shop	..	1	..	..	..	..	1
153 Bde. Gp. W/Shop	..	1	..	..	..	..	1
154 Bde. Gp. W/Shop	..	..	..	1	..	..	1
Pro. Coy.	..	2	..	5	..	..	7
Recce Regiment	1	12	5	42	..	3	63
Totals	87	1071	286	3364	17	564	5399

CHAPTER V.

THE THIRTY-NINE DAYS

"A chlanna na con thigibh an so's gheibh sibh feoil."
(Sons of the hounds come here and get flesh.)

"I have said, and repeat it, Malta is the direct road to Sicily."
HORATIO NELSON.

SICILY! The place was never mentioned during those pleasant days and nights on the Algerian coast, where the men of the Highland Division, with French civilians and American soldiers, swam in a happy sea, sang cheerful songs in their quarters, drank wine and treated quite seriously as good fun the embarking and disembarking from landing-craft.

The Division was visited by the Secretaries of State for War and Air, and Sir James Grigg was reported as being "even more highly impressed than he expected." A Divisional piping competition was held, and the winning tune by Lance-Corporal W. Macdonald of the Seaforth from Invershin was named "The Wadi Akarit."

While at Djidjelli Brigadier Murray fell sick and had to be evacuated home.[1] At the battles of Alamein, Mareth and Akarit, besides in many a smaller action, he had played a distinguished part. No essential detail was too small to escape George Murray's attention, and thoroughness was his keynote. Thus the Division regretfully said farewell to the last of the three experienced regimental soldiers who had led their Brigades to victory at Alamein, now some 2000 miles away.

The combined training with the Navy made it clear that a new type of warfare was before the Division, and that fact, in itself, was a great relief to a desert army. Where was the new job to be tackled? Someone had picked up a map of Crete—dropped a' purpose; someone had heard the "high-ups" discussing Greece—too loudly a' purpose. But the only sure information was that there were to be landings somewhere, and the rocky beaches round Djidjelli were the new form of those old battle-practice areas which had been constructed behind El Alamein—

---

[1] George Murray had commanded the 152 Brigade for over two years, and at fifty years of age was reputed to be the oldest combatant officer in the Division.

it seemed so long ago. Under battalion auspices officers and N.C.O.s were lectured on combined operations with the ever-helpful Senior Service, and later were given practical exercises. Then in similar tactical schemes the instructions were passed on to the men—and it did not take much time to make them proficient in this new form of warfare, for they were, by their long experience, well-trained soldiers with a very complete knowledge of the use of their weapons. The new entry from home was soon broken in by the old hounds, and the " A " and " Q " Staff, under Lt.-Col. Jack Colam, assisted by Majors Jock Gray (Gordons) and Geordie Ross (Seaforth) of Cromarty, worked long hours in ensuring that equipment and reinforcements were of the best obtainable in Africa. The whole Division was a very " happy ship."

Three Brigade exercises were held, and finally a full Divisional one, during which every manœuvre was performed exactly as it was to be carried out when the real landings on the still unnamed beaches were to take place. The result was that, except for actual place-names, dates and times, the Division knew its job thoroughly. Divisional and Brigade staffs were worked exceedingly hard. They had to prepare complete written instructions for the landings. When the time came to leave the Djidjelli area all the necessary copies of those instructions were ready and sealed.

So good-bye to that pleasant Algerian shore, with no reminders of real war except some night bombing which caused a few casualties, and back to Sousse—the troops by sea, the transport by land. Between the paths of the ships and the motor-vehicles lay Carthage, the ruins of which must have suggested to some minds the earlier defeat of the Romans in Tunis, and their later flight to Gela in Sicily. But there was little time for reflection, for the Division was soon concentrated in the neighbourhood of Sousse and Sfax, with all the discomfort of dust and flies and all the pleasure of bathing in the cleansing waters of the Mediterranean and of listening to the cheery songs of Will Fyffe. A much bemedalled small detachment from the Division had had the luck to be sent to see His Majesty the King in Algiers, and General Wimberley afterwards sent the following letter to unit commanders dated 29th June :—

" When I met H.M. the King in Algiers, he instructed me that he wished all Unit Commanders in the Division to know how sorry he was that he was unable to come and visit us. He said that he had tried two separate dates, but both clashed with our Exercises, with which he felt he could not interfere.

"So far as I can recollect, his actual words were somewhat as follows :—

"'... I determined that the next best thing was to send for some of you to come and see me, because I felt I could not possibly go home without having seen the Highland Division.'

"From our point of view, it is at least satisfactory that the last troops of any of the three Services that the King should inspect, before he stepped into his plane to leave North Africa and to return to Great Britain, should be found from our Division."

The same detachment had also the good fortune on 24th June to march past General Eisenhower, who wrote :—

"If this detachment is at all typical of your Division, I can well understand why your organisation has established such an enviable record as a fighting team."

The Division's destination was not yet public property, but, from the point of view of the sequence of this narrative, here is a very short résumé of the plan projected by the Supreme Commander. The American 7th Army was to land in Sicily from the Gulf of Gela, was to drive north and west and, having cleared the western half of the island, was to sweep east along the north centre and the north coast to Messina, where it would make a final junction with the 8th Army. The three Corps of the 8th Army were to reach the north-eastern corner of the island as follows :—

The 13th Corps was to land two Divisions from the Gulf of Noto in order to capture Siracusa. The 30th Corps was to land two Divisions (of which the Highland Division was one) on the Pachino Peninsula at the extreme south-eastern tip of the island. The left-hand Division (1st Canadian) would keep in touch with the right flank of the American 7th Army, but the general line of the Corps advance was directly north. The 10th Corps was left in reserve in Tripoli.

The plan as finally thrashed out and agreed upon by Admiral McGrigor,[1] that most distinguished Scotsman who had charge of the whole naval side of the 30th Corps landings, was that the 51st Division were to land on a four-battalion front on the very point of the peninsula with, on the right, the 231 Infantry Brigade, now commanded by the Highland Division's late G.S.O.1, Roy Urquhart. The Highlanders were to capture the town of Pachino and then to advance as fast as possible to the Noto-Avola road, where they would contact and relieve

[1] Admiral McGrigor eventually commanded the Home Fleet, and at the time of writing is First Sea Lord.

the 50th Division (13th Corps). They were then to push ahead on to the high ground towards Palazzolo and carry on to Viccini.

So much for the general plan. Now back to the vicinity of Sousse for the details. The initial assault was to be made by 154 Brigade Group (Brigadier Rennie), which was divided into two parts—154 Brigade Group proper, consisting of the 1st and 7th Black Watch, 7th Argylls, 11th R.H.A., 50th Royal Tanks (less two squadrons), two companies of Middlesex machine-gunners, 244 Field Company R.E., 176 Field Ambulance, and certain other details; and, attached for the operation, the 1st Gordons Group, with 1st Gordons, 456 Battery R.A., one squadron 50th Royal Tanks, "C" Company of the Middlesex, 275 Field Company R.E., 174 Field Ambulance, and certain other details. Portopalo Bay was to be Corps maintenance beach. It was thought to be well defended, so beaches were chosen on either side of it; the Gordon Group (under Lt.-Col. Fausset-Farquhar) were to land on the north beaches, named "Green," and the 154 Brigade Group on the west beaches, named "Red." The two groups would then act as the jaws of pincers and squeeze out the opposition on Portopalo. When the beaches had been secured the tanks and artillery were to be landed.

Landing-craft were of many different types. Each Landing Craft Assault (L.C.A.) carried a full infantry platoon; Landing Craft Motor (L.C.M.) two to three vehicles; Landing Craft Infantry (L.C.I.) two hundred men plus such stores as they could handle; Landing Craft Tank (L.C.T.) eight tanks or twelve vehicles; Landing Ship Tank (L.S.T.) sixty vehicles; Landing Ship Infantry (L.S.I.) fifteen hundred troops. The last-named ships carried L.C.A.s and L.C.M.s slung like boats on davits. The L.C.I.s and L.C.T.s were to move by two stages, first to Malta and then to Sicily; the others were to sail direct from Africa to within seven miles of the Sicilian coast, where they were to rendezvous with the lesser craft from Malta. There were also supporting vessels—Landing Craft Gun to carry searchlights, Landing Craft Support to cover craft making for the beaches, and Landing Craft Rocket to put down block barrages round the beaches and to silence the enemy batteries. Destroyers were also to be in readiness in case heavier artillery bombardment of enemy positions proved necessary. 10th July was to be zero day.

Certain changes had now taken place in the Highland Division as far as commanders were concerned. Brigadier Gordon MacMillan (Argylls) had succeeded Brigadier Murray (Seaforth) in command of

152 Brigade, and the Division was fortunate to get the services of this already distinguished Highland officer, at last released at his urgent request from duties on the staff. Brigadier H. Murray (Camerons), who had now recovered from his Alamein wound received when commanding the 1st Gordons, had succeeded Brigadier Graham (Cameronians) in 153. Brigadier T. Rennie (Black Watch), also recovered from his last wound, had succeeded Brigadier Stirling (Seaforth) in command of 154 Brigade. Few Divisions can have gone into a new campaign with better Brigade Commanders; all three were to lead Divisions with great distinction before the war was ended.

Also among the Lt.-Cols. there were a number of changes. Lt.-Col. Dunlop (Argylls) had succeeded Lt.-Col. R. Urquhart as G.S.O.1 on the latter's well-earned promotion to command 231 Brigade; Lt.-Col. Sorel-Cameron had succeeded Lt.-Col. Miers with the 5th Camerons; Lt.-Col. Blair had taken over from Lt.-Col. Roper-Caldbeck in the 1st Black Watch; Lt.-Col. Mathieson had succeeded in the 7th Argylls Lt.-Col. Lorne Campbell, who had been promoted to the command of the 13 Brigade in the 5th Division.

When the convoys went to sea, and the destination was made known, Wimberley's message to the Division was released :—

"You will by now have realised, if you had not sensed it before, that we of the Highland Division were chosen, before even the fighting in North Africa ended, to form part of the Empire's spearhead. For that reason and for that reason alone, we were denied the satisfaction of being present at the last surrender of our desert adversaries. We were, moreover, deliberately chosen for this very rôle because we have proved ourselves in many an action and because we had thereby shown them we in our generation could still live up to our great national motto of 'Second to None.'

"Now we are called upon once more to enter Europe. As, therefore, the time approaches again to go forward into battle, never must we forget that we of this Division, helped by our English comrades, are ever the proud bearers of that ancient motto, and, in bearing it, that we carry with us Scotland's renown, Scotland's fair name, and Scotland's prayers." [1]

On 5th July the crossing to Malta began, and by the afternoon of the 6th, troops were disembarking from Valetta harbour and moving into excellent camps on the outskirts of the town. Lord Gort inspected

[1] Of this message, the Lord Chancellor, Viscount Simon, stated in a speech : " There could not be more moving words, nor words better calculated to evoke heroic deeds from a proud race."

various units, and on the 7th General Montgomery (accompanied by Brigadier H. Murray) visited each of the camps in an open car. The men were drawn up in hollow square, and when the General had stopped his car in the centre he shouted out, " I cannot speak to you out there. All come in a bit." So the men crowded in round the car, and Montgomery proved himself " a fellow of infinite jest." He interspersed the information he gave about the coming attack with jokes and remarks, and, as the historian of the 7th Black Watch writes, " Each man left the parade feeling that he had spoken personally to General Montgomery. As a result of this the morale was exceedingly high."

The men had a good time in Valetta, but that was offset by the exceedingly bad time they faced when they went to sea again, for the weather was very rough. In fact one man actually died of sea-sickness. Some doubt was expressed if landings would be successful under such unsatisfactory weather conditions, but it was decided to go ahead. The rendezvous with the larger vessels, which had sailed direct from Africa, was duly accomplished, and the first landings were made approximately at zero hour.

At 2.45 A.M. on the morning of 10th July the 7th Argylls (Colonel Mathieson) were on their beaches. They met no enemy resistance, except that from somewhere a grenade was thrown into one landing-craft and, as a result, fifteen men of " D " Company were wounded. As the light improved the various prominent features on the landscape were easily recognised from the memory of photographs seen in the training days, and, after the navy had plastered the shore defences with some eight hundred 20-pound rocket bombs, the Italians manning the coast batteries called it a day, put up their hands, and the Argylls formed their bridgehead without any opposition. All forenoon tanks, guns, and supplies were landed on the beaches behind the Argylls and, twenty-four hours after landing, the Battalion passed through the town of Pachino and established themselves on a ridge some eight kilometres farther to the north-west. Then by a series of gruelling marches they made Noto on the evening of 12th July, and after a few hours' rest moved forward again some twelve miles to a position in the hills about Palazzolo. There their transport caught up with them and carried the Battalion to a position two miles north-west of Palazzolo.

The 7th Black Watch (Lt.-Col. Oliver), the other attacking Battalion of 154 Brigade, were not quite so successful in their initial landing. " C " Company made it all right, but the commanders of the craft carrying the other Companies failed to find the arranged beaches in the rough seas, and landings had to be made somewhat higgledy-piggledy. It was a quarter past six in the morning before the 7th Black Watch could move forward from the beaches to tackle their ridge objectives. Like the Argylls they met no opposition, but lost one officer and ten other ranks, who were wounded by anti-personnel mines. By seven o'clock, however, all their objectives were taken, they moved forward on much the same line as the Argylls and by 14th July were in position near the Palazzolo railway station. In due course the 1st Black Watch (Lt.-Col. Blair) made their landings—very wet ones indeed, one of their jeeps actually finding a watery grave—and advanced into position on the right of the 7th Battalion.

The 1st Gordons (Lt.-Col. Fausset-Farquhar) Group had a relatively comfortable landing. This Group's objectives were Capo Passero Island, the village of Portopalo, a tunny factory, a lighthouse, and finally a 200-foot-high ridge which commanded the approaches to Pachino. One pre-landing incident could borrow its title from Conan Doyle's Sherlock Holmes story, 'The Greek Interpreter.' A Greek officer had been attached to the 1st Gordons as a kind of " camouflage." His business was to spread the idea that Greece was the Division's objective, and in his enthusiasm for his job he even went the length of recognising Greek hills and capes, etc., on the Sicilian maps. He was supposed to return to Cairo before the landings, but so keen was he that he accompanied the Gordons on shore and was with them till the end of the Sicilian Campaign. As the various craft neared the beaches, the troops could recognise in the black masses ahead the features they had seen on the training photographs, which masses where silhouetted against the flashes from the supporting gun-fire. Also away to the left could be heard the noise of the landing of 231 Malta Brigade. " B " Company of the 1st Gordons landed first and cleared up the defenders of the tunny factory, " A " Company made the island their own, and " D " Company were advancing on Portopalo. " C " Company made for the high ground and by nine o'clock in the morning the ridge was securely held. Slight hitches did occur, but Lieutenant Bird with his platoon and Lance-Corporal Robert Taylor with his section attacked the enemy posts that were proving troublesome. They carried out their jobs with grenade and bayonet, and then returned with complete composure to continue bringing up ammunition and stores. Italian prisoners were formed into unloading parties on the beach, and just after midday advance parties were in Pachino, junction had been made with the 5th Black Watch (Lt.-Col. Thomson) and the 1st Gordons returned to their Brigade.

The 153 Brigade's training in the Djidjelli area had been somewhat different from that of 154. Since 153 was not required to form a bridge-head at the landings their training had been confined to rock-climbing and mountain warfare generally. Though the Brigade's job was to pass through 154, there was always the possibility that it might be called on to help complete the initial action of either the 154 Group or the Gordon Group. But the success of 154 landings left 153 to proceed with their initial purpose. By 6.30 on the morning of the 10th the Brigade began to disembark on " Red " beach. The 5/7th Gordons moved by the left of Pachino and the left of the main road north of that town. They were unfortunate in losing the services of their commanding officer, Lt.-Col. Hay, who was wounded by a bullet from a tommy-gun which was accidentally dropped on the ground. The 5th Black Watch (Lt.-Col. Thomson) were left to clear up the whole beach area, and then moved level with the 5/7th Gordons on the right of Pachino. The Gordons met some opposition, but with the help of two troops of Sherman tanks that opposition was overcome without much difficulty. A strong-point surrendered to the 5th Black Watch without firing a shot, and that unit now made contact with 231 (Malta) Infantry Brigade on their right. At this point, as has been noted above, the 1st Gordons came again under command of their own Brigade, and next day went into reserve behind the other two battalions.

The 152 Brigade and Tactical Division Headquarters landed on " Amber " beach on 10th July without opposition and with their transport close behind them. The 2nd Seaforth (Lt.-Col. Horne) moved on the 11th to a position between Noto and Rosolini. Next morning they relieved the East Yorks (50th Division) near a town called Floridia, and on the 13th passed through Palazzolo and Buccheri to an area seven miles south of Francofonte. The 5th Seaforth (Lt.-Col. Walford) landed without any trouble, advanced by the Rosolini–Noto road, then north of Avola, and finally by Palazzolo and Buccheri to the area of Francofonte by midday on the 13th. The 5th Camerons (Lt.-Col. Sorel-Cameron) landed safely but were subjected to a certain amount of bombing, during which the R.Q.M.S. was wounded in the leg. The Camerons led the Brigade advance through Pachino and on the road to Rosolini. Some five miles beyond Pachino " C " Company ran into anti-tank fire. The Battalion dug in for the night, and next morning " C " Company attacked a small piece of rising ground occupied by the Italian enemy. The position was taken and a number of guns captured with barely any casualties, as were other enemy strongpoints farther down the road. The Camerons then made Noto, and on the 13th moved behind 5th Seaforth to within three miles of Francofonte, though there had been hard marching in hot weather with heavy loads and no transport to help.[1]

So far all had been plain sailing : now the trouble started. But let us consider for a moment what had been happening to the troops on the Highland Division flanks.

The position with the 13th Corps on the right was as follows. At their landings they had had to contend with heavy seas and heavy shelling, but they gained a footing in the coast-towns of Noto, Avola, Casanuova and Cassibile, marched on and took Siracusa, and then proceeded to advance north on Augusta which, after overcoming strong counter-attacks by German tanks, they took on the night of 12th-13th July. Montgomery then decided to push into the Catania Plain, for it became very obvious that that area was to be the main point of enemy resistance.

The Canadian landing on the left of the Highland Division had been quite successful, as had the landings of the 7th United States Army from the Gulf of Gela. The Germans put up a determined counter-attack with tanks against the Americans, but were heavily repulsed, forty-three tanks being destroyed. Contact was made between the Americans and the Canadians in the area of Ragusa.

Now back to the Highland Division.

On the morning of the 13th the 5th Seaforth were the advance battalion of 152 Brigade and were marching on the village of Francofonte. No particular opposition had been met so far and, when their own advance party reported some sniping ahead, it was not considered too seriously. A Royal Tank squadron of the 23rd Armoured Brigade and their own carriers were in the van of the Seaforth advance on the road. All seemed peaceful in the village of Francofonte, which appeared to be asleep on its hill sheltered by groves of orange and olive growing on terraces on the hillside, in circumventing which the road into the village took a nasty hairpin bend. The cemetery lay to the south side

---

[1] A few deserted perambulators were commandeered and were pushed down the roads loaded with Bren guns, ammunition and mortar bombs ; bicycles were also used for the same purpose.

of the village. But the peace was suddenly broken by a German 88-mm. anti-tank gun, and it got the leading Seaforth carrier fairly and squarely. Enemy machine-guns joined in from the cemetery, and the 5th Seaforth had to get out of their trucks and take what shelter they could. Lt.-Col. Walford decided to concentrate first of all on the anti-tank gun, but the Germans at once withdrew and our tanks proceeded up the road on which they had to continue as far as the hairpin bend, where they met a shower of projectiles from automatic and other weapons. It was obvious that the defence of the village was not only a determined one but was in the hands of first-class troops. In fact it was later discovered that the defenders were the 2nd German Parachute Regiment. The fight went on all day, and at nightfall the 5th Seaforth were not in any happy position among orange and olive trees smouldering all over the hillside. The following morning the Highlanders were still holding on to forward areas, but the C.O. decided to withdraw to a defensive position along the line of the road.

Then our artillery began to pound the village and the 2nd Seaforth were sent up by MacMillan to pass through the 5th. Under cover of the barrage, " A " Company of the 2nd were able to get close in and to take on the German defenders in hand-to-hand fighting. The other Companies were held up by the difficulties presented by the terracing, and one German position named " The Red House " presented a very serious problem. It was decided to wait until nightfall and to attack in the moonlight. But by that time the Germans had quitted the village,[1] and in the early morning a party of the 2nd Seaforth captured a German escort, who, unaware that the village had been entered, were marching off some British prisoners they had taken the previous day.

Private A. Thomson of the 2nd Seaforth particularly distinguished himself in this action. He was No. 1 of a Lewis machine-gun team and so well did he handle his weapon that he broke up a German counter-attack and assumed control of a very vital point of the front. " I consider," wrote his commanding officer, " that his personal example, courage and leadership restored a dangerous situation." Private John Cormack, 5th Seaforth, played his part well after being taken prisoner near Francofonte. He succeeded in escaping on 7th August and rejoined our forward troops three days later. During all the period of

---

[1] In this action the 5th Seaforth had 87 casualties, and the 2nd Seaforth about the same.

his imprisonment he kept both eyes and ears very wide open and, with the idea of escape ever in his mind, noted everything that was going on around him. As Colonel Walford wrote of him on his return, " He was able to give information concerning the strength of the enemy, their probable date of departure from Sicily, the source of supply from which their food and ammunition came, the state of their transport, their reaction to our bombing and shelling, and their state of mind generally. He also described various guns, weapons and equipment he had seen. Very little seemed to have escaped the notice of this soldier, and the alertness of mind shown by him is commendable."

The 5th Camerons also took part in the Francofonte attack. They went into the battle behind the 2nd Seaforth and were pinned down in much the same way. Colonel Sorel-Cameron was wounded while directing mortar-fire, and Major Noble temporarily took over command. Sergeant McLean made himself worthily conspicuous by leading a bayonet charge, shouting the war-cry of his clan, and forcing a large party of the enemy to abandon the position whence they were holding up the whole of his Company. The Camerons did their best to serve things as hot as possible for the German transport, which was making considerable use of the road which ran north to Lentini. In the evening " A " Company got astride that road, and on the morning of the 15th the Camerons moved northwards up the road and were in touch with the rearguard of the enemy who were obviously making for Scordia. Finally " D " Company and " B " Company, each acting as a jaw in a pincer movement, closed in north of Scordia. The Cameron carriers entered Scordia and a considerable number of prisoners were taken. In fact some thousand prisoners passed through the prisoner-of-war cage, including one Italian General.

The tanks gave support to the infantry in the Francofonte battle, and " C " Squadron of 23rd Armoured Brigade had a very tough time. A German parachutist " stalked " one tank and dropped a magnetic anti-tank mine through the driver's hatch. He was killed by fire from the next tank. Only one tank of this squadron was left in action by the night of the 14th. It was commanded by Corporal Maplesden, who continued to support the infantry and on his own initiative carried out all sorts of tasks with great determination and gallantry.

Great assistance was also given to the infantry by the Middlesex machine-gunners, especially by Captain Victor Thomas and Lieutenant Henry Dawson. Another outstanding machine-gunner was Private

Percy Crowhurst. With his gun he knocked out two troop-carrying vehicles and killed or wounded all the crew of a Spandau. Next day (14th July) by bringing his gun to bear on a German counter-attack, he held up the enemy for two hours and allowed our own infantry to withdraw to a more commanding position. He finished up a magnificent day's work by bringing a seriously wounded man back to safety. A similar show was put up by another Middlesex private, Edward Dickson, while Sergeant Harold Wedon also distinguished himself.

The interests of other units in this battle are exemplified in the following noteworthy deeds. Lieutenant James MacKintosh (Camerons) with Corporal N. Paterson of the Divisional Provost Company were marking the route to be followed by 152 Brigade from Cassibile to Francofonte. Just beyond Buccheri they captured a couple of Italians, but were then attacked by two separate parties of the enemy armed with machine-guns. Corporal Paterson was wounded and Lieutenant MacKintosh covered his withdrawal, still holding off the enemy. Paterson, hearing one of our vehicles approaching, crawled, although he was in great pain, round a corner of the road and prevented the crew of the vehicle running into the area covered by the enemy's fire. On 13th July, at Francofonte itself, Sergeant Alexander Smith of 275 Field Company Royal Engineers showed the stuff that Royal Engineers are made of by removing mines *behind* the enemy's lines and by penetrating into Francofonte village. Next day he successfully cleared two tanks which were blocking the road, and again penetrated right into the village to investigate a suspicious object in the street.

On 16th July the whole Brigade moved into position on to the line of hills overlooking the Gorna Lunga River, with 153 Brigade on the left. There were two crossings on the Gorna Lunga River and the Camerons were instructed to send out patrols to report if and when the enemy abandoned them. Lieutenant F. E. Bright commanded one of those patrols. Bright's carrier ran into an ambush and received a direct hit from an anti-tank gun. Bright and his driver were killed by small-arms fire. The other member of the crew, Private MacKinnon, was thrown out of the carrier and wounded. Lance-Corporal Brody, who was on a M/C behind the carrier, collided with it and was thrown to the ground, but he immediately went to the assistance of the carrier crew, found that Bright and the driver were dead, lifted MacKinnon on to his shoulders and, under a hail of small-arms fire, carried the wounded man through a field of blazing barley and kept going thus for two miles till he contacted the other members of the patrol. No Military Medal was ever more gallantly won.

Meanwhile, on the 14th, 153 Brigade were making urgent preparations for an attack from the west on the town of Viccini, the garrison of which was holding up the whole advance. This town, like Francofonte, also sat on the top of a hill (2000 feet above sea level), and the garrison had so far resisted all efforts of the 231 Malta Independent Brigade to oust them from the east. The 153 attack was made by 5th Black Watch on the left and the 1st Gordons on the right from the south-west of the town. All are agreed that this was, as far as the temperature of the weather was concerned, the hottest day experienced by the Division. Water was scarce, cover negligible, and no smoke available. But our troops did very well. The 5th Black Watch fought their way to the outskirts of the town, moving forward with American troops on their left, and, permission having been granted by Brigadier H. Murray, Colonel Thomson, the C.O., sent a patrol followed by the remainder of its Company, later reinforced by a second Company, into the south-west of the town itself. The garrison offered considerable resistance, but by next morning, being now attacked from two different directions, they had all packed up and gone.

The 1st Gordons had, at first, lost touch with Brigade Headquarters, but by nine o'clock at night it was found that they also had two Companies on the outskirts of Viccini and had occupied the top of the cathedral tower, where riflemen lining the parapet commanded most of the town. An artillery bombardment was put down on the right half of the town, and when it lifted before dawn the following morning the 1st Gordons moved in, capturing many prisoners and a great quantity of stores. Meanwhile the 5/7th Gordons took up a position between Buccheri and Viccini, the 1st Canadian Division moved up in the rear of 153 Brigade and passed through Viccini on their way to Caltigirone.

There was one unfortunate happening in this battle. The 1st Gordons of 153 Brigade fired a success signal when they had occupied the eastern half of Viccini and, unfortunately, some supporting artillery mistook that signal for an S.O.S. from 153 Brigade demanding defensive fire. Battalions of 154 Brigade had been moved up to attack from the east through the Malta Brigade, and the fire fell on them with the result that the 1st Black Watch, who had penetrated into the town from the east, suffered some thirty casualties before the bombardment could be stopped.

SFERRO BRIDGE
From the original painting by Ian G. M. Eadie

GERBINI BATTLEFIELD
From the original painting by Ian G. M. Eadie

By courtesy of the   Imperial War Museum

Gerbini

Night 20/21 July 1943

PROFANE not with profundities these casual graves,
    Words are but platitude to the dead.
Raise no echoes among these blackened trees;
    Their tale is best untold.
Here, where they died in twos and threes,
    Leave them in their brotherhood.
Nor regiment in well-kept rows among the flowers
    Those whose last hours
Ran in this shell-tormented wood.
Rather let the earth cave in upon their grave
    And their cross decay,
Or let the cactus with its prickly fruit
    Be symbol for their Resurrection Day.
What if Death's moods are various?
We cannot find out why, to fulfil what secret laws,
    His choice should pass us by and fall on either side.
But we know the stray bullet cannot make a hero,
    Nor blood more sanctify our cause.
So, mock not these dead with words they cannot understand.
But, to commemorate this dust
Raise a plain stone pillar, if you must,
And write upon it, in a soldier's hand.

"What man can suffer, These have suffered,
What man can do, They did."

Let all other praise be silent
And, like our grief, be hid.

Demolitions and not enemy action now held up the Division for some time in its further advance on Scordia, but on the 15th that town was in our hands.

It is necessary at this point to consider the map of east-central Sicily. You will observe that the Gorna Lunga has a succession of tributaries, the first—the Monaci—flowing into it in a north-easterly, the other two—the Dittaino and the Simeto—in a south-easterly direction. The main stream and its tributaries all act as a series of "trenches," defending the Catania Plain from attack from the west. On the 15th July the Highland Division was holding a line from Scordia to Palagonia, and had forward elements in the vicinity of the River Monaci.

It was decided on the 16th that 152 Brigade, with the 23rd Armoured Brigade in reserve, would advance on the right, while 154 was to move through the outposts of 153, effect a crossing of the Monaci and take the village of Ramacca. The 154 Brigade was carried by transport to Palagonia, and then moved on foot with the 7th Black Watch on the right, the 7th Argylls in the centre and 1st Black Watch on the left. The 7th Black Watch suffered a few casualties from shelling, but, covering the last part of the journey in transport, reached the Ramacca area on the night of the 17th. The Argylls also made Ramacca, as did later the 1st Black Watch who, owing to stiff resistance on the westerly edge of the Catania Plain, had been ordered to change direction and move forward behind the Argylls, who were ordered to attack a ridge north of the village. To do so a bridgehead had to be established beyond the River Gorna Lunga. The Argylls had a sharp bout with the enemy but were successful in their purpose. Then by a series of well executed leap-frogging tactics 152 and 153 Brigades came forward, and on the night of the 18th established bridgeheads across the next tributary, the River Dittaino.

The gallantry exhibited in the establishment of those bridgeheads is featured in the details of the actions of Captain John Grant of the 1st Gordons. Captain Grant had already made a name for himself as an officer of courage and resource, when, in command of a carrier screen near Medenine in March 1943, he was attacked by one hundred and fifty of the enemy supported by artillery. Grant withheld his fire till the last moment, and definitely halted that infantry attack. He was then attacked by enemy tanks, when he most skilfully withdrew his screen. During the following week's fighting he manœuvred his screen with

CAMPAIGN IN SICILY, 10TH JULY–20TH AUGUST 1943

great success, inflicted heavy casualties on the enemy and did not lose a single man or a single carrier. This was the capable officer who was now sent out with his carriers to secure the crossings of the Dittaino. In bright moonlight Grant went forward driving enemy machine-gunners in front of his carriers. Next day he covered the advance of the Brigade with great skill, and on the 18th he pushed across the vital bridge over the Dittaino, advanced a mile in the face of very heavy enemy opposition, got his anti-tank guns and carriers very cleverly positioned, and held his bridgehead until reinforcements arrived. This bridgehead was of first importance to the Divisional attack, and General Wimberley, who witnessed Captain Grant's action, very warmly congratulated that Gordon officer on his remarkable achievement.

The crossings of the Dittaino having been secured, 154 Brigade moved forward, under their determined Brigadier, with the intention of capturing without loss of time the village of Gerbini with its aerodrome, barracks and railway station, and then of pushing into the Catania Plain across the River Simeto. The 1st Black Watch were leading and were to be responsible for capturing a road junction some half-mile beyond the bridgehead, which led to Gerbini village. The junction secured, the 1st Black Watch were to move in and capture the barracks and the railway station. The 7th Black Watch were to advance by the airfield to the Simeto River where, if the road-bridge were not destroyed, they were to hold it, when the 7th Argylls would pass through them and form a bridgehead in the Catania Plain. But things did not go according to plan.

As General Wimberley has stated, "Emboldened by the speed at which we had gone forward we were now too hasty and took rather 'a bloody nose.' We found the Germans holding the airfields of Gerbini with wire and concrete belonging to the old aerodrome defences. We had come so fast that we had not been able to get the detailed aeroplane photographs which we obtained for more deliberate attacks, and I made the mistake of attacking the enemy within twenty-four hours of getting over the river."

The 1st Black Watch met trouble long before they reached the cross-roads, but they finally did capture them, only to discover that the barracks on the ridge in front were very strongly held. There was an anti-tank ditch some eight hundred yards north of the cross-roads, and the C.O. decided to hold this flank. This delay naturally held up the 7th Black Watch, but in due course that Battalion advanced and reached their objective on the edge of the aerodrome where they dug in, without the Germans realising they were there. When the morning of the 19th broke, however, the enemy got busy, and the 7th Black Watch under Colonel Oliver had a very sticky time. At this point Rennie, the Brigade Commander, decided to change the function of the 7th Argylls who were ordered, instead of crossing the river, to come up between the two Black Watch Battalions and reduce Gerbini. There was nothing for it now but a full scale frontal attack and that was put in on the night of the 20th. The brunt of the battle was borne by the Argylls, who, with tank support, advanced roughly by the line of the railway on the barracks and railway station. The 7th Black Watch moved round by the right and advanced up the road in an endeavour to clear it as far as the railway station. The Argylls had everything against them, deep wire, machine-guns and tanks. Their Commanding Officer, Lt.-Col. R. Mathieson from Stirling, was killed, their Second-in-Command, Major John Lindsay Macdougall of Lunga, severely wounded and captured (later he died of wounds in the hands of the enemy), many other officers were killed or wounded, and what was left of " A " Company, which took a fearful mauling, was captured.

Sergeant Alexander of the Argylls was in charge of an anti-tank gun. He was unable to dig it in, but for twenty-four hours he kept it in action in the open. He withheld his fire till targets were absolute certainties. For example, he waited till one armoured car was within twenty-five yards of him and then opened up. The crew jumped out and Alexander promptly disposed of them with his Bren gun.

In all eighteen officers and one hundred and sixty other ranks of the Argylls were killed, wounded or missing. Finally the Battalion was withdrawn to the line of the anti-tank ditch. The 1st Black Watch did in the end reach the barracks, which they found abandoned by the enemy, but they could not get in touch with the Argylls. Their C.O., Colonel Blair, was severely wounded in the leg, and a vicious counter-attack forced back the advanced Companies of this Battalion, which now also withdrew to its original position in the anti-tank ditch. Major Baker-Baker took over temporary command.

Private John Travena, of the 1st Black Watch, who was batman to his Company officer, was beside that officer when the latter was killed. Travena did what he could for him and then went forward to his Company. When the order to withdraw was given, Travena saw a wounded officer of the 7th Argylls lying in the open ground. Travena bound up that officer's wounds and then dragged him down the hill. Realising, however, that he could not get him away by day, Travena pulled the officer into a deserted Bosche dug-out and remained with him till darkness; the enemy meanwhile were patrolling and searching the dug-outs. The officer's need for water became imperative and Travena twice went for it to a well actually in the village. In the early morning he tried to get the officer back to our lines, but his strength was exhausted. He laid the officer down and got into the 7th Black Watch defensive position. He found an officer and said to him, " I have a wounded Argyll officer about five hundred yards away. I have carried him all night, and I simply cannot manage another inch." Men went out and brought in the officer, who would probably have died of his wounds, and would certainly have been made prisoner, if it had not been for Travena's courage and determination.

There were sights to see at Gerbini, and long will the men of his Company tell how they watched Lieutenant " Mike " Wingate-Gray of the 1st Black Watch seize a Bren gun, jump into a carrier and order the driver to drive straight at an enemy machine-gun post which was causing considerable trouble. Standing up in the carrier Wingate-Gray kept firing at the post, the occupants of which broke and ran with the carrier after them. Wingate-Gray killed five and wounded several others.

By this time General Montgomery, who had studied the whole position, decided to shift the axis of the 30th Corps farther west, and the Brigade was withdrawn behind the Dittaino River, with the 7th Black Watch still holding the bridgehead on the enemy side.

A footnote to the Battle of Gerbini took the form of an illustrated poem, written by Captain Hugh Murray Baillie, Divisional Intelligence Officer, and published in ' Punch.' It is reproduced here facing page 113.

" B " Squadron of 46th Royal Tanks had a very heavy time in the Gerbini engagement. As they advanced to support the infantry, one tank was ditched and another " bellied " on a 2000-lb. bomb. At dawn they moved into the wood of Gerbini and took up a defensive line alongside the Headquarters of the 7th Argylls. Five tanks were knocked out, and Major J. S. Routledge, the C.O., was killed in his tank with Colonel Mathieson, the O.C. 7th Argylls, while the latter was using the tank-wireless to get orders through to his forward Companies. In this action the Royal Tanks lost one officer and five other ranks killed, one officer and nine other ranks wounded, and one officer and eleven other ranks missing—heavy casualties for an armoured squadron.

"A" Squadron 50th Royal Tanks, which moved forward between Sferro and Gerbini, suddenly came under bombardment from a concealed battery of 88-mm. guns. Six tanks were knocked out, as was a scout car in which Lieutenant Waddell was travelling as wireless link between the carriers and the regiment. Waddell wirelessed for another car, went forward and picked up a number of badly wounded and burned men. He brought them to safety. He made several such journeys, and in all rescued eleven men. The remainder of the crews (two officers, nineteen other ranks) were all lost. Later it was discovered that all tanks save one were completely burned out. "Corporal Smith commanded his tank," a 50th Royal Tank record states, "with great courage and determination. He exchanged fire with the 88-mm.s until his tank was hit for the fourth time and his driver killed. He then brought the remainder of his crew out safely, picking up survivors on the way back."

The Sherman, with which all armoured regiments in Sicily were equipped, was not entirely satisfactory when being used with infantry. As the Commander of 23rd Armoured Brigade, Brigadier G. W. Richards, wrote : " The peculiar construction of the Sherman tank . . . makes it difficult for the tank and infantry soldiers to converse easily on the battlefield without unduly exposing themselves ; added to which there is no means of attracting the tank commander's attention (*e.g.*, the bell on the Valentine)." On 23rd July Brigadier Richards, whose Brigade had so excellently supported the Highland Division from Alamein, was promoted to be Brigadier Armoured Fighting Vehicles 8th Army, and Brigadier Arkwright took his place.

Between the 18th and 21st Brigadier H. Murray handled his 153 Brigade with skill and determination. On the night of the 18th, 153 Brigade advanced in the direction of the village of Sferro, which was up the Dittaino River some three miles from Gerbini. An Armoured Brigade was to clear up whatever enemy were on the west side of the Dittaino, then the 5th Black Watch were to advance over the river and capture Sferro. Our artillery set fire to all the trees and crops on the hillside where the village was situated, and the Black Watch got into position between the river and the hillside. There they lay pinned down through all the burning hot hours of 19th July and spent what Colonel Thomson described as " a really damnable day." The men of his Company will long remember the water brought forward to them under heavy fire by Lance-Corporal Low, while Private Cranedge was a kind of Horatius on the Sferro Bridge.

During the night the 1st Gordons and two Companies of the 5/7th Gordons passed through the Black Watch to face what has been referred to as "the heaviest shelling the Battalion (1st Gordons) had experienced, both in the North African and Sicilian Campaigns." The railway line leading to the village had many sidings, all packed with trucks and wagons, very considerable obstacles to the fully equipped infantryman. Some of those wagons had been loaded with tar, which flowed like molten lava down the line. But the railway station was cleared of the enemy. The 5/7th Gordons had reached the village, but there they were blasted with every kind of projectile and were made the object of vigorous counter-attacks. Still they held their ground, and on 21st July a definite defensive position was formed. Two Company stretcher-bearers, Privates William Stenton and James Edward, gave a great display of cool courage in going forward and carrying in wounded under intensive fire. Our artillery registered very well, and the troops were especially heartened when one of the anti-tank guns blew a very annoying German 88 to pieces with a couple of shots.

The 5th Black Watch were now brought up to relieve the 5/7th Gordons and had to withstand very nasty raiding. The show this Battalion put up under its gallant commander, Lt.-Col. "Chick" Thomson, on this occasion can be described as most excellent.

Mention must be made here of the daring of Private J. Hyland of the 1st Gordons. Hyland offered to act as a forward observer in no-man's-land, and "disguised as a stook" in the darkness he took up a position some two hundred yards from the enemy's advanced lines. He stayed there all day, while the enemy moved round about him, made himself acquainted with the enemy's location and defences, learned also of a raid the enemy intended making, and returned in the darkness with his information, which proved invaluable to his own side. On the 24th the 1st Gordons were relieved by the 5th Camerons, who in their turn were relieved by the Gordons two nights later.

The work of the Forward Observation Officers of the Royal Artillery in those actions was worthy of great praise. For example, on the night of 19th-20th July at Sferro, Major K. W. Pooley was acting as F.O.O. with the 5th Black Watch. The bridge at Sferro had been rushed silently and successfully, but the enemy brought a terrific concentration of artillery and other fire on it. It was obvious that the enemy intended counter-attacking. Our artillery had advanced and taken up new positions, but in the darkness survey and registration were impossible, and they did not know just where our forward infantry were. Major

Pooley, walking across the bridge through a perfect inferno of fire, made contact with the farthest advanced units of our infantry. He then returned through the same hell to his wireless truck and proceeded to get his guns to register well in front of our infantry. He then bit by bit brought the fire back, until the enemy fire slackened, when he laid on the full weight of his regiment's fire. Time and again he moved between his truck and the forward infantry to ensure that all was well. There is no doubt the bridge was held as a result of Major Pooley's combination of natural courage and technical skill.

Tribute is here paid to the devotion to duty of all the Padres in the Division in recording the action of Captain (Rev.) David Wedderburn Rutherford attached to the 1st Gordons. Right from the time of the landing Captain Rutherford carried out all his duties under fire and in the most trying conditions with the greatest bravery. In the Sferro bridgehead, when enemy fire had made movement during the day well-nigh impossible, Captain Rutherford found his way daily from slit trench to slit trench right to our farthest forward position, and his offer of a cigarette or his telling of a good story cheered the men beyond all recording. He was seriously wounded in the foot on 20th July, but refused to have any attention given to his wound till other casualties around him had been treated. The O.C. records of him that, " By his devotion to duty and his selflessness, Rev. Rutherford was a shining example of what a Padre should be. The men of the Battalion found inspiration in everything he said and did." The coolness displayed by Sapper Kenneth Hendry Smith of 239 Field Park Company R.E. on 22nd July was well worthy of record. Smith was in charge of a bulldozer working on a track known as Marine Drive. An enemy counter-attack had driven back the infantry behind the Drive. Smith however continued with his work until ordered to withdraw by an officer.

It was at this point that Montgomery changed his plans. He decided as a result of the stubborn resistance on the Catania Plain met by the 50th and Highland Divisions to shift his attack to points farther west and north.

In a personal letter written in pencil to Wimberley, and dated 21st July 1943, Montgomery wrote :—

"MY DEAR DOUGLAS,

" I have decided to make the right flank of the Army front a defensive front, and to pull in to the best positions—ready for offensive action at a suitable moment later on.

THE THIRTY-NINE DAYS

" Meanwhile I am pushing the offensive hard on the left, where the resistance is not so strong.

" In ten days we have captured practically the whole of Sicily, and the enemy is now hemmed in at the north-east corner—rather like the Cape Bon Peninsula.

" Please tell all your soldiers that I think they have done magnificently. They have marched and fought over a very long distance in great heat, well up to the best standards of the Highland Division.

" I am sending you 50,000 cigarettes as a present to the Division.

" Yours ever,

" (Sgd.) B. L. MONTGOMERY."

The 13th Corps on the right had certainly had hard fighting, and both 5th and 50th Divisions were distinctly requiring a breather, so the Army Commander halted them on a line some twelve miles south of Catania. The Highland Division was on the left of the 13th Corps, and 154 Brigade was now withdrawn back over the River Dittaino. No further attack was made on Gerbini, and it appeared later that after our withdrawal the enemy did not reoccupy it. The 7th Black Watch under Colonel Oliver continued to hold the Dittaino bridgeheads, but on the night of 25th July 13 Brigade of the 5th Division, now commanded by Brigadier Lorne Campbell, V.C., late of the 7th Argylls, took over those bridgeheads. Lt.-Col. Dunlop (who had been G.S.O.1) had now assumed command of the Argylls, who were sent back to Ramacca to reorganise and, for a period of five days, their place in the Brigade was taken by the 1st Battalion (Lt.-Col. R. Macalister) of the same regiment, relieved from their duty as a Beach Group Battalion. The 7th Royal Marines were also attached to the Brigade for a few days.

153 Brigade was holding the Sferro bridgehead and 152 Brigade was in reserve. The Division's left flank was still in the air, so Montgomery brought up the 231 Infantry Brigade to fill the gap between the 51st and 1st Canadian Division. The Army Commander also brought over the 78th Division from Sousse and attached it to the 30th Corps. He then proceeded to do all his " pushing " on the extreme left of the 30th Corps front. On that front the 7th United States Army were regrouping to attack north of Etna on Messina. Next the 1st Canadian Division were pushing due east from Leonforte by Agira towards Adrano to the south of Etna, the 231 Infantry Brigade were moving north to join the Canadians beyond Agira, the 78th Division

were pushing from Catenanuova into Centuripe, and on their right the Highland Division's job was to cross the Dittaino and the Simeto and make for Paterno.

The 51st's first objective was the road that ran between Sferro and Catenanuova, so that the Corps artillery might get forward and be in a position to shell Adrano. But it was obvious that if that road were to be brought into use, the enemy must be driven off the Sferro range of hills which lay to the east of it. It was decided that a deliberate Divisional set-piece attack on these hills should be made by MacMillan's 152 Brigade on the right and Rennie's 154 Brigade on the left. Lt.-Col. N. D. Leslie (Camerons), who had newly succeeded Dunlop as G.S.O.1, had accordingly plenty of work on his hands.

In the right Brigade attack the 5th Camerons had the leading rôle, the 5th Seaforth coming up behind them, with the 2nd Seaforth in reserve. Imagine a ridge of hills running north-west and south-east. At the north-west end is a high tor known as Point 224. Some quarter of a mile along the ridge, but in a fold in the hills, lies Iazzovechio Farm. Five hundred yards farther along and in another fold a little higher up lies Angelico Farm, with behind it and right up to the ridge a thick olive-grove. On the Camerons' left flank the valley of the Fontana Muralato ran down from the hills and passed below the railway and the main road to the dried-up bed of the Dittaino River. The upper regions of the valley were known to be mined and to hide anti-tank gun nests. It was arranged that a Bofors gun should fire tracers up this valley to indicate the direction to be taken by the Camerons who were supported by a squadron of Sherman tanks and a platoon of the 1/7th Middlesex. The whole prospect could be viewed from the slopes of Mount Turcisi, which was the starting-point for our attack, and from which General Wimberley made his detailed reconnaissance.

On the night of Saturday, 31st July, the Camerons, now under Lt.-Col. A. Monro of Auchenbowie, set out, with some difficulty negotiated the almost dry bed of the Dittaino and then proceeded to the attack behind a lifting barrage at the rate of one hundred yards in three minutes. The leading Companies met much opposition on the top of the ridge,[1] and had so many casualties that " B " and " D " Companies of the 2nd Seaforth in Brigade Reserve were sent up as reinforcements. Lance-

---

[1] After the battle the body of a leading Company Commander, Captain A. M. Macleod of Skeabost, Skye, was found on the point, and near him the body of Lieutenant Henry of the Camerons lying on top of a dead German under-officer.

Sergeant James Graham (Seaforth) went forward with one man, silenced a machine-gun post and took five German prisoners. He found one prisoner could speak English, so he made him lead the way to a point where another post was holding up his platoon. Graham attacked this post alone with his tommy-gun, adding another couple of prisoners to his bag. But the opposition was very stiff and a heavy concentration of smoke and shells from 128th Field Regiment's guns was put down on Point 224. Then the Germans put in a very strong counter-attack with tanks and infantry. Fighting continued all Sunday, and on Monday it became obvious that the enemy were pulling out. Cameron carrier-patrols were able to make their way down the reverse slopes of the hills on to the Strada di Palermo and towards the crossing of the Simeto River.

In the rear of the Cameron advance had come the 5th Seaforth (Lt.-Col. Walford). They had been held up by a nasty traffic jam in a very dangerous gully, but in due course they moved through the right of the Camerons and made Angelico Farm, to find the olive-grove behind it was "hotching" with the enemy. "C" Company worked over the crest on the edge of the grove only to find that the trees continued down the other slope. But they got to the foot of the wood and dug in. It was greatly owing to the courage and resolution of two private soldiers, James Graham and James McLauchlan, that this grove was partially cleared of the enemy. The Seaforth now held a line on the top of the ridge, and the counter-attack on them and the Camerons by German tanks and lorried infantry was smashed up by the Divisional Artillery and in particular by Brigadier Jerry Shiel's ever-ready guns of the 128th Field Regiment.

The 5th Seaforth also received excellent support from 13 Platoon of the 1/7th Middlesex. The platoon commander, Lieutenant Wrampling, a reinforcement officer, who had joined the Battalion only ten hours before the attack began, was ordered to reorganise on a small "pimple." He advanced to survey the area, found it strongly held by enemy machine-gunners and was very severely wounded. Before he was evacuated, however, he was able to get three of his own guns into action some eighty yards below the crest. Corporal Dean, the senior N.C.O., then assumed command, ordered two of the guns to continue firing while he rushed the third across the open to the top of the crest, where the sub-section was lucky to find an empty trench. Into this they dropped, mounted their gun and concentrated on an olive-grove some two hundred yards away. The other two guns had meanwhile silenced their opposition. The platoon sergeant, Sergeant Fisher, now brought up the fourth gun and led the section to some olive-groves on the left, where the Seaforth were having very bitter fighting. He moved his guns into a captured enemy machine-gun post and gave invaluable support to the Highlanders.

At the same time 154 Brigade, as left attacking Brigade, were advancing up the high ground on the left of the Camerons, with the two Black Watch Battalions attacking and the Argylls in reserve. The 7th Black Watch was immediately on the left of the Camerons and moved forward along the tapes on the night of 31st July. There was a deep gully separating the left flank of the Camerons from the right flank of the 7th Black Watch, whose main axis of advance was up the shoulder next that gully which was a comparatively gradual slope right up to the crest. " D " Company were to the left of that shoulder and had to attack the main crest up an extremely steep scree. This main crest immediately in front of " D " Company was very rocky and extremely strongly held. " C " Company advanced and disappeared over the crest ; " B " Company reached the crest and came under very heavy fire from troops who had apparently allowed " C " Company to pass unmolested. From the Battalion Headquarters' position it was observed that " D " Company had apparently reached the crest itself up the steep scree, but very heavy fighting ensued and " D " Company were pushed back off the crest. They made their objectives on the ridge of the hills, and " A " Company carried on down the other side.

" C " Company ran into an ambush and were badly knocked about, Captain Scott, the Company Commander, being wounded and taken prisoner. The enemy were putting down heavy machine-gun fire from positions among large rocks on the top of the hill. Lance-Corporal Forbes climbed up those rocks and single-handed captured a position containing a Spandau and its crew. He held the position against counter-attacks, and his courage and coolness were quite outstanding. " D " Company also ran into an ambush and were roughly handled. Major Bobby Hutchison, the Company Commander, was wounded. Private David Nicol was acting as runner to the Company Commander and was wounded in the head and face, but entirely on his own initiative he made his way forward to the platoon which had the next senior officer to report that the Company Commander was a casualty. He continued under heavy fire to visit the other two platoons, and having found out their positions, he returned to Company Headquarters and gave valuable information to the acting Company Commander. Nicol kept on acting as runner during the whole of the action although suffering great pain from the wound in his face. In addition, Nicol for some time defended Major Hutchison against several Germans, one at least of whom he shot with his officer's pistol. Major Hutchison later died of wounds. The Germans vigorously counter-attacked all next morning, but by evening they had had enough.

For their excellent shooting on every one of the battalion fronts in this battle great credit goes to the Divisional Artillery. The 126th Field Regiment actually fired 2000 rounds per gun in support of the 7th Black Watch. As Major Russell relates : " An interesting sidelight on the effect of this shelling was revealed only after the war, when Captain Scott, ' C ' Company Commander (7th Black Watch), who had been wounded, reported how when he had been for some hours in a German officers' dug-out during which several attempts were made to evacuate him, but had to be abandoned owing to our very heavy shelling, he was at last put on to a half-track armoured vehicle and was followed the whole way down the hill and along the track at the back by unpleasantly accurate shell-fire. He himself was lying on a stretcher on top of the half-track and he found it most unpleasant, especially when, as the half-track was moving down the hill, one shell passed so close to his head that he was able to watch it travelling away from him and bursting farther down the hill." In the battle the Division had again under its command as Medium Artillery, to the delight of all parties concerned, the Scottish Horse. It proved a most efficient Medium Regiment.

The 1st Black Watch had an easier time and took their objectives with only some two dozen casualties. Major Patrick Sholto Douglas led a particularly successful attack on enemy machine-gun posts.

Among the ambulance men who distinguished themselves during the battle of the Sferro Hills was Driver Charles Cox of the 175th Field Ambulance. Evacuation of casualties from certain Aid Posts could only be effected under the direct observation of the enemy. It was decided, therefore, to hold all casualties for the first twenty-four hours of the battle. But before dawn on 1st August an urgent appeal for an ambulance car was received from a Regimental Aid Post. It was not possible to carry out the return journey in darkness, but Driver Cox took forward his car for several miles under direct enemy observation and shell-fire. He collected several cases from the Regimental Aid Post and then returned in full daylight along the main road which was even closer to the enemy. He made similar journeys on successive days along those dangerous roads until after the enemy had withdrawn.

So ended a short sharp battle, and, from the Highland Division's point of view, a most successful one.[1]

The Corps Commander, Sir Oliver Leese, was most complimentary, and gave it as his opinion that the Division's successful attack on the Sferro Hills had much to do with the whole German withdrawal on the front of the 30th Corps, if not of the 8th Army. That opinion was endorsed later by statements found in a captured German document.

That same afternoon (1st August) the reserve Battalion, the 7th Argylls, were ordered to advance on Pietraperciata, a high ridge to the left of the 1st Black Watch position. They had even less trouble than the 42nd had had in the attack proper, for they completed their job with only one man wounded. From their ridge they could see the town of Centuripe on the top of a distant hill, and in front of that hill another ridge culminating in the top known as Mount Spezia. It had been decided that 153 Brigade should attack that position, but an Argyll patrol, supported by Middlesex machine-gunners, found the position held by nine Germans, who were only too pleased to call it a day.

Here and now we may follow the remainder of the story of 154 Brigade in the Sicilian Campaign. By the 3rd of August it was obvious that the enemy were all east of the Simeto River. Brigadier Rennie therefore advanced his Brigade as right flank cover for the 78th Division, whose attack on Adrano was timed for the night of 6th-7th August. On the evening of the 3rd, the 1st Black Watch (Lt.-Col. John Hopwood[2]) had pushed forward patrols to the high ground at Cocola, and when dawn broke on the 4th, moved along the track from Massa Parlata, the 7th Argylls (Lt.-Col. Dunlop) holding the Cocola foothills, and the 7th Black Watch (Lt.-Col. Oliver) remaining in reserve across the track. On the morning of the 5th, the 7th Argylls and the 1st Black Watch moved forward to force and secure the crossings of the Simeto River. The two Battalions carried out their job with great success and few

---

[1] The enemy left behind him a battery of ten howitzers intact. When captured by a Cameron carrier patrol under Captain J. Elliot, one gun was still loaded.

[2] Hopwood, after being Second-in-Command the 7th Black Watch throughout the North African battles, had taken over command of the 42nd when Colonel Neil Blair was wounded. Hopwood had already proved himself to be an outstanding fighting soldier and, as C.O. of the 42nd right up to the end of the war, he was to become one of the best-known characters in the Division.

casualties. "B" Company of the Argylls particularly distinguished itself that day by capturing a German officer and fourteen other ranks, a motor-cycle combination, a self-propelled 75-mm. gun, and a Mercedes ten-seater carrier, one of the most varied "bags" of the campaign. Corporal Forsyth of the 1st Black Watch, in an attack on a fortified farmhouse, ran round an outside wall and got two Spandau men from the flank with his tommy-gun, thus saving many casualties which would have resulted if those men had been left active during the frontal attack. Then both Battalions made crossings of the river, and a Black Watch patrol advanced close up to Biancavilla which fell to 152 Brigade the following day. The 7th Black Watch and the 1st Argylls remained in reserve. The latter Battalion, the old 91st Argyllshire Highlanders, to the regret of the whole Division, was then withdrawn from the 51st, and the Brigade were given a rest period in the vicinity of the Simeto crossings.

On 17th August 154 Brigade was moved up to Messina and Rennie took over from the 3rd United States Division on the 20th. The enemy had moved across to Italy and the Brigade's job was to guard bridges and other important works on the edge of the Straits against possible sabotage, for there appeared to be little chance of the enemy making any attempt at a re-invasion of Sicily. The Brigade was mostly occupied accepting the surrender of Italian soldiers who had been left behind on the island after the German evacuation. Their next job was to keep accurate observation across the Straits so as to cover the landing of the 13th Corps on the Italian mainland, and their final one was to cross behind the 13th Corps and hold a bridgehead round Reggio. The 13th Corps crossed without difficulty, and on 5th September 154 Brigade was ferried over the Straits and formed base around Reggio and Reggio aerodrome. On 8th September they were all ferried back again to Messina, where they had a two months' rest.

On 2nd August Murray with his 153 Brigade was moving north-eastwards to take and hold the high ground at Spezia and Guzzarano so as to cover the right flank of 78th Division's advance on Adrano. The 5th Black Watch occupied the position after passing through a very heavily mined area where one of their carriers was blown to bits. The 1st Gordons moved forward in support of the 5th Black Watch, with the 5/7th Gordons in reserve some thousand yards west of the village of Muglia. But the Brigade was not asked to do any further fighting in this area, for the 78th Division occupied Adrano on 7th August.

The 153 Brigade had now to play a somewhat different rôle. It had to take over the sector of the front held by 13 Brigade of the 5th Division on the south-east side of Mount Etna. On 13th August the 1st Gordons led the way to Milo, but great difficulty was experienced in getting transport forward, for the enemy had blown up all the bridges on the road, and "D" Company were turned into a kind of carrier company. But by night-time the forward troops had reached some high ground overlooking the Linguaglossa–Piedmonte valley, from which across the last northern chain of Sicilian hills could be seen the shores of Italy. A curious predicament, which had never been met before in the whole of the North African and Sicilian Campaigns, occurred at this point. Eight pioneers had carried forward the necessary cable and instruments for communications, only to discover that, when everything was installed, the result was nil owing to the fact that the peculiarly dry lava soil rendered useless the "earth return" circuit. A diarist of the 1st Gordons records that : " Shortly after midnight thirty pack-mules arrived. The animals were not in the best condition, having had no food since nine o'clock the previous morning. They were taken off the lorries, saddled and brought forward without a halt. Perhaps the animals' pleasure at being once again on solid earth made up for their fatigue. Once loaded there was hardly any holding them and they were sent forward with their Indian muleteers in small packets of two or three. Each packet was guided by a member of the Intelligence Section—and perhaps it says something for their training that, when the mules returned at first light, the muleteers were still walking while the guides rode."

The Battalion pressed forward down the hills to Linguaglossa, at which point the 5/7th Gordons passed through them and occupied the town of Castiglione. Meanwhile the 5th Black Watch had been acting as road repair squads, and at that point the news came that Messina had fallen and the curtain was rung down on the campaign.

The 152 Brigade had been left behind temporarily in reserve, but, after the fighting ceased, the 5th Seaforth advanced to Biancavilla on the slopes of Etna, and then to Pisano where, as Alistair Borthwick puts it, " we were left among the vineyards of Pisano to eat grapes and rest." There they had the company of the 2nd Battalion, who later advanced to Fleri. An interesting Regimental Reunion was held at Catania when the massed pipe-bands of the 2nd, 5th, 6th Seaforth (5th Division) and the Canadian Seaforth Highlanders together beat

DIVISIONAL MEMORIAL AT SFERRO, SICILY

By courtesy of the IMPERIAL WAR MUSEUM

HER MAJESTY QUEEN ELIZABETH WITH Brigadier OLIVER AT AMERSHAM

By courtesy of the Press and Publicity Photographic Company

"Retreat." On 10th August the Pipes and Drums of the Camerons beat "Retreat" in Biancavilla in the presence of the Corps Commander, and on the 16th the Camerons moved to Zafferrana.

As soon as the fighting stopped in Sicily training again began at once, as was customary in the Division. In particular, some time was spent for exercise purposes fighting over again in the actual areas the battles of Gerbini and Sferro.

At the end of that battlefield tour General Wimberley broke the news to the assembled officers that he was now going home to take up the appointment of Commandant of the Staff College, Camberley, and that his place as Divisional Commander was to be taken over by Major-General Bullen-Smith, late Commander 15th Scottish Division in the United Kingdom. Bullen-Smith was a K.O.S.B. who had served as a Staff Officer in the 3rd Division when General Montgomery commanded it in France in 1940.

At about the same time Wimberley released two congratulatory messages sent to him :—

From General Montgomery—

"Now that the campaign in Sicily is over I would like to tell you how well I consider your Division have done. One never imagines that the Highland Division can do otherwise than well, and in this short campaign the Division has lived up to its best traditions.

"I have always been proud to have the Highland Division in the 8th Army.

"Please tell all your officers and men how well I consider they have done."

From the Corps Commander, Sir Oliver Leese—

"Now that the campaign in Sicily is over I want to write to congratulate your Division on your magnificent fighting during the campaign.

"I am convinced that the foundation of your success lay in the immense amount of trouble you took in all the arrangements for the landing. Everything went according to plan. I realise the stress and strain of the preliminary days and I congratulate you on the results.

"After that the Division fought continuously until the last week of the campaign. Your advance towards Paterno and your operations on the River Salso entailed very heavy fighting. I know what this cost you in casualties amongst officers and men. I also realise the difficulties with which you had to contend in intense heat in the low ground ; when you were under direct enemy observation from the high ground on front and flank. Your Division fought splendidly in these battles and culminated their efforts with your highly successful battle for the high ground west of the Sferro bridgehead—an action which I feel had a decisive effect on the enemy decision to withdraw earlier than we had expected from his Etna Line.

"I hope you will congratulate and thank all ranks of your Division on my behalf. I am very proud that the Division has fought in a second successful campaign with 30 Corps. . . ."

Wimberley also published his own farewell "*Order of the Day to all Ranks of the 51st Highland Division*":—

"On giving up command of the 51st Highland Division, in which I have served for the past three years, the Division, moreover, in which I was so proud also to have been numbered in the last Great War, I find it difficult to express to you what I feel.

"It is naturally easiest on this occasion merely to recall to memory some of the milestones passed in the long road which we have travelled together, ever onwards, from Scotland right across Africa and into Europe.

"For instance, the many tributes which your spirit, discipline and behaviour brought from those leaders best qualified to compare us with other Divisions in those now far-off days at home.

"ALAMEIN, and that moonlight night, when you went into your first battle, new and untried as individuals, but bearing in your historic tartans and your Pipes an inheritance of centuries of gallantry from your forebears, and each bearing Scotland's banner in your hearts.

"MERSA BREGA and its mines, and our gallant Engineers who died as we went on.

"BUERAT, and the rapid advance to TRIPOLI, when your spirit to get forward, from the leading Highlander to the very back of the Division's Administrative Services, resembled a living flame.

"MARETH, when you showed that the Highland Division could defend as well as attack.

"The race for SFAX. That hard fight at AKARIT, when you pressed through mines and wire and defences as on a field-day, but paid the inevitable price for your gallantry.

"The SICILIAN beaches; and now FRANCOFONTE, GERBINI, SFERRO and its hills, almost still reverberating with the crash of our artillery as our Gunners hammered the German infantry and tanks, and as our 'Die-hard' machine-gunners fired their belts on the bullet-swept tops of SAN ANTONIO.

"By your deeds, it is not too much to claim that you have added to the pages of military history, pages which may well bear comparison with the stories of our youth, telling us of our kinsmen who fought at Bannockburn, Culloden, Waterloo, the Alma, and at Loos. Further, in achieving this, you have earned, as is indeed your due, the grateful acknowledgments of your Country.

"All this, however, belongs to the past. All this can be summed up by one verse recently written of the Division in the Scots Press :—

> '*Ye canna mak' a sojer wi' braid an' trappin's braw,*
> *Nor gie him fightin' spirit when his back's ag'in the wa'.*
> *It's the breedin' in the callants that winna let them whine,*
> *The bluid o' generations frae lang, lang syne.*'

"It is the future which matters most. It is concerning the future about which I would therefore remind you to-day, and especially those thousands of you who have joined the Highland Division since we left Egypt.

"No individual, no Regiment, no Division can afford to rest on its laurels. Just as your fathers in the Highland Division won their proud position as the premier fighting formation in 1917 and kept it through many weary months, so must you, in this generation, maintain your reputation to the end of the road. To do this, you must ever set your own standards, you must ' gang your ain gait ' ; you must choose the hard and not the easy path. Your discipline and behaviour, your saluting, your battle drill, your battle technique must continually be overhauled and be kept at the highest level, come what may.

"Provided all this is maintained, then, with your national background and your great morale, you will, in due course and God willing, fight your last battle as bravely and successfully as you fought your first—proud that all must still grant to you your Alamein motto of ' Second to None.'

"For myself, I can best thank you in the farewell words of my great predecessor Sir Colin Campbell, who led our same famous Highland Regiments to such glory nearly one hundred years ago—

From the bottom of my heart."

A day or two was spent in good-bye visits, and then the General who had led the 51st, in training and in battle for over two years, left by air for Britain. A note followed him from Montgomery which spoke of "the magnificent Highland Division which played such a large part in the victories gained in Africa and Sicily."

And here is a final picture in Sicily of that distinguished leader. It is given by Sergeant Barker (1st Gordons) of "The Balmorals"[1] :—

"Wimberley was a great character and someone for whom I personally had a great admiration. His interest in ' The Balmorals ' (which we were sadly to miss) lasted until the day he left. As his car turned out of Divisional Headquarters on the way to the airfield he passed Bunny Playfair and Archie Angus in the road. He stopped the car and threw something out of the window. ' Sing this ! ' he shouted to them as the car pulled away. They bent down and picked up a copy of the words and sheet music of a song called ' Good Old Fifty-First,' which months before he had promised to try

[1] See footnote, p. 24.

and get me. It was published in the last war and had long been out of print. It had been written by Eric Stanley who ran ' The Balmorals ' then, and had been inspired by the fact that on 22nd March 1918—the second day of a German offensive when the Highland Division was still holding its original positions—there had been dropped from a German balloon the message : ' Good old Fifty-First, still sticking it ! ' I only wish the song had been up to the standard of the men who inspired it.

" Unfortunately for modern tastes it was not quite good enough, and we could never use it. It worries me that the last order given by Major-General D. N. Wimberley, D.S.O., M.C., as Commander of the Highland Division was disobeyed."

It is no exaggeration to say that every single man in the Division knew General Wimberley, and the news that he was leaving the Division came as a very great shock to everyone. The General was regarded by all ranks as an essential part of the Division, and it was very difficult to think of the Division without him in command. He was certainly the mainstay of the success which the Division had achieved under his command. Wimberley had served in the Highland Division in the 1914-18 war when it was commanded by General " Uncle " Harper, and the lessons which he had learned in the Division then had made a lasting impression on him—thoroughness in training and in preparation for battle,[1] the vital importance of the Division's *esprit de corps* and morale (and no one knew better than the General how to raise that morale to a really high level and to keep it there). As he left the Division in Sicily his thoughts must have gone back to those early days of 1941 when he took over command of the Division in Scotland and to the many and strenuous exercises carried out by the Division over the whole of the north of Scotland during the period he was training it and getting it ready for war. It must have been a tremendous satisfaction to him to know how well all his efforts on behalf of the Division had succeeded. What he could not know at that time, but what was to be amply proved later on was that, although he was to be no longer with the Division himself, the spirit, which he had imbued, and his ideas of what was essential for its success in battle, were to last right through the war.

We say good-bye to Sicily near the Gerbini battlefield amid the great rains which usher in that island's winter. On the dreich day of

[1] General Maxse, commanding 18th Corps, wrote of the 51st in 1917 : " What has struck me most is the thoroughness of the organisation within, and the fact that all the usual war problems had been thought out beforehand, discussed in detail, and are embodied in simple doctrines well known to all ranks. The result is, the Division always fights with gallantry."

4th November representatives of the Highland Division gathered once more close to that point where had taken place the heaviest fighting of the campaign, and there a stone Celtic Cross was unveiled as a memorial to all those gallant men who fell with the 51st in Sicily. It is interesting to note that even at this time, when it had suffered some 7000 casualties within a year, 81 per cent of the officers and 72 per cent other ranks in the Highland Regiments of the Division were Scotsmen. Perhaps these figures are the best evidence of Douglas Wimberley's influence in the Highland Division.

The time of rest before the Division came home for its next task was not particularly happy. Malaria was rampant; the local population were sad and miserable people, thankful enough to know that Italy had dropped out of the war, but gazing in mute despair on their broken cities and their ruined fields.

So the 51st were ordered by Montgomery to come home to train for yet another campaign, and the transports with the Highland Division aboard sailed from Catania, and the mists that hide the island, into the darkness of the Mediterranean night " while Jove's planet rises yonder silent over Africa."

51ST HIGHLAND DIVISION—BATTLE CASUALTIES SICILIAN CAMPAIGN

From 10th July 1943 to 16th August 1943

	Killed		Wounded		Missing		Total Casualties	
	Offrs.	O.R.s	Offrs.	O.R.s	Offrs.	O.R.s	Offrs.	O.R.s
H.Q. 51 Div.	..	..	..	..	..	..	..	..
H.Q. R.A.	..	..	..	..	..	..	..	..
126 Fd. Regt.	..	..	..	1	..	..	..	1
127 Fd. Regt.	1	6	4	16	..	..	5	22
128 Fd. Regt.	..	4	4	19	..	..	4	23
61 A.-Tk. Regt.	..	3	2	39	1	2	3	44
40 L.A.A. Regt.	1	..	3	7	..	..	4	7
H.Q. R.E.	..	..	1	1	..	..	1	1
239 Fd. Pk. Coy.	..	..	..	..	..	..	..	..
274 Fd. Coy.	1	1	..	12	..	..	1	13
275 Fd. Coy.	1	1	..	2	..	..	1	3
276 Fd. Coy.	..	..	..	3	..	..	..	3
16 Div. Sigs. and L.A.D.	..	..	..	1	..	..	..	1
H.Q. 152 Bde. Def. P.I. and L.A.D.	..	1	..	..	..	..	..	1
Sig. Sec.	..	..	..	..	..	..	..	..
2 Seaforth	6	24	2	99	6	71	14	194
5 Seaforth	5	22	7	82	1	28	13	132
5 Camerons	4	17	7	41	1	10	12	68
H.Q. 153 Bde. Def. Pl. and L.A.D.	..	1	..	2	..	..	..	3
Sig. Sec.	..	..	..	..	..	..	..	..
1 Gordons	1	16	6	57	..	2	7	75
5/7 Gordons	..	8	6	38	..	10	6	56
5 Black Watch	2	14	7	95	..	2	9	111
H.Q. 154 Bde. Def. Pl. and L.A.D.	..	..	..	2	..	..	..	2
Sig. Sec.	..	..	..	..	..	..	..	..
1 Black Watch	1	26	9	99	1	20	11	145
7 Black Watch	2	13	4	61	1	45	7	119
7 A. & S.H.	4	26	11	105	6	92	21	223
1/7 Middlesex	1	11	4	47	..	2	5	60
" A "	..	..	..	..	..	..	..	..
" B "	..	..	..	..	..	..	..	..
" C "	..	..	..	..	..	..	..	..
H.Q. R.A.S.C.	..	..	..	..	..	..	..	..
525 Inf. Bde. Coy. (152)	..	..	..	4	..	..	..	4
526 Inf. Bde. Coy. (153)	..	..	..	..	..	..	..	..
527 Inf. Bde. Coy. (154)	..	..	..	..	..	..	..	..
458 Div. Tps. Coy.	..	..	..	..	..	..	..	..
174 Fd. Amb.	..	..	..	..	..	..	..	..
175 Fd. Amb.	..	..	..	..	..	..	..	..
176 Fd. Amb.	..	..	..	..	..	..	..	..
5 F.D.S.	..	..	..	..	..	..	..	..
6 F.D.S.	..	..	..	..	..	..	..	..
29 Fd. Hyg. Sec.	..	..	..	..	..	..	..	..
H.Q. R.E.M.E.	..	..	..	..	..	..	..	..
152 Bde. Gp. W/Shops	..	..	..	..	..	..	..	..
153 Bde. Gp. W/Shops	..	..	..	..	..	..	..	..
154 Bde. Gp. W/Shops	..	..	..	..	..	..	..	..
Pro. Coy.	..	..	..	1	..	..	..	1
Div. O.F.P.	..	..	..	..	..	..	..	..
	30	194	77	833	17	284	124	1312

CHAPTER VI.

THE ETERNAL TRIANGLE

" Gabhaidh sinn an rathad mór, olc air mhath le càch e."
(We will take the King's highroad whether well or ill in the opinion of others.)
OLD GAELIC SONG.

" Fair stood the wind for France,
When we our sails advance,
Nor now to prove our chance
Longer will tarry."
DRAYTON.

THEY were lucky in one way, unlucky in another, those elements of the Highland Division who, after their experience of Africa and Sicily, were brought home to the kindly shores of the Clyde. It was pleasant to make Scotland on a 1943 November morning, to appreciate once more " the smells of her and the sounds of her," that sweetness of a land of green pastures, with " the music of the waters running down " ; it was not so pleasant to be pushed at once into a train, and carried away across the Border to the meadows of Buckinghamshire and Hertfordshire. But home-leave came along in due course, and then back the troops went to Amersham and Berkhampstead, to Great Missenden and to many other places in those two Home Counties.

The Division settled down first of all to play—for London was not far away—and work. A beginning was made immediately to build up the strength of the various units, and certain changes took place in some of the higher commands. As was stated above, Major-General Charles Bullen-Smith of the K.O.S.B. had taken over from Wimberley in Sicily just after the fighting there had ceased. Bullen-Smith had had a first-class fighting record in World War I., and came to the 51st with excellent reports as a trainer of troops during his eighteen months' command of the 15th (Scottish) Division at home. As regards the three Brigadiers, Brigadier Gordon MacMillan of 152 had left in Sicily to command the 15th (Scottish) Division at home, and Brigadier Thomas Rennie of 154 now said " good-bye " on taking over the 3rd Division. But fortunately for the 51st that " good-bye " was in each case an " *au revoir.*" About the time when hostilities ceased in Sicily, that distinguished Battalion Commander, Lt.-Col.

James Oliver of the 7th Black Watch, took over 152 Brigade on Macmillan's promotion. As Bernard Fergusson has recorded [1]: " His [Oliver's] departure from the 7th Battalion was a sad occasion, but it was a gain to the Division : for he was now to prove himself as good a Brigade Commander. All that 154 Brigade was concerned with was that one day, if Thomas Rennie should have to go, James might come back in his room." Now that Rennie had gone, Oliver was transferred from 152 Brigade to 154. Brigadier D. H. Haugh (Seaforth) was in command of 152 until 26th June, when Brigadier A. J. H. Cassels succeeded him. Cassels was a product of Rugby and Sandhurst, was commissioned in 1926, and served for six years in India, for some time as A.D.C. to his father, General Cassels, who was C.-in-C. of the Army there. In 1939 Cassels was a Captain in the Seaforth, and went to France with the 52nd Lowland Division.[2] Brigadier " Nap " Murray of the Camerons continued in command of 153. Of the three Brigadiers, Cassels, Murray and Oliver, Colonel Martin Lindsay (R.S.F., attached Gordons), under the date of 8th August 1944, writes in his ' So Few Got Through ' [3]: " I should not think that any Division anywhere had three better or more trusted Brigade Commanders."

The chief change in units was that the 2nd Derbyshire Yeomanry took the place of the Highland Reconnaissance Regiment and became known as Divisional Cavalry.

The play-and-work business was changed to work-and-play as soon as a typical Scottish welcome had been given to New Year 1944, in the early days of which the Division had many distinguished visitors. On 15th February General Sir Bernard Montgomery, who was now commanding the 21st Army Group, inspected the Division at Berkhampstead, and expressed his personal pleasure that once again the 51st was under his command ; on the 24th the newly appointed Supreme Commander Allied Expeditionary Force, General Eisenhower, watched some of the units training ; on the 28th Their Majesties attended the beating of " Retreat " by the Massed Bands of the Division at St Albans. Other visitors were the Moderator of the Church of Scotland and, not the least welcome, Major-General Wimberley.

Hardening training for the infantry was made less monotonous by

[1] By permission of Colonel Bernard Fergusson and Messrs Collins, publishers of ' The Black Watch and the King's Enemies.'
[2] Cassels in 1951 commanded the Commonwealth Division in Korea.
[3] By permission of Mr Martin Lindsay and Messrs Collins.

combined manœuvres with tank units, by river-crossing exercises, by night operations, and by demonstrations of the new "Wasp" flame-throwers, which, mounted on carriers, could project their fiery breath one hundred yards.

At the end of March units of the Division were moved to various stations in East Anglia, where not the least interesting part of the training was that conducted in the Limehouse Street-Fighting Area, while loading and landing exercises were carried out at Lowestoft. A certain amount of comic relief was provided by the tests of the waterproofing of vehicles. "This," wrote an officer in the 152 Brigade, "had become the obsession of all Regimental M.T.O.s and everyone else who had any responsibility in getting the Brigade ashore on the Continent with all its vehicles. Every time a water-splash was used, it was surrounded with spectators, both those out to learn and those out to laugh. It was funny to see intrepid Jocks driving all types of vehicles hell for leather into a deep pool, disappearing up to their necks in water, and emerging at the other side of the pool, bedraggled but triumphant. Those drivers, who did not emerge triumphant, had perforce to become more bedraggled still."

On 5th April the Division was transferred to the 1st Corps, and left the 30th Corps, with which they had fought so many victorious battles, with much regret.

It is doubtful if ever a secret were better kept than that of where exactly the landings in Europe were to be made. Everyone knew that the Division was to take part in an invasion, but the secret of where and when and how was as well preserved as had been the secret at Djidjelli of the Sicilian landings. There was a Planning H.Q. at Divisional Headquarters, but no papers were allowed to be removed from that office. An exercise, "Fabius," was held, which took the form of a full-dress rehearsal of marshalling and concentration, and on 16th May Major-General Bullen-Smith briefed representative staff and regimental officers from the whole Division. Lectures were given in huts surrounded by many barbed-wire fences. The invasion operation was known as "Overlord," and in those huts the huge maps of the landing-areas were covered with place-names borrowed from Scotland and America.

The final move was to Embarkation Assembly Areas on the London-Southend road, and then in the early days of June to various craft lying in the Thames.

Since the 152 and 154 Brigades had made the initial landings in Sicily, it was 153's turn now; but before we "set sail" with the 5th Black Watch and the two Gordon battalions let us look at Montgomery's plan. The Army Group Commander was to invade the Normandy coast from the Carentan Estuary, which is at the south-east corner of the Contentin Peninsula, to just east of the mouth of the Orne River, a distance of some forty-five miles. A United States Airborne Division was to land in the Carentan area on the extreme right of the attack; the First U.S. Army were to land to the left of their Airborne Division roughly on the line Carentan-Bayeux; the British Second Army (30th Corps on right and 1st Corps on left) to the left of the Americans, between Bayeux and the mouth of the Orne, and the British 6th Airborne Division in the centre of the triangle Ornemouth, Caen, and Cabourg. The assaulting Divisions on the British Second Army front were the 3rd British, 3rd Canadian and 50th, and it was good to know that in the Commanders of two of these three Divisions—General Thomas Rennie, 3rd British, and General Douglas Graham, 50th—the Highland Division had old friends who a short time previously had both served in the 51st as Brigadiers.

The Highland Division in the 1st Corps were to spend some two very unpleasant months in that Ornemouth area, and were to take some very nasty knocks there; for it was in that area that the Germans were not only to resist most determinedly but were to counter-attack most strongly until the Americans had swung round in the great "left-form" movement, which was to result in the German disaster at the Falaise Gap, the completion of that "left-form" movement, and the advance to Paris and northern France. But there was not much to be seen of all that by the Highland Division in 1944's very "leafy June" in the Bavent woods.

Back then to 153 Brigade moving out of the Thames Estuary through the Straits of Dover west towards Portsmouth, and then straight south to the Normandy beaches. Brigadier "Nap" Murray had gone overland to Portsmouth, whence he and the Seconds-in-Command of his battalions were to ship across first with markers of various kinds which were to tell the troops where to go. It should be noted here that the first landings (behind Brigade Headquarters) were to be made by the rifle companies. All transport, etc., was following on at a later date. Lt.-Col. "Chick" Thomson was in command of the Brigade as it sailed from Tilbury in the same kind of craft which were used for the landings in Sicily. They left on the 5th June (D − 1 Day) and at dawn on the 6th they were some ten miles off Normandy. There was a very well-buoyed channel along which they were piloted by a naval officer, who later became famous in the literary world as the author of 'The Cruise of the *Conrad*.' But before they came near the shore they passed the ship carrying the Brigadier and the Seconds-in-Command. So far the leaders had been unable to land, but Murray succeeded in shouting instructions to Thomson in which he advised the Black Watch officer to get in touch with the Canadians, who were directly in front. By two in the afternoon of D Day 153 were still some mile and a half from the beach. It appeared to be quite quiet and did not look difficult. It somewhat resembled the West Sands of St Andrews. But when the ramp was let down from the leading L.C.I., Colonel Thomson found that the water was to reach over his head. In the end, however, they tied up to a kind of amphibian bulldozer and made the shore. Thomson advanced inland with his three battalions and placed them in close proximity to each other in the woods. He then proceeded up a road which, he took it, would lead him to the Canadians. By the side of this road he found a very excellent motor-cycle, and also a push-bike. He was accompanied by an officer, who mounted the push-bike, while Thomson himself took over the motor-cycle. It was a kind of fairy-tale adventure this moving in the dim greenness of unknown woods on those machines which appeared to have been produced by an unseen fairy godmother. In time the two Scots made the headquarters of a Canadian Brigade, and Thomson offered whatever help he could give. The Canadian Brigadier, however, thought everything in the garden—at the moment—was lovely, so Thomson returned to his three battalions to await whatever might befall.[1]

Next morning (7th June) the Divisional General landed from H.M.S. *Hilary* and contacted Colonel Thomson. Bullen-Smith had an order from Corps that a battalion should be sent to reduce the radar station at Douvres, where it was said that a pocket of Germans were holding out. Colonel Thomson was given the job to do with the 5th Black Watch, and he had attached to him two armoured vehicles of the Royal Engineers. There is a wood that lies to the east of Douvres,

[1] To appreciate fairly the position of the 51st at this point, it must be clearly understood that the Highland Division was a "follow-up" Division, and as such had to be used piece-meal to fill in holes in the front wherever and whenever it was so ordered. Many units of the Division were fighting hard before 154 Brigade landed.

and Colonel Thomson was assured that all Canadians were well south of that wood. It was very thick and movement was very difficult in it. Troops were encountered, who were taken for Germans. They were, in fact, Canadians. But after that little trouble had been sorted out, Thomson got ahead. There was a wide open space beyond the wood and between it and the radar station. This was being swept by a murderous enemy fire, and it was evident that the station was much more strongly held than had been supposed. An 88-mm. gun, firing somewhere from Douvres village itself, accounted for the two R.E. vehicles.

It was impossible for the Black Watch to get forward, and Lt.-Col. Thomson sent back asking for additional troops. He was, however, instructed to withdraw, and, although he planned a new form of attack from the rear of the objective, orders came that he was to by-pass the radar station, which was left to be shelled by the Navy. In actual fact, it was some considerable time later when it was taken by commandos. Lt.-Col. Thomson was instructed to move by Hermanville to the bridge across the Caen Canal (named Pegasus Bridge, since it had been taken by the gallant 6th Airborne and marked with their Divisional sign, the flying horse of Mediterranean mythology). The 5th Camerons, who were temporarily attached to 153 Brigade, were left to keep an eye on the radar station.

And here we can laugh for a moment—for there is little to laugh about for some considerable time—at the fate of certain Highland Divisional signs in the vicinity of the Normandy beaches. Part of the Division did not arrive on the beaches till D + 7, and some humorists of the 3rd Division, who had been the first to land, and were commanded by Tom Rennie, added a 7 to the 51st Divisional signs, so that they read H.D.+7.[1]

Lt.-Col. Walford, commanding the 5th Seaforth, had taken over the command of 152 Brigade in the embarkation area, just as Lt.-Col.

---

[1] Very shortly after the landings in Normandy, an American officer, Major Basil Filardi, was posted to the Division for liaison duties with the civil population. Major Filardi, who had previously served in the American Air Force, soon became very well known in the Division and, in fact, an essential part of it. He had all the versatility which one expects from the New World and he seemed to be as equally at home with forward troops under very unpleasant conditions as he was when pacifying and consoling elderly French peasants who had just seen their homes and all their possessions ruthlessly destroyed by the ravages of modern warfare. He became a most ardent Highland Division supporter and even wore Highland Division flashes on his American uniform with, he stated, General Eisenhower's personal permission to do so.

Thomson had taken over command of 153. His rifle companies plus transport embarked on 5th June, and the ships steamed off on the morning of the 6th (D Day), and early on the morning of D+1 anchor was dropped just off the Normandy beach-head. The marching troops were all ashore very quickly, but considerable time was lost before transport could be ferried in. It was not till midday on D+3 that the Brigade (with 60 per cent of its transport) was concentrated in an area north of the radar station at Douvres and received orders to cross Pegasus Bridge and attack certain villages in the area of the 6th Airborne Division. The 4th Armoured Brigade was to support 152.

The 154 Brigade landed on the beach-head in the early hours of D+4, and the main body, as in the case of 153, arrived in advance of its advance party. A 1st Black Watch observer recorded: " The Channel crossing was quiet and uneventful, and one awoke on a glorious sunlight morning to find oneself a solitary dot in the midst of a boundless Armada. A line of blockships was quietly settling down whilst others manœuvred into position; small landing-craft darted from ship to beach and back again; a few massive and ponderous battleships could be seen slowly steaming back and forth, and a cruiser hurled a steady stream of shells at some German post miles inland. On the beach itself everything appeared to be quiet. Sapper parties could be seen and heard exploding mines, laying Sommerfelt tracking, and improving the exits which led to solid roads on the soil of France. For the soldier afloat there was nothing else to do but await the orders of the Navy, and then transfer as quickly as possible to landing-craft, rolling and pitching alongside, and be carried to the beach." The Brigade was held in 1st Corps Reserve, and it was not until 13th June that the 7th Argylls moved across to the east of the Orne, to be followed on the 18th by the remainder of the Brigade. The 154 was temporarily placed under orders of the 6th Airborne Division.

Meanwhile, very unpleasant things had been happening to units of 153 Brigade. The 5th Black Watch, temporarily under the 6th Airborne Division, had been ordered to march on Breville, the 5/7th Gordons south to Touffreville, and the 1st Gordons to what was afterwards to be known as the Triangle, a triangle within the triangle mentioned above. The 5th Black Watch advanced along the road from Ranville to Breville and ran at once into opposition. The ditches at the side of the road were full of Germans, and the whole of the front was swept by very accurate fire. The result was that " A " Company was practically wiped out; in point of fact, every man in the leading platoon died with his face to the foe. Lt.-Col. Thomson then decided to occupy the grounds of the Château de Breville some half-mile south of the village. The Germans put down a very heavy fire on the château and grounds and then put in a strong frontal attack. The enemy were extremely brave and, as a result, made good targets. They were killed literally by the hundred. But despite everything the Germans could do, the much-depleted 5th Black Watch stood their ground, and the Germans withdrew. But not before a very ugly thing had happened. Some men of the 5th far out on the flank had been captured. The captors shoved them up against a wall and shot them in cold blood. All were killed but one man, who feigned death, and later was able to get away and tell the story—a very different story from that concerning the chivalrous behaviour of the German 90th Light Division in Africa. But there was no doubt about its truth. While what was left of this battalion was seething with anger resulting from this incident, a German prisoner was taken, and it looked as if something pretty ugly might be his lot; but that was not the way of British troops— all that did happen to him was that a Jock gave him a cigarette.

The Gordon battalions were luckier than the Black Watch unit. They occupied their positions without opposition, and the 5/7th Gordons also put up a very good show against a German counter-attack. Sergeant Aitkenhead of " B " Company of that battalion was captured by the enemy and taken to a German headquarters. He was left there with a single guard, whom he stabbed with a knife which had been overlooked when he was searched. Aitkenhead rejoined his battalion later in the day.

Meanwhile 152 Brigade, less the 5th Seaforth, who had been put temporarily under command of 153, were given the job, in an operation named " Smock," of reducing two villages, St Honorine (full name St Honorine la Chardonnerette) and Demouville. The 5th Camerons had to look after the former and the 2nd Seaforth the latter. The Camerons, under Lt.-Col. " Sandy " Monro of Auchenbowie, concentrated in the Ranville area, and moved to the attack on the morning of the 13th. Very heavy enemy bombardment of the start-line resulted in considerable delay, and of the four tanks supporting the infantry three went west before coming into action at all, and the fourth joined them at the beginning of the assault. The Camerons took positions in and on the flanks of the village, but had to sit under an incredibly heavy artillery bombardment, which was followed by an infantry attack strongly supported by tanks. Sergeant A. Mackenzie got three of one column of tanks with his gun and gave " B " Company some respite, while Private C. Sands of " D " Company, although wounded in both legs, kept his Bren gun going with very marked effect. But by 10 A.M. so reduced was the rifle strength that the Companies were ordered to withdraw. " C " Company did not get the order and held on for some time, but finally was ordered back, and what was left of the battalion re-formed at Longueval on the Orne. The whole attack seems to a historian to have been hastily arranged, and, as unfortunately is apt so often to happen with the fluid battle, it would appear that in the higher command there was a lack of specific knowledge of the actual situation in and about St Honorine.

The failure of the Camerons' initial attack on the 13th, and the tremendous concentration of German artillery fire, made it impossible for the 2nd Seaforth to advance south to Demouville, so they were put into a defensive position on the high ground north of St Honorine, and the 5th Seaforth, back from 153 Brigade, filled up the gap between their 2nd Battalion and the Camerons at Longueval.

On 22nd June the Camerons were sent back to have another shot at St Honorine. There was to be no artillery support, but tanks had to be and were in position in the captured village by dawn. By half-past eight in the morning the Camerons were well and truly in the village, and by ten o'clock mopping-up had been practically completed. The Camerons had to withstand several very vicious counter-attacks, and held the position until relieved that same night, when they went back to Herouvillette.

After the Camerons' second attack on St Honorine, the 2nd Seaforth, detachments of which had assisted the Camerons, relieved, and in their turn were relieved by their 5th Battalion in that village of evil memory. Here it was that 152 Brigade first made acquaintance with " Moaning Minnie," the German 6-barrelled rocket-propelled mortar, which had a devastatingly terrible effect on the nerves of the troops. On the night of 1st-2nd July the 5th Black Watch relieved the 5th Seaforth. Meanwhile the Gordon battalions had put in a considerable amount of both offensive and defensive fighting in and about Escoville and St Honorine.[1]

[1] Sergeant Faiers of the 1/7th Middlesex picked up an enemy map in St Honorine, which, on being examined by Divisional Intelligence Staff, was found to contain the Order of Battle of the whole enemy Battle Group from Troarn to Caen. The information proved of great value, and his Commanding Officer sent Sergeant Faiers a special message of congratulation for his initiative.

How fared 154 Brigade ? On 14th June the 7th Argylls (Lt.-Col. John Meiklejohn) had been placed under command of the 6th Airborne Division, and were sent east across the Orne to take up a position in defence of the bridges. Enemy attacks, however, were frustrated by our own artillery fire, and the Argylls rejoined 154 Brigade in a defensive position in the Bois de Bavent. The 7th Black Watch (now under command of Lt.-Col. Charles Cathcart, one of the original Territorial officers of the Battalion) had a very sticky time from heavy mortaring, and the enemy made a determined effort to infiltrate into their positions. They were beaten off not without loss, among our killed being Captain R. E. Cape, the Padre of the Battalion. The 42nd (Colonel John Hopwood) had taken a hand in watching the radar station at Douvres, and one non-commissioned officer (Lance-Corporal McPhail) did a little reconnaissance on his own and returned with a prisoner and two very large portraits of Hitler and Goering. Then the Battalion joined the remainder of 154 Brigade in the Bois de Bavent, and in the heavy shelling there on the 26th the Adjutant, Captain Ronald Milligan, C.S.M. McGarry, and many others were killed.

So the strange story of the Orne bridgehead went on, one battalion being perforce sent here, another being attached there. All three Infantry Brigades were in the line, and, when aggressive action was ordered, there were no reserves to draw on. Readjustments had to be made in the holding troops. The southern point of that bridgehead on the Orne was at Longueval, from thence it moved north-east along the road to Ranville. After Ranville village it ran south-east to Herouvillette, then still south-east to the ghastliest hole of all—the Triangle (to which this chapter owes its heading) and to the brick-works north-east of Touffreville ; then the line turned back directly north through the Bois de Bavent, and so by Breville and Amfreville to Sallenelles, which is very nearly at the mouth of the Orne.

The reason why the Triangle was such a horrible place was that the Germans surrounded it on two sides, and our failure to capture St Honorine until 22nd June left the whole of the right flank in a precarious position. The fact must be faced that at this period the normal very high morale of the Division fell temporarily to a low ebb. There were many factors responsible for this condition ; for example, this was the first occasion in two long years of fighting when the Division had been asked for weeks on end to play a defensive rôle—and a defensive rôle in thick woods, far, far different from the open spaces of

Africa and Sicily. A kind of claustrophobia affected the troops, and the continual shelling and mortaring from an unseen enemy in relatively great strength was certainly very trying. In Africa and in Sicily there had been a tradition that the Division fought always as a Division. In Normandy this could not be so. Battalions were sent here and there and everywhere under all sorts of commands. Both in Africa and in Sicily, when an attack was mounted, the briefing had always been most thorough, and sufficient troops had been available and were always used to ensure that the job was done. In Normandy, in what attacking there was, accurate information was harder to obtain in the much more confined terrain, and briefing was consequently correspondingly poorer ; a platoon was accordingly at times sent to do the work proper to a company ; a company to do that of a battalion ; a battalion to do that of a Brigade. There had already been misfortunes and now there was to be almost disaster, and that was in the tragedy of the attack on Colombelles.

Colombelles may have been a village, but as far as our attacking troops were concerned it was a huge factory, with several immense chimneys. It lay a mile to the east of Caen, and it dominated the landscape. The 153 Brigade were sent to take it by night, and let it be known now that in the end it took two Divisions to carry out the job. The chimneys were said to be German O.P.s. In fact, the whole factory stood in such a position that it was one almighty O.P. The plan laid down for 153, to which the 7th Black Watch had been attached, was as follows. The 1st Gordons were to advance on the right flank from Longueval and attack the village of Colombelles ; the 5th Black Watch were to make for the north-east corner of the factory and hold a cross-roads there ; the 7th Black Watch were to pass through the 1st Gordons and occupy the factory area ; Divisional R.E.s were to destroy the chimneys. Then all troops were to withdraw. It was reckoned the job could be done in twenty-four hours.

At one o'clock on the morning of 11th July the attack began. The two right-hand companies of the 1st Gordons moved along the Orne towpath and entered the western corner of Colombelles village. But the other two companies on the left were held up by very heavy artillery, mortar, and small-arms fire. The 5th Black Watch reached their position at the cross-roads and occupied some houses there. At four o'clock in the morning orders came to withdraw the two left-hand Gordon companies, so that they might re-form and attack at dawn. But the

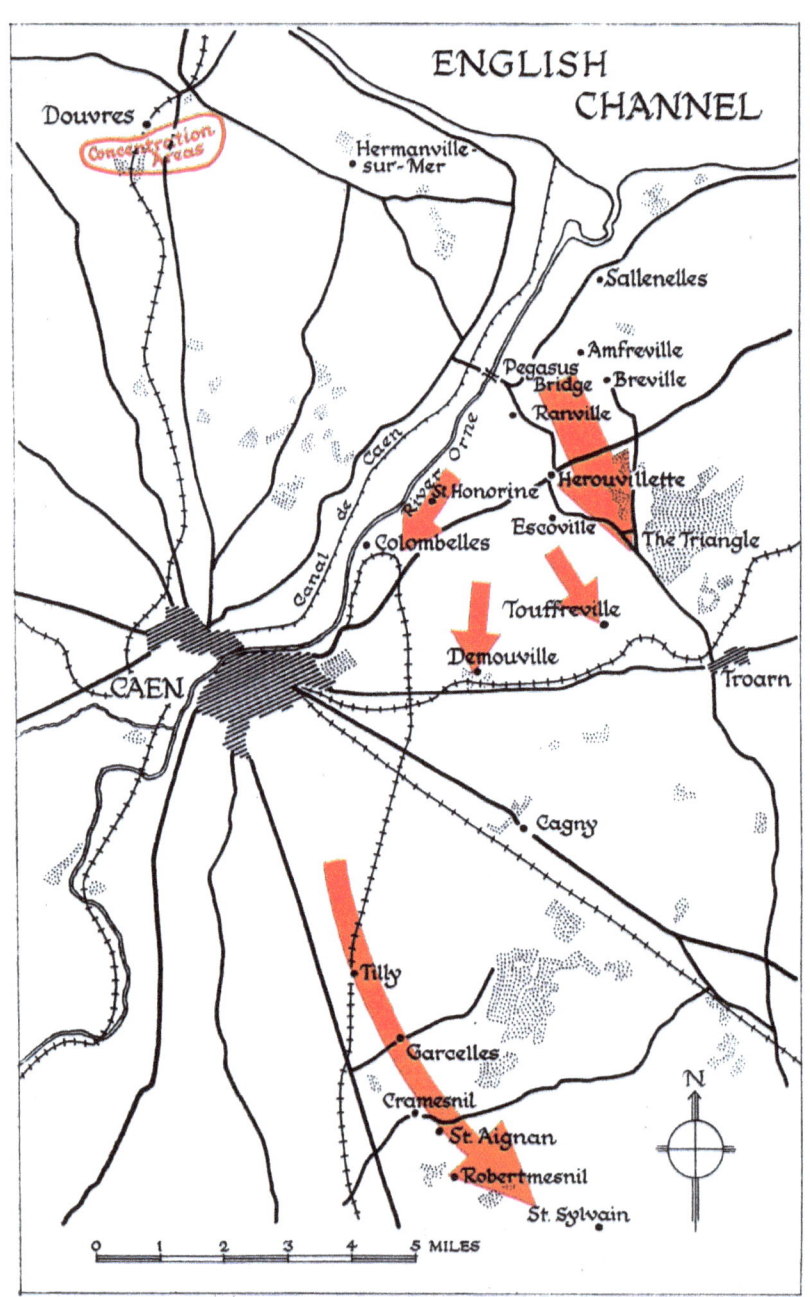

NORMANDY, D DAY, 6TH JUNE 1944. ST SYLVAIN, 9TH AUGUST 1944

enemy supplied quite enough light by means of flares, and the retiring Gordons suffered very severely. The Commanding Officer, Lt.-Col. Stevenson, was wounded, and Major the Hon. Cumming-Bruce took over the battalion.

The 5th Black Watch were now in a most unenviable position. The ground in their area was too hard for them to dig in, and the Germans from their excellent positions in the factory had them under direct observation and simply pasted them with mortar and artillery fire. The enemy on their right flank also poured in a devastating enfilading fire. Then, to complete the nerve-racking situation in which the Black Watch found themselves, at half-past six in the morning from the southern end of the factory three Mark VI. and two Mark IV. German heavy tanks waddled forward, and ten of our eleven Sherman tanks were knocked out. Our available tank weapons had no effect on the German Mark IV.s and Mark VI.s. At 8.30 in the morning orders came that all our infantry were to withdraw to their original positions in St Honorine and Longueval. Our men suffered very heavily during this operation, which was completed by 9.30. The 7th Black Watch were not asked to carry out their part of the attack, but had several casualties from shell-fire as they waited in the assembly area. They remained at Longueval until the 15th, where, as their historian tells, the only incident of note was the arrival of two Germans on a motor-cycle and side-car in the battalion's lines one morning. " They were taking rations to their forward troops, and did not seem to be unduly perturbed at their mistake."

But some battalions were still due for unhappy times in the bridgehead. The 5th Seaforth under Lt.-Col. John Walford had taken over from the 7th Black Watch on the edge of the Triangle, which was now in the hands of the Germans, on 9th July, and were now to have their first really offensive action in the bridgehead battle. The Triangle was isosceles, with a 300-yard base and two 800-yard sides, and was completely surrounded by woods. It pointed south, and the Germans held the south and east apexes, which were made by cross-roads. It was necessary to get them out. Some of them got themselves out, for a steady trickle of Poles and Russians, who had been forced into German uniforms, kept deserting and coming into our lines with at times very useful and accurate information as to opposing units, strong-points, etc.

On 18th July the 5th Seaforth attacked as part of the general operation " Goodwood," and were completely successful. A tremendous concentration of heavy bombers played the part of curtain-raisers, followed by a terrific artillery bombardment. The Seaforth had a new and strange companion in their onset—the Crocodile tank, which was a Churchill with a flame-thrower, and which might best be described as Lewis Carroll's " Jaberwock," which

> " With eyes of flame,
> Came whiffling through the tulgey wood
> And burbled as it came ! "

Spandaus just faded out before it.

Once the 5th Seaforth had done their job, the 2nd Seaforth and 5th Camerons carried on and smashed their way south past the Triangle apex down the Troarn road. They took their objectives, but had many casualties. The Camerons had then grimly to hold the gained area for ten days, when they were shelled literally every hour. Two acting C.O.s (Major H. W. Cairns and Major C. A. Noble) were wounded in succession, and, when the battalion finally was relieved, Lt.-Col. D. B. Lang took over command. The relieving troops were the 7th Black Watch, who had been as far south as Demouville, a small village just east of Caen. The 152 Brigade was completely relieved by 153, and crossed to the west of the Orne to a " rest " area round Gazelle, where the 5th Camerons spent their first couple of hours being shelled by a German long-range gun.

On the 21st Lt.-Col. J. E. G. " Scrappy " Hay, who had commanded the 1st Gordons at Alamein after Lt.-Col. Murray was wounded, and who was now commanding the 5/7th Gordons, was wounded in the head by shell-fire when crossing Pegasus Bridge. Colonel Hay had proved himself an efficient commandant of a Divisional Junior Leaders' Training School at Rothes in 1941, and had helped train many of the young officers and N.C.O.s of the 51st. Later in the desert his common-sense and leadership became equally apparent.

In the operation " Goodwood " very excellent work was done by the Division in removing mines so that the armour could get through, and Commander 1st Corps received a letter from Commander 8th Corps which contained the following :—

" In particular, will you please convey my thanks to the 51st Division for the wonderful work they have done in removing the minefields and so enabling our armour to pass through. It is greatly appreciated by everyone in this Corps."

But it was obvious that all was not well with the Division. They had long been accustomed to thinking of themselves as invincible, and second to none—British or German ; and now the proud Division, which had been acclaimed "most to be feared" by the Germans in the whole British Armies in 1917, had, almost for the first time since High Wood in 1916, met failure—not in the splendid isolation of St Valéry, but in the sight of other formations, formations too which had never aspired so high—" and that was the bitterest pill of all ! "

Deep down, the officers and men of the 51st knew what they still could do, and remembered what they themselves had done in battle after battle in the 8th Army, while other Divisions, now fighting, had been resting and training at home ; and so, as the inevitable price of failure in battle, changes in command were made.

CHAPTER VII.

THE BREAK-OUT

*" Brisemaid o cheile an cuibhreach ;
agus tilgeamaid dhinn an cuing."*
(Let us break their bonds asunder :
and cast away their cords from us.)
Psalm ii. 3.

*" Now is the winter of our discontent
Made glorious summer."*
SHAKESPEARE.

ON the 26th July there arrived at Divisional Headquarters a well-known figure with his arm in a sling, and soon, very soon, the Division came into its own once more.

The man with his arm in a sling was Major-General T. G. Rennie, who took over command of the Division at one o'clock on the afternoon of 26th July. Rennie, it will be remembered, had gone to France as G.S.O.2 with the Division in 1939, had been taken prisoner at St Valéry, had made a thrilling escape, had been given command of a battalion and later of a Brigade in the re-formed Highland Division, and had then gone to command the 3rd Division, which was the first British Division to make the Normandy beaches on D Day. He had been wounded once more on that occasion ; hence the sling. Now he was back, and with him back came once again all the enthusiasm and high spirit and confidence which had characterised the Division in the good days in Africa and Sicily. Rennie was a man who believed in his own star. As a Battalion Commander he *knew* that a Brigade waited for him, as a Brigadier he *had no doubt* that a Division was to come his way. Perhaps he even hoped that it would be the Highland Division. He was killed at the height of his successful soldiering, when he had seen that Division across the Rhine into Germany. An officer who had served under him both as Battalion Commander and as Brigadier wrote of him thus :—

" Such a record of important and difficult tasks successfully accomplished can seldom have been equalled by a soldier of General Rennie's age and seniority, and could never have been achieved had it not been for the outstanding qualities with which he was imbued and which were immediately apparent to all who served under him and who will never forget his tremendous determination and unshakable tenacity of purpose, together with the ability never to allow himself to become harassed or weighed down by difficulties. He had a great flair for doing things the right way, and, equally important, complete confidence in his ability to do so and in his own judgment. He knew at once what was essential and refused utterly to bother himself at all or take the slightest interest in anything which was not. He had great personal courage and was blessed with an optimistic outlook with which he was able to infect all who served under him. He could be completely ruthless when he considered it necessary to be so, but he always retained a great sense of humour and he realised to the full how vital cheerfulness is in war. He had a spontaneous—almost schoolboyish, in fact—sense of fun which manifested itself so often just at the right moment. He was the least pretentious and unassuming of Generals, and he was so approachable that everyone, however junior, felt completely at ease with him. The knowledge and experience which he had gained first hand, both as a Battalion Commander in battle in this war and later as a Brigadier, stood him in great stead as a Divisional Commander, and, coupled with his own outstanding ability and strength of character, enabled him to enjoy the complete confidence and implicit trust of everyone who served under him.

In spite of all his outstanding qualities, General Rennie was not, and certainly never pretended to be, in any way perfect. He had his faults like everyone else, and no appreciation could be really sincere which pretended otherwise. He could be intensely vague—sometimes, admittedly, intentionally—and at times complete understanding of what he really wanted done became almost an acquired art requiring an intimate knowledge of his own particular ways of working and thinking. His determination of mind and purpose sometimes appeared to cause him to be rather too inflexible, with the result that at times he was inclined to allow his first impressions to continue to influence him too long and after they had, sometimes even on his own admission, ceased to be applicable.

Sometimes as a hobby and as a diversion to military problems he painted, and even the results achieved would never convince him that his talents did not lie in this direction. The fact that his efforts to portray horses grazing in the Seine valley were not successful was, it was made quite apparent to everyone, more due to some fault on the part of the horses themselves or the Seine valley rather than the painter himself. These various idiosyncrasies only tended, however, to show that, notwithstanding all his brilliant qualities as a soldier, he was intensely human, and all who had the privilege of serving under him will long retain the happiest and most grateful memories of an outstanding commander and an inspiring leader."

It is well in " a time outworn " to " get free of the nets of wrong and right." It was well that, in the circumstances, the Division should get clear of the Corps of which it had formed part since the time of the Normandy landings. In the First World War in 1917 the Highland Division had felt particularly at home in the 17th [1] and 18th Corps, and never very comfortable in the 4th Corps, and here was history repeating itself.

In the opinion of many experienced regimental officers the operations they had been asked to carry out in France had, so far and for some reasons unknown to them, seemed to lack the skilful planning arrangements which had existed in the 30th Corps in North Africa and Sicily under General Oliver Leese and which were also found to exist in the 12th and 30th Corps when the Division served under these Corps later in the European Campaign, and also in the Canadian Corps under the command of which the Division was always happy, and was now to take part in operation " Totalise."

It may be profitable at this juncture, in order to understand the part played by the Division, to take a quick glance at the general picture in Normandy. By 12th June the Americans had captured Carentan, the beach-landings had been securely linked, and 326,000 men, 54,000 vehicles, and 104,000 tons of stores had been landed. By 29th June Cherbourg was in American hands, and all was set for the general attack southwards. By 3rd July the British were in Caen, and by the 10th thrusting Americans were in St Lo and were holding positions on the ground west of that town, positions, as Montgomery put it, " required for mounting the major break-out assault operations to the south." That break-out was launched from 25th to 27th July, and it heralded the American advance that was to cut off the Brittany peninsula. That advance was then to swing east to a line Le Mans–Alençon.

On 30th July the British 2nd Army drove south from the Caumont area, and, after the capture of Vire on 6th August, Montgomery issued his orders for an advance towards the Seine. The 1st Canadian Army was to do its utmost to reach Falaise, with its axis on the Lisieux–Rouen road ; the 2nd British Army was to drive for Argentan. The Allies were considerably assisted by the personal interference of Hitler, whose order read : " The Fuehrer has ordered the execution of a break-through to the coast to create the bases for the decisive operation against the Allied invasion front." By this order the German armour, very short of petrol, was wasted, and its destruction greatly helped the Allies towards the formation of the Falaise pocket.

[1] Then commanded by the father of Colonel Bernard Fergusson, historian of The Black Watch.

THE BREAK-OUT

But let us return to the 1st Canadian Army ready to launch their "Totalise" attack down the Caen–Falaise main road on 7th August.

The Commander of the 2nd Canadian Corps was an able soldier named Lt.-Gen. G. G. Simonds, who as a Divisional Commander had fought alongside the 51st in Sicily. He was a man of imagination and ideas, and he first of all set about destroying certain accepted principles. The first one was that tanks could not operate in darkness, because they were easy meat for enemy infantry. Simonds argued that there need not be complete darkness, and he proceeded to show how "artificial moonlight" could be employed. Searchlights were placed as near the start-lines as was compatible with a certain degree of safety, and their beams were directed on low-hanging clouds. The reflected light was invaluable to our advancing troops, but the nature of the reflection was such that it did not help the enemy to see their attacking opponents until the latter were close on them. Simonds also collected a large number of "Priest" self-propelling guns, and removed the guns. In the space thus left vacant in each vehicle it was found possible to pack in ten fully equipped infantrymen and to get them forward fresh and fit to any point where Bosche were to be found. Owing to the marsupial suggestion, the de-gunned carrier became known as a "Kangaroo." Simonds' next bright idea was that, if his advance column could ignore the German front line, and get in behind it, that front line could be cleaned up by succeeding columns, and the advance column would be saved the very heavy casualties which infantry invariably suffer from defensive shelling and mortar-fire during their approach on foot to enemy front-line positions in a large-scale attack such as this was to be.

So Simonds decided that his Corps would advance on a two-Brigade front on each side of the Caen–Falaise main road. The 154 Brigade was to advance on the left with a Canadian Brigade on the right. The 33rd Armoured Brigade, consisting of the Northamptonshire Yeomanry and the 144th and 148th R.A.C. Regiments, was to support 154 Brigade. This was the Division's first contact with this excellent armoured formation, and so successful was the co-operation in the forthcoming battle that the Armoured Brigade thereafter became the affiliated Tank Brigade of the Highland Division. The Brigade was commanded by Brigadier H. Scott of the Royals, a veteran of the North African Desert Campaigns, who had taken part in many of the great tank battles there, and it was soon found that he was a commander and leader after the Division's own heart, and that he had all the right ideas about infantry and tank co-operation. The three Tank Regiments of the Brigade were later affiliated to the three Infantry Brigades as follows :—

With 152 Brigade . 148 R.A.C. Regiment (Lt.-Col. R. Cracroft [R.T.R.]).
With 153 Brigade . 144 R.A.C. Regiment (Lt.-Col. A. Jolly [R.T.R.]).
With 154 Brigade . The Northamptonshire Yeomanry (Lt.-Col. D. Forster).

Soon after the Brigade joined the Division, Colonel Cracroft was killed, and the East Riding Yeomanry, commanded by Lt.-Col. T. C. Williamson (5th Royal Inniskilling Dragoon Guards), took the place of the 148th R.A.C. as the Regiment affiliated to 152 Brigade.

The Division and this Tank Brigade were to fight many battles together and the support given to the infantry by their armoured friends was always first-class. As will be seen later, the Northamptonshire Yeomanry was equipped with and trained in the use of amphibious tracked vehicles so that it could swim the Division across the Rhine. Complete confidence and understanding between infantry and their supporting tanks are very essential for success in battle. That confidence and that understanding were very quickly achieved with the 33rd Armoured Brigade and the closest possible liaison and co-operation existed between the two formations.

The 154 Brigade (under Brigadier Oliver) was to drive straight through the German front defensive line to a depth of some 5000 metres and do its best to occupy and hold the area Cramesnil–St Aignan–Garcelles–Secqueville. The 153 and 152 Brigades would then come up in that order, increase the size of the salient, and then two Armoured Divisions would follow and fan out to the south and south-east. The 154 was to advance in two columns : on the right the 7th Argylls (Lt.-Col. Meiklejohn) with the 144th R.A.C. were to make for Cramesnil ; behind them in the same column were to come the 7th Black Watch (Lt.-Col. Cathcart) with the 148th R.A.C., and they were to be responsible for Garcelles–Secqueville ; the left-hand column was to consist of the 1st Black Watch (Lt.-Col. Hopwood) and the Northamptonshire Yeomanry, who were to go for St Aignan. In all, 350 armoured track vehicles were employed by 154 Brigade in this attack. The ground to be covered in the advance was quite flat. A large proportion was under cultivation, but the crops were still uncut. The fields were divided by strips of woodland ; the roads were sunken with thick poplar hedges growing on the high embankments. The countryside was strewn with villages, which consisted usually of a kirk, surrounded by peasants' stone-houses, and round those apple-orchards, and thick hedges, sometimes of bramble, sometimes of poplar.

This was to be a crucial battle—crucial from the point of view of bringing to an end the Caen period of the Normandy Campaign and the final closing of the Falaise Gap, and crucial from the point of view of the Division itself, since a successful offensive battle was vital to restore both its own confidence and the confidence of the higher command in its ability to live up to its 8th Army reputation. Very careful planning and preparations were made, including a full-dress rehearsal at night with all the armoured and tracked vehicles which were to take part in the Brigade attack.

On 7th August General Rennie sent out a message to be read to all troops. In it he wrote :—

" The Highland Division is about to take part in a battle under command of the 2nd Canadian Corps. This may well prove to be the decisive battle in France. The Division has an enterprising part to play, well suited to its particular characteristics. The battle also bears a strong resemblance to some of those great battles in North Africa in which the Division added laurels to its reputation of the last war. In Africa we fought side by side with Australians and New Zealanders. Now we are with Canadians and it is a coincidence that during the closing stages of the Great War we were also fighting beside a Canadian Corps.[1] The Highland Division fought at El Alamein, which great victory was the turning-point in our fortunes. Now we are to take part in what may be the decisive battle of France. The success of the battle depends on the determination and offensive spirit of every Commander and Soldier in the Division and in the 33rd Armoured Brigade and other units with the Division. Good luck to every one of you."

If ever a message contained sound battle psychology, that one did. Let it be remembered that there were, even in high places, those who were at that time whispering that the Highland Division was now " punch drunk "—it had, it was said, fought too many battles since Alamein. It had been admittedly a very great fighting Division, but now its star had waned. It now contained, so it was said, too many men who had crossed the starting-line once too often.

Rennie knew full well of this undercurrent of talk, and that knowledge underlies what is written in his message, with its emphasis on the particular comradeship of the Highlanders with Dominion troops, the

[1] Near Valenciennes in October 1918.

reminder of the glories of 1916-18, and of Alamein and Akarit, fought alongside Australian, New Zealand, and Indian troops.

Steeped in the tradition of a very great regiment of the Highland Brigade, Rennie knew of what all his famous fighting regiments were capable, and what they had done under Wolfe and Wellington, under Colin Campbell and Harper. With all the concentration of a brain trained to the selection of essentials and to decision, the Divisional Commander made absolutely sure that for this battle, so critical in the fortunes of the 51st, his Division would be launched to a fair start.

Montgomery's message of 11th August, as always a very shrewd one, contained the following :—

"We have been through some difficult times since D Day, and, on occasions, great patience and confidence were necessary if we were not to falter. When the struggle was in its most critical stage there were some who had doubts as to whether we would win through, but you and I had no doubts—not one ; we knew that so long as we did our duty all would be well ; and to-day, all is well. What a change has come about in the last few weeks. The whole of the Cherbourg peninsula is in our hands, and most of Brittany also ; our armies are moving relentlessly eastwards into France ; many hundreds of towns and villages have been liberated. The prisoners taken are well over 100,000 and great quantities of enemy equipment and war material have been captured or destroyed. And, best of all, the great bulk of the German forces in N.W. Europe are in a bad way ; we are round behind them in many places, and it is possible that some of them will not get away. They will fight hard to avoid disaster ; that we know. But let each one of us make a tremendous effort to write off this powerful German force ; it has caused us no small trouble during the last two months ; let us finish with it, once and for all, and so hasten the end of the war."

Allied bombers had put down a huge amount of explosive on the flanks of the area which was to be attacked, and at half-past two in the morning of 7th August, in the glow of "artificial moonlight," the columns moved forward with Bofors firing along the flanks so that direction could be kept, and with the artillery firing green smoke on the objectives. Each column advanced four vehicles abreast, with some twenty yards between each line of vehicles, some "Flail" tanks moving near the head of each column in order to beat a way through any minefields which might be encountered. The routes from the forming-up area to the start-line had been lit by lamps (green right, amber left) placed on five-foot stakes. The Argylls (Lt.-Col. Meiklejohn) were unlucky to lose, in a crater about half-way to their objectives,

THE BREAK-OUT

the tanks containing the navigators, and also came in for some hand-grenade throwing. One grenade landed in a Kangaroo, but Private Jarvis of H.Q. Company (Signals) promptly picked it up and threw it back. The crossing of a railway caused further disturbance in the column, but at four in the morning the battalion debussed, and, despite heavy ground mist, the companies reached their objectives. " A " Company had the toughest time, but got there all right. Major T. R. Lorrbond of the 144th R.A.C. was killed in his tank after leading his command in a most fearless manner. As one of his own people wrote of him : " The death of Major Lorrbond was a severe blow to the regiment. No one was more loved and respected by officers and men alike, and his superb leadership during this action had a direct bearing on the success of the operation."

The 1st Black Watch (Lt.-Col. Hopwood) also had hold-ups during their advance, due to sunken roads with high embankments. The only enemy opposition came from a self-propelled gun, which knocked out two Kangaroos. But the Black Watch, having advanced in their carriers right through the cornfields up to St Aignan, debussed at exactly the place that had been arranged on the map, formed up, and launched their attack, all according to plan and as had been rehearsed and practised beforehand. By six o'clock all objectives had been taken, and the battalion proceeded to dig in. One anti-tank gunner of the 42nd distinguished himself by dashing into a house where a Spandau had opened fire and killing the crew manning the enemy gun. The 7th Black Watch (Lt.-Col. Cathcart) also had trouble with an anti-tank gun, but reached their debussing area up to time, and took their objectives after some severe fighting, during which Lieutenant McAllister, who had accounted for several machine-gun posts, lost his life. Daylight arrived a bit early, with the result that mortaring took its toll of the battalion before they were properly dug in.

But it was the 1st Black Watch who had to bear the brunt of the Bosche counter-offensive, and to the discomfort caused by heavy German artillery and mortar fire was added the fact that American bombing planes came over and dropped some of their bombs in the battalion area, killing two of " B " Company's signallers. Then the Germans counter-attacked with infantry and tanks, but the Northamptonshire Yeomanry (Lt.-Col. Forster) put up a splendid show, advancing in great style and knocking out four Tiger and seven Mark IV. tanks. All three Tank Regiments of the 33rd Armoured

Brigade had given first-class support to the infantry, and the Jocks, naturally inclined to be critical of other arms, were already firm supporters of those armoured units. The Divisional Artillery (Brigadier Shiel) also put up an excellent defensive barrage.

The Polish Division had not too satisfactory an experience. They passed through the Black Watch making for Robertmesnil, but one hour later they came back and took up a position behind our lines. The recorder of this particular 42nd action points out that " it should be borne in mind that, owing to a lack of reinforcements, the Battalion had (as had many battalions at Akarit) been reorganised on a three-company basis since 7th August. On 16th August three officers and ninety-seven men of the Oxford and Bucks. Light Infantry were posted to the Battalion."

The job of Cassels' 152 Brigade was to clear up the enemy left in the front line through which 154 had passed. It was thought that this would be relatively simple, since it was presumed that the Germans in that front line, knowing that British armour and infantry were in full action *behind them*, would clear out as soon as they could. But the enemy stayed to fight, and very tough they proved, especially in the village of Tilly-la-Campagne. The 2nd Seaforth were to make the initial attack on Tilly, but so stubborn were the defenders that a company of the 5th Seaforth were sent up to reinforce the 78th. That company ("D") also found themselves very much up against it, and their C.O., Grant Murray, was killed along with ten of his men. Captain Murray was found lying in front of the German defensive line with the dead of No. 17 Platoon round about him. They had obviously had a fierce hand-to-hand struggle with the enemy, for one or two bodies were found actually in the German line with dead Bosche beside them. When daylight came in, a squadron of tanks was sent back from 154 Brigade to attack Tilly from the rear. Twice they drove their way through the village, and on the second journey made prisoners of one German officer and some thirty of the 1055th Infantry Regiment. Meanwhile the 5th Camerons had advanced, through fields of wheat, where many snipers were concealed, on the village of Lorquichon, which they captured without difficulty and with the loss of only seven men killed. They then moved through the wood to the village of Poussy, some two miles farther south, where they dug in.

The 153 Brigade provided the firm base for "Totalise" and on 8th August the 1st Gordons (Lt.-Col. Cumming-Bruce) were taken up to the Garcelles–Secqueville area in Kangaroos. From that point the battalion attacked Secqueville-la-Campagne with very satisfactory results, two German officers and ninety other ranks being taken prisoner. Lieutenant Mitchell was seriously wounded—he had to have an arm cut away with a jack-knife—but otherwise casualties were very light. The 5/7th Gordons were in action in the woods west of Conteville. The 5th Black Watch had an adventurous start. A heavy bomber dropped his load all round about the two jeeps, in which were the C.O., the adjutant, and R.A.P. personnel. All were blown out of the transport vehicles, but none of the officers was wounded. The battalion advanced and occupied the village of Soliers.

None had been more thankful to get out of the Orne bridgehead woods than the machine-gunners of the 1/7th Middlesex. There they had been able to indulge in only very close-range shooting, but now in that first break-out targets were excellent, and the Middlesex expended on them 250 bombs from each of their mortars and 44 belts from each of their machine-guns.

So on 9th August the Highland Division were once again able to report, as they had so often reported before in battle, that they had taken all their objectives in the first phase of the break-out : and now for the road to Lisieux and the east. The woods round the village of St Sylvain, which had been captured by the Polish Armoured Division and were being held by the 5th Black Watch and 1st Gordons, were " hotching " with Huns, and 154 Brigade was ordered to clear them. The 7th Argylls and 1st Black Watch were chosen for the venture. The two battalions passed through the 7th Black Watch positions near Robertmesnil. The Argylls moved forward first in a " silent " night attack. They passed through St Sylvain and at once ran into very intensive machine-gun fire from three sides. They, however, continued to advance, and next day were subjected to several very heavy counter-attacks. The 1st Black Watch had much the same kind of experience, and as Bernard Fergusson writes [1] : " In the memory of the 1st Battalion the St Sylvain position is associated with one, Private Moncrieffe, a signaller whose job it was to maintain the telephone lines. He bicycled cheerfully about them, ignoring the fire and accompanied by a doll, small, slender and attractive, which was lashed uncomfortably to the cross-bar of his machine, pointing one leg disdainfully at the sky. Moncrieffe was decorated for his performance during these days at

[1] See footnote, page 136.

St Sylvain, but was unfortunately killed in similar circumstances outside Le Havre later on."

The positions of the Argylls and Black Watch was also made more uncomfortable by the failure of the Polish Armoured Division to advance through the Scots and fan out to the east. A German counter-attack from the south-west destroyed a number of Polish tanks, and the remainder withdrew. Two days later the Poles were replaced by the 10th Canadian Armoured Car Regiment, and the 2nd Derbyshire Yeomanry also came up to strengthen our offensive. The same night the 7th Black Watch relieved the Argylls, and the 5/7th Gordons improved the situation by clearing a ridge to the left front, from which the enemy had been very troublesome. In general, the Canadian tanks had been having a bad time. One gallant regiment lost its C.O. and all its squadron commanders, and in all fifty-three of sixty-five tanks had been knocked out.

It was on that same day (12th August) that news arrived that the ever-cheerful and highly experienced Brigadier, "Nap" Murray (Camerons), had been given command of a Division in Italy, where he was destined still further to enhance his reputation. Badly wounded at Alamein when commanding the 1st Gordons, Murray had led 153 Brigade right from the invasion of Sicily, and the Division was indeed sorry to see him go.[1] He was succeeded by Roddy Sinclair of the Gordons, later to be Earl of Caithness, who had commanded a battalion in the 15th (Scottish) Division.

Another change had previously taken place in 153 Brigade: Lt.-Col. "Chick" Thomson, who had been with the Black Watch in the 1939 adventure in France, and who had commanded the 5th Battalion, after Thomas Rennie, in every battle right through Africa, Sicily and Normandy, had gone home for a well-earned rest and to take over the 10th Black Watch. He had been succeeded by his great friend, Lt.-Col. "Bill" Bradford.

It was during this period that, for some reason unknown to the Highlanders, liaison between the infantry and Bomber Command seemed to fail. In warfare of quick movement unhappy episodes of this nature are inevitable, but now for a time they exceeded what the troops considered were fair risks! On 15th August, for example, Allied bombers actually bombed the gun-lines behind 154 Brigade

---

[1] Lt.-Col. Cumming-Bruce (now Lord Thurlow) acted as Brigadier for a few days, and during that same period Major Lindsay commanded the 1st Gordons.

Headquarters, and the 1st Gordons lost thirteen of their sixteen " A " Echelon trucks through this same extraordinary mishap. Time and again our front-line infantry were bombed from our own planes and were also attacked by fighters. On the 18th August Typhoons kept strafing the road behind our lines and the Divisional General had a narrow escape. They hit Brigadier Cassels' headquarters, and his Brigade Major, John Thornton (Seaforth), was killed.

But the advance went on with 153 Brigade to the left of the line. The 1st Gordons took the village of Doux Marais and moved into the château at St Marie-aux-Anglais, a village with a sixteenth-century tower, held by the English in the Maid's day. On the 1st Gordons' left came their 5/7th Battalion. They had had some stiff fighting in the St Sylvain woods, where Sergeant Briley of " D " Company particularly distinguished himself. The Company Commander had been wounded, 50 per cent of the company were casualties, and Briley took over command and reorganised the remainder into a very effective fighting unit. The Battalion, in a combined action with the 5th Black Watch, made a satisfactory crossing of the River Dives.[1] The 1st Gordons then made a most successful attack on the village of St Maclou. In pitch darkness they marched fifteen miles on the night of 16th-17th August, landed slap-bang on their objective, and completely surprised the enemy, of whom they killed and captured a considerable number. Captain Jamieson came across a Bosche observation-post, where he found a telephone connected to a German headquarters. He informed the Hun at the other end, in German, that they should come out with their hands up, since the " English swine " had arrived. The Germans thought this an immense joke, and received it with loud laughter. The demand was again made ; this time over the telephone came sounds of hurried departure, and then the line went dead. Some people took objection to Captain Jamieson's phrase. They thought he should have said " Scottish swine," and it has been suggested that, if Wimberley had been in command, he might have been severely reprimanded.

The Germans had not evacuated the French civilians from St Maclou, so this was the first place since the break-out that a unit of the Division was welcomed by the local French people. The 1st Gordons had taken this place without any preliminary shelling or bombing, and for that reason the local welcome was all the more enthusiastic. But there was little time for rejoicing. That same night (18th August) the

[1] See below, page 162.

5/7th Gordons moved to the attack on Grandchamp,[1] on the bank of the Vie River, and on the way up that very gallant soldier, Lt.-Col. Blair Imrie of Lunan, who had come to command the Battalion from the 5th Black Watch, was killed. The attack was quite successful, the River Vie was crossed, and a bridgehead formed.

On the 22nd the Battalion entered Lisieux, where, against very strong opposition, " D " Company (a practically new company from the East Lancs.) fought with great distinction. The enemy contested each street, each square, each house. The Gordons drove them out in bitter hand-to-hand fighting. A patrol went to the railway line, which was held by S.S. troops. When they reached their objective the enemy opened at point-blank range with Spandaus and grenades. Under intense fire half the patrol gained the cover of a ruined house. The German fire then increased in violence, and movement seemed quite impossible, when Private Redican of " C " Company, entirely on his own initiative, leaped into the open, and, defying the hail of bullets, commenced firing at the enemy from the hip, burst for burst. Hit in both legs, Redican fell to the ground, but reloaded and continued to fire despite great pain. His action drew the enemy's attention to him and enabled the remainder of his platoon to move to a flank and neutralise the enemy's fire. The records of the period give particular notice to the work of the stretcher-bearers under Sergeant Watt. During the break-out period the 5/7th Gordons had been responsible for some 500 prisoners. They had suffered 155 casualties.

On 14th August the 5th Black Watch, under temporary command of 154 Brigade, had made a successful attack on La Bû-sur-Rouvres and took some 200 prisoners. They were greatly assisted by some Canadian infantry and tanks which had got lost, but, seeing there was good work to be done where they were, the Canadians settled down to do it with the Black Watch. On the 16th the Battalion moved to Percy and enjoyed the pears and peaches left by the 1st Gordons. Next day they moved forward to St Pierre, crossed the River Dives into the 154 bridgehead, and then advanced north parallel to the enemy's lines to contact with the 1st Gordons at Ecajeul. Much difficulty was caused by French refugees who were sleeping on the sides of the roads and in abandoned German dug-outs. On the 18th the Battalion was required to take part in an operation with the 5/7th Gordons designed to make a bridgehead over the Vie River and to

[1] For details of this action, see below, page 163.

occupy a horseshoe feature about three-quarters of a mile on the north side of the river, which was held in strength and which overlooked the river itself. The plan was that the 5/7th Gordons, who were already holding the river line, were to form a short bridgehead to enable the one and only bridge at this point, which had been destroyed, to be reconstructed and so enable the Black Watch to pass through and to seize the high ground. The early part of the operation went off reasonably well, and the Gordons, although having a difficult passage, made their crossing and attempted to reconstruct the bridge. This latter part of the operation had to be done under fire and the 5/7th suffered casualties as a result.

At about midnight the bridge was in condition to take infantry but not vehicles, and the Acting Brigadier of 153 (Lt.-Col. Cumming-Bruce) decided to launch the 5th Black Watch on its part of the operation, so that it might try to occupy the high ground before first light. The first two companies of the Black Watch set out and appeared to be making some progress when Battalion Headquarters, which were situated about quarter of a mile on the south side of the river, came under extremely heavy shell-fire. For a short time chaos reigned there. Lt.-Col. Bradford was wounded; Captain Forfar, the Signals Officer, Captain Home, the Carrier Officer, Major Ken Aitken, the Supporting Battery Commander, and practically all the signallers were killed, and Major Dunn and R.S.M. Palmer were the only two executives left to carry on the operation at Headquarters. They were entirely without communications—either with the companies, with Brigade, or with the guns—as all wireless sets had been destroyed. To make matters worse, the head of " A " Echelon transport column had come on the scene and vehicles were being damaged by shell-fire. Major Dunn decided that, the leading two companies having been launched, the operation must go on, otherwise those companies would be cut off. At this juncture the Commanding Officer of the 5/7th Gordons, Lt.-Col. Hugh Blair Imrie, was killed and his Second-in-Command was not fully aware of the position across the river. Work was still proceeding on the bridge, and the Gordons, although in great trouble, announced that they thought the bridge could take transport. The two remaining companies of the Black Watch were then called forward and pushed over the river. By first light the leading two companies were fighting their way on to the horseshoe feature. A number of casualties were suffered and the 5th was now strung out on a fairly long and tenuous line of communication.

It was not possible to get any transport forward until first light and thereafter attempts were made to get a few vehicles to the forward companies with reserve ammunition and to collect casualties. These vehicles had to run the gauntlet of small-arms fire on a very open piece of road north of the river, but three or four eventually got through. The two leading companies of the Black Watch managed to get themselves established on the ridge but could make no progress over it.

At this stage Lt.-Col. Bradford, who had been sufficiently bandaged, took over command, although he was suffering considerable pain. He called up a troop of tanks, and, although these were reluctant to go out into the open, Bradford actually sat on top of one of them and insisted on its driver driving right up into the forward position, where it established itself and brought confidence to the troops on the ground. The position gradually resolved itself and the Battalion were comfortably established at about midday on the horseshoe feature. The 1st Gordons were then called up and under the covering fire of the Black Watch took up the position on the left flank of the horseshoe feature. It was as the Battalion were advancing into their position that Major Grant, who had distinguished himself in Africa and Sicily, was killed. Both Battalions repulsed counter-attacks during the day, and by nightfall the horseshoe feature was firmly held. Communications had been re-established and new gunner liaison fixed.

A message from the Divisional General read: " Well done, 5th Black Watch! "

The Battalion took over from the 5/7th Gordons in Lisieux two days later. On 26th August a letter was received by the Commanding Officer from Lt.-Col. Cumming-Bruce (1st Gordons), who had been acting as Brigade Commander, from which the following is an extract: " The two major attacks at Bretteville (Ecajeul) and Grandchamp, when you ' achieved the impossible,' are to my mind the two finest feats that a Battalion has ever accomplished in my own experience."

A Divisional Engineer has left a valuable note on the crossing of the Vie. " The line of the River Vie was perhaps the trickiest of the minor obstacles so far met. The development of the now familiar ' hook ' took one axis considerably to the south to the vicinity of Grandchamp, where 153 Brigade intended to form a bridgehead and push a curving hook to the main axis beyond St Julien. The countryside was extremely open and extremely unsuited for bringing forward bridging equipment. The bridgehead was, from the Engineer point of view, small to the extent of being almost negligible. A daring daylight reconnaissance by Lieutenant O. H. Watkins of the 276th Field Company produced information that a satisfactory crossing was possible using Folding Boat Equipment, and the suggestion was duly adopted. But even then, the original intention of constructing the crossing to take Class 9 loads by using trestles and no boats proved impossible, and only by determined and skilful work was the equipment made to fit together to produce a Class 5 bridge [1] using two half-floating bays. It is interesting to note that this bridge was reported sunk by shrapnel the following day, just as the original Class 9 plan was being completed. On salvaging the equipment, however, it came to light that the cause of the trouble had not been enemy action at all, but overloading of the bridge by our own vehicles, no doubt by some misguided person or persons, so frequently met with, who consider that load restrictions are a fad of the sappers used to make things even more difficult."

After crossing the River Vie and fighting alongside the 5th Black Watch, the 1st Gordons on 21st August occupied a village, La Forge Vallée, the largest buildings in which were a stud-farm and training establishment. But the Acting Brigadier had been there before them, and had left a note on the training establishment door: "This place belongs to an Englishman. Respect it." The Englishman concerned was a man called Sam Ambler, and later on the 1st Gordons found him busy in his underground cavern, when he told them that he had his race-horses hidden away in small farms. On the 23rd the 1st Gordons reached Lisieux and were ordered to advance to some high ground beyond the town, and one company had forty casualties. Here the Highlanders' old friends, the 7th Armoured Division, came up and cleared the ridge, and the 1st Gordons moved to an area south-east of Lisieux, where Lt.-Col. Cumming-Bruce again took over command.

In 152 Brigade the 5th Seaforth (Lt.-Col. Walford) on 14th August began their advance towards Lisieux and had their first hold-up at Favières, with the 78th on their right. Favières was on a high plateau commanding considerable ground to the east. By 9 P.M. on the 15th the 5th Seaforth had established their position. Next day they moved through St Pierre-sur-Dives, which was held by the 5th Camerons, and thence in troop-carrying vehicles along the main Lisieux road to about

[1] A Class 5 bridge took loads up to five tons.

a mile short of the River Vie. And then the usual trouble began. The Camerons had actually had to stop advancing because Spitfires had knocked out every wireless vehicle on their establishment. Now Lightnings began to strafe the Seaforth and kept doing it time and again. Nevertheless, let the civilian reader remember that, had the Division not had the air superiority they were enjoying, strafings by hostile planes would certainly have been very much worse.

The 5th Seaforth crossed the Vie at St Julien-le-Fauçon. They had many days of hard fighting with determined German rearguards, and on one occasion had an unexpected breakfast party, when, as the water for the tea was coming to the boil, they were suddenly attacked by the enemy. But the East Riding Tanks invited themselves as well, and soon the unwelcome visitors were either dead or prisoners. In their advance into St Pierre-des-Ifs the Seaforth had, as a guide, the seventy-year-old village flesher. Then, dead-beat physically but in the best of spirits, they reached the Lisieux milestone of their journey on the 22nd.

When the 5th Camerons (Lt.-Col. D. Lang) left St Pierre on 18th August they were taken in carriers to within a mile of St Julien-le-Fauçon, where, supported by Shermans of the East Riding Yeomanry, they had as their main purpose of attack the crossings of the Vie. " The evening ended," writes one of them, " with a final attack by a Lightning formation which bombed and strafed the whole area. Next day the Air Force left us alone." On the 20th the Camerons crossed the Vie and then attacked southwards parallel to the main Lisieux road, finally digging in for the night at St Fressard-le-Chère. Next day they moved to St Pierre-des-Ifs, where they remained until 26th August. The 78th had fought from the Vie crossing on the 5th Camerons' left, and on the 28th they were established on a spur overlooking Lisieux.

The 154 Brigade's advance from La Bû-sur-Rouvres was made on a system devised in Sicily. That system was to move forward on a one-battalion front, bringing up the other two battalions in transport. When the leading battalion had completed its task, the next battalion took over, with the result that the attacking unit was always fresh for the fray. Should the leading battalion at any time be held up, then an alternative line of advance was adopted by the next battalion, so that the enemy strong-point could be outflanked. The 7th Black Watch led the Brigade advance on 17th August towards St Pierre-sur-Dives. The river was crossed successfully and the Battalion

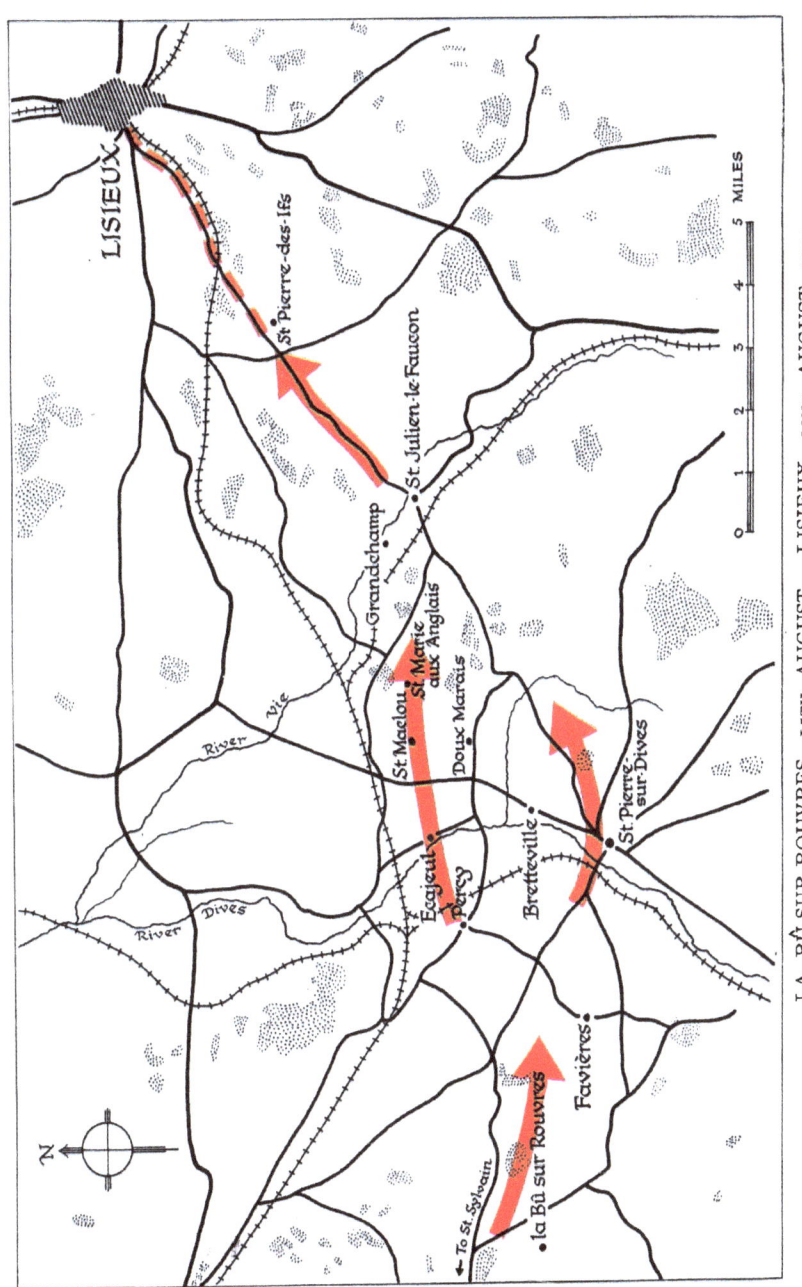

LA BÛ-SUR-ROUVRES, 15TH AUGUST. LISIEUX, 22ND AUGUST 1944

proceeded to attack the high ground at Le Godet with the tanks of the 1st Squadron Northamptonshire Yeomanry in support. Unfortunately, in crossing the open ground in front of the objective, ten of the tanks were knocked out by accurate fire from opposing enemy tanks. An attack in the darkness by the infantry came up against strong opposition.

In the morning the 7th Black Watch renewed their assault and at last took their objectives, when the 7th Argylls passed through them and continued the advance, their objective being the cross-roads about a mile short of St Julien. They had not gone very far when they came under heavy mortar-fire, and the old Triangle trouble of mortars bursting among thick foliage and branches was with them again. When they got out on the open road they were under direct observation from the high ground above St Julien, and the C.O., Lt.-Col. Meiklejohn, was wounded in both legs; two Company Commanders were also wounded. But the objective was finally reached, although at the cost of two officers killed and seven wounded, eighteen other ranks killed and fifty wounded.

Next day the 1st Black Watch took over the advance, their objective being St Julien. It was thought possible that the enemy had gone, and a patrol, led by Sergeant Stevenson, entered the town. They had one small scrap in which they were successful, and they got back word to Lt.-Col. Hopwood that all was clear. Major I. S. Douglas, who had fought with the Division since Alamein and who was now Second-in-Command, was seriously wounded. The Battalion occupied St Julien and remained there till 21st August, when they passed through the 7th Battalion, who had moved beyond the La Corne cross-roads, and occupied their objective without casualties. On 25th August the Brigade Group moved to a concentration area at Marolles, east of Lisieux, where Lt.-Col. David Nicoll (Black Watch) took over command of the 7th Argylls.

The final mopping-up of Lisieux on 23rd August brought to a conclusion what has been officially described as undoubtedly one of the most strenuous periods of continuous fighting which the Highland Division had experienced in the course of both World Wars. Since the night of 7th August the Division had fought without respite for seventeen days against a courageous and determined enemy, who took every advantage of terrain to carry on rearguard actions across thirty miles of country. Every unit of the Division fought at least four main

THE BREAK-OUT

actions, in which splendid support was given by all other arms of the Division, by 33rd Armoured Brigade, by Corps Artillery, and by other units which came under command. During this advance the Division took over 1600 prisoners.

The gallantry and efficiency of the Divisional Sappers is well exemplified in their final bridging of a wide stream just outside Lisieux. During the night of 22nd August the 275th Field Company were building a 100-foot Bailey bridge in rain and darkness and the showering of enemy shells. Morning found only a small part of the bridge complete, and the company "all in." The 274th Field Company carried on with the job, and completed the bridge. Lieutenant Carter, who had been in charge, was killed by shell-fire while resting beside his truck on return to camp. The bridge was named Carter Bridge.

The 2nd Derbyshire Yeomanry's (Lt.-Col. Serocold) work during the whole advance was invaluable, and many individual acts of courage and initiative were performed by members of the regiment. On 15th August Trooper Bake of "C" Squadron was driving his troop leader's armoured car, when that car was set on fire by a direct hit from an enemy shell, which wounded the officer. Bake, with the assistance of the operator, lifted the officer out of the blazing car and hid him in a culvert. Bake then set out for help. He was unarmed. He encountered two Germans in a slit trench. He jumped on them, made them prisoners, and got hold of a rifle. He got back through the enemy lines to his own Squadron, and later brought forward an armoured car troop and rescued the wounded officer and the operator.

The very speed of the Division's forward movement does much to explain the tragic results of the R.A.F. and American Air Force bombing of our troops. But it is very satisfactory to be able to record that the infantry all along "thought the world of their gunners."

Montgomery's words at this point in the campaign were :—

"On the 11th of August I spoke to the officers and men of the Allied Armies in north-west France. I said we must 'write off' the powerful German force that was causing us so much trouble ; we must finish it, once and for all, and so hasten the end of the war. And to-day, ten days later, it has been done. The German armies in north-west France have suffered a decisive defeat ; the destruction of enemy personnel and equipment in and about the so-called 'Normandy pocket' has been terrific, and it is still going on ; any enemy units that manage to get away will not be in a fit condition to fight again for months ; there are still many surprises in store for the fleeing remnants. The victory has been definite, complete, and decisive. . . .

"The victory in north-west France, south of the Seine, marks the beginning of the end of German military domination of France. Much still remains to be done, but it will now be done the more easily.

"And what next? Having brought disaster to the German forces in north-west France, we must now complete the destruction of such of his forces as are still available to be destroyed. After knowing what has happened to their armies in north-west France, it is unlikely that these forces will now come to us; so we will go to them. The end of the war is in sight; let us finish off the business in record time."

Best of all, and reminiscent once again of Africa and Sicily, General Rennie received the following message from General Crerar, G.O.C.-in-C. 1st Canadian Army, through Commander 1st Corps :—

"Please congratulate Highland Division on fine aggressive work. The 51st of this War is showing the same unbeatable spirit which the Canadians got to know and admire in 1918." [1]

The following reply was sent by General Rennie :—

"Thank you very much for your message. I am glad you consider the Highland Division is living up to the reputation it earned during the Great War. We, of the 51st, are proud to be in your Canadian Army and to be fighting side by side with Canadians. We could wish for no better comrades in battle."

General Rennie's own message to his Division was as follows :—

"In its advance from TILLY to LISIEUX, the Highland Division has played a major part in the Battle of France. During that advance the Division for fifteen days fought continuously in its most intensive period of fighting in this war. We sustained some 1761 casualties but took over 1600 prisoners, in addition to killing and wounding a very large number of Germans and to overrunning great quantities of German equipment.

"The Canadian Army Commander has congratulated the Division on its 'fine aggressive work,' and it is to that aggressive work that we owe our success. The German is no good when his tail is down, and we undoubtedly kept it down. Great scope for revenge lies ahead both SOUTH and NORTH of the River Seine. Remember that on the 12th of June 1940 a portion of the Highland Division, including its Headquarters, 152 Brigade and 153 Brigade, were captured by a large German force at ST VALÉRY-EN-CAUX, due NORTH

---

[1] On 29th March 1918, after the British retreat, when the 51st was transferred from 3rd to 1st Army, General Byng sent the Highlanders a message, in which he wrote of the Division's "splendid conduct during the stage of the great battle which is just completed. By their devotion and courage they have broken up overwhelming attacks and prevented the enemy gaining his object—namely, a decisive victory."

from our present position. That magnificent Division was sacrificed in a last effort to keep the French in the war. True to Highland tradition, the Division remained to the last with the remnants of our French Allies, although it was within its capacity to withdraw and embark at LE HAVRE.

"The Division drew on to ST VALÉRY the German 4th Corps of four Divisions, a Panzer and a Motor Division, in all six Divisions, and thereby diverted this force from harassing the withdrawal of other British troops on LE HAVRE and CHERBOURG.

"General Victor Fortune ordered the surrender of the Division at ST VALÉRY when it had run out of ammunition and food and when all prospects of evacuation, which had been carefully planned by him, had failed.

"The discipline of that Division remained up to Highland Division standard to the last. I was there, so I know.

"We of the Highland Division must not rest till we have freed our kith and kin of the ST VALÉRY Highland Division and avenged their misfortune to the full."

CHAPTER VIII.

THE RETURN

" Cuimhnich air na daoine bho 'n d' thainig thu."
(Remember those you come from.)

" Sweet sounds the ancient pibroch
O'er mountain, loch, and glade,
But the sweetest of all music
The pipes at Lucknow played."
(*From* J. G. WHITTIER'S Poem commemorating the
Relief of Lucknow by the Highlanders in 1858.)

AFTER Lisieux the majority of the units of the Highland Division had a few days' rest—and they needed it. The Germans had taken a terrific pounding, and the Division could claim seventeen days of undiluted victory. But it was the end of a round, and there had to be a short breathing-space. The Germans were in a bad way. The Falaise pocket had meant tremendous losses to them, and as a result their High Command had decided on a complete withdrawal from France and Belgium, and a retiral to the defence of positions in Holland and behind the old Siegfried Line. The Canadian and British troops had turned north towards the upper reaches of the Seine; the Americans were already across that river and coming in on Paris from both west and east. So back the Germans went; but, in order to deny the Allies easy access to the western harbours on the European mainland for reinforcements of men and equipment, they left garrisons in all the larger Channel and west coast ports from Le Havre eastwards. The Highland Division's next job was to cross the Seine, and, still under Canadian command, to cut off the Le Havre Peninsula, and after occupying St Valéry-en-Caux, where their predecessors had so gallantly fought, to move down and capture that harbour of Le Havre whence 154 Brigade had embarked in the sad days of 1940.

So the Highland Division moved from Lisieux practically due east by way of St Georges-du-Vievre, then north-east to Bourg Achard, and so into a haugh on one of the Seine loops, which river the Division crossed at Duclair and Mauny. Tough Nazi rearguards held the high ground which covered the approaches to the Seine, and some four

THE RETURN

battalions had a certain amount of fighting to do. The 5/7th Gordons (Lt.-Col. G. D. Renny) made five attacks in the Mauny loop before breaking through those rearguards, and so allowing the armour to advance. The Gordons took some hundred prisoners. German barges ferrying their troops across the river provided excellent targets for artillery and machine-gunners. After crossing the Seine, the Division held east again to Elbœuf and Rouen, where a tumultuous welcome awaited them; and so right across country to St Valéry-en-Caux. At the same time the Canadians made for Dieppe. As a result, the Le Havre Peninsula was quite cut off, and the garrison of that port could be dealt with in due course.

Once across the Seine, 152 Brigade Group found no opposition, and the Derbyshire Yeomanry, who were acting as scouts in armoured cars, sent back the information gained from civilians that the Germans had completely evacuated the area and that there were no mines to worry about. On went 152 Brigade some eighty miles north-west across country, kissed and garlanded, cheered and wined, handing out the " cigarette pour papa " in the beflagged villages, until the leading battalion, the 5th Seaforth, found themselves in Veules-les-Roses, a little seaport just north of St Valéry, whence a few of the Highland Division had got away in 1940, but where many of them had found a last resting-place.

It will always be a matter of debate who were the first Highland Division troops to enter St Valéry in this hour of return. The Derbyshire Yeomanry were undoubtedly there before any others, but they were not connected with any of the regiments which had known the place four years before. The 5th Seaforth claim that Captain Dawson, with a patrol from that battalion, was the first infantryman to enter. The 5th Camerons also sent in a patrol, and, when the Seaforth and Cameron Colonels met in the Station Square on that morning of 2nd September, the race was judged a dead heat. The Camerons had their pipers with them, and it was " Blue Bonnets over the Border " that skirled the return to St Valéry. Five of the original 4th Battalion of the Camerons were selected to play a set in the Square. Their names should go on record. They were: Sergeant A. MacRae, Pipers J. Chisholm, R. McNeil, J. MacLean, and Lance-Corporal A. MacDonald. Then the Maire of St Valéry presented each of the Commanding Officers, Lt.-Col. Walford and Lt.-Col. Lang, with a bouquet of flowers.

Colonel Walford of the 5th Seaforth, who, as a Company Commander, had managed to get away in 1940 from St Valéry, found his old company shield and sign in a farm-house. In all, four military cemeteries were discovered, and each of them had been carefully and lovingly tended. Originally they had been constructed by the Germans, but they had been looked after by French civilians. Each grave had a cross, on which was inserted the name and number of its occupant. When it had been impossible to identify the soldier, on the cross were the words " Anglais inconnu." In World War I., when all the regiments of the 51st were dressed in the kilt, it would have certainly been " Ecossais inconnu," as it was in the Peninsula and at Waterloo.

The Camerons made the acquaintance of two old ladies, in whose house men of the 4th Battalion had spent that terrible June night in 1940. The old ladies remembered particularly the work of the M.O., Captain MacKay, and they still possessed a sheepskin coat with the name R. MACKAY on it. The people of St Valéry had actually hidden six British soldiers for six months after the Germans had taken the town. They finally got those soldiers away to Paris, but one man was injured in a train-smash. In hospital the Germans found the address of the gallant lady of Veules-les-Roses who had hidden him. By order of the Gestapo she, along with another woman and a man, was condemned to death. The sentence, however, was changed to life imprisonment.

Some Black Watch men came across a board with a notice: " Honour the Black Watch Regiment who fought with courage in 1940." It had not been destroyed by the Germans. On the road between Veules-les-Roses and St Valéry abandoned vehicles, which had originally belonged to 152 Brigade, were discovered. The Staghead crest, the vehicular sign of the Division at that time,[1] was still to be seen on them in the Brigade colours.

General Rennie chose as his headquarters the château at Cailleville which had housed General Fortune's last headquarters. He also placed 152 and 153 Brigades in positions as close as possible to those which their predecessors had occupied in 1940, and on 3rd September the Massed Bands of the Division beat " Retreat " at Cailleville, when Rennie delivered the following address :—

" Officers and men of the Highland Division. This is a very great occasion in the history of our famous Division.

Here, at ST VALÉRY on the 12th June 1940, a portion of the Highland

---

[1] The HD sign had been forbidden, much to the annoyance of the Division.

Division, including its Headquarters, 152 and 153 Brigades, was captured by a large German force.

That magnificent Division was sacrificed in a last effort to keep the French in the war. True to Highland tradition the Division remained to the last with the remnants of our French Allies, although it was within its capacity to withdraw on LE HAVRE.

The Division drew on ST VALÉRY the German 4th Corps, a Panzer and a Motor Division—in all six Divisions—and thereby diverted this force from harassing the withdrawal of other British troops on LE HAVRE and CHERBOURG.

General Victor Fortune ordered the surrender of the Division at ST VALÉRY when it had run out of ammunition and food and when all prospects of evacuation, which had been carefully planned by him, had failed.

That Highland Division was Scotland's pride; and its loss, and with it the magnificent men drawn from practically every town, village, and croft in Scotland, was a great blow. But this Division, then the 9th Highland Division, took its place and became the new 51st Highland Division. It had been our task to avenge the fate of our less fortunate comrades and that we have nearly accomplished. We have played a major part in both the great decisive battles of this war—the Battle of EGYPT and the Battle of FRANCE—and have also borne our share of the skirmishes and those costly periods of defensive fighting which made these great victories possible. We have lived up to the great traditions of the 51st and of Scotland.

I have disposed the Division, as far as is possible, in the areas where it fought at ST VALÉRY. General Victor Fortune had his H.Q. here, 152 Brigade held the sector to the WEST, and 153 Brigade to the EAST. The Lothians and Border Horse held the sector to the SOUTH. The 154 Brigade and 'A' Brigade ('A' Brigade was at that time operating with the Division) embarked at LE HAVRE.

I hoped by disposing the Division in that way to make it easier for some of you to find the graves of your relatives or friends who lost their lives with the ST VALÉRY 51st. You will find at ST VALÉRY and in the village cemeteries around, that the graves of our comrades have been beautifully cared for.

We have to-day playing with the Pipes and Drums of the Highland Division those of the Scottish Horse. There are also officers and men of the Lothians and Border Horse at this meeting."

"The Flowers of the Forest" was played by the pipe-majors of the Division in memory of the men of the 51st who had fallen at St Valéry in 1940. Later a deputation headed by the Mayor, and bearing their standards, were greeted by the Divisional General.

Meanwhile to that last great battle in the east rolled the carriers of the whole U.S.A. Forces and our 21st Army Group. But the Highland Division had something to do before they could follow up. Along with the 49th Division they were ordered to reduce Le Havre, where a very determined German General, whose wife and children had been killed in Berlin, had made up his mind to resist to the last. The Highland Division was returned to the 1st Corps for this particular operation. Le Havre was very well defended. For four long years the Germans had held it, and during that time they had constructed every kind of barrier about it. In concrete dug-outs lived their troops; from concrete dug-out emplacements fired their guns. A great stretch of minefields acted as the outside perimeter, and each possible tank-approach was broken by an anti-tank ditch. At the point of a peninsula lay Le Havre, with the broad Seine estuary on the south side, the broader sea on the north-west, and this great defensive line cutting across from one waterway to the other. At some parts that defensive line was as much as a mile in depth. The plan put forward by the 1st Corps was that the 49th Division should attack from the east and the 51st Division from the north. But General Rennie pointed out that, since the Germans had obviously always considered that the likeliest attack on Le Havre would be in the form of an invasion from the sea, the defences on the edge of the sea would be strongest. He suggested—and the suggestion was approved—that a purely deceptive form of attack be made from the north to delude the enemy and that the main thrust by the Division be put in from the area of Montevilliers, which is on the Lezarde River. The 154 Brigade was to hold the line from which the attack was to be made; 152 Brigade, followed up by 153, was to reduce the defences in, and clear the Forest of Montgeon up to the outskirts of the town; then 154 Brigade would advance into the town itself. It should be pointed out here that the whole scheme for our attack was greatly helped by information from civilians concerning the positions of the enemy, their guns and their minefields. One Frenchman had actually stolen the German fire-plan and presented it to our Intelligence Staff.

So 152 Brigade moved away from St Valéry on 4th September. Their records at that period contain an interesting note regarding their transport. It reads: " In the break-out from Caen many German vehicles had been overrun especially at the Seine. Each battalion (of the Brigade) had upwards of thirty captured enemy vehicles, and, in addition, there were many privately owned push-cycles. In particular, that part of the Battalion and Brigade Headquarters columns carrying ' B ' Echelon looked hybrid. Grotesquely shaped and painted wagons

MAJOR-GENERAL BULLEN SMITH, DIVISIONAL COMMANDER AT NORMANDY LANDING, WITH (*Left*) BRIGADIER "NAP" MURRAY

NORMANDY BEACH-HEAD. JUNE 1944

By courtesy of the   IMPERIAL WAR MUSEUM

MAJOR-GENERAL THOMAS RENNIE, DIVISIONAL COMMANDER FROM NORMANDY
TO THE RHINE, WITH HIS A.D.C., LIEUT. DOUGLAS TWEEDIE

GENERAL RENNIE AND FRENCH DEPUTATION AT ST VALÉRY. SEPTEMBER 1944
By courtesy of   MAJOR D. F. O. RUSSELL

from practically every country in Europe punctuated the uniformity of W.D. vehicles, and it seemed as though the more grotesque a vehicle was, the more fun the driver got out of driving it. It was laughable to see the great sun-tanned Jocks trying to look sedate and unconcerned in the back of a big Mercedes car, but failing to do so completely, and turning their faces inwards to each other in the endeavour to hide the wide grins which covered them."

The 152 Brigade had attached to them a naval officer from H.M.S. *Erebus*, which was to shell such coastal defences as the infantry requested. The requests were made, the shelling took place, but the German artillery reply was so effective that *Erebus* had to limp home to Devonport for repairs.

10th September was D Day for the Le Havre operation, which was named "Astonia," and the 5th Seaforth attacked from a start-line roughly a mile to the east of Fontaine-la-Mallet. In a darkness from which the searchlights gave little relief, the Seaforth advanced, their main objective being a Bosche strong-point on high ground slightly to the north-east of Fontaine-la-Mallet. From the start-line onwards they were very heavily shelled, and the anti-tank ditch, which was their first obstacle, proved an obstacle indeed. No bridge was available, and everything had to be man-handled down into the ditch and up the other side. In the same way all casualties had to be brought back. But the German infantry were not in such good heart as their gunners, and, as the Seaforth went forward, they encountered little opposition from riflemen. The actual nature of the ground proved a much more difficult opponent; but the Seaforth kept pushing ahead, Germans kept on surrrendering, and the 5th were able to dig in on or near their objectives. Morning disclosed to them a Fontaine-la-Mallet literally in complete ruin after the aerial bombardment.

The German guns also took toll of the 5th Camerons who followed the Seaforth, Major A. L. MacNab and the Intelligence Officer, Captain D. W. Milne, both being killed. But the Camerons reached a strong-point in the outer defences, where Major A. N. Parker, later himself to be killed in action, made use of the German telephone, got through to the enemy's Supreme Commander in Le Havre, and asked him to make the choice of surrendering or being annihilated. Parker got no satisfactory answer, so the Camerons carried on to Fontaine-la-Mallet, where, like the Seaforth, they dug in. The 78th meanwhile were being held in reserve behind Brigade Headquarters. By now the Germans were showing white flags right and left, and next day Le Havre surrendered.

The 153 Brigade had also moved up, and a company of the 1st Gordons had advanced with the Camerons. The remainder of the Gordons were mostly employed collecting prisoners, who advanced showing copies of printed bills dropped by our aeroplanes, which gave full details of how kind we were to prisoners, and finished up: " This man is to be well treated and sent back from the front as soon as possible." The bills were signed by Eisenhower and Montgomery. The 5/7th Gordons, now commanded by Lt.-Col. Douglas Renny, were particularly fortunate not only in the number of prisoners they made but in the quantities of food and drink captured in the fort. " For the first time in the memory of those present, the Jocks had champagne in their tin mugs when they ate their evening meal. The news of the loot spread like wildfire and we had to establish firm control to keep out hordes of the most desperate looters we have ever seen," wrote their Commanding Officer. As the Brigade Major (153) remarked: " It was harder to get into the fort after the 5/7th had captured it than when the Germans held it."

As for 154 Brigade, so well had the other two Brigades succeeded, that Brigadier Oliver's command had a relatively easy time. The 7th Black Watch, with Northamptonshire Yeomanry in attendance, moved right away to Cap de la Heve at the north of the town, where they collected some fourteen hundred prisoners. The Commander of the garrison and his staff in their best uniforms, medals and all the rest, looked forward to some high formality when they threw in their hand, but, as Major David Russell, Second-in-Command of the 7th, who was seriously wounded during this attack, writes : " Their hopes were soon dispelled, however, when they were hustled off by a diminutive Jock, who looked keen to use his bayonet." The 1st Black Watch and 7th Argylls were not required to take part in the attack.

And so Le Havre fell. On 13th September General Rennie issued the following message to be read to all troops :—

The capture of Le Havre is another important task successfully accomplished by the Highland Division, this time in close co-operation with the 49th Division.

The casualties suffered by the Highland Division were 13 officers and 125 other ranks, and our prisoners totalled 122 officers and 4508 other ranks. The number of enemy casualties is not known, nor has it been possible even to estimate the number of weapons which have been captured in this heavily defended fortress.

The capture of the port of Le Havre should make a great difference to the future course of operations and will speed up the final destruction of the German army.

For the ten following days units of the Division were employed on garrison duties, quite popular on this occasion, for the Germans had stocked up well for a long siege. Massed Pipes and Drums played " Retreat " in the Square, and wreaths were laid on the town war memorial. Montgomery issued the following personal message on 17th September :—

" I want to-day, 17th September, to speak to all soldiers in the group of armies under my command. What a change has come over the scene since I last spoke to you on 21st August. Then we were moving up towards the Seine, having inflicted a decisive defeat on the German armies in Normandy. To-DAY the Seine is far behind us ; the Allies have removed the enemy from practically the whole of France and Belgium, except in a few places, and we stand at the door of Germany. And by the terrific energy of your advance northwards from the Seine, you brought quick relief to our families and loved ones in England—by occupying the launching sites of the flying bombs. We have advanced a great way in a short time, and we have accomplished much. The total of prisoners captured is now nearly 400,000 ; and there are many more to be collected from those ports in Brittany and in the Pas de Calais that are still holding out. The enemy has suffered immense losses in men and material ; it is becoming problematic how much longer he can continue the struggle.

Such a historic march of events can seldom have taken place in history in such a short space of time. You have every reason to be very proud of what you have done. Let us say to each other :—

' This was the Lord's doing, and it is marvellous in our eyes.'

And now the Allies are closing in on Nazi Germany from the east, from the south, and from the west ; her satellite powers have thrown the towel into the ring—they have had enough of the Nazis, and they now fight on our side. Our American Allies are fighting on German soil in many places ; very soon we shall all be there.

The Nazi leaders have ordered the people to defend Germany to the last and to dispute every inch of ground ; this is a very natural order, and we would do the same ourselves in a similar situation. But the mere issuing of orders is quite useless ; you require good men and true to carry them out. The great mass of German people know that their situation is already hopeless, and they will think more clearly on this subject as we advance deeper into their country ; they have little wish to continue the struggle. Whatever orders are issued in Germany, and whatever action is taken on them, no human endeavours can now prevent the complete and utter defeat of the armed forces of Germany; their fate is certain, and their defeat will be absolute.

The triumphant cry now is ' Forward into Germany.' "

And now we have to follow Oliver's 154 Brigade on a little ploy of their own. The German garrison in Dunkirk was particularly strong, and there was a certain amount of worry that they might make raids on the 21st Army Group's lines of communication, which ran through Cassel, a town only some fifteen miles south of Dunkirk. The 4th Special Service Brigade were acting as the Dunkirk investing troops, and 154 were sent to relieve them in order that they might proceed north for operations which were to commence in the Walcheren area. The investment of Dunkirk was under control of the 1st Canadian Army, so 154 Brigade came under that particular command, and on 26th September relieved the 4th Special Service Brigade. The 7th Argylls took up position right on the coast four miles north-east from Dunkirk at Bray-Dunes Plage, a beach with many 1940 memories of the escaping B.E.F. Three miles south of them and inland lay the 7th Black Watch at Ghyvelde, while right at the other side of the town to the west were the 1st Black Watch. There were twenty-five miles of perimeter, but, owing to extensive flooding, the possible exit routes were covered by those three battalions, except in the case of the main road to Bergues, a fine old French frontier fortress town constructed by Vauban, the man who built the Arras citadel so well remembered by the Division of the 1914-18 War. The carrier platoons from each battalion in the Brigade, with some tanks, all under the command of Major I. Campbell, 7th Argylls, guarded this road. The command was known as Campbell Force. All the Divisional Artillery had been sent off to bombard Calais, so that an Anti-Aircraft Brigade of four regiments, which was already in position on the perimeter, was put under Brigadier Oliver's command. Brigade Headquarters was right away back at Wormhoudt, a town twelve miles from Dunkirk.

The 15,000 German garrison seemed to have been quite well aware of the relief, for they immediately proceeded to make trouble. On the night of 26th-27th September a strong fighting patrol of very determined men attacked " B " Company of the 7th Black Watch. They got into the main street of Ghyvelde, demolished the windmill, which was being used as an observation-post, set fire to several houses, and took back five prisoners with them, obviously for identification purposes. Later in the morning of the 27th, the 7th Argylls were also attacked and the German patrol actually forced its way into that battalion's headquarters. They wounded the adjutant, Captain W. O. Williamson, and killed two other ranks, but two dead Germans were left behind. In each case several enemy prisoners were taken.

And now the Brigade had a novel experience. A deputation arrived from the French Red Cross requesting Brigadier Oliver to arrange a thirty-six-hour truce with the commander of the German garrison in Dunkirk, during which period the French civilian population might be evacuated. The Army intimated their approval of the idea, and on 2nd October a letter was sent to the German Commander through the French Red Cross, in which the suggestion for the thirty-six-hour truce was made. It was left to the Germans to fix a meeting-place and the route to it. The Germans approved, and 154 Brigade Intelligence Officer, Captain Wingate-Gray, a fluent speaker of both French and German, entered the outskirts of the town under a flag of truce, was blindfolded, and then conducted to German headquarters. The German Commander agreed to the terms of the truce, provided that no changes in military dispositions were made during the period when it was in force. Written personal guarantees to this effect were given by the German Commander and Brigadier Oliver, and the truce began at six o'clock in the morning of 4th October. Almost twenty thousand civilians were evacuated along with some seriously wounded German soldiers. A wounded Allied soldier was also evacuated with each wounded German. The truce was extended by twelve hours to allow the garrison to replace mines and demolish bridges. It should be recorded that the conditions of the truce were scrupulously observed by both sides.

On 8th and 9th October, 154 Brigade were relieved by the Czech Brigade, and set off to rejoin the Division, which was lying in the area of St Oedenrode, between Eindhoven and Nijmegen, in Holland. Brigadier Oliver's command had added their name to the list of besiegers of the tragic town of Dunkirk, which besiegers included the French kings of the thirteenth to the sixteenth centuries, Condé who had Tromp and the Dutch fleet as his allies in 1646, the Spaniards in 1653, Turenne in 1658, and the Duke of York in 1793.

CHAPTER IX.

GATEWAY TO THE FATHERLAND

" Lean gu dluth ri cliu do shinnsre."
(Follow close in the footsteps of your fathers.)

" And with our armie this night joyned we
Not far from Newmego it now was."
" The Remembrance,"
by JOHN SCOT, Soldier in the Scots Brigade.
1701-1711.

BEFORE 154 Brigade rejoined the Division they had another troke to carry out. The move north to Holland was to be a two-day one, with an overnight stop near the town of Alost, which is close to Brussels, and on the second day across the Belgium frontier into Holland to St Oedenrode. The first day (9th October) was one of revolving old memories of the 51st of 1916-18, for the Brigade moved by Abbeville, Bethune, Ypres, the Menin Gate, Courtrai, and so across towards Brussels. But on the second day Brigadier Oliver received a wireless message to report to Corps Headquarters at Turnhout, a small town just south of the Belgian border. He was instructed to concentrate his Brigade at Zeelst, which was the airfield for and about three miles west of Eindhoven. So let us tarry there with the Brigade if only to hear the story entitled " THE TOP SECRET."

Just north of Eindhoven lay the Wilhelmina Canal. The Germans were on the northern bank of that canal. The Royal Air Force were making full use of the Zeelst airfield. But the night before 154 Brigade arrived there the enemy had made a raid across the canal and had penetrated the edge of the airfield defences. The troops guarding the airfield were units of the R.A.F. Regiment, who had not, until this occasion, come into close contact with the enemy. They had suffered several casualties. Now the " top secret " was that His Majesty the King, in the course of the next few days, was to fly over to visit his troops in the Eindhoven–Nijmegen corridor and was to land on the Zeelst airfield. It was therefore thought advisable by Corps that the airfield should be guarded by a force of not less than a Brigade with some considerable experience of combat with Germans. The 154 Brigade was selected, and Brigadier Oliver and his Brigade Major were told exactly why. But no other person was to be made aware of the fact that the King was coming to Zeelst. The Brigade took over, and the Brigadier was billeted in the house of the local schoolmaster. That evening he was holding a conference of his senior officers, none of whom knew anything about the Royal visit, when there was a knock on the door of the room, and the daughter of the schoolmaster, a charming *meishe* of some fifteen summers, entered. She asked very politely if she might speak to the Brigade Commander, and, on permission being granted, she said: " What time does your King arrive at the airfield to-morrow for his visit to Nijmegen and General Montgomery ? " His Majesty did arrive, but the Germans took no action ; so all was well.

On 16th October orders came that 154 Brigade was to hand over to the Royal Netherlands Brigade, rejoin the Division who were holding the line in the Nijmegen corridor, and relieve 158 Brigade of the 53rd (Welsh) Division, which Brigade had temporarily been taking the place of 154 in the Highland Division. The 154 moved from Zeelst on 18th October.

We left the rest of the Division in the Le Havre area, bathing in the sea, and fraternising with the "much-relieved" French people. The R.A.S.C. had been put on 3rd line supply, and the gunners (Brigadier Shiel) had gone to batter Boulogne and Calais. Areas were mapped out in which it was possible to carry out exercises with live ammunition. Much long-distance marching was a feature of the training programme. On 26th September, however, orders came that the Division was to move up into Belgium. The 153 Brigade led the way along roads on the sides of which the little people of France stood and waved and cheered. So on they went by places old in the Division's story—Amiens, Cambrai, Valenciennes, and Mons. And always now and again they would pass one of these beautifully kept collections of white crosses; and sometimes a bigger memorial, erected in one instance to keep in memory the 9000 killed in the battle of Cambrai, " who have no known grave."[1] The Germans had treated those cemeteries with respect ; except that they had removed the books containing the lists of names, which once had been preserved in the porches

[1] In November 1917 at Cambrai the 51st lost 2500 soldiers. The Corps Commander wrote : " I am proud and delighted with the Division as they might well be themselves with the grand fight they put up."

leading to the cemeteries. So 153 Brigade came to Brussels on the last day of September, and took over a part of the line from a Brigade of their sister Division, the 15th Scottish.[1]

The 152 Brigade moved up two days later. On the last day of September they reached the Amiens area, and the following night that of Valenciennes. In those districts the French hosts—and every Frenchman wanted to be a host—were full of memories, and kept telling those new liberators stories of 1914-18, and how well their fathers fought " in the brave days of old." On 2nd October the Brigade moved into Belgium, by Mons and Waterloo to Brussels, and then to the district of Herenthals–Herenthout, which lay midway between Turnhout (Corps Headquarters) and Malines. The Belgians were as enthusiastic about the Division's arrival as were the French, and did everything they could for the troops. The Brigade was ordered to take over the line from 46 Brigade, 15th (Scottish) Division, at Best on 4th October. They left the Herenthout area on 3rd October and debussed at Eindhoven–Vught, just south of the Wilhelmina Canal. They then moved into the line, where the 78th relieved their own 7th Battalion and the 9th Cameronians, while the 5th Seaforth relieved the 2nd Glasgow Highlanders, the 5th Camerons relieved the 2nd Gordons, and the 2nd Derbyshire Yeomanry relieved the 2nd Argylls. The holding line was so extensive that the 243rd Anti-Tank Battery and the Derbyshires were employed as infantry. Two platoons of " H " Company, 1/7th Middlesex, were also in the line.

To take the place of the Dunkirk besiegers, 158 Brigade from the 53rd Division was put under command.

To understand the position of the Highland Division at this period it is necessary to have a general picture of the situation of the 21st Army Group. In the west of Holland the 1st Canadian Army were cleaning up the area round the estuary of the Scheldt and the approaches to Antwerp. The aim was to get the port of Antwerp in working order as soon as possible. The attack on Walcheren had begun, the ultimate purpose of which was to capture Beveland and liquidate all the enemy south of the Maas as far as Geertruidenberg. The British 2nd Army took up from that point, with the Highland Division on its left. It was holding a line from the southern environs of Tilburg to just north

---

[1] Then commanded by the well-known six-foot-six Cameron officer, Major-General (now Lt.-General Sir Colin) Barber, who, as Major Barber, had been G.S.O.2 when the Highland Division had originally landed in France.

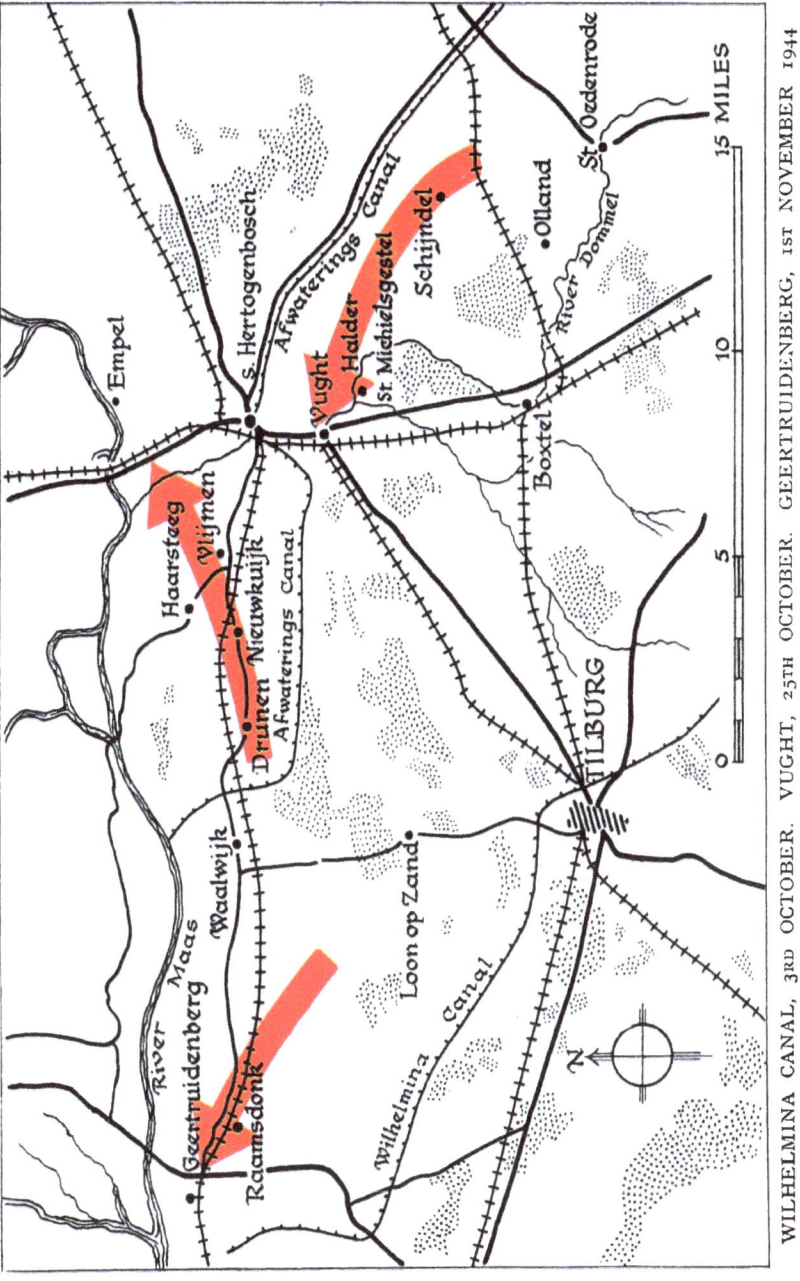

WILHELMINA CANAL, 3RD OCTOBER. VUGHT, 25TH OCTOBER. GEERTRUIDENBERG, 1ST NOVEMBER 1944

of St Oedenrode, then up to Nijmegen by the west side of the corridor and down the east side to Helmond. Now the idea was that the army should, as it were, push out its elbows and so enlarge the corridor. On the left this pushing would result in squeezing the Germans across the Maas on the whole line west to Geertruidenberg, and so linking up with the Canadians. The main object of the movement, as has been stated above, was to get the port of Antwerp opened as the main supply base for practically all the Allied armies. This clearance was being made under the direction of the 12th Corps, commanded by that distinguished Black Watch soldier and ex-Commander of the 51st, Lieut.-General N. M. Ritchie, and the troops to be employed included the 7th Armoured, 15th Scottish, 51st Highland, 33rd Armoured, and 53rd Welsh Divisions.

For a couple of weeks the Highland Division had a peaceful enough time in the line. The 5th Seaforth specialised in sniping. One expert, a Mackenzie of that battalion, collecting the pay-books of his victims, as a Red Indian might have collected scalps, "Chust so as all wass knowing his shooting." The 2nd Derbyshire Yeomanry made a good showing as infantrymen, for, on their own feet, with four Churchills following up, they raided an enemy position and took every man in it prisoner. And here is another of the good stories, that of "The Man Who Would Not Desert His Comrades." About an hour after the Derbyshires had returned from their raid, a German soldier, complete with suitcase, walked into our front line. He explained that the call of duty had necessitated his being absent from the position which the Yeomanry raided. As soon as he returned, and learned what had happened, he packed his grip and hastened to rejoin his comrades.

Unfortunately, Germans of that type were few and far between, and when the 1st Black Watch came into the line they experienced a very daring raid on the part of the Germans. The 42nd had relieved the 1/5th Welsh, and, at the first morning stand-to, over came a strong fighting Bosche patrol, consisting of an officer and twenty men. It got as far as "C" Company's headquarters without being spotted. The C.S.M. challenged two men whom he could not recognise and got his answer from an automatic rifle. He replied with a couple of grenades, and the conversation became general. The Bosche collared two batmen and a jeep-driver, and then began their return journey. Unfortunately for them they ran into No. 14 Platoon, who opened fire on them. In the ensuing mêlée the three prisoners broke away from their captors and killed the Bosche officer. In fact, only five Germans got back to their own lines. The 5th Camerons sent out one patrol, which found a German fast asleep in his slit trench. He was roused only when he was lifted out and dumped on the ground. He appeared to be quite delighted with this rude awakening.

At this time Major Du Boulay, Second-in-Command of the 5/7th Gordons, who had fought with the Battalion ever since Alamein, left to go on a lecture tour to America.

And so to the Battle of the Maas, or Operation " Colin " as it was called. It was to take place on 23rd October, the anniversary of El Alamein, and it was to be the Highland Division's business, with the support of the 33rd Armoured Brigade, to attack directly north from the St Oedenrode area, clear the town of Schijndel, and then swing north-west and seize crossings of the Dommel and Halsche Rivers, just south of s'Hertogenbosch. The day before the Division attacked, the 53rd (Welsh) Division and 7th Armoured Division were to clear up the area between the Zuidwilhelms Canal and s'Hertogenbosch and, the day after, the 15th (Scottish) Division were to capture Tilburg and then move north. The Highland Division plan was that 153 Brigade would go for Schijndel, while 152 would clear up the woods east of the Dommel. The 154 Brigade (in Kangaroos) would be held as an exploitation force.

The 153 Brigade advance began at midnight, 22nd-23rd October, with the 5/7th Gordons (Lt.-Col. Renny) going in on a silent attack on the village of Wijbosch, close to Schijndel. This attack was quite successful, although the Gordons suffered many casualties, and the 5th Black Watch passed through them *en route* for the south-east end of Schijndel, and, in particular, for a large factory which appeared to dominate the whole town. The 1st Gordons set out at 8 A.M., found no obstacles at all in their way, and occupied the south-west of Schijndel. They captured some two dozen paratroopers.

The 152 Brigade moved forward to clear the area between the Schijndel dyke opposite Boxtel, east by north to Schijndel itself and south-east to Olland. The 5th Camerons (Lt.-Col. D. Lang) moved off at 11 P.M. on the 22nd, and no sooner were they in the open than they met intense machine-gun fire. " B " Company reached its objective, but " A " Company's opposition was particularly powerful. The O.C. Company (Major Nigel Parker) was hit and later died of wounds. " D "

Company, in attempting a flank movement, was also held up, but "C" Company was finally sent round on a wide detour and succeeded in taking "A" Company's original objective. Thus the Camerons by evening were concentrated on their objective in the woods of Schijndel. The 2nd Seaforth made their objective without difficulty, and the 5th Seaforth (Lt.-Col. J. H. Walford) "walked on" to theirs without opposition, the Germans having withdrawn from Olland nine hours before the attack began. A crashed Dakota pilot, who had been hidden by members of the Resistance Movement, and two priests came into the 5th lines with a great deal of valuable information about the German withdrawal, so that the 5th Seaforth moved north towards s'Hertogenbosch almost as far as the Zuidwilhelms Canal, when they were held up on account of a blown bridge.

In the case of 154 Brigade, the 7th Argylls (Lt.-Col. A. MacKinnon), with half a squadron of tanks, moved off at eight o'clock on the morning of the 23rd to protect the Division's right flank. Mines provided the chief opposition, but by 1 P.M. they had reached their objective. The 7th Black Watch made a start at 11.15 A.M., moved through Schijndel, and so towards St Michielsgestel. Tanks cleared the road-blocks and "A" and "D" Companies penetrated into the town. They were within one hundred yards of the bridge across the river when it was blown by the enemy, but about four o'clock a platoon of "A" Company crossed in small boats, and the pioneer platoon erected a Class 9 bridge. By 9 P.M. the whole battalion had crossed and were followed by the 1st Black Watch (Lt.-Col. Hopwood). The two battalions formed a very strong bridgehead, which earned them a special word of praise from the Divisional Commander himself. The positional situation necessitated putting the 5/7th Gordons under command of 154 Brigade and the 7th Argylls under command of 153.

The next move was to get across the Halsche Water at Halder, and this was accomplished by the 1st Black Watch. The bridge had been blown, but a whole company made its way across over the wreckage, and, under a smoke screen, the Pioneers fixed up a new bridge, which in its turn was replaced by a heavier one constructed by the Engineers. This bridge carried over the armour and the carriers, but a platoon of the latter making for s'Hertogenbosch ran into a strong German counter-attack by self-propelled guns and was badly mauled. The 7th Argylls to the rescue! They came up, passed through the 1st Black Watch, and made for the town of Vught. But half-way on the road what has been well described as a " pitched battle " took place. The honours were fairly even, and the Argylls consolidated at the point they had reached. Next morning the 7th Black Watch came up and passed through them with a troop of tanks in support. The Fife Battalion met some considerable opposition, among the enemy being several of the " Green Police," unmentionable guards from the equally unmentionable concentration camp in the vicinity of Vught ; but in the early afternoon the 7th had taken the town and were busily engaged cleaning up.

Meanwhile 152 was also thrusting towards Vught. The 5th Camerons had moved forward into an assembly area near Groenendal, whence they advanced to the main Vught–Tilburg road, and the 5th Seaforth took up position in the woods to the south of the same road. The 2nd Seaforth were on the left of the 5th Battalion. The Brigade then advanced, supported by a tremendous concentration of artillery fire, got into the positions required of them, and halted there until it could be found out what the 7th Armoured Division were doing.

As a matter of fact, the 7th Armoured Division were held up in front of the village of Loon op Zand, so the Highland Division were moved in support. The credit for the capture of Loon op Zand goes to 153 Brigade. On 27th October the 5/7th Gordons had occupied Holeind ; 5th Black Watch, Haaren ; and 1st Gordons, Oisterwijk. Next day that last-mentioned battalion, despite determined opposition, took the northern half of Loon op Zand ; the 5th Black Watch passed through them and pushed ahead up the road to the north, reaching Horst on the morning of the 29th. The 5/7th Gordons were advancing meanwhile on Kaatschevez, and along with their senior battalion occupied Sprang on the 30th. The 154 Brigade were sent to the west to prevent as many Germans as possible crossing to the north of the Maas, and to get to Geertruidenberg and join up with the Canadians. The 152 and 153 Brigades were to push north to s'Hertogenbosch.

The 1st Black Watch led 154's advance to the west at midday on 29th October, and moved to Hooge bridge, where the Germans occupied a strong defensive position. In the advance Lieutenant Viney, who was in command of the leading platoon of " A " Company, suddenly found himself cut off by the fall of a tree, brought down by gunfire. He had to kill five Germans before he fought his way out of this bit of trouble. The Battalion advanced on the village of Waspik, where the bridge appeared still intact. They had to fight very hard to secure this place. Lieutenant Cox died of wounds received here, and Major Anderson was severely wounded. The 7th Argylls came up, and were directed to make straight for Geertruidenberg. They set off in Kangaroos, but owing to strong enemy opposition were forced to halt half-way and take up a defensive position for the night. They continued their forward movement in the morning, and after a very stern battle with an advancing German column they reached Raamsdonk, where they were ordered to halt.

The 7th Black Watch were now detailed to take over; their advance being led by Lieutenant I. Donaldson, with a platoon of "A" Company. This officer had two tanks in front, two Kangaroos following, and two tanks bringing up the rear. Half-way to their objective this small force ran into Spandau-fire, the origins of which were dealt with. Then a self-propelled gun was seen moving on to the road out of a side-track which the two leading tanks had already passed. Donaldson, without hesitation, ordered his Kangaroo driver to put on full speed and charge the gun. The action was entirely successful, the gun was immobilised, and, though the Kangaroo capsized in the ditch, all the platoon got clear and dealt with the self-propelled gun-crew, killing every one of them. The platoon then withdrew to Raamsdonk. Another platoon was sent in a far-out flanking attack and succeeded in cutting the enemy's escape route at Geertruidenberg. Next day the area received the usual mopping-up, and a 7th Black Watch carrier patrol proceeded as far as the bridge over the Maas, which they found blown. General Rennie had a special word of praise for the battalion that afternoon, and next day it was withdrawn to Vught.

The 5th Camerons were now ordered to advance on Waalwijk, a town on the Maas. Everything went well, for, by the time that town was reached, cheering inhabitants and not aggressive Germans met the Camerons. That battalion spent a couple of days in Waalwijk, when they were relieved by elements of the 7th Armoured Division.

There were two pockets south of the Maas still to be cleared up. The one demanded an attack across water in boats, and Corps had purposed to give this job to the 53rd Division. West of the town of s'Hertogenbosch ran the thirty-yard-wide Afwaterings Canal, which cut across the foot of a piece of land in a bend of the Maas River, and the tops of the dykes of which were ninety yards apart. That piece of land was known as the "Island" and was some six miles in length by four miles in width.

When the 53rd Division were preparing for this attack, news was received that the Germans had launched a major assault on an American Division, which, temporarily under command of the 2nd Army, were holding a part of the line on the Meuse, just at that point where the Dutch-Belgian-German frontiers meet. The enemy had made a considerable penetration some twelve miles to the west of Roermond, and were only some twenty miles from Eindhoven. Instructions came to the 12th Corps to send a Division immediately to reinforce the Americans on the Weert sector, to use another Division to clean up the " Island," without delay, and then to arrange for a Corps attack that would drive back the enemy from the west of the Meuse between Venlo and Roermond. The 53rd Division were selected as the Weert reinforcement and the Highland Division were given the " Island " problem to solve. So on 2nd November 154 Brigade was sent to s'Hertogenbosch to relieve 152 Brigade, which, along with 153, were to make preparations for an attack on the " Island."

Cutting through the middle of the island was a road, which ran through the town of Drunen. That town was to be the objective of the 5th Camerons. Some three-quarters of a mile east of Drunen and on the same road was Groenwoud. The 5th Seaforth were to go for that. The 2nd Seaforth's objective was the cross-roads at Drunen. On the right 153 Brigade were to capture Nieuwkuijk, Vlijmen, and Haarsteeg. The 154 Brigade, along with 131 Brigade, were to stage diversionary attacks. The operation rejoiced in the name of " Guy Fawkes," the 5th of November being only one day away. Collapsible canvas boats, each capable of carrying sixteen men, were to be used for navigating the canal. A tremendous barrage was laid down, first on the dyke. But both dyke and canal were crossed with very few casualties, and the northern dyke (Drunesche Dyke), which was supposed to be the German main line of defence, proved no obstacle to our advancing troops. The 5th Seaforth found Groenwoud empty. The 78th and 5th Camerons achieved complete success, the latter battalion providing us with another of our little stories. This one is entitled " How It Works." C.S.M. Gordon of " C " Company came across one German soldier who was trying without result to get his Spandau to function. Gordon took the gun from him, and, holding him by the scruff of the neck, explained to him exactly what was wrong with the weapon. He then broke the Spandau to bits and sent his pupil back to the prisoners' cage. The Camerons continued right on to the line of the Maas and captured the river town of Helsden.

The 153 Brigade attack also went very well. The 1st Gordons and 5th Black Watch led, and, once their first objectives were taken, the 5/7th Gordons passed through them. The 5th Black Watch then made for Haarsteeg, and by six o'clock on the evening of 5th November all the Brigade objectives had been taken and their area was clear of Germans right up to the Maas. The 5/7th Gordons found Nieuwkuijk ablaze and the church in ruins.

The other small German pocket on the south side of the Maas was at Empel, due north of s'Hertogenbosch, where the enemy were holding a bridgehead. To liquidate those troops the 7th Argylls were sent up on the night of 6th November. The new C.O. of the Argylls handled this affair. He was Lt.-Col. A. MacKinnon, Second-in-Command, and had taken over from Lt.-Col. Nicoll, who left to take up a staff appointment. Colonel MacKinnon had been with the Division in France in 1940 and had been awarded the M.C. there. He rejoined the Division in 1944 shortly before it crossed to Normandy. The Argyll attack was all that was desired. There was little opposition, and what Germans were left were very willing to become prisoners. South of the Maas was clear.

The following message from the Divisional Commander, dated 8th November, was read out to all troops of the Division :—

"We of the Highland Division, with the 33rd Armoured Brigade and those units who have been working with us, can look back with satisfaction on the successful operations just completed. During the period 23rd October to 7th November the Division, by its thrust from SCHIJNDEL to GEERTRUIDEN-BERG and its activities later east and north of s'HERTOGENBOSCH, cleared an area of some 300 square miles of HOLLAND, denied the Germans their bridge escape route at GEERTRUIDENBERG, and captured or annihilated most of the German rearguards south of the River MAAS. The operations included the assault crossing of two rivers, the forcing of the narrow causeway from WASPIK to GEERTRUIDENBERG, and the assault crossing of the AFWATERINGS Canal.

The success of the operations was due to the forceful and offensive spirit of commanders and troops, and to the successful co-ordination of all arms.

The casualties of the Division during this period amounted to 44 officers and 630 other ranks, of whom 7 officers and 115 other ranks were killed. Prisoners captured amounted to a total of 30 officers and 2378 other ranks, and enemy casualties must have been heavy.

The Commander of the 2nd Army [General Dempsey] writes of these

BAILEY BRIDGE OVER THE MAASTRICHT-NORDER CANAL

MAJOR-GENERAL MACMILLAN, DIVISIONAL COMMANDER FROM THE RHINE TO BREMERHAVEN, WITH HIS A.D.C.

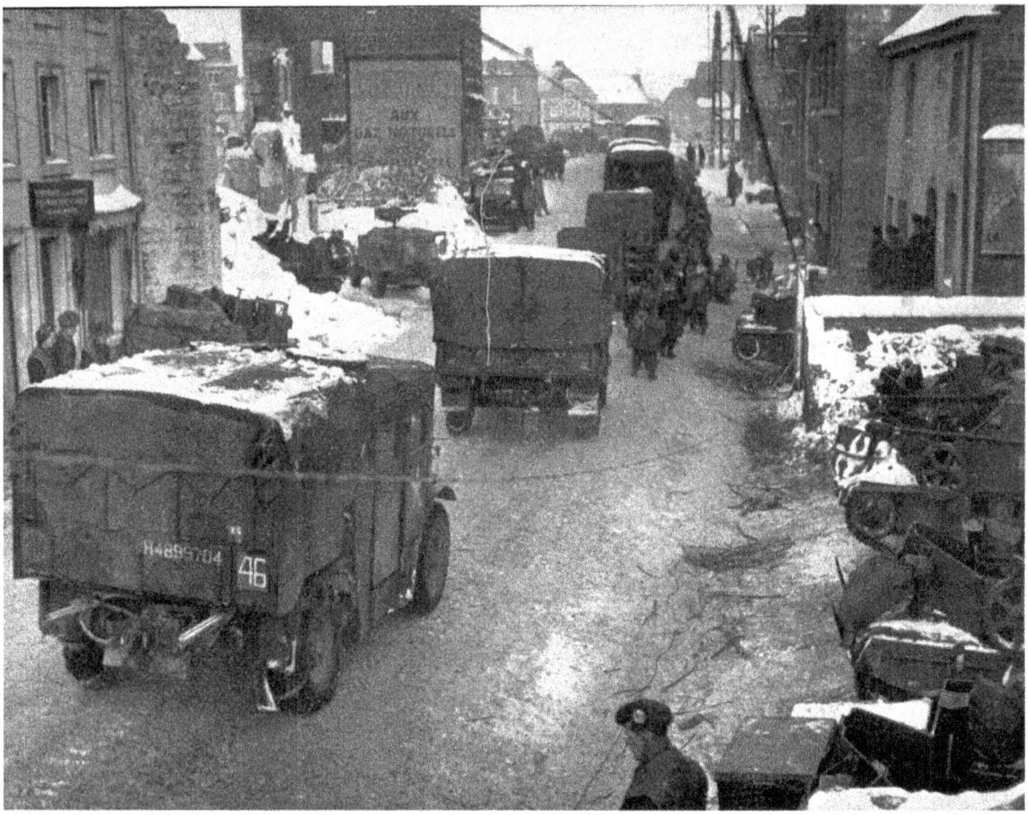

By courtesy of the IMPERIAL WAR MUSEUM

THE ROAD TO THE ARDENNES FRONT

A PATROL IN THE ARDENNES

By courtesy of the IMPERIAL WAR MUSEUM

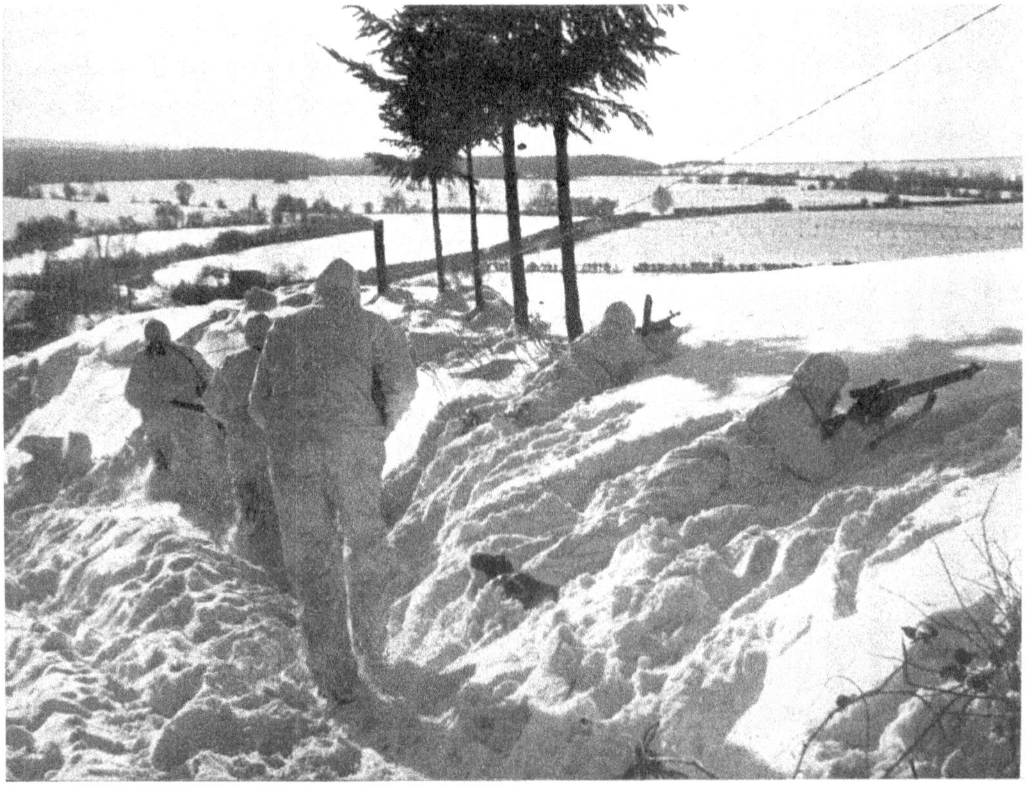

[*To face p.* 193

operations: 'Now that you have entirely cleared the country south of the River MAAS, I want to tell you how greatly I appreciate the splendid way in which your Division has fought during the recent operations. You had a great many difficulties to contend with; you overcame them all in the best possible way. Please give the Division my very sincere congratulations.'

We will undoubtedly have some heavy fighting to contend with before the war is won, and we shall encounter better troops than those we have seen lately. It is the duty of every one of us to ensure that the fighting spirit of the Highland Division remains 'second to none.'"

CHAPTER X.

THE LOWLANDS OF HOLLAND

"Theid an deagh shaighdear gu h-aoibhneach suilbhear an dail gach tuiteamais a thig'na chrannchur."
(The good soldier will advance with spirit and cheerfulness to any service that comes his way.)
Address to soldiers of the Highland Brigade at the end of the eighteenth century.

"In 1632, an alliance having been concluded between the States and Gustavus Adolphus, then in the midst of that career of victory in Germany, which owed so much of its success to the hardy valour of his Scottish Brigade, Prince Frederick Henry made another great effort to permanently increase the dominions of the United Provinces. Venlo, Stralen, and Ruremonde successively surrendered—the three Scottish regiments forming part of his army."
'Scots Brigade in Holland.'

THE River Maas (Meuse) rises in the French Departement of Haute-Marne and runs through that country by Verdun and Sedan. It takes a northern course through Belgium, approximately parallel to that of the Rhine, and practically on the German border, where it flows by Namur, Liège, and Maestricht. Just south of Nijmegen it turns due west and keeps that airt till it reaches the sea. Half-way between Nijmegen and Maestricht it passes Roermond on the Belgium-Holland border, and in that area the Highland Division were now to continue their battle. All Germans had been cleared from the south side of the Maas from the point where that river takes its final turn to the west, but the enemy were still scattered about on the western side of its course from south to north. The German offensive against the Americans, which the 53rd Division had been sent down to stem, had not been too successful, but it had enlarged the enemy's bridgehead across the Maas, and his forces were spread out between Venlo and Roermond and offered a continual threat to Eindhoven. Once and for all he must be pushed back across the Maas, and the Highland Division was sent down to lend their weight in that scrum. The operation was named "Ascot," and the Division's part in it was to push the enemy out to the south of the Weert–Roermond road some five miles north of the Belgian frontier and then to turn and push him across the Maas right up to Venlo. The 53rd Division were to attack south of the 15th (Scottish) Division, north of the Highland Division.

It was an unhappy time of year in an unhappy countryside. Rain poured down on a chilly world of drenched fields and miserable villages, which had been battered to pieces by both sides, and especially during the latest German attack. The enemy's strong-point was an area near the village of Nederweert, where the Noorder and Wessem Canals joined. Being in possession of the lock-gates near the Maas the enemy could at will flood or empty those canals, which, in order to get at that enemy, the Division must cross.

D Day for "Ascot" was 14th November, and the Divisional plan was for 152 Brigade to cross the Noorder Canal and 153 the Wessem Canal. The 154 Brigade was to be responsible for the capture of the lock-gates at the junction of the two canals, and so make certain of some kind of crossing, should the other two Brigades find their bridging problems unsolvable. If 153 were successful, 154 was then to advance and capture the town of Heyhuijzen, the half-way house to the Meuse. The 152 and 153 Brigades moved south on 6th November, and 152 relieved part of the 7th United States Armoured Division in the line at Nederweert. The take-over was a new type of experience for the Brigade. Being armoured troops the Americans had quite understandably little knowledge of and little zest for actually holding ground. In the eyes of an experienced Infantry Division like the 51st their defence system was practically without any organisation whatever. Enemy patrols had been crossing the canal at night and laying mines all over the place. However, the take-over was completed by 7th November, and the Americans clattered off westwards into the darkness. The frontage to be held by 152 Brigade was so great that the 2nd Argylls[1] from the 15th (Scottish) Division were temporarily brought under command, and were put into the line on the left of the 2nd Seaforth. On 9th November 154 Brigade came south and relieved 152 in the line. On the 12th the 1st Gordons took over from the 93rd Highlanders, who returned to the 15th (Scottish) Division.

And so to the attack. It required some preliminary training for 152 and 153 Brigades. The method of crossing the canals was to be by assault boats and Buffaloes.[2] The tanks of the East Riding

---

[1] The 91st Argyllshire Highlanders had been attached in Sicily. Now it was pleasant to have the 93rd Sutherlands with the Division.

[2] The Buffalo had a slightly armoured large body with spades fastened to the tracks, which, as a result, acted as paddles when the vehicle was travelling through water. It had a tail-board, which could be dropped, so that a carrier could be taken on board. It could accommodate thirty men.

Yeomanry were given the job of dragging the assault boats on sledges to the banks of the canal, and the launching crews had to put in a good bit of practice. Further training was also required on the part of the infantry in embarking on and disembarking from Buffaloes. But at length D Day arrived.

Buffaloes were loaded with jeeps and anti-tank guns, and the men, trained to lift the boats from the sledges, carried them down to the canals. In the advance by 153 Brigade the 1st Gordons got across without difficulty, although they had to submit to considerable mortar-fire, but their Buffaloes proved ineffective craft owing to the steepness of the Wessem banks. The 5/7th Gordons (Lt.-Col. Renny) had a somewhat unusual experience in the first half-hour of their attack, for during that period the well-known broadcaster of the time, Chester Wilmot, brought up a B.B.C. recording van and gave a running commentary. The 5/7th crossings were entirely successful, and all objectives were taken on the other side of the canal.

The 5th Black Watch, who followed on the heels of the Gordons, had also a satisfactory show; the 5th Camerons and 5th Seaforth made their Brigade's initial crossings over the Noorder Canal, the 152 Buffaloes, in contradistinction to the 153 " animals," proving a great success. The Germans, however, had worked the lock-gates well, and " B " Company of the Sutherland Battalion had a veritably sticky time in the thick black mud exposed when the canal waters disappeared. But they made a bridge with boats, got across on it, and the Battalion took all its objectives some thousand yards farther on.

The Camerons also had a successful crossing, Piper McLean playing his pipes all the way on " C " Company's leading Buffalo. " The advance on the canal," writes a Cameron eye-witness, " was an extraordinary sight, reminiscent of mobile columns in the desert : infantry on tanks, infantry on Buffaloes, infantry on their feet, all rolling southwards, spread out on a front of half a mile with a tremendous barrage screaming overhead. The great pains which had been taken over details paid a high dividend. Not only was the canal crossed without difficulty, but all objectives were taken in less than the ambitious time allotted." In due course the Brigade crossing was successfully completed by the 2nd Seaforth.

When 154 Brigade went for the lock-gates, they took with them an A.V.R.E. bridging-team and a bridge completely built and long enough to span the canal at the lock-gates. This bridge was carried forward on a Churchill tank. The 154 crossing was initiated by the 7th Argylls, who had also to clear a small island at the junction of the canals. At five o'clock on 14th November the leading Argyll platoon was over the lock-gates and another platoon was on the island. Schu-mines proved the main opposition.[1] Many of them were camouflaged as bricks, and a certain number of casualties resulted from their unavoidable detonation. The A.V.R.E. bridge was quickly got into position, and against only slight resistance the Argylls made themselves masters of the village of Hulsen. Bosche fleeing from that locality ran into elements of the 5/7th Gordons, who were moving up from their bridgehead. The 1st Black Watch had had one brief encounter with the enemy some time before the crossing. A German patrol infiltrated into the 42nd lines and took prisoners, some Middlesex gunners and three Seaforth. But, as they were returning in the direction of the canal, the raiders ran into a Black Watch standing patrol, who broke up the party, and the prisoners escaped. The 42nd crossed the Bailey bridge in the 153 bridgehead on the morning of 15th November, and advanced in Kangaroos to Leveroi, where the road was blocked by houses destroyed by our bombers and artillery. At this point the 7th Black Watch were passed through the senior battalion with a squadron of tanks in support, and made for the town of Heythuijzen. Mines having been responsible for the destruction of two tanks, the infantry took to their feet, occupied the town, which had been evacuated by the enemy, and sent patrols out in the direction of Roggel. Next day " D " Company occupied the town of Neer, and two days later the Battalion was concentrated in Onder.

In its final advance to Baarlo the 1st Black Watch kept meeting self-propelled guns at every turn of the road ; but those were liquidated satisfactorily. Major Peter Taylor, as on many previous occasions since the Division started battling at Alamein, again distinguished himself. Towards the end of the advance the 42nd also went forward on foot through the village of Bong to Baarlo. All through this advance the German shelling was particularly heavy and accurate, testimony to that heaviness and accuracy being borne by the tale of " The Tin

---

[1] This mine was in the form of a small wooden box. No metal was used in its construction so that it was impossible for it to be " spotted " by any form of mine-detector. Its top was hinged. The unfortunate soldier who put his foot accidentally on the top of this lid detonated the charge, and, as a result, generally lost the lower part of a leg. These mines could be produced at a very small cost, and the Germans had littered the ground with them.

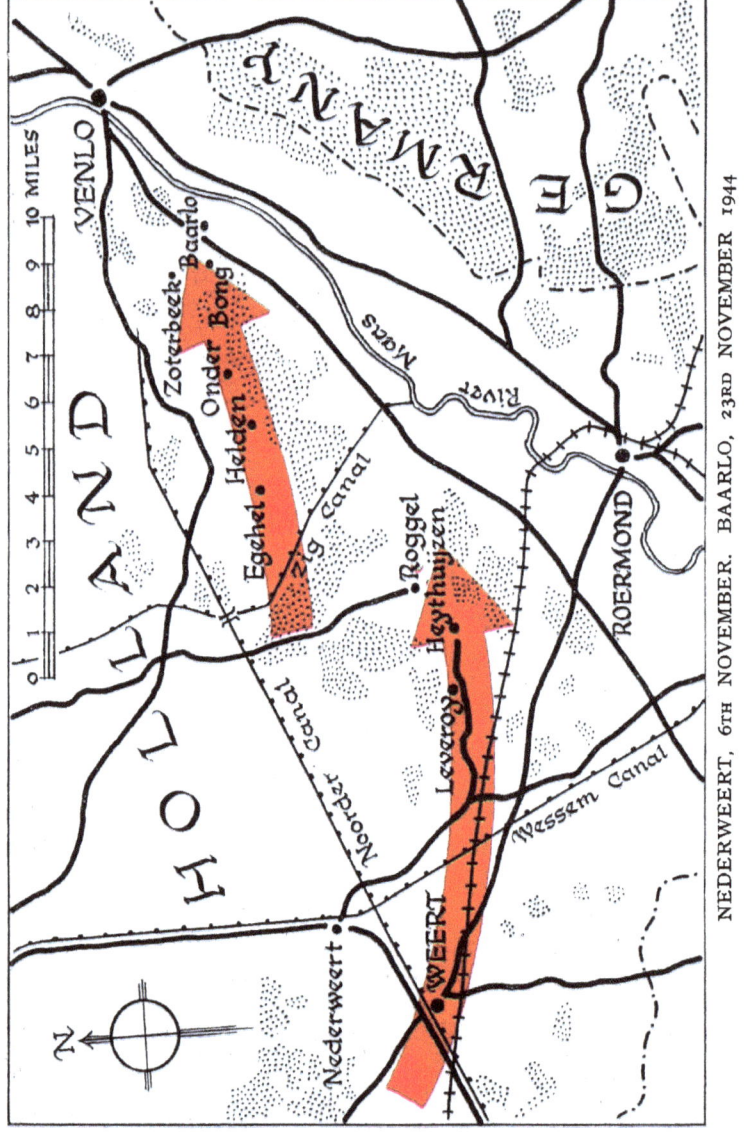

NEDERWEERT, 6TH NOVEMBER. BAARLO, 23RD NOVEMBER 1944

Hat." During the height of the shelling the Brigade Commander, Brigadier James Oliver, came up to see Colonel Hopwood. On returning to his headquarters the Brigadier was asked what it was like up there. His reply was not only a cryptic and vivid impression of the state of affairs, but also a tribute to a very brave officer. He answered : " John is wearing his steel helmet."[1] On the 26th the 42nd were relieved in Baarlo by the Welch Regiment.

Meanwhile 152 Brigade were also getting ahead, and the 5th Camerons under Lt.-Col. Lang earned a special Corps clap on the shoulder for their action in crossing yet another canal. On the night of 16th November the Camerons sent forward patrols to find out the position of the enemy as far as the Uitwaterings Canal (locally known as the Zig Canal) was concerned. The patrol reported enemy in the vicinity of a blown bridge at the junction of this Zig and the Nederweert Canals. At first light on the 17th " C " Company made a dash across the broken bridge and dug in on the far side. They came under heavy shell and mortar-fire. Then " A " Company crossed at the sluice-gates, and the enemy fire was intensified. The Germans also put down a smoke-screen in an endeavour to hamper the work of our tanks, which were supplying the Highlanders with covering fire from the far bank. Then the enemy put in a vicious attack, but at that point Captain Douglas Tilly, the F.O.O. of the 492nd Highland Battery, who had crossed the canal with " C " Company, brought down the full weight of fire from both field and medium artillery on the advancing enemy. Yet, despite all this obstruction added to by mortar and small-arms fire, the enemy displayed the highest courage in pressing home his attack.[2] The fighting went on till after midday, and, when the Germans did withdraw, the Cameron companies had almost exhausted their supplies of ammunition. During the night a Class 40 bridge was constructed in the area of the blown bridge. For obvious reasons it became known as " Cameron Bridge." General Sir Neil Ritchie's message, sent after this action, read : " Had not the 5th Camerons held on to their foothold on the east bank of the Zig Canal, the advance of the whole Corps might well have been delayed for an appreciable time." A D.S.O. was Major

---

[1] It had been something of a tradition in the Highland Division that the Balmoral bonnet, as the sign (for all to see) of a Scots soldier, should be worn in battle except when particularly heavy shelling made such a practice foolish.

[2] The enemy artillery were particularly accurate at this period. It was estimated that on the 17th the Division had to stand up to the heaviest shelling since the days of the Bois de Bavent in Normandy.

Melville's reward, while Major R. M. Munro, Captain D. H. Cameron, and Sergeant D. Calin were also decorated.

In the heavy rain and churned mud of that miserable night, the 5th Seaforth advanced from the Cameron bridgehead towards Zelen, with the 78th moving with them on their left flank. It was really a very remarkable accomplishment that under such dreadful conditions those two battalions should have arrived and dug in (still in the darkness) on the exact positions they had set out to reach.

On the 17th also the 1st Gordons and 5th Black Watch made the crossing of the Zig Canal to divert some of the trouble that was being showered on the Camerons. They all got over safely, and were followed next day by the 5/7th Gordons, who occupied the Keup–Egehel area. A day later they were practically on the bank of the Maas, and on the 24th the two Brigades were relieved by units of the 53rd Division.

It was considered that, with the capture of Baarlo, Bong and Zoterbeek, the Highland Division had completed "Ascot" as far as was required, and the 15th (Scottish) Division were allotted the task of attacking from farther north against what was left of the German bridgehead on our side of the Maas across from Venlo. Further, there was work for the Highland Division in the Nijmegen bridgehead, and to that area they moved on 28th November, where they relieved the American 101st Airborne Division. At this time Lt.-Col. Cumming-Bruce (1st Gordons) was posted to command the 44th Infantry Brigade, 15th (Scottish) Division, and Lt.-Col. J. A. Grant-Peterkin took over the Battalion.

As far as the 21st Army Group's sector was concerned, there were now no Germans south or west of the Maas. In actual fact the Group held one bridgehead across that river. That bridgehead extended from Cuyjx, which is some ten miles due south of Nijmegen, to Driel, some six miles north-east of s'Hertogenbosch, the width limits of the Nijmegen corridor. Nijmegen itself was in the corridor. When the Rhine turns west to the sea it breaks into two parts; the southern, on which stands Nijmegen, is named the Waal, and the northern, the Neder Rijn or Lek. The Corps had an advanced bridgehead in the area between those two river branches. It was in that area that those great battles had taken place, when our ground forces had striven in vain to get through to the beleaguered airborne troops who had been dropped around Arnhem. The bridgehead was known as the "Island," and it was with no great enthusiasm that the Division turned north to share

THE LOWLANDS OF HOLLAND

in its defence. The 49th Division, under command of the Canadian Corps, were holding Nijmegen with one Brigade, and they had their other two Brigades on the " Island." The Highland Division came in on their left.

But Nijmegen did not turn out to be as much a harassed town as the Division had imagined. In fact, the Dutch population were going about their lawful occasions without any very great interruptions from the German artillery and air force. The bridge at Nijmegen across the Waal, which carried the main road to the " Island," although in full view of the enemy, was shelled (but very accurately) only on occasion. The " Island " itself was not a " nasty " place. It was, of course, very flat, with innumerable dykes, large farms with very large orchards, and small villages connected by roads built on the causeway principle. The troops occupied the villages and farm-houses. There was any amount of livestock (especially poultry) wandering about ownerless, so that soldiers in Randwijk, Heteren and Opheusden, front-line villages roughly on the south bank of the Lek, and in the reserve positions at Zetter, Andelst and Valburg, lived literally on the fat of the land. Occasionally it was necessary during the night to make track-marks in the open fields to delude the Germans into thinking that a big attack was in the offing ; occasionally the enemy laid on a heavy mortar bombardment on one or other of the villages, but that was about the extent of the discomfort. Some battalions had casualties as the result of Schu-mines, and one Black Watch officer was taken prisoner while on a reconnaissance patrol. But the battalions, even in the front line, held a very satisfactory St Andrew's Night.

On 2nd December Private James Kerr, 11th Parachute Brigade, who had succeeded in evading capture after Arnhem, came into the lines of the 1st Gordons, and on the same day a loud explosion was heard : the Hun had burst the Lek dyke and flooded the island. Operation " Noah," which had been prepared in case of this eventuality, was set a-going, and the 49th Division drew back their front to higher ground. The 152 Brigade immediately sent most of its transport south over the Nijmegen bridge, and the Ross-shire Buffs and the Sutherlands followed. The Camerons were withdrawn on the 4th along with the 5th Black Watch and 1st Gordons. The 5/7th Gordons were put under command of 154 Brigade, who were left to hold the " Island." But the flooding increased to such an extent that on 7th December only the 1st and 7th Black Watch remained north of the

Maas. By this time all civilians had been evacuated from the "Island," where all their homesteads were in a state of desolation and ruin. There were occasional clashes between water-borne patrols. In one of these the 7th Black Watch brought back five soldiers of the 13th Paratroopers. The 152 Brigade came back on the "Island" on 19th December and relieved the two 154 battalions there.

These battalions, who had been driven off the "Island" by the floods, had had a very pleasant time in various villages in the s'Hertogenbosch–Nijmegen area. They had settled down to training for future battles and preparations for a not-so-distant Christmas. The battalion flags were flown, guards paraded whenever possible in the kilt, there were Highland dancing and piping and dining, cinema-shows, parties given by enthusiastic Dutch civilians, football matches between units. The Moderator of the Church of Scotland visited the Division, and Field-Marshal Montgomery held an investiture at which the 7th Argylls provided the Guard of Honour. One of the highlights of that relatively happy fortnight was "Retreat" played in Nijmegen (and repeated in s'Hertogenbosch) by the Massed Pipes and Drums of the 5th Camerons, the Queen's Own Cameron Highlanders of Canada, and the Cameron Highlanders of Ottawa; hard-bitten old Colonel Cameron of Erracht would have been the proud man to have seen it.[1]

On 19th December, when the 154 battalions left the "Island," Major-General Rennie took his Brigadiers on a reconnaissance to the farthest east position of the Nijmegen corridor in the vicinity of Cuyjx. Here the line was held by elements of the 2nd Canadian Army, whose eyes were turned to a point in the west where lay the Reichswald on the Dutch-German border. The Brigadiers were informed that in the first week of 1945 an offensive would be opened on this front (Canadians on the left; 30th Corps, in which was included the Highland Division, on the right), the object of which was to clear out all Germans between the Maas and the Rhine. As far as the 51st Division was concerned, the initial attack was to be made by 154 Brigade with 153 on its heels.

It was arranged that meanwhile officers commanding battalions, and their seniors, should take home-leave and be back in time for the "party." The news about leave was very welcome, as was the information about the Highland Division's attachment to the 30th Corps, in which the 51st had seen practically all of its African and Sicilian fighting, and in which it was now to remain until the end of the present

[1] He raised the 79th Cameron Highlanders in 1793 at Fort William.

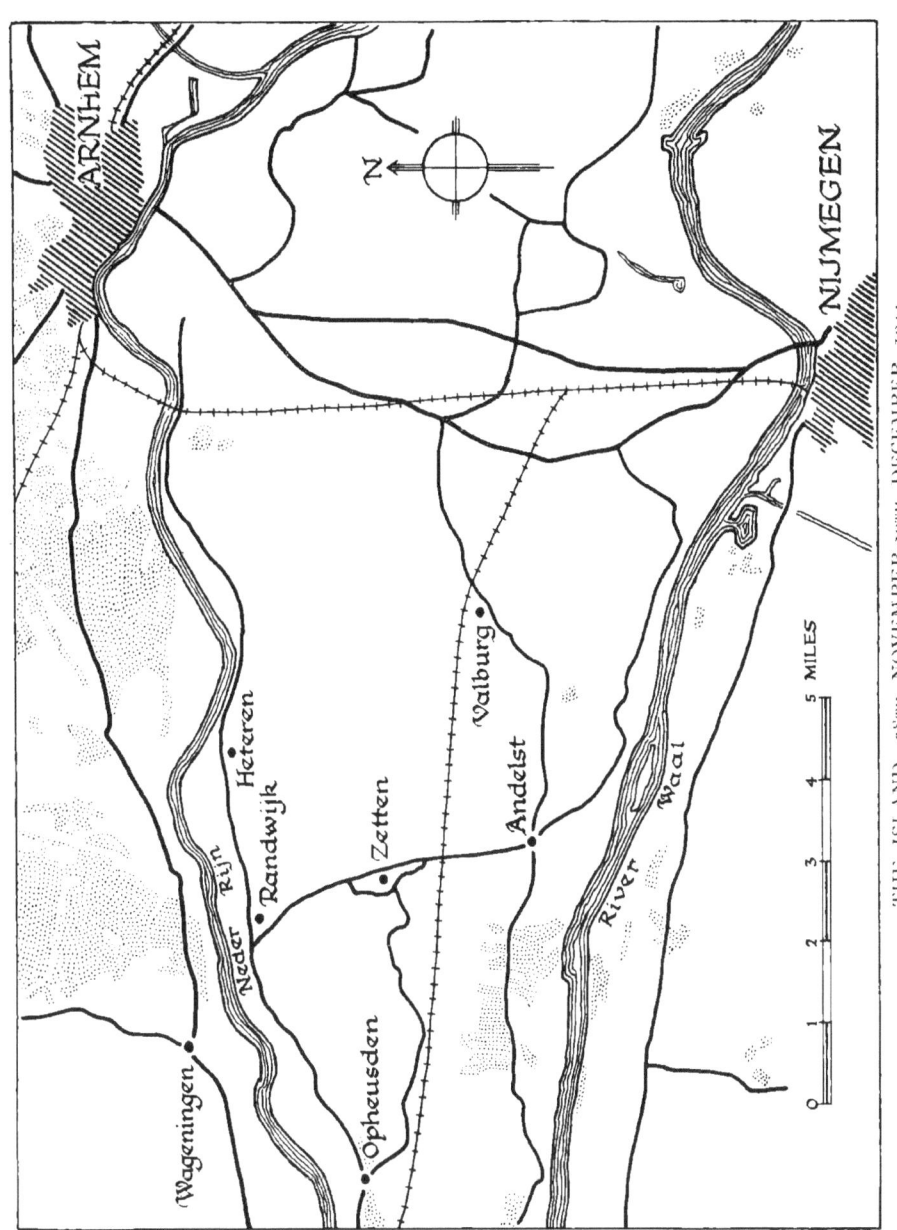

THE ISLAND, 28TH NOVEMBER–19TH DECEMBER 1944

campaign. As the recorder of the doings of 154 Brigade points out :
" The Corps was now commanded by Lieut.-General B. G. Horrocks, who appeared to be one of the most brilliant Commanders in the British Army. It was generally understood that he would have commanded the 2nd Army had he not been seriously wounded at Bizerta at the close of the North African Campaign. He had been fit to return to duty only a month or two after the Normandy landings in June 1944. He immensely impressed everyone in the Brigade with his tremendous drive and energy and his brilliant leadership and command of the 30th Corps."

But in this case Montgomery proposed and the Germans disposed. That same night word came to the Division that the enemy had made a break-through in the Ardennes area, and that the Highland Division must move south at once to help stop the gap.[1] At least two Battalion Commanders had to vacate the seats they were occupying in the leave-plane at Brussels and return to their units.

[1] The few members still serving with the Division, who remembered 1914-18, may well have recalled how the 51st on St Andrew's Day 1917, resting just after the Cambrai battle, was hastily entrained to meet the German threatened break-through in their counter-attack against the shoulders of the British salient.

CHAPTER XI.

THE BARRING O' THE DOOR

" Là a' Bhlàir's math na Càirdean."
(Friends are good in the day of battle.)

> "LAROCHE is a popular little summer resort, the 'heart of the Ardennes,' strikingly situated in a loop of the Ourthe. The neighbourhood abounds in charming walks and excursions."
> 'Guide Book.'

IT was Hitler's idea, this last desperate throw by which he hoped to drive a wedge between the British and American Armies, and so disorganise them that he would be able to reorganise his own defensive front. He hoped to seize our supply bases of Liège, Brussels and Antwerp, and then to drive the second part of his offensive southward from the areas he still held in Holland. For his Ardennes offensive he used three armies—6th Panzer in the north, 5th Panzer in the centre, and the 7th Army in the south. His first objectives were crossings over the Maas (Meuse) between Liège and Givet, just south of Dinant. He parachuted a Brigade of Panzer troops, dressed in American uniforms, into the American area, and he sent in any number of civilians and individuals in Allied uniforms to act as a kind of Fifth Column. The Americans "got wise" to those people, and regulations for entry into the zone were very strict. In fact, when the Highland Division did come down from the Nijmegen area, many individuals and groups were put through a kind of third degree by American guards.

Hitler's armies in the initial attack on 16th December had smashed right through the 1st U.S. Army's forward troops, and three days later had reached as far east as Hotton, Marche, and Bastogne. The way looked clear to Brussels. On that same day (19th) the Supreme Commander ordered Montgomery to take over command of the 9th U.S. Army, as well as the part of the 1st Army which was holding the north line of the enemy wedge. All Allied offensives were halted, and it was then that the 30th Corps were ordered south into the Louvain-Maestricht area. But the enemy was halted, and made no crossings of the Meuse. He reached Celles, close to Dinant, but that was the farthest west point of his infiltration. The American garrisons in

St Vith and Bastogne gallantly refused to give in, and, when on the 22nd December the fog, which had shrouded the whole battlefield since the beginning of the German offensive, lifted, our air force got going and that was the beginning of disaster for the Germans.

On the same day on which Montgomery had taken over his new command, the Highland Division moved south, and were placed under command of the 9th American Army. Organisation at top level was no doubt all that it should have been, but it must be recalled that the Division had a very unsatisfactory time from 20th to 23rd December, when they were pushed from pillar to post all over Belgium and elsewhere. On the 22nd they were at Maestricht, and on Christmas Day they were ordered to move to Liège.[1] Christmas dinners were eaten somehow, but there were many burned mouths as a result of food grabbed hastily.

Some troops were able to enjoy the Christmas puddings generously gifted by Her Majesty The Queen, while a CHRISTMAS MESSAGE FROM THE DIVISIONAL COMMANDER was read to all. It ran as follows :—

"I had intended starting a week ago to visit every company or equivalent unit in the Division and to wish you a Happy Christmas and New Year, and to thank you all for what you have done for the Highland Division, but events have made that impossible. I am afraid Christmas will not be as well organised as it might have been, but I hope the food and drink turn up, and that you will all have as happy a Christmas as can be under the circumstances.

The present German offensive has been, to a large extent, established, and the flanks of the break-through are firm, so in the next few days we must expect a counter-offensive to be launched by the Allies which should have far-reaching results—results which, we hope, will shorten the war and make the task of forcing the defensive and river obstacles between us and BERLIN easier.

For the present we are serving under the command of General Simpson, who commands the Ninth United States Army, and we are held in reserve to counter-attack in the event of a German break-through on this front. General Simpson told me he was very proud to have the Division under his command and he knows of our great traditions. We must therefore be sure to deal with any tasks we are given in true H.D. fashion.

Another year of great achievements and deeds is drawing to a close and let us hope that next spring will see final victory and our task of bringing the Germans to utter defeat completed.

Good luck, and a Very Happy New Year to you all."

---

[1] In this area the Division had their first experience of the "buzz-bomb." The Liège area received some fifty to sixty per day.

The Division were given guard duties on certain of the Maas crossings between Liège and Namur on the last day of the year. They were on those positions for one week, and on 7th January moved forward in the great counter-offensive on a line that was to bring them by Hotton and Laroche to Houffalize. The concentration area was in the vicinity of Marche, the small town which at one time marked the "march" between the Duchy of Luxembourg and the Prince-bishopric of Liège. This was also the "routing" place of Quentin Durward's enemy, William de la Marck, "the wild boar of the Ardennes." This forest is on an extension of that plateau, the Eifel of West Germany, and is made a kind of country of fairyland romance by the beautiful valleys (those of the Maas, the Ourthe, and other rivers) on the bluffs surrounding which stand many castles old in story, and between which torrents foam.

The Highland Division had already fought in Europe over many kinds of terrain and under varying weather conditions—sun and storm, vineyard and wood, mud and flood. Now they were to experience the rigours of snow and ice in a land where roads were few, and those few choked by snowdrifts. Of the romantic valleys the one which interested the Division was that of the Ourthe, foaming through a deep gorge—difficult to attack, easy to defend. Infantry could move over the open country, tanks could not. The Division had to attack down the Ourthe valley, and General Rennie developed a very interesting method of advance. The main south road through the valley was joined at intervals by cross-roads moving east and west. General Rennie's idea was to send a Brigade over the open country to the right. Immediately it reached one of those cross-roads it was to bear along it to the left and follow it down to the main road in the valley. As soon as this Brigade was impressing its power on the enemy, then another Brigade would advance down the main road to that point, and having established themselves there, the two Brigades would hold until their transport could be got up the main road. Artillery could move only on the roads, so the guns were brought into action actually on the roads. Tank support was supplied as usual, and as excellently as usual, by the 33rd Armoured Brigade. Their tracks were "sharpened"; that is, they were fitted with special snow studs. As in the case of the earlier attacks on the canals, sledges were brought into use so that ammunition and supplies could be got forward quickly to the infantry.

General Rennie decided to entrust the advance on the right to

153 Brigade, while 154 were to make their way up the main road. At eight o'clock in the morning of 9th January, 153 Brigade set out. In artificial moonlight the 1st Gordons (Major Lindsay : Lt.-Col. Grant-Peterkin had gone on leave) led the way from the little village of Verdenne, and moved up through the forest of birk and fir—very reminiscent of a Scottish hillside—while the sun slowly took over the duties of the searchlights. The Gordons reached the plateau after some two hours' climbing. Then they crossed a valley and climbed up the farther side, where they met their first enemy in the form of mines. But the sappers got going and cleared row after row. The Gordons had made a firm base in the buildings of a farm named du Chauvaiment, which the Germans now began to shell. The medical officer, who had set up an aid-post there, was killed. But the 1st Gordons reached their objective, and the 5th Black Watch (Lt.-Col. Bradford) and 5/7th Gordons (Lt.-Col. Irvine [1]) passed through them down the track to Hodister.

The 5/7th Gordons had been quartered earlier in Heure, and it is on record that, being in the country of wild boars, they organised a boar-hunt on 6th January. The hunters claimed to have wounded a fox and to have killed a mouse.

In their initial advance on the 9th, the 5/7th Gordons' only trouble was the treacherous surface of the ground. After passing through the 1st Gordons, a bulldozer led and cleared the way through the drifts. The 5/7th occupied Hodister without opposition in the early evening.

Meanwhile, 154 Brigade had been moving straight down the defile road of the Ourthe to the town of Laroche. The road entering Laroche is cut out of solid rock. At eight o'clock in the morning of 11th January the 1st Black Watch (Lt.-Col. Hopwood) set off on foot to Laroche, with a troop of Derbyshire Yeomanry in armoured cars in the lead. As the first car turned a bend on the rock-carved road near the outskirts of Laroche, the crew found themselves gazing into the muzzle of a Tiger tank gun. It took them a considerable time to realise that the tank had been abandoned some time before by the enemy. So the 42nd came in to the ruined streets of the once beautiful town, and it was only when they got to the farther side that they found themselves being opposed from a ridge beyond the town. On a house on that ridge a party of the enemy held up the 1st Black Watch, so the

---

[1] Lt.-Col. Renny, who was a K.O.S.B., had left to command a Brigade in the 52nd (Lowland) Division. Lt.-Col. Irvine, of the ancient family of Drum, Aberdeenshire, had served with the Division throughout.

7th Battalion, who were following close behind, were passed through up a heavily wooded hill on the right, and made for the village of Hives. They were also held up until the hours of darkness by a German tank which was firing down the only track leading into the village. Under cover of night, however, the 7th entered the village, and after confused fighting took some forty prisoners. Meanwhile the 1st Black Watch continued their attack on the ridge and finally cleared it, but at the expense of four officer casualties. Later they moved into the village of Erneuville, and next morning contacted the Americans coming up from the south. The advance of both Black Watch battalions had been assisted by armoured bulldozers, which had driven a way through the main street of Laroche, up till that time completely blocked by fallen masonry. That meant that a way was clear for the tanks, which moved up to the assistance of the Black Watch battalions. " Weasels " also had given very great assistance.[1]

On 12th January the 5th Black Watch were put under command of 154 Brigade, and they advanced from Laroche on the left of the 1st Black Watch. They had a very thin time for they met strong opposition from German infantry, who were supported both by self-propelled guns and tanks. The road along which they were advancing had been barricaded by fallen trees and had also been mined.

One of the Northamptonshire Yeomanry tanks supporting the Argylls was knocked out, and that battalion were subjected to considerable fire from Spandaus, mortars, and Panther tanks. The Argylls lost their " A " Company Commander, Major Peter Samwell. Major Samwell was the author of that volume, ' An Infantry Officer with the 8th Army,' which contains a first-hand account of his experiences with the Division in the desert. That same evening the Argylls took the ridge of Lavaux, and on the 13th they made their final objective, Beaulieu, knocking out one Panther tank on the way.

On the 12th, 153 Brigade had continued their advance. The 5/7th Gordons came into Laroche after 154 Brigade had passed through, and next morning advanced and took Roupage and Ortho without opposition.

On the 14th an S.O.S. from elements of the Reconnaissance Regiment in Varempage was received. The Gordon relief party were instrumental

---

[1] A " Weasel " was a new kind of light carrier with rubber tracks and no armour. It could use its track to float and swim, and " could go anywhere under any conditions."

in capturing a considerable number of the forty-five prisoners taken on this occasion.

The 5th Black Watch had now returned to 153 Brigade, and on the 13th the 1st Gordons, who had passed through Laroche, were sent up to support them. They joined forces in Hubermont, after a Gordon officer reconnaissance party had had a brush with the enemy. The Gordons then advanced on Nisramont, but their tank support came under heavy fire from German tanks, with the result that three Shermans and one of our self-propelled guns were knocked out. Since there was no cover of any kind, it was necessary to wait for darkness before the attack could be continued. At eight o'clock in the evening the Gordons moved up the slope, only to find that the Bosche had also taken advantage of the cover of night to evacuate the village.

The 152 Brigade's main duties in this attack were mopping-up and patrolling. The 5th Camerons (Lt.-Col. Lang) moved forward across the Laroche–Marche road on the 10th and spent their time cleaning up the woods towards the Champlon cross-road. They also captured the village of Ronchamps. The scout platoon and an "A" Company platoon finally linked up with the patrols of a 3rd American Army unit moving up from the south. On the 9th the 5th Seaforth took the village of Genes. The 2nd Seaforth occupied Halleux and proceeded to relieve the Camerons in Ronchamps. The 5th Seaforth were sent forward to reduce the village of Mierchamps on 11th January, and it will always remain somewhat of a puzzle in the memory of that battalion why they were not wiped out as they crossed the featureless valley from Vecmont. They entered the village about nine o'clock in the evening, and took some seventy prisoners, only six of whom put up any fight whatever. What had gone wrong with the lately triumphant enemy? The situation is perhaps best explained by Alastair Borthwick, the historian of the 5th Seaforth. He writes [1]:—

"The postscript to the Ardennes offensive is best given in the words of two Belgian boys, because their description of what they saw during the fortnight of German occupation shows in miniature the whole course of the offensive—the sweeping advance, the first check, the cutting of the supply lines by our planes, the massing of our forces, the final disillusionment.

'They came on Christmas Day,' they said. 'They made a feast and the toast was *To Paris, Brussels, Antwerp*. But they did not go forward. And when that happened, they knew. In five days, in five days only, the soldiers

[1] See footnote, page 35.

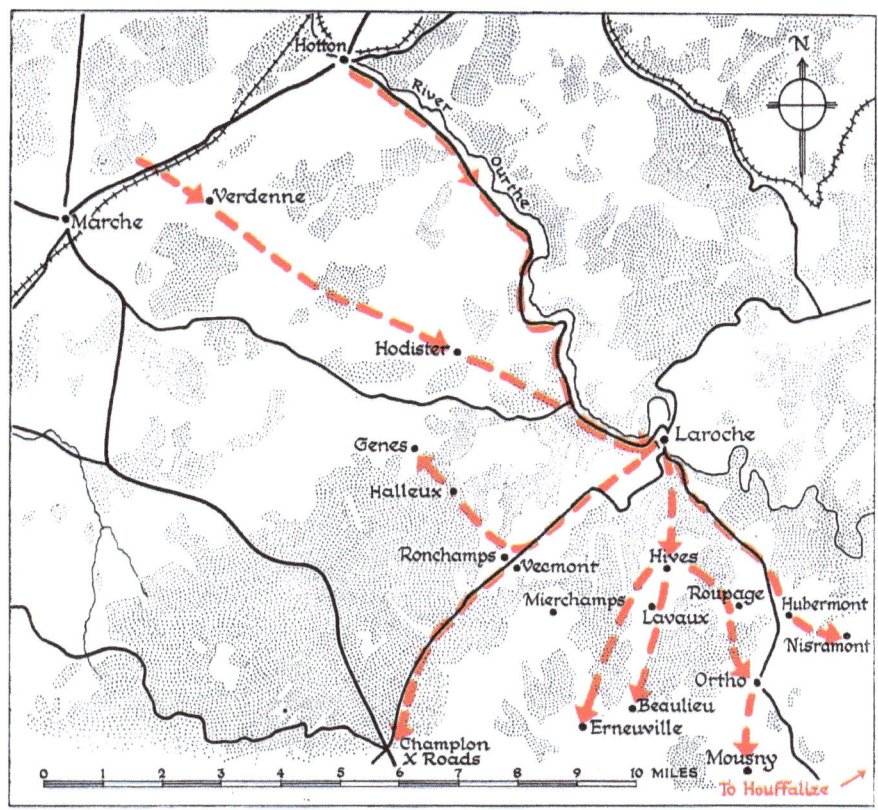

THE ARDENNES. MARCHE, 7TH JANUARY; NISRAMONT, 13TH JANUARY 1945

were saying Von Rundsted was a traitor who had led the Wehrmacht into a trap. Then there was fine weather, and your planes came. By New Year's Day they were slaughtering our beasts because they had no food. Already they had used all our petrol—those vehicles you took, they could not drive them away because of that. They became very miserable. They said they were betrayed by their officers. They knew nothing of the battle. A shell would land, and one would say : *That is British*. And another would say : *No. It is German*. They knew nothing, except that the British were creeping in. They stayed in one place, but it was as if the country round them had moved. When you came, they were in great fear and ran to the cellars. They made the old people sit on their knees so that they would be protected by them. Paris, Brussels, Antwerp ! Aaah, the bandits, the dirty bandits ! ' "

And so the Highland Division moved north once more from the Ardennes snow, with the memory of the destruction of the Laroche fairy valley, of the terror spread amongst the inhabitants of Liège by the arrival of the " V " bombs, but most of all of the anguished faces of the Belgian people, and their piteous cry as they looked towards the threatening German east : " You will not let them come back again ! "

It has been estimated that his Ardennes offensive cost the enemy 120,000 men and 600 tanks and assault guns. It was a bold venture, but one that could not hope to succeed without air supremacy. When the fog, which blanketed the German initial infiltration, lifted, and the Allied Air Force got going, the situation was hopeless as far as the enemy was concerned. His lines of communication were battered to pieces.

The Allies, however, had temporarily lost the initiative. It was up to them now to regain it without delay, and to see that they held it right to the end.

CHAPTER XII.

THE PATH THROUGH THE WOODS

> "*Dh' aindeoin co theireadh e.*"
> (Gainsay who dare.)

> "My luve's in Germanie,
> Fighting brave for Royalty."
>   OLD SCOTS SONG.

AND to gain that initiative was mounted the operation known as "Veritable." In an earlier chapter it was stated that on their northerly courses the Maas and the Rhine run more or less parallel. The capture of the area between those two rivers was the idea in "Veritable," and a simple method of comprehending the Allied move is to consider that area between the two rivers as another Normandy, and the Maas as the English Channel. The Nijmegen bridgehead was, as it were, the first and most northerly of the Allied landings, and was made by the 1st Canadian Army and part of the 2nd Army. Again those armies would form a kind of pivot. They would hammer away in a direct attack on the German defences, and would so hope to draw the enemy's reserves to their opposition. Then in the southern area the Americans would make their "landings" (Maas crossings) and would sweep north to join the Canadians and British in what might prove to be the last great battle of the war, because in it the Germans might be so heavily handled that they would not be able to put up much of a show later on the east bank of the Rhine.

The whole of the Canadian attack had to be pushed across the Maas by temporary bridges in the Nijmegen area and concentrated in the relatively small bridgehead there. Preparations had to be made for two types of weather conditions: frost and snow, or thaw, mud and flooding. Both Rhine and Maas had overflowed their banks during the December rains, and the ground between the rivers was very sodden. The Canadian attack had to overcome some three lines of defence. Before the Reichswald Forest could be reached, a strong belt of defences over a mile in depth had to be reduced. These consisted of an anti-tank ditch and strong-pointed farms and villages. Having broken through this belt, the attack would have to cross some two miles of relatively open country to the northern extremity of the

Siegfried Line, which ran from a point on the Nijmegen–Cleve road southward through the close-growing trees of the Reichswald to the strong-point of the town of Goch. This part of the Siegfried Line consisted of an elaborate trench system punctuated by pill-boxes, and behind it a second line of defensive works from Cleve to Goch. Some six miles farther to the east was another line, named by Montgomery the Hochwald "lay-back"—a new High Wood.[1] The 9th United States Army had to cross the Roer and advance up the east bank of the Maas to meet the 1st Canadian Army.

The 30th Corps was to lead the Canadian attack—a Corps front was all the width at their disposal. The troops making this break-in would have to widen their front as much as possible, so that the 2nd Canadian Corps might come in on the left on this now two-Corps-width advance. The 30th Corps attack was to go in at 10.30 on the morning of 8th February, and was to be made by six Infantry Divisions, two Armoured Divisions, three Armoured Brigades, and many specialised regiments in all sorts of armoured vehicles—*e.g.*, flame-throwing tanks. A thousand guns would supply the initial bombardment, and the Allied Air Forces were to be there in very great strength. Five Infantry Divisions would advance together in the initial move. The 3rd Canadian Division would be on the left flank, and then in order left to right were the 2nd Canadian, 15th Scottish, 53rd Welsh, and 51st Highland Divisions.[2] It was well that consideration had been given to all possible weather conditions, for the hope that the frost would hold was shattered a week before D Day. So the preparations for an advance over soaking, boggy ground were put in train.

General Rennie decided that, since his Divisional jumping-off frontage was so narrow, he would use only one Brigade for the initial break-in, and he selected James Oliver's 154, strengthening them by putting under their command the 5/7th Gordons (Lt.-Col. Irvine). This jumping-off line was entirely suitable for the beginning of a daylight attack, since the sight of it from the enemy's point of view was hidden by a heavily wooded ridge. The 7th Black Watch (Lt.-Col. Cathcart) were the right-hand battalion in the attack, and on the night of 6th February they were moved in troop-carriers to the assembly area. With the aid of a sand-model and large-scale maps the men were all briefed the following day.

---

[1] A battlefield of the Somme of 1916 where the 51st had fought.

[2] The other Divisions in the Corps were the 43rd Wessex and the 52nd Lowland—all five were Territorial Divisions.

At five o'clock on the morning of the 8th the artillery opened the ball with a bombardment the like of which the Division had not experienced since Alamein. Every possible type of gun went into action. Three and a quarter hours later the 7th moved from the assembly area on to the start-line, and at 10.46 A.M. the leading companies began advancing close behind the barrage. " A " Company took the first objective, the village of Breedeweg, without much difficulty, but " D " Company were less fortunate, for some determined German snipers killed three officers, among them Major K. A. Lowe, who had served with the unit in Africa, where he was twice severely wounded, but had rejoined in Sicily, and had been with the Battalion ever since. Tanks put paid to the snipers' accounts, and the 5/7th Gordons then passed through the 7th Black Watch.

A few minutes before 11 A.M. the 1st Black Watch moved off towards their objective just inside the Reichswald trees. They got there by 1.20 P.M., an important hour on an important day. In reply to their message, " Positions taken," came back one from General Horrocks congratulating the 42nd on being first on German soil. Colonel John Hopwood had gone on leave, so that it was actually Major Peter Taylor who was commanding on this auspicious occasion. It put the hallmark on the career of this 1939 6th Battalion private, now commanding the 1st Battalion in battle in Hitler's Reich.

So far so good. But soon congestion on the track became everybody's headache. The anti-tank ditch had given the leading infantry little trouble, but now it had to be bridged for vehicle-crossings, and this also led to confusion. However, all was accomplished in time, and the 5/7th Gordons got into the edge of the forest just as darkness fell. They had very stiff fighting there. At one cross-roads among the trees " C " Company found themselves taking part unofficially in a German take-over. " C " Company did not hesitate to attack, with the happy result that the take-over never took place, and they collected 148 prisoners.

Meanwhile the 7th Argylls (Lt.-Col. MacKinnon) had been waiting in another forest—a forest of abandoned gliders left in the open ground in front of the Reichswald by the 82nd U.S. Airborne Division's 1944 summer bid for victory. The 7th Argylls moved up through the 1st Black Watch and carried on the confused but intense fighting in the dense clumps of the trees.

The 152 Brigade (Brigadier Cassels) followed on the heels of 154. The 5th Camerons (Lt.-Col. Lang) went in behind the 5/7th Gordons, and their progress was both slow and costly, but by mid-afternoon they had reached their first objective in the forest. At 7 A.M. on the 9th the 5th Seaforth, now commanded by Lt.-Col. J. M. Sym (Lt.-Col. Walford [1] having gone home to a very well-deserved rest to command the 9th Battalion), moved in and passed through Breedeweg village. In the afternoon the Seaforth advanced through the forest half a mile north of the Camerons and ran slap into a German counter-attack. But they pushed the enemy back with the bayonet and proceeded to dig in some thousand yards farther into the forest than any other of our troops. The 2nd Seaforth (Lt.-Col. Andrews) had advanced through the 5th Camerons, but found themselves held up by an enemy strongpoint. There was nothing to be done but lie down and wait for the first light of 10th February, when, with the assistance of a troop of Crocodiles, they cleared out the enemy positions.

The 153 Brigade's business was to form a firm base on the high ground at the south-west corner of the Reichswald, to dislodge the enemy from the wooded plateau to the west of that point, and then to cut the Mook–Gennep road. They were not to move from their start-line on the 8th till 154 Brigade had taken their first objectives, since both Brigades had to advance on the one and only axis. The 5th Black Watch moved forward at four o'clock in the afternoon. This was a Second-in-Command battle for many battalions. In the case of the 5th Black Watch, Lt.-Col. Bradford was on leave, and Major George Dunn, another stalwart of the Division and one of its most experienced fighters, had taken over. The Battalion took its objective in the forest, and on the following morning made a right wheel and moved southwards. Through a thick smoke barrage they captured several defended houses, and then got ready for the third day attack on the small township of Gennep on the banks of the River Niers, a couple of miles east of the Maas.

The 1st Gordons (also led by their Second-in-Command, Major Martin Lindsay: in this case the C.O., Lt.-Col. Grant-Peterkin of Grange in Moray, was commanding the Brigade in the absence of Brigadier Roddy Sinclair, who was in hospital) moved forward at 5.20 in the afternoon, left most of their tank support in the mud,

---

[1] To appreciate what Colonel Jack Walford's bravery had accomplished, one has only to read 'Sans Peur,' the Regimental History of the Sutherlands. Towards the end his men became superstitious about him. They believed that, if they stuck close enough to him, they would not be hit.

waited patiently while the forward troops vacated the tracks, and soon occupied their first night positions. One vehicle did get forward—a Weasel carrying five hundred tins of self-heating soup. Next day the Gordon Battalion spent in mopping up what Germans still remained in the villages of St Martensberg and Grafwegen, the country in between, and the valley to the south. That valley gave some trouble, but at length tanks did get forward, and settled that difficulty. On the far side of the valley the Germans had very strongly fortified entrenchments, but after an artillery " stonk " " C " Company occupied these and the village of Del Hel beyond them. The 5th Black Watch by this time had cut the Mook–Gennep road, but " A " Company of the 1st Gordons were held up by a strong-point, and, until that was dealt with, the road could not be used for Corps axis purposes. Major Lindsay, who collected a very good D.S.O. for this show, personally took command of his leading company, fought his way through a nasty ambush, attacked the strong-point, and, as he himself records [1] : " There was a cheer and a burst of Sten, and a wild surge forward, and in a moment a shout of ' Kamerad ' and a column of Huns, seventy-one in number, came running out with their hands up. The front platoon fanned out and we went forward in the moonlight, climbing over broken walls and piles of rubble interlaced with a honeycomb of trenches. I was afraid that some enthusiast in front might shoot at us, so I passed the word back to the two pipers with Company H.Q. to play the regimental march, and before long we heard the distant strain of ' Cock o' the North '—we heard the pipers of the Camerons of Canada and knew we had not far to go."

Beyond the Reichswald the country becomes more open, sloping down from the woods to a kind of plain, cut through by tributaries of the Maas, chief of which, as far as Highland Divisional responsibilities were concerned, were the Niers and the Kendel. On the far bank of the Niers lay the town of Kessel, a German strong-point, and the river itself in its flooded condition was a natural and perfect anti-tank ditch. So far the attack on the Reichswald had been a success, despite the lack of roads and the tragic thaw. The 53rd (Welsh) Division on the 51st's left were well forward, while on their left the 15th (Scottish) were making for the town of Kranenburg.

What Corps required now was a secure axis for a further advance, and that axis was controlled by the township of Hekkens. That town-

[1] See footnote, page 136.

ship lies on the southern edge of the Reichswald at the cross-roads of the Gennep-Cleve and Kessel-Goch highways. The Siegfried Line (second line it might be called) ran through Hekkens, at which point it was heavily defended by concrete constructions. It was essential that this village should be reduced, and such reduction had been one of 152 Brigade's objectives. But 152 had come up against a very difficult obstacle, the southern portion of the German anti-tank ditch, which was lined by a determined enemy armed with all sorts of automatic weapons. The 5th Seaforth had to go to ground in a road ditch some fifty yards from the Germans, and for a whole night and day they were held there until, under tank-fire cover, they withdrew back into the forest. The 5th Camerons, in their advance, had made several brilliant bayonet charges. Sergeant McClew, when his platoon officer had been wounded, took over command and with great bravery led his men, sadly reduced in numbers, across a hundred yards of open country to the enemy's lines, where he liquidated twenty Huns who had been manning five machine-guns. For this spirited action he gained his D.C.M.

But one of the most interesting "charges" of the day was made by Lieutenant J. R. Le Mesurier, who was attached to the Camerons from the Canadian Army. He had fired off all his ammunition, so he picked up a shovel, charged an enemy machine-gun team, and knocked them out. Then on their final objective on the road, an incident occurred in the Cameron lines which illustrates very well what was meant by the term "confused fighting" in reference to the Reichswald battle. A Cameron corporal collected some full mess-tins from the cooks' truck, and was walking back to his platoon's position, when in the dusk he saw three figures coming towards him also apparently carrying mess-tins; members of his own platoon he presumed, undoubtedly seeking their own breakfast. The corporal recovered from his surprise quicker than did the three Germans, who were making for the wrong cook-house, with the result that, as a chronicler puts it, "the corporal brought home his three prisoners with the bacon." The 2nd Seaforth, who had been fighting on the right of their 5th Battalion, were also withdrawn into the wood. In those positions 152 Brigade remained while 154 were ordered to reduce Hekkens.

On the afternoon of 11th February General Rennie gave Brigadier Oliver his instructions regarding Hekkens, and arranged for the whole Corps artillery to concentrate on the village. Night fighting amid the

Reichswald standing trees, and the paths blocked by the fallen ones, was a hopeless business, so it was decided that 154 Brigade should do their best to make Hekkens their own before darkness came down. An attack beginning at 3.30 in the afternoon would have the use of some ninety minutes of daylight, and at that hour the two 154 Black Watch battalions moved off from a start-line some mile and a quarter north-east of Hekkens. If ever an action was won by complete co-operation of gunners and infantry, it was this one. It was like an attack of the First War, in General Harper's day. The infantry kept so close behind the barrage that they were in on the Huns before the latter knew what was happening, and by seven o'clock in the evening both battalions were firmly established in the village and had taken a couple of hundred prisoners. After the capture of the village, Lt.-Col. John Hopwood returned to command the 42nd, Major Taylor at the same time being appointed chief instructor at the Divisional Battle School.

Major Dunn with the 5th Black Watch had also, as arranged, captured the important village of Gennep on the third day. He ferried his men over the River Niers in assault boats; the village was taken without difficulty, but just beyond it there was much heavy fighting in which the 1st Gordons, who had also crossed the Niers, joined. There is one strange story of this village of Gennep. It has been told again and again, but always with a sense of wonder. Captain Donald Beales of the 5th Black Watch was standing in the doorway of a house in Gennep, where he had established the headquarters of his company. He sent his runner, Private Smith, on a message, who, as he moved down the roadway, shouted back to his officer: "I'll see you in twenty minutes, sir." The next minute Beales was killed, as was Smith exactly twenty minutes later.

And now the Niers waterway problem faced the other battalions of the Division. This river is normally only some thirty yards wide, but its width had been more than doubled by flooding, and the approaches from both sides were soggy in the extreme. From the high ground on the far bank of the Niers the enemy had the whole Corps axis road under observation, so that, although junction had been made between 153 and 154 Brigades, and the whole highway was clear, the road could not function under this direct Bosche observation. It was, therefore, necessary that the river should be crossed, the high ground—the enemy's observation-post—cleared, and a bridgehead formed which would include the village of Kessel, which lies on the main road to the comparatively large town of Goch, the Division's final objective. That town was also the final objective of the 43rd Division, which had not been used in the initial attack but which was now advancing through Cleve on Goch. The Highland Division was to go in from the west.

General Rennie ordered 154 Brigade to mount this attack over the Niers. The Reichswald runs down to the river bank north-east of Kessel, and the 7th Argylls were positioned in the woods at that point early on 12th February. Buffaloes were supplied to take the two Black Watch battalions over the swollen Niers on the night of the 13th-14th. The 7th Black Watch moved first in order to establish a small bridgehead to include the villages of Kapelle and Villers. Their crossing at a loop of the river south-west of the Hekkens cross-roads was not opposed. Kapelle offered slight resistance and then a batch of fifty prisoners. Villers was a little more difficult, very definite resistance being put up from a house in the middle of the village which ultimately yielded one hundred prisoners. But the Buffaloes down by the river were not having an easy time. They were shelled badly, and, when the time came for the 1st Black Watch to cross, it was found that only three were serviceable. The 1st Black Watch passed through the 7th, but ran into trouble from defended isolated buildings. One of these buildings was rushed in a sortie led by Captain Hogg, the R.A. Forward Observation officer. The breakdown of the Buffaloes, however, had presented the Battalion with an ammunition problem, and Germans began to infiltrate into the company positions. A standing patrol was captured, and Colonel Hopwood reduced his perimeter. The 5th Camerons, however, came to the rescue by sending forward an infantry company and some anti-tank guns with ammunition, and Typhoons swept over and blasted the German positions.

On 14th February the 7th Argylls were ferried across into the Black Watch bridgehead and at 10.15 P.M. moved on Kessel, which they took along with seventy prisoners, and which they proceeded next morning to put in a state of defence. Twenty-four hours later Churchill tanks came through, advanced some three hundred yards, cleared out a German dug-out-defended line, and doubled the Argylls' prisoner bag.

On the 16th, tanks (Crocodiles with flame-throwers) got up to the 1st Black Watch positions. These tanks comprised a squadron of the Fife and Forfar Yeomanry, and they advanced with the 42nd on the railway station of the village of Hassum, which was taken. But no sooner was that done than the enemy put down an artillery bombardment on the village, as a result of which the Black Watch had several casualties, among them two officers. One of those officers was Major Ian Molteno of Garth in Perthshire, the one-time home of that earliest of Black Watch historians, General David Stewart. Molteno had lost an eye in Africa, but had managed by gallant importunism to force his way back to the side of his comrades.

It was now 152's turn to lead the way. The two Seaforth battalions, which had sustained many casualties during their strenuous 8000-yard advance, had had four days out of action. The Camerons were holding Hekkens, and had sent over one company into the Black Watch bridgehead to strengthen the line. That company, however, was not required to go into action. Now the Brigade was to advance down the main road to Goch, and to clear a triangle of villages on the way. The 78th were to take Grafenthal, 5th Camerons Asper, and 5th Seaforth Hervost and Asperden. The Fife and Forfar Crocodiles went with them. The 2nd Seaforth led off from Kessel at 7 P.M. on 16th February for Grafenthal. An hour and a half later they reached the road-fork to the village. By half-past eleven they had made their final objective, which was a large hospital building in Grafenthal, taken by a bit of dash and daring on the part of Major Andrew Todd and his men.

The Sutherlands passed the 78th's road-fork as soon as it was known that the 2nd Battalion was home, and made for Asperden, which had been rocketed by Typhoons during the afternoon and strafed all evening by the artillery. Also they had the support of a new Allied form of rocket attack, known as a "Mattress." This Mattress was fired from a collection of something of the nature of the Stokes guns of the earlier war, joined up in a kind of Pipes of Pan arrangement, plywood instead of reed. These guns were mounted on a carrier and each fired, on the old mortar principle, a canister carrying ten pounds of high explosive. Some ten such carriers were concentrated and all their rockets fired simultaneously, with the result that some three hundred of them (a Mattress) landed on to a small target.

In Monty's "fake-moonlight" Asperden's defenders were put to sleep under three "Mattresses," and by midnight the wearers of the Sutherland tartan had made the village their own. The Germans proceeded to shell it in the same way as they had shelled Grafenthal. There the 5th Camerons had moved through the 2nd Seaforth, and,

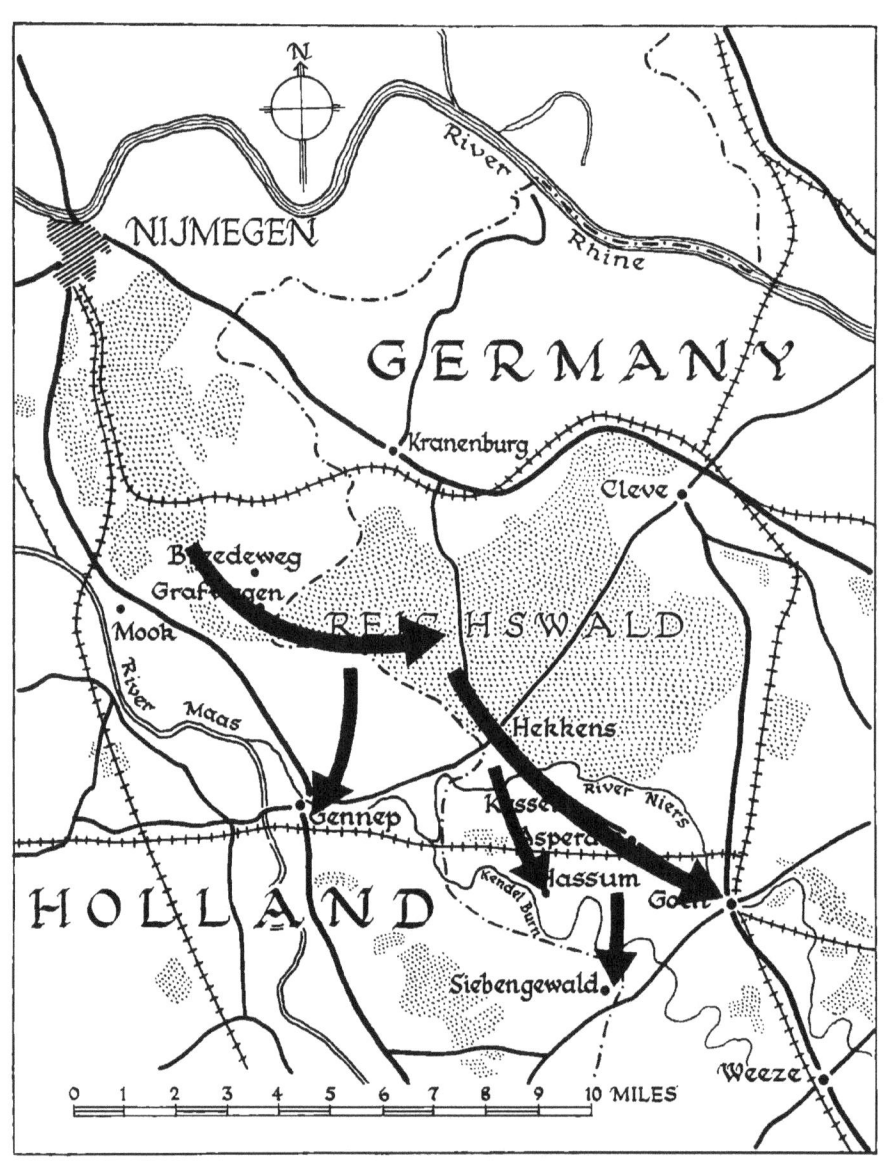

THE REICHSWALD, 8TH-18TH FEBRUARY 1945

although suffering casualties from mines, they took Hervost, and next day cleared up some pill-boxes in the area, one of which, defended by self-propelled guns, required to be smoke-screened and shelled before the Jocks could reduce it. A word of remembrance here concerning the action of the members of the Camerons' Pioneer Platoon. They climbed on the top of this recalcitrant pill-box and dropped thirty-six grenades down the ventilators. General Horrocks sent his personal congratulations to the Seaforth and Cameron Brigade for their work in this advance.

And now 153 Brigade were presented with their " pigeon "—the strongly fortified town of Goch, which was surrounded by an anti-tank ditch on three sides and a river on the fourth, and had many pill-boxes. We left the 5th Black Watch (Major Dunn) on 11th February in the town of Gennep, where they were joined by the 1st Gordons (Lt.-Col. Grant-Peterkin), who had a spell of very hard street-fighting. The Gordon method, which is illustrative of the general street-fighting technique of the Division, was to clear one side of a street by using the back-gardens as the line of attack on each individual house, then crossing at the end of the street, and clearing the other side in the same way. By the morning of the 12th, Gennep was fairly clear of the enemy, the 5/7th Gordons (Lt.-Col. Irvine) had moved over the river, and with their 1st Battalion captured the ridge features that overlooked the town. Next day the 1st Gordons had to stand up to a counter-attack, the first made by the enemy on that battalion since the June affair at Escoville. Three self-propelled guns shelled their position before the German infantry attack came in. But well-directed 3-inch mortar-fire astride the road stopped the Germans, who later on withdrew.

On the 18th, 153 Brigade received its orders for the attack on Goch. The 5th Black Watch were to be the leading battalion, and were to do their best to enter the town in the early hours of the 19th. They were to be responsible for the capture and clearance of that part of Goch which lay south of the river, which area included the main square. The 5/7th Gordons were then to pass through the Black Watch and clear the streets from the main square to the railway. The 1st Gordons were to be responsible for the main road leading out of the town to the south-west, and were to clear certain cross-roads and several large buildings, including a school and a factory.

The 152 Brigade had been ordered to make a crossing over the anti-tank ditch which surrounded Goch on three sides. The 2nd Seaforth made a very good job of this operation on 18th February, and the A.V.R.E. bridge was in position before midnight. The 5th Black Watch advanced across that bridge and entered Goch, where they found the defenders mostly peacefully asleep in cellars. The 5/7th Gordons then came in to clear their part of the town, but their Huns were awake upstairs and waiting for them. Street-fighting continued throughout the whole day and the following night, and owing to the amount of rubble in the roadways tanks were unable to get forward. The 1st Gordons again had some severe street-fighting, and " A " Company's Commander, Major A. J. Thomson, was shot through the head by a sniper. Major Thomson had only been three days with the Battalion. The 1st Gordons cleared a housing estate, and by this time tanks and Crocodiles had come up and were giving excellent support. The Gordons spent the night in the cellars of the housing estate, and next morning advanced with armoured cars in their van towards Thomashof, a group of farm buildings a mile to the south. They put in their attack round about five o'clock in the morning, and, in the confused fighting in houses on the road, Captain Kyle and some fifty men were taken prisoner by the Germans. After much heavy house-to-house scrapping, " B " Company took Thomashof. The 5th Black Watch then passed through the Gordons and attacked some buildings on a road a quarter of a mile farther east. On the following day the same battalion cleared up other positions round about Thomashof.

The 153 Brigade had been very much reduced in numbers during the attack on Goch, so the 7th Black Watch (Lt.-Col. Cathcart) was put under command, attacked through the 1st Gordons on the 20th, and ran up against very stiff opposition from both infantry and self-propelled guns concentrated in a large barracks building. In the morning a troop of Fife and Forfar Yeomanry put in appearance and " brewed up the barracks most efficiently." The 7th Argylls (Lt.-Col. MacKinnon) had moved into Goch on the 21st and took up a position on the outskirts, while the 1st Black Watch took over from their 5th Battalion just south of the town. The 7th Black Watch had returned to 154 Brigade, through which the 53rd Division now passed on their way to attack Weeze.

It looked as if the Division's interest in " Veritable " had ceased, but that was not the case. On 24th February General Rennie instructed

THIS WAY FOR THE REICHSWALD!

5/7TH GORDONS MOVE UP TO THE REICHSWALD FOREST. FEBRUARY 1945

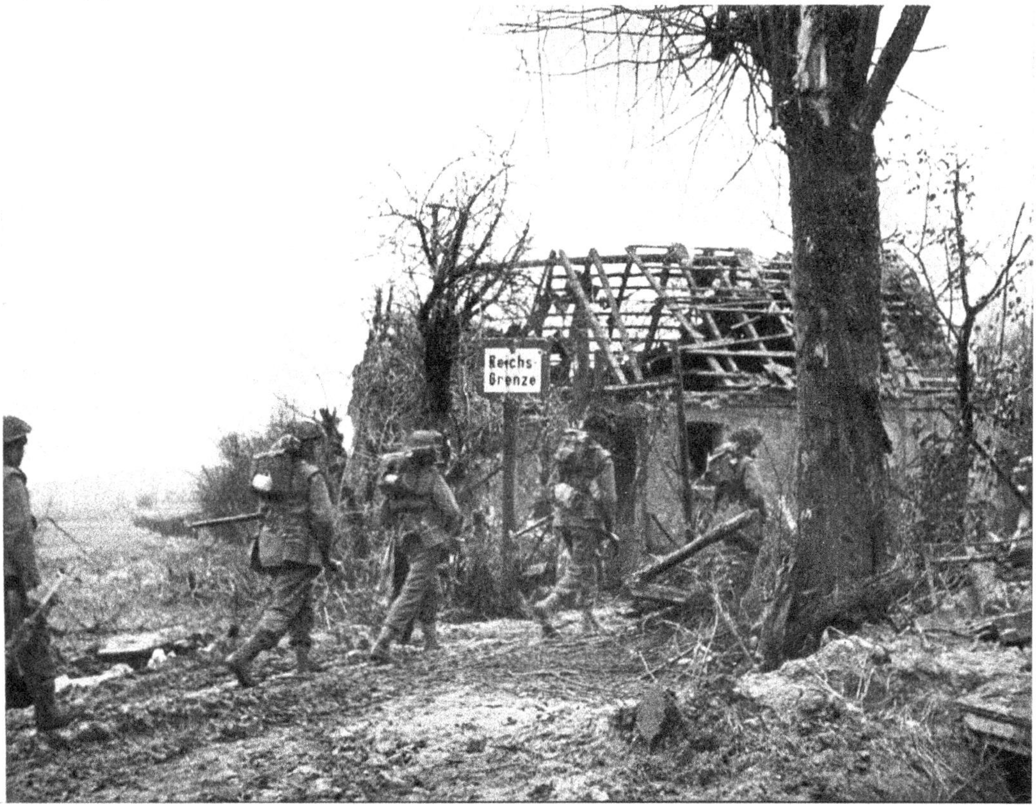

HEKKENS CORNER. FEBRUARY 1945

From the original painting by
IAN G. M. EADIE

By courtesy of the
IMPERIAL WAR MUSEUM

his Brigadiers to prepare for a still further advance. Some distance south of Goch flowed a tributary of the Niers, the River Kendel, the method of progression of which was rather on the lines of the Links of Forth. Beyond the Kendel ran another lateral road, which would be Corps' next axis, and which required to be opened at once. The Highland Division were to be responsible for such opening and were also to mop up all the area south-west of Goch to this road. The 152 Brigade set the ball rolling by moving south from the Asperheide district and capturing the village of Boeckelt, which is south-west of Goch and in the north side of one of the Kendel loops. The 5th Camerons had advanced on Boeckelt, which was surrounded on three sides by an anti-tank ditch and had the river behind it. It was known to contain three pill-boxes, and to be garrisoned by two full-strength infantry companies. At 10 P.M. on the 25th the Camerons made for the anti-tank ditch, and with only one casualty—the victim of a Schu-mine—crossed it and captured two of the pill-boxes. " C " Company then set out in search of the third pill-box, which they could not discover, until Lieutenant Van Rockel, the Dutch liaison officer, seized a prisoner and ordered him to lead the way to it. The prisoner, with a sort of " the customer is always right " smile, did lead the way to a farm-house, which turned out to be the pill-box in disguise. It was discovered from prisoners that, when the Cameron attack came in, every officer of the garrison was absent attending a conference. So low now was the morale of the German other ranks here that prisoners admitted that they had all agreed not to fire on the advancing Allies, but rather to use their guns on any Germans who made any attempt at defending the village. The Cameron bag of prisoners accordingly exceeded two hundred.

The Division suffered a severe loss at this time when Lt.-Col. Ralph Carr, the C.R.E., was severely wounded. Carr had joined the Division in North Africa, where he had had great experience as a Field Squadron Commander with the 7th Armoured Division, when Colonel Sugden, the previous C.R.E., was wounded. Carr had proved himself to be a worthy successor to Sugden, and the work accomplished by the Divisional Engineers under his command was outstandingly good. Sappers have a far more unpleasant time in war than most people realise—they take part in every battle with the forward troops, and at times, when other troops are enjoying a well-earned rest, they have to lay and lift mines, build bridges, and carry out other unpleasant tasks often under heavy shell-fire, and, even when there is no actual contact with the enemy, they have to work day and night repairing roads and bridges. Only sappers commanded and led by cheerful and determined people like Carr, and Sugden before him, can hope to do all that is expected of them, and the Division was indeed fortunate in having such excellent C.R.E.s. The standard which they set was maintained right through the Divisional Engineers, and, without their constant aid, few, if any, of the Divisional tasks could have been accomplished.

On the night of 25th-26th February the Guards Armoured Brigade put a Kapok bridge across the top of one of the loops of the Kendel just south of Boeckelt, which the 2nd Seaforth crossed in order to capture the farm-houses of Terpoten and Blumenthalshop, which lay at the base of the peninsula formed by this loop. But both farms were strongly garrisoned and defied all the efforts of our infantry and artillery to reduce them. The 5th Seaforth crossed into the isthmus behind the 78th, waiting to hear of that battalion's success before advancing on Siebengewald, which was on the proposed axis road, and was the Brigade's final objective. " C " Company of the 5th Seaforth was then sent forward and a fierce artillery bombardment was put down on the farm of Terpoten, while that company moved beyond and behind it into the farm of Jenkenshop, which was found to be undefended. In the morning, when the Germans in Terpoten realised that the Highlanders had established themselves behind them, they surrendered at once, as did the garrison of Blumenthalshop. The result was that the 5th Seaforth moved into Siebengewald without any opposition of any kind. On the evening of the 27th 152 Brigade was relieved by 156 Brigade of the 52nd (Lowland) Division, and next day began their journey back to Nijmegen.

The 154 Brigade had made an advance on the 25th on the left of 152, when the 7th Argylls crossed the Kendel loop on the west of 152 and captured Hulm. Just after midnight the 1st Black Watch crossed the river and took the town of Winkel. They then joined up with the 5th Black Watch in the village of Robbenhof, and next night the 7th Black Watch attacked Boyenhof. Elements of both Black Watch battalions had waded breast-high through the ice-cold water, but no one took any ill-effects. A smart little action with some Germans on the bank had warmed up the 7th for their attack on Boyenhof (led by Major Sam Small, who had fought with the Battalion continuously since Alamein), which they took with few casualties. But as Major

Russell writes: "Unfortunately, Lieutenant Duncan Colquhoun, A. and S.H., and Sergeant Hewan, C.M.P., both of Brigade H.Q., who had lit the route forward from Goch most ably, were killed by mortar-fire after their task had been completed. It can safely be said that no Brigade Staff had done more for its battalions throughout this campaign than that of 154 Brigade, whose efforts were quite untiring." On the 27th 154 Brigade was also relieved by the 52nd (Lowland) Division and went back to the neighbourhood of Goch.

The Division was the recipient of many congratulatory messages after the Reichswald battle. On 23rd February General Horrocks wrote: "I have seen the 51st Highland Division fight many battles since I first met them just before ALAMEIN. But I am certain that the Division has never fought better than in the recent offensive into Germany. You breached the enemy's defences in the initial attack, fought your way through the southern part of the Reichswald, overcame in succession several strong-points of the Siegfried Line such as Hekkens, etc., and then finally cleared the southern half of Goch—a key centre in the German defences. You have accomplished everything that you have been asked to do in spite of the number of additional German reserves which have been thrown in on your front. No Division has ever been asked to do more and no Division has ever accomplished more. Well done, the Highland Division."[1]

And in passing that message round the Division, General Rennie wrote: "I am sure the operations of the Division, which culminated in the capture of the Siegfried bastion of Goch, will go down in history as one of the finest achievements of the Fifty-First. Although the brunt of the fighting has necessarily been borne by the infantry, who were magnificent, success was only made possible by the great co-operation of all the arms and by the determined effort of every single man in the Division to give of his best. I thank every one of you for what you have done towards the destruction of the German Army. There may be tough times ahead but the end is at last clearly in sight. Good luck to you all."

Those messages were sent also to the 107th Regiment Royal Armoured Corps, The Scottish Horse, "A" Squadron 1st Fife and Forfar Yeomanry, "D" Squadron 1st Lothians and Border Horse, and

---

[1] Nearly two hundred years earlier William Pitt had said of the newly raised Highland Regiments: "I sought for merit wherever it was to be found. I found it in the mountains of the north."

222nd Assault Squadron A.R.E., who formed part of the Highland Division during " Veritable."

As a finale to the operation, Mr Churchill, accompanied by Field-Marshal Montgomery, General Sir Alan Brooke and Lieut.-General Crerar, visited the 51st at Grafenthals on 4th March, when the Massed Pipes and Drums of the Highland Division and of The Scottish Horse played " Retreat." [1] The Prime Minister broadcast to the Parade, when he complimented the Division on its work in " Veritable." Mr Churchill said that the achievement of the Division equalled those of any other formation in the Army, and that, although the Division had suffered grievously at St Valéry, the spirit of Scotland had never wavered.

[1] The Division always considered the Scottish Horse as a part of the 51st. They had been in it throughout the long years of training in Scotland, they picked it up again in Sicily, and they were with it in almost all the battles in France. On 20th February an interesting conference took place in a cellar in Goch between Brigadier Sinclair, who had previously served in the 15th Scottish Division, and Brigadier Cumming-Bruce, now commanding the 44th Brigade, who had previously served in the 51st. Present also was Lt.-Col. Grant Peterkin (1st Gordons), who had commanded the 15th Division Recce Regiment. The 15th (with their five Highland battalions) and the 51st were always closely linked together in spirit and in comradeship.

CHAPTER XIII.

ONE MORE RIVER

" Na diobair caraid 's a charraid."
(Forsake not a friend in the fray.)

" Bring on the Tartan ! "
General Sir COLIN CAMPBELL, at Lucknow, 1858.

MONTGOMERY'S message at the beginning of March, which was addressed to all troops in the 21st Army Group, sums up the situation at that date. It reads :—

" On the 7th February I told you we were going into the ring for the final and last round ; there would be no time limit : we would continue fighting until our opponent was knocked out. The last round is going very well on both sides of the ring—and overhead. In the WEST, the enemy has lost the Rhineland, and with it the flower of at least four armies—the Parachute Army, Fifth Panzer Army, Fifteenth Army, and Seventh Army ; the First Army, further to the south, is now being added to the list. In the Rhineland battles the enemy has lost about 150,000 prisoners, and there are many more to come ; his total casualties amount to about 250,000 since 8th February.

In the EAST, the enemy has lost all POMERANIA east of the ODER, an area as large as the Rhineland ; and three more German armies have been routed. The Russian armies are within about 35 miles of Berlin. Overhead, the Allied Air Forces are pounding Germany day and night. It will be interesting to see how much longer the Germans can stand it. The enemy has in fact been driven into a corner, and he cannot escape. Events are moving rapidly. The complete and decisive defeat of the Germans is certain ; there is no possibility of doubt on this matter.

21ST ARMY GROUP WILL NOW CROSS THE RHINE.

The enemy possibly thinks he is safe behind this great river obstacle. We all agree that it is a great obstacle ; but we will show the enemy that he is far from safe behind it. This great Allied fighting machine, composed of integrated land and air forces, will deal with the problem in no uncertain manner. And having crossed the RHINE, we will crack about in the plains of Northern Germany, chasing the enemy from pillar to post. The swifter and the more energetic our action the sooner the war will be over, and that is what we all desire : to get on with the job and finish off the German war as soon as possible.

Over the RHINE then let us go. And good hunting to you all on the other side. May the Lord mighty in battle give us the victory in this our latest undertaking as He has done in all our battles since we landed in Normandy on D Day."

To prepare for the crossing the Highland Division was moved up to billets in the Roermond-Nijmegen area, where " a pleasant time was had by all." The local inhabitants were most hospitable. The battalions had brought north with them what in the earlier war would have been termed " souveneered " livestock, and with plenty to eat, and dances and cinemas, all " went merry as a marriage bell." There were regimental reunions, as in the case of the Gordons. The Massed Pipes and Drums of the 1st and 5th Battalions were joined by those of the 92nd Highlanders, and all played " Retreat " together. The 5/7th Gordons outdid most units as far as smart appearance was concerned by having white sporrans for their band, with white spats and diced hose. But the Camerons put the cap on it all by turning out each man in a kilt. There were football matches and competitions in the use of various types of weapons. Several changes in commands were announced, and many congratulations came the way of Major George Dunn of the 5th Black Watch, who was given command of the 2nd Seaforth. Another reason for satisfaction was the return to the Division of the Northants Yeomanry, who had been away for some time training in the use of the Buffalo. When the day came, they were to ferry the Division's attacking Brigades across the Rhine.

On 9th March General Rennie held a conference of all officers down to Company Commanders in the Model Room of the Main Headquarters 12th Corps at Eysden, where a model of the Rhine was set up showing Corps' suggested layout for the Marshalling, Loading, Waiting Areas, Traffic Control, and also for Dispersal Control on the far bank. Leading Brigades were to cross in Buffaloes, and reserve Brigades and battalions in storm-boats. A further conference was held on the 11th at Divisional Headquarters for Brigade staffs, when the outline plan for the attack (to be known as Operation " Plunder ") was explained, and arrangements made for a full-scale exercise in river-crossing on the 14th, the Maas to function as the Rhine. The exercise was known as " Slosh," and was practised both by day and by night. It was not too successful inasmuch as the banks of the Maas were very steep, which made it difficult for the Buffaloes to take the water. The area for the exercise was limited owing to the presence of a great number of mines on the far bank, not yet cleared, and the fact that the steering arrangements in the Buffaloes were not all that they should have been, some of the troops in the night exercise marvelling at the short time it had taken them to get across the river. They were somewhat disgruntled when they discovered that they had merely turned back and landed at their embarking point.

And now to the general plan. The crossing of the Rhine was to take place on a two-Corps front, the 30th Corps (Lieut.-General Horrocks) on the left and the 12th Corps (Lieut.-General Neil Ritchie) on the right. The honour of making the initial assaults was given to two Scottish Divisions, the 51st Highland for 30th Corps and the 15th Scottish for 12th Corps.[1] The Highland Division was to attack on a two-Brigade front. On the left (the extreme left of the whole attack) 154 Brigade was to cross the Rhine near the village of Honnepel; on the right 153 Brigade was to cross on either side of Rees. The 152 Brigade was then to follow up 153, and the 9th Canadian Brigade 154. The Canadians were to act as a kind of flank guard. The 154 Brigade's purpose was to hold the east bank of the Rhine as far north as Wardmannshof, to capture the villages of Klein Esserden, Speldrop and Bienen, thence to advance northwards, using the 9th Canadian leading battalion (H.L.I. of Canada), to Millingen and Grietherbosch. The 153 Brigade was to capture the village of Esserden, block the approaches to Rees from north, north-east and east, take Rees itself, and then move northwards on the Rees-Isselburg road, with the leading battalion of 152 (2nd Seaforth) under command. The other two battalions of 152 Brigade were to capture Mittelburg, Groin and Haldern, and move north on the Haldern-Isselburg axis. The 43rd Division was then to follow up.

The countryside, in which were the various concentration areas, was a strange sight. The plain that ran right down to the banks of the Rhine was well cultivated and dotted with farm-houses. But the farmers and their families had gone across the river with the departing Germans, and only their cows and pigs and hens wandered about the deserted steadings and fields. The 3rd British Division was holding the line of the river.

It is not often that one finds ancient history referred to in Intelli-

[1] All three Scottish Divisions (15th, 51st, and 52nd) took part in the Battle of the Rhine.

gence Reports in modern warfare ; nor should one expect to find such information marked " Secret." But in Part II. of the Highland Division Intelligence Summary for 12th March, you may read that the first recorded crossing of the Rhine " was made (*c.* 55 B.C.) by Julius Cæsar, who built a bridge across the river from Gaul to Germany at an unidentified point between Andermach and Coblenz. The following is an excerpt from Book IV. of Cæsar's Commentaries, translated by the 1st U.S. Division.

" For these reasons Cæsar decided to cross the Rhine, but he did not deem it worthy of either himself or the Roman people to make the crossing by boat. Therefore, although the width, fast current, and depth of the river made the construction of a bridge extremely difficult, he believed that a bridge would have to be attempted or the crossing would not be undertaken at all. . . .

Ten days after starting to bring up bridging materials, the structure was finished and Cæsar and his army crossed the river."

H Hour for the attack of the Highland Division was fixed for 9 P.M. on 23rd March (D−1). H Hour was the actual moment when the assault troops began crossing the Rhine. The artillery's preliminary bombardment was to begin at 5 P.M., and the whole near bank of the Rhine was screened by smoke so as to hide our forward movements from the enemy. Special D.D. tanks, fitted with a swimming device, and manned by the Staffordshire Yeomanry, had been provided so that the Jocks would have tank support even before bridges could be built across the river. By the use of air tentacles the leading Brigades could get into direct communication with fighter-bomber aircraft, and there were always planes in the sky to accept and act on such messages. An immense amount of work was done with regard to the various forms of ferry-craft which would have to do all the transport work until bridges could be built. All vehicles were pre-loaded, and each had its place on a priority list. Material could thus be sent over to the assaulting Brigades on demand. Those Brigades moved into the Divisional marshalling area on 21st March, from which date the smoke-screen covered all movement. The time was spent by the troops in being briefed in the last detail by their officers, and in looking on in amazement while Mr Churchill and the C.I.G.S., Sir Alan Brooke, drove round the area, the Premier as usual enjoying his cigar.

At 5 P.M. on 23rd March our bombardment of enemy infantry and artillery positions was in full swing. On the left Brigadier James

Oliver had taken up his H.Q. in the little village of Honnepel, some few hundred yards from the near bank of the Rhine, and at 8 P.M. the 7th Black Watch, the extreme left-hand battalion of the whole assault, began to embus in Buffaloes. As in the case of all the assault battalions, the transport was divided as follows: F1 Echelon was ready in the loading area, and comprised such vehicles as anti-tank guns, mortar-carriers, F.O.O.'s carriers, ammunition carriers and medical jeeps, all of which were to be ferried over before dawn; F2 Echelon was in the assembly area, ready to move forward on call, and would also be taken over in Buffaloes; "A" and "B" Echelons would have to wait till bridges had been constructed.

At 9 P.M. the crossing began, and the two and a half minutes that it occupied scarcely allowed time for much appreciation of this memorable incident. There was bright moonlight that showed up the strange uncouth shapes of the ferrying craft. Above was the continual roar of our shells, but very little was coming the other way. Within six minutes from the start, 154 Brigade H.Q. received word from Lt.-Col. Cathcart and Lt.-Col. MacKinnon that both the 7th Black Watch and 7th Argylls had landed on the other side, and a message from Corps contained congratulations from the Commander on the fact that the 7th Black Watch were "the first Allied troops from whom word had been received that they had landed on the far bank." We can imagine how James Oliver felt.[1] The 7th Black Watch lost one of their Buffaloes by a Teller-mine, and had a certain number of casualties from Schu-mines after the troops had been debussed. They were particularly unlucky as regards their Unit Landing Officer's party under Major T. L. Rollo, a pre-war Fife Territorial who had done yeoman service with his battalion and was now Second-in-Command. Captain Duncan Kermack and Corporal Wright were both killed, while Major Rollo himself had a very narrow escape, one bullet lodging in his pack and another in his haversack. Battalion H.Q. established themselves in Pottdeckel, which "B" Company had captured, while "A" Company took Scholtenhof. "D" Company had the assistance of two Wasps in their reduction of Wardmannshof, so that by dawn the Battalion had done all that was required of it, and was in position for a further advance with a platoon of Middlesex machine-gunners under command.

The 7th Argylls also crossed the river without any interference, and made their landings exactly where they had been planned. They

[1] He commanded the 7th Black Watch throughout Africa and Sicily.

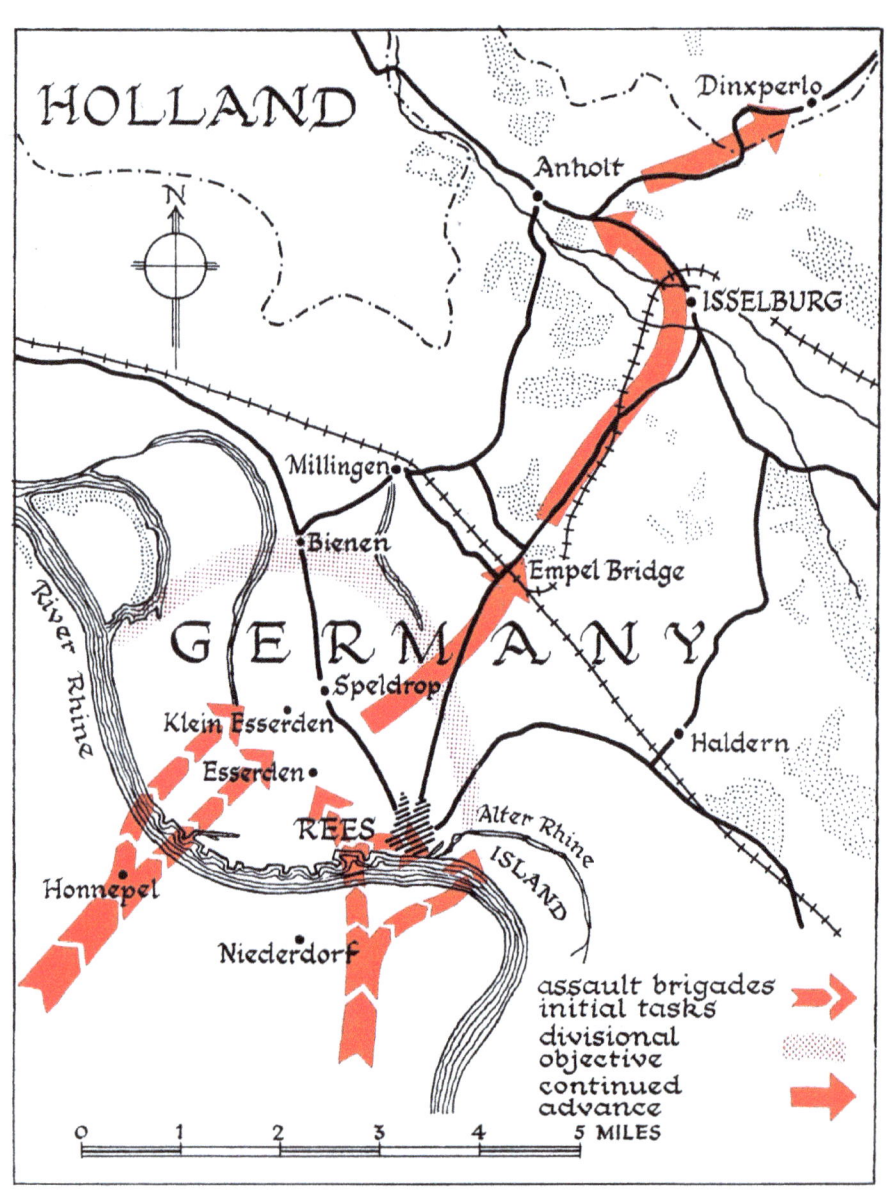

THE RHINE CROSSING, 23RD MARCH 1945

took the village of Ratshoff and the cross-roads beyond it. An hour and a half after the two leading battalions had crossed, the 1st Black Watch (Lt.-Col. Hopwood) climbed into their Buffaloes, were ferried over, disembarked, and passed through the 7th Argylls. The central point of their attack was a creamery outside Klein Esserden, which was apparently a very strong strong-point. The 42nd came under very heavy mortar-fire, and the R.A. officer's carrier went up on a mine, the wireless set being destroyed. Major Richard Boyle (O.C. " B " Company) was killed. " A " Company, however, took the creamery without much difficulty, and " B " Company moved forward on Klein Esserden. Only one officer was left in that company, so Colonel John Hopwood sent up the whole of " A " Company in support. " C " Company moved up on Speldrop, and by six o'clock in the morning Tactical H.Q. received news that both Klein Esserden and Speldrop were clear of the enemy.

Headquarters moved up to the creamery, but in half an hour word filtered back that all was not well with " C " Company. A very heavy enemy counter-attack had infiltrated into Speldrop. It was decided to withdraw both " C " and " B " Companies into the creamery area. One platoon of " C " Company, however, could not pull out, and a nineteen-year-old subaltern, Robert Henderson, set off with a patrol to try to get in touch with it. On going along a hedge the patrol came under machine-gun fire, and Henderson, with one Bren gunner for company, continued his advance, crawling along a shallow ditch not far from the embankment on top of which ran the main road. A machine-gunner from this embankment fired on the Black Watch couple, killed the Bren gunner, and knocked Henderson's revolver out of his hand. Henderson seized the shovel, which he was carrying on his back, went bald-headed for that machine-gunner and caved his head in with the spade. He then signalled his patrol to come up, and led them into a house. He himself went back some sixty yards under heavy fire, retrieved his dead gunner's Bren, and returned. This officer and his party were forced to evacuate the house which was set on fire, but moved to another, from which the enemy failed to dislodge them.

In the morning the 1st Black Watch, who had been reinforced by a troop of tanks, some anti-tank guns and a platoon of Middlesex machine-gunners, advanced and retook Klein Esserden. But Speldrop still held out, and again the Battalion withdrew to the creamery area. In the evening the Highland Light Infantry of Canada, the Brigade's supporting battalion, went in behind a heavy artillery bombardment, and after much stiff fighting cleared the village and made contact with the detached parties of Black Watch who had been isolated there and who had all held out against every enemy effort to dislodge them.

During the day the 7th Black Watch had had to withstand a fierce enemy counter-attack on Kivitt. All day the enemy shelled and mortared the area, and in the evening a 9th Canadian Infantry Brigade battalion relieved the 7th, who went into reserve at Pottdeckel. During the day also the 7th Argylls captured Rosau, but failed in their attack on Bienen. That village was in the end taken by two Canadian battalions, with the good names the Nova Scotia Highlanders and the Canadian H.L.I. No wonder the comradeship between the 51st Jocks and the Canadians was so strong.

Brigadier Roddie Sinclair (153 Brigade) had as his leading battalions the 5th Black Watch (Lt.-Col. Bradford) on the left and 5/7th Gordons (Lt.-Col. Irvine) on the right, and on the right of Rees. The 1st Gordons (Lt.-Col. Grant-Peterkin) were to follow the 5th Black Watch as soon as the latter's Buffaloes could return to the near side of the river. The 5th Black Watch encountered few difficulties to begin with, and by morning had taken all their objectives, the main one of which was the southern part of Esserden, south of Klein Esserden, and not to be confused with it. During the night bitter house-to-house fighting had taken place in the northern part of the town, but in the morning all was cleared, including the railway station.

The 5/7th Gordons also crossed the Rhine without difficulty. There is a kind of island formed by the main river and a strip of water named the Alter Rhine to the right of Rees, to clear which was the first objective of the Gordons. The bridge across this Alter Rhine had been blown, but on the " island " itself the Gordons made themselves masters of the farm-houses and took a number of prisoners. Morning found them in very exposed positions overlooked from the far bank of the Alter Rhine, and more or less at the mercy of snipers. No movement was possible during that day, but the following night assault boats were carried across the " island " by the Carrier Platoon. The opposition, however, was so great that the attempt to get to the east side of the Alter Rhine was called off, and for another day the Gordons had to grin and bear it on the exposed plain. During the second day (25th), however, the 5th Black Watch, who had made the south-eastern corner of Rees, were ordered to capture the east bank of the Alter

Rhine, so as to allow " C " Company of the Gordons to cross by a bridge still intact in that area. This move was a complete success and the Gordons crossed.

Rees was a sorry sight as far as being a town was concerned. In the early days of 1945 the R.A.F. had drenched it with high explosive and incendiaries. The houses were gaping ruins, the streets a mass of craters and rubble-heaps. The Germans' main funk-holes were a series of tunnels, of which the attacking forces had no knowledge. The result was that the enemy could appear in a most disconcerting way from openings in the ground after the clearing troops had passed forward. Broken-down trees, mines, and trenches were further obstacles in the path of 153 Brigade.

The 1st Gordons had followed up the 5th Black Watch, and a battalion diarist has left the following note on their crossing of the Rhine : " On either side flat green fields slowly dip down to the river where the banks are shingle. The river looked all the 450 yards it was, the current, however, being not very terrible. The Buffaloes slowly crawled over the fields, then dipped down into the water, became waterborne, and then one had the feeling of floating down out of control, yet each Buffalo churned without any difficulty out of Germany's greatest barrier and at the right place by the green flicking light. Once aground the Buffaloes with vehicles took one two hundred yards inland, those with troops depositing their load on the green fields, now baked hard by the recent fine weather, at the water's edge; two dunes, each about ten feet high, stood up against the skyline, otherwise the flatness of the country was unbroken. The night of the crossing was as perfect as it could be—warm, still, and with a three-quarter moon ; the normal peace, however, was shattered for the whole night and next succeeding three days by a crescendo of gun-fire which out-Alameined Alamein and out-Veritabled Veritable."

The 1st Gordons crossed without a single casualty. " D " Company took their first objectives—some farm-buildings—but those were set alight by an incendiary, and the Gordons had to vacate certain of their positions. " B " and " C " Companies made for the bund across some three hundred yards of open grassland, where they had the benefit of a smoke-screen, and after considerable fighting in isolated house-positions they also were successful. By 7 A.M. " B " Company had made a further advance, had reached the Rees–Speldrop road, had turned right towards Rees, and fought their way up to the cemetery, leaving a clear road for " C " Company's advance on Rees itself. " C " Company reached the town, proceeded to a slow but methodical clearing of houses and streets, and by ten o'clock were joined by " A " Company, who had entered Rees by way of the bank of the river. " D " Company came in and liquidated opposition all the way to the main square. By midday " B " Company had cleared up the northern edge and the three companies had united. The rest of the day and the following night were spent in town clearance, and at 7 P.M. " D " Company took a strong-point which was situated in the ruins of the cathedral.

Every Gordon was enthusiastic about the support given the Battalion in this town clearance by a gun-crew of 454 Mountain Battery (3.7 Howitzers) commanded by Captain McNair. The general public are familiar with this type of gun from film-pictures of teams competing at exhibitions, taking the gun to pieces, clearing an obstacle, and reassembling it. These gun-teams had put in some three years' hard training in the Inverness area, and had been sent out specially for the Rhine crossing, since the guns could be carried in a Buffalo. Major Lindsay, who took over command of the 1st Gordons when Colonel Grant-Peterkin was hit in Rees, writes in his ' So Few Got Through ' : " This was McNair's first action, and such enthusiasm for battle as he showed can seldom have been seen before—in fact, it was rather easy for some of our more battle-weary officers to be quite funny about it. For each situation in this street-to-street battle McNair had some excellent suggestion for using his gun. He hauled it over rubble, rushed it round corners, layed it on a house that was giving trouble, dodged back again, prepared his charges, and then back to fire them. He even took it to bits and mounted it in an upstairs room. ' Exactly which window is the sniper in ? ' he said, and then, when the sniper fired at him, ' Oh, that one ! ' and layed his gun on it. It set houses on fire as well as any Crocodile, and the effect on the enemy was devastating. This very brave officer took incredible risks ; finally he ran out into a street which was under fire and pulled in a wounded officer. He and his gun became the talk of the companies, and already, in a few hours, he has become an almost legendary character ! " [1]

The 5th Black Watch had now cleared the station and its environs, and the only sore spot remaining was an area of some ten thousand square yards in one corner of the town. Shortly after darkness had fallen this pocket was also liquidated. " Thus," concludes the diarist, " ended forty-eight hours of continuous fighting against the most

[1] See footnote, p. 136.

determined enemy we had seen since D Day." The Corps Commander and the Divisional Commander paid special visits to the 1st Gordons to congratulate them on their capture of Rees, and the Brigade expressed the opinion that it was the best thing the Battalion had ever done.

But, alas, the Divisional General who visited the Gordons was not Thomas Rennie. On the morning of 24th March that gallant soldier had been on a visit to the Tactical Headquarters of 154 Brigade. He had left in his jeep to come back to the L.V.T. Ferry. He called out "Good luck" to Captain Stewart, Adjutant of the 7th Argylls, who was passing in a carrier. In the jeep along with the General were his A.D.C., Lieutenant Tweedie (K.O.S.B.), and Lance-Corporal Craig, Royal Signals wireless operator. A concentration of mortar bombs fell, and the jeep received a direct hit. General Rennie fell out on to the grass verge. Tweedie was unhurt, but Craig was wounded. " Are you all right, sir ? " asked Tweedie. There was no reply. General Rennie was carried to 176 Field Ambulance, which was only some thirty yards away. He died almost immediately after admission. We of an undemonstrative age live in a kind of terror of sentiment. Yet there is every reason why Thomas Rennie should be lined up with John Cameron of Fassiefern of the 92nd Highlanders at Quatre Bras, or James Wolfe as Fraser's Highlanders streamed across the Plains of Abraham. He had died like them in the hour of victory, his warfare surely accomplished. They laid him to rest (four Black Watch men acting as pall-bearers) at Appeldorn to the sound of the pipes and in the presence of his Staff, of Lieut.-General Horrocks, his Corps Commander, and the Commanders of the 3rd British Division and 3rd Canadian Division. The Senior Chaplain to the Forces took the Service. And now we go to the poet Collins for his requiem :—

> " How sleep the Brave who sink to rest
> By all their country's wishes blest !
> When Spring, with dewy fingers cold,
> Returns to deck their hallow'd mould.
> She there shall dress a sweeter sod
> Than Fancy's feet have ever trod.
>
> By fairy hands their knell is rung.
> By forms unseen their dirge is sung :
> There Honour comes, a pilgrim grey,
> To bless the turf that wraps their clay ;
> And Freedom shall awhile repair
> To dwell, a weeping hermit, there."

Brigadier Oliver took over command of the Division until the arrival of Major-General G. H. MacMillan of the Argylls, affectionately known to the Army as " Babe," and fortunately well known to the Highlanders. He had been Brigadier of 152 in Sicily, and now came back home to the Highland from the 49th Division. On the morning after General Rennie's death, MacMillan[1] crossed the Rhine with his G.S.O.1, Colonel Leslie.

And so to the experiences of 152 Brigade (Brigadier Cassels) in " Plunder." The 2nd Seaforth (Lt.-Col. George Dunn) had crossed the Rhine in storm-boats under command of 153 Brigade just before midnight on the 23rd, and by five in the morning of the 24th they had successfully taken all the positions, their hardest job being to reduce a pipe factory just at the north end of Rees. They were followed in the early morning by the 5th Camerons (Lt.-Col. Lang), who, when they reached the 5th Black Watch area, realised that the position was such that they could not hope to attack Mittelburg, as had been planned, by first light. The attack was held back till a tank squadron became available, and then went in at 7 A.M. An anti-tank ditch caused a spot of bother, and three of the four leading tanks were knocked out by self-propelled guns concealed in houses on the fringe of Mittelburg. It was decided to hold off further attacks until darkness, when " A " Company went in on the left and " B " Company on the right. Straw and phosphorus grenades were used to clear snipers from the upper storeys of houses, and Major A. W. Lee led his company in a very spirited attack on a strongly defended brick-works. Mittelburg was finally reduced, and the Camerons garrisoned it for two days.

The 5th Seaforth (Lt.-Col. Sym) had been held back to the last and they crossed at dawn on 24th March. That crossing took a long time, for a great number of storm-boats had been knocked out, and the Seaforth had to be content to cross in penny numbers. They moved to a position just south of Esserden, where they had to sit, without reply, under a really devastating enemy bombardment. Then they were ordered to the factory area north of Rees, where they became entangled with the Camerons, held up on their way to Mittelburg. When, however, the Camerons captured Mittelburg, the 5th Seaforth were ordered to take Groin, a small village which covered a main road into Rees. No enemy reinforcements must be allowed along that road. Many of the houses in Groin were on fire, but all the others—

---

[1] MacMillan took the 15th Scottish Division to France in June 1944.

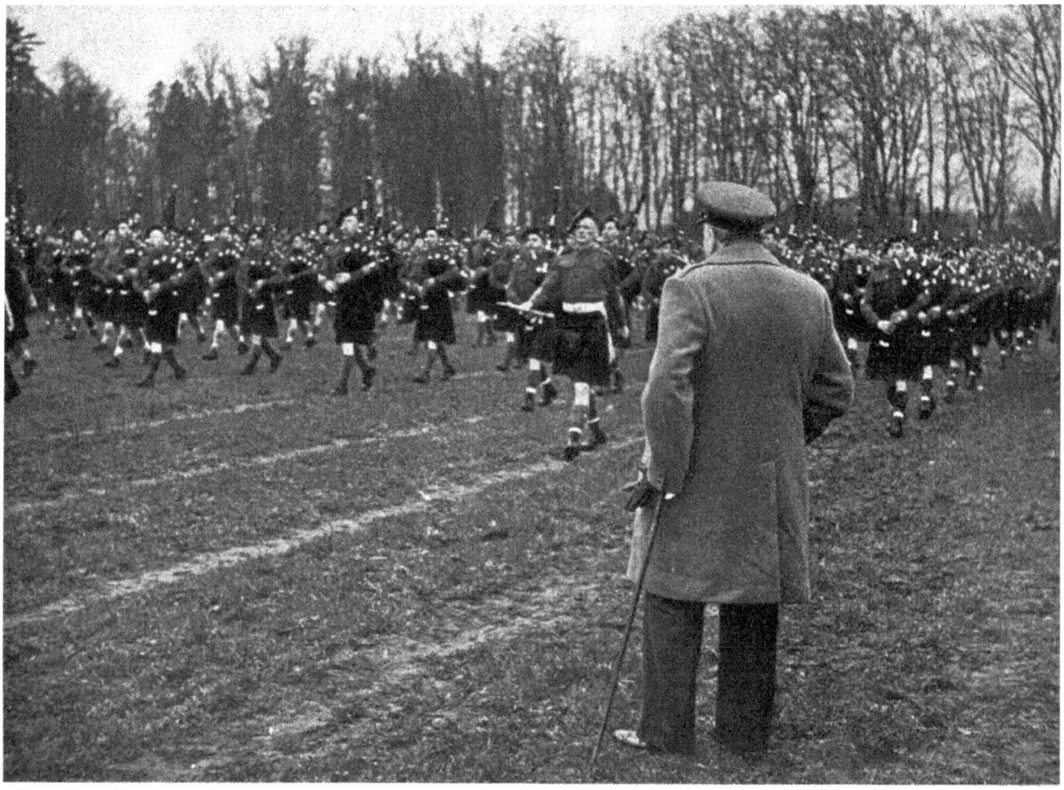

By courtesy of the Imperial War Museum

THE PRIME MINISTER WATCHES DIVISIONAL MASSED PIPE-BANDS. 5TH MARCH 1945

GERMAN MUD

By courtesy of the Imperial War Museum

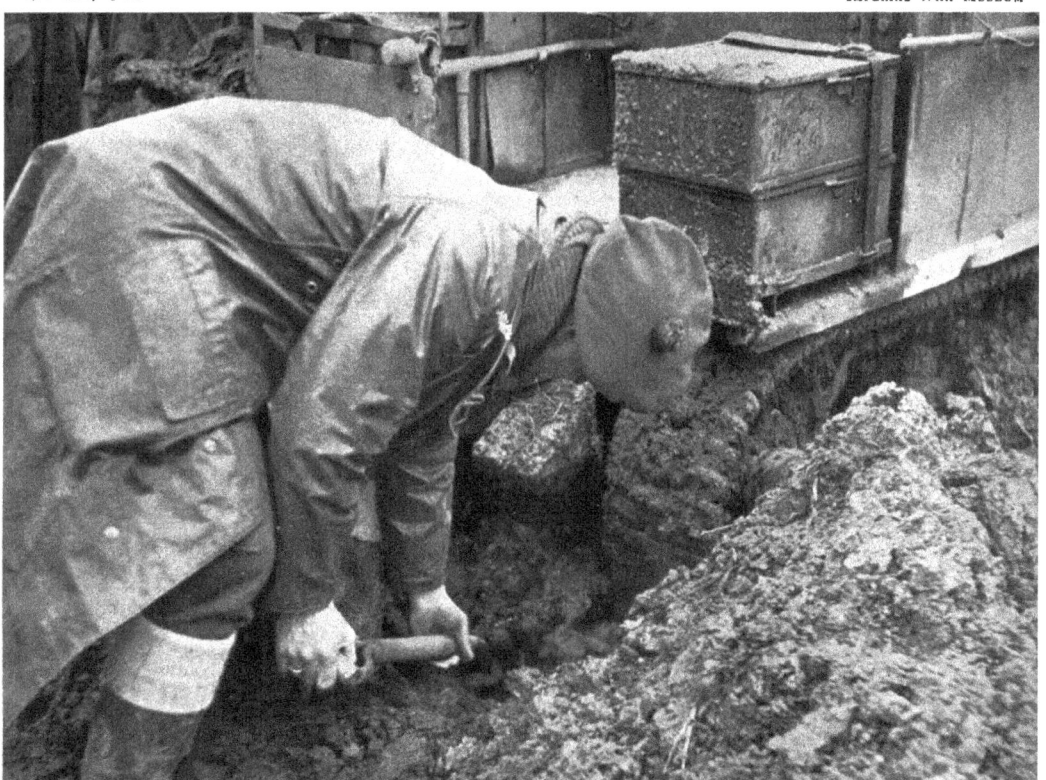

JEEP AMBULANCES ON BUFFALOES MOVE UP TO CROSS THE RHINE

D.U.K.W.s CROSSING THE RHINE

the majority of them farm-buildings—were strongly defended, and Alastair Borthwick claims that "Groin was the hardest village fight the Battalion ever fought."[1] Each building had to be tackled separately, and it must be admitted that the honours went to the Germans in the first few rounds of the fight. Morning was not far away, and it was essential that the reduction of Groin should be completed in the darkness.

The Sutherland Battalion had the whole village clear by 7.30 that morning. One outlying farm was left in enemy hands. It was named Hollands Hof, and was a solid building. "D" Company was sent to attack it in daylight with D.D. tanks in support, and took a very bad hammering. As a result of terrific mortar, artillery and Spandau fire, only two officers were left unwounded in the company, but yet Captain Gardiner did not give in. With his two remaining tanks putting everything they had into the building, the remnant of the company under Lieutenant Evans rushed the house, and fought it room by room, outbuilding by outbuilding. But orders came for Evans to withdraw back to Groin. That night "A" Company attacked Hollands Hof, only to find that the enemy had had enough and had cleared off.

The 1st Gordons had been clearing up houses on the river east of Rees, and now the whole of 152 Brigade (relieved by the 9th Brigade of the 3rd British Division) was ordered to take Isselburg, and to form a bridgehead over the Issel River. A Gordon patrol had discovered that the enemy had withdrawn from Isselburg, so that on the morning of the 28th the 5th Camerons entered that town without opposition, and the 2nd Seaforth crossed the river by a bridge which the enemy had failed to destroy properly. The Germans put down a very intense artillery concentration on Isselburg, and the 78th were held up by a strong-point in a wood north-west of their bridgehead. But Typhoons came to the rescue and rocketed that strong-point to pieces. Next day a bridge, capable of carrying tanks, was being thrown across the Issel, and the 5th Seaforth, supported by a company of Camerons, were instructed to advance and seize the crossings on the Astrang River. The enemy were still occupying both Anholt and Astrang, so that the 5th Seaforth, when they took one of the Astrang bridges (the other had been blown), had enemy on both sides of them. The position became worse when the Germans decided to evacuate Anholt, and the

[1] A most excellent account of this Seaforth fight is given in Mr Borthwick's 'Sans Peur.'

garrison marching down to Dinxperlo made for the crossing held by the 5th Camerons (without tanks). The Germans overran the 5th Seaforth headquarters, and for a period Colonel Sym was actually a prisoner. "C" and "D" Companies on the far side of the river made a strong-point of their joint headquarters, and then our tanks came. Two hundred and six prisoners surrendered to the Seaforth, and all their own prisoners, including Colonel Sym, were recovered.

And now over the bridges clattered the Allied armour.

The 154 Brigade on the 25th advanced towards Empel Bridge on the road to Isselburg. The 7th Black Watch were to capture that bridge and, if it was still intact, to advance across it and form a bridgehead on the farther side. On their way they had to capture a certain number of farm buildings, but they reached Empel Bridge without difficulty and found it intact. A platoon was sent across, and immediately heavy fire came down on the bridge area from the direction of the village of Empel. Lance-Corporal Macbride, with five unwounded and several wounded men of the platoon who had crossed the bridge, took up a position in a house on the far side of the stream and negatived the attempt of a German patrol who crawled forward with the intention of blowing up the bridge.

At ten o'clock that night the 1st Black Watch moved through the 7th Battalion, crossed the stream some distance from the bridge in the good old Northants' Buffaloes, and after a conflict with German self-propelled gunners, advanced and took Empel. The 7th Argylls had followed the 1st Black Watch across the swollen stream (in certain reports referred to as a lake) also in Buffaloes, and managed to account for several of the self-propelled guns which had been giving trouble to the 42nd. Next morning the 27th Brigade of the 43rd Division passed through 154. For two days 154 Brigade had what might be termed a comparative rest, while 152 and 153 Brigades moved on and beyond Isselburg. On the 29th Brigadier Oliver received instructions to capture the town of Dinxperlo. All his three battalions were used in this attack, which went smoothly. At first light next morning the Guards Armoured Division passed through.

The Rhine crossing was an action in which the Jocks salute with admiration all the other arms of the Services which supported them with so much courage in their spirits and so much accuracy in their actions—those Bank Control experts, those Buffalo "skippers," those R.E. mine-lifters and bridge-builders, those mountain-battery gunners, those D.D. and other tank crews, the R.A.M.C. under Colonel Kerr, the A.D.M.S. and pre-war Territorial who had been with the Division all through the war, and the R.A.S.C. under Lt.-Col. Nichols, the artillery and the air force and all the others. Never, perhaps, since Alamein had there been such an interlocked unity of purpose and achievement.

And a special word must be said of the Highland Divisional Signals under the indefatigable Lt.-Col. James Cochrane. Before the crossing of the Rhine they had placed a controlling Test Point in a farm cellar just below the near-side bund. The cable was laid by hand to the bank of the Rhine as soon as the first Buffaloes had taken the water. The Signals then broke down part of the bank for a launching site for their D.U.K.W. which was to carry the line across. About thirty yards out the D.U.K.W. was holed by a splinter from a shell, and its crew had to swim back to the bank. They then took the water again in a spare D.U.K.W., and the submarine cable was safely laid and established on the far bank. Line parties set out to connect up with the Tactical H.Q.s of the Brigades, and by half-past three in the morning all that work had been done. The rest of the night was spent by the men in patrolling those lines, which were being regularly cut by mortar-fire and crushed by tracked vehicles crossing them. An observer records : " Looking back on the scene on the banks of the river lit up as it was by artificial moonlight from searchlights, it is difficult to imagine how these line-men managed to lay and keep their lines through. Out of the darkness of the river came all types of craft and out of them vehicles and assaulting troops. It was perhaps the finest operation done by these line-men, most of whom had served with the Highland Division ever since the days of Alamein. It is the proud honour of the unit that an immediate reward of the D.S.O. was awarded to Major Henderson and Military Medals to Signalmen Clark and Reilly, who were the leading hands of the cable crews on that crossing."

The Divisional Commander received the following letter, dated 31st March, from Sir Miles Dempsey, Commander 2nd Army : " Now that the Battle of the Rhine has been won, and the break-out from the bridge-head is well under way, I would like to give you and your magnificent Division my very sincere congratulations. Yours was one of the two Divisions[1] which carried out the assault crossing of the river,

---

[1] The other was the 15th Scottish, who also received a similar congratulatory message from the Army Commander.

defeated the enemy on the other side, and paved the way for all that followed. A great achievement—and I am sure you are all very proud of it."

This account of the Rhine crossing finishes not with a military tail-piece, but with one of a civilian on the far bank of the Rhine on the afternoon of the 24th of March. He had been ferried over where 154 Brigade had made their crossing the night before. He was Winston Spencer Churchill.

CHAPTER XIV.

THE LAST LAP

" Cha do chuir a ghuallainn ris nach do chuir tur thairis."
(None ever set his shoulder to, who did not what he sought to do.)

" For I've nae skill o' lands, my lads,
    That kenna to be free ;
Then Scotland's right, and Scotland's might,
    And Scotland's hills for me.
I'll drink a cup to Scotland yet
    Wi' a' the honours three ! "
                                H. S. RIDDELL.

For the first few days of the last April of the war, the main part of the Highland Division rested in the area of Isselburg, where on that April's first afternoon a Memorial Parade Service was held for General Rennie. The service was conducted by the Senior Chaplain to the Forces, General Rennie's successor, General MacMillan, read the lesson, and the nine Pipe-Majors of the Highland regiments played " The Flowers of the Forest." On parade, with representative officers and C.O.s of the Division, were General Crerar, Commander of the Canadian Army, Lieut.-General Guy Simonds, Commander 2nd Canadian Corps, Major-General Barber, Commanding 15th (Scottish) Division, with his Brigade Commanders, and the Commander 33rd Armoured Brigade.

On 3rd April orders came to MacMillan that the Division were to concentrate some forty miles north in the area of the Dutch town of Enschede, and 153 Brigade moved there on the 5th. Enschede had been lucky. It had experienced little bombing. So in the clean happy homes of the Dutch inhabitants, with boxes bright with flowers on every window-ledge, the Brigade were given time to do some refitting and to take stock of things. At this point we may also take stock of the situation. Montgomery has stated that, during the month of March, Germany's losses in prisoners alone averaged some 10,000 a day. Hitler had no reserves to replace such enormous wastage of man-power, and had therefore to withdraw inside a much shorter perimeter. The Ruhr was a beleaguered fortress ; American armour was energetically careering here and there over Central Germany ; the Russians were practically at the gates of Berlin. But the enemy still held the north of Holland, and it fell to the Canadian Army, with the 30th Corps under command, to advance through Arnhem and clear the enemy out of north-east Holland and the coastal belt up to the mouth of the Elbe.

The general route the Highland Division were to take in the 30th Corps' advance was from Enschede some twenty miles east to Salzbergen on the main Lingen–Rheine road, then due north on that road some fifteen miles to Lingen, north-east thirty miles to Quakenbrück, another eighteen miles to Vechta, eighteen miles north-west to Wildeshausen, another twenty to Delmenhorst, ten miles to the outskirts of Bremen, thirty miles to Bremenvörde in the centre of the Weser–Elbe peninsula, and then twenty-five miles west to Bremerhaven. This movement was to be somewhat different from anything so far undertaken by the Division. It was obvious to everyone that Hitler had shot his bolt, and that the war was more or less over. But such knowledge leads to an unhappy frame of mind in most people—the idea that it would really be too bad to be hit now. Fighting was to be spasmodic; advances were all to have about them a kind of question mark. As our troops went forward into the unknown, German prisoners streamed past the other way to the cages, forced labour cheered from the roadsides, and then from somewhere there would come a burst of Spandau-fire, and there was another name or two to add to the casualty list. In the larger areas of population the Allies found themselves responsible for hospitals full of German wounded, and the taking over of German houses for billets was an uncomfortable business. The British soldier has no scruples in dealing with men, but when enemy women and children have to suffer inconveniences, he feels embarrassed.

During the advance, 154 Brigade discovered that the civilian telephone service in the area was still in working order. This service was immediately used for military purposes. When it appeared that opposition was likely to be encountered in any centre of population on the line of the Brigade's advance, an officer, with a knowledge of German, got through to the town or large village by phone, demanded speech with the local burgomeister, and informed that functionary that, unless he surrendered his town immediately and gave an assurance that it would not be defended in any way, it would be blown to bits by our guns, burned out by our flame-throwing tanks, and generally obliterated. The method of declaring such surrender was to display white sheets on prominent buildings in the area—church steeples, for example. The telephone system worked very efficiently and brought good results.

In the advance, 153 Brigade (Brigadier Sinclair) batted first. On 5th April they moved from Enschede to relieve the 5th Guards Brigade, 5th Black Watch at Schüttorf, 1st Gordons at Gildehaus, and 5/7th Gordons at Bentheim. Black Watch patrols, manœuvring beyond the Ems tributary in front of Schüttorf, met some infantry opposition. When bridges had been constructed over this river, the 5/7th Gordons moved through the 5th Black Watch and pushed on to Emsburen. They met considerable opposition both in front and on their flanks, but by the morning of the 7th they had occupied the town, where they rested for three days, their main occupation being football matches, in which they beat the 1st Gordons by 7 goals to 2, but lost to the 5th Black Watch by 6 goals to 3. They were on the move again on the 12th and next day reached Amerbusch, whence they turned north to Wildeshausen, where they took over from a unit of the 3rd British Division. The 1st Gordons had rested in Leschede for four days before crossing the Ems. They then moved on to Goldenstedt.

On 8th April Oliver's 154 Brigade had relieved the 9th Infantry Brigade south of Lingen. Two days later they relieved the 5th Guards Brigade in the area of Fürstenau, and next day the 7th Argylls led off the advance to Ankum, which they captured without difficulty. There the two Black Watch battalions of the Brigade passed through them. The same night the 7th Argylls moved on to Badbergen, on the following day to Lohne, and later to Vechta. On the 16th they took over at Harpstedt from the 2nd Royal Ulster Rifles of 3rd Division. The 7th Black Watch, now commanded by Lt.-Col. Berowald Innes, who had come out from the 4th Black Watch at home, were, on the 8th, on the Dortmund Canal near the village of Albergen. Innes took over the Battalion from Charles Cathcart, who had been with it in practically every battle since the Division began its fighting career in North Africa. Cathcart had given great service to the Battalion, first as a junior Company Commander at Alamein, when he was awarded one of the first D.S.O.s won by the Division, then as Second-in-Command, and later as Commanding Officer throughout the long and strenuous journey across Europe. He had now gone home to a training appointment and well-earned rest there. The Battalion moved on the 9th through very dark woods to Mundersum, and on the 11th had occupied the pleasant town of Quakenbrück without a shot being fired. Some difficulty was encountered next day in reconnoitring the bridge over the Lager-Hase River. They then moved to Vechta, where they remained till 16th April.

On the 10th the 1st Black Watch passed through the Guards Armoured Division at Loxton, with instructions to capture the village of Badbergen. Then advanced in Kangaroos "steered" by "C" Company of the 2nd Staffordshire Yeomanry through woods and villages and over small streams. Felled chestnut trees hiding mines were the main type of road-blocks encountered, but nothing could stop the 42nd in their determination to reach Badbergen. The Battalion had the interesting experience here of being visited by the German burgomeister of Dinklage, a village a little farther on, who explained that he and the inhabitants were very tired of our shelling, and that he wished to surrender his village. The Battalion accepted the offer and occupied Dinklage.

On 10th April, 152 Brigade (Brigadier Cassels) relieved the 8th Brigade of the 3rd Division in Lingen, the 2nd Seaforth taking over from 1st South Lancs, the 5th Camerons from 2nd East Yorks, and the 5th Seaforth from 1st Sussex. They too joined in the advance, and on 12th April the 2nd Seaforth relieved the 7th Black Watch in Quakenbrück. The Brigade then moved by way of Vechta to Goldenstedt, where the 5th Seaforth surprised some hundred of the enemy in bed. The 152 continued to lead the Divisional advance, and here note must be taken of the invaluable work done by the Derbyshire Yeomanry. As advance scouts they were excellent.[1]

On the morning of the 13th, the 5th Seaforth moved off in Kangaroos to take the villages of Ambergen, Holzhausen, and Barglay. Ambergen gave no trouble, and, despite the boggy ground in front of Holzhausen and Barglay, which necessitated an advance on foot, all went well. The 5th Camerons meanwhile occupied in turn Visbek and Varnhorn, into which villages they were followed by the 2nd Seaforth, who next day contacted elements of the Guards Armoured Division some two miles west of Visbek. At the same time the 5th Camerons contacted the 43rd Reconnaissance Regiment, and it is recorded that they had a pipe-band practice to celebrate the occasion. The Germans objected to the tune of four 105-mm. shells, which "failed to put the drum-major out of step." The 152 Brigade then went into Divisional reserve.

[1] The Yeomanry were commanded by Lt.-Col. Pearce Serocold, who had taken over the Regiment soon after the landings in Normandy.

THE LAST LAP

On the 14th the 5/7th Gordons of 153 Brigade took over the town of Wildeshausen from a battalion of the 3rd British Division, and, in attempting to fill craters on the road out of the town, came under heavy shelling from self-propelled guns. The Gordons, however, completed the job and also took the village of Dotlingen, where they had sporting targets presented to them by the garrison attempting to escape on push-bikes. On the 14th, the 1st Gordons also advanced, and, against some very determined resistance, cleared the villages of Hockensburg and Brettorf.

The 154 Brigade set the ball rolling in the Division's advance on Delmenhorst by clearing the main road half-way to that town. This operation took them to Ippener and Annen, and from that position 152 Brigade again took the lead. It was left to the 5th Camerons later to fight the stiffest action in this part of the campaign, when they made a night attack on the area of Adelheide, which included the village, an airfield, and two bridges. The attack was rendered memorable by the noise made by a kind of Mad Mullah of a German, who kept up a continuous shouting of " Heil Hitler " while he blazed away with his bazooka. One heavily defended bridge required to be shelled before it fell to the Camerons. Not long afterwards the second bridge, the airfield, and most of the village were in their hands, and the following afternoon " D " Company, with Crocodiles and Flails in support, cleared the cross-roads at the north end of the village. This Adelheide affair was the real battle for Delmenhorst, where stiff opposition had been expected. But after the Cameron victory the Derbyshire Yeomanry advanced on Delmenhorst only to find that the enemy had cleared out of it altogether.

During the remaining days of April the Division was not involved in what could be termed serious warfare. On the 21st, 154 Brigade relieved a Brigade of the 3rd British Division, and on the 25th were in their turn relieved by 153 Brigade. Bremen was to be the " pigeon " of the 43rd and 52nd Divisions, and 154 Brigade was placed on the right of the 43rd to protect that flank. When it became obvious that all was going well with the Bremen-attacking Divisions, the 51st was moved north-westward to link up with the Guards Armoured Division. It was left to 154 Brigade to clear the Germans from the far bank of the Wümme, and this Brigadier Oliver achieved by leaving the 7th Black Watch on the near bank to keep an eye on the enemy, while his other two battalions moved through Robertburg and came in on the German

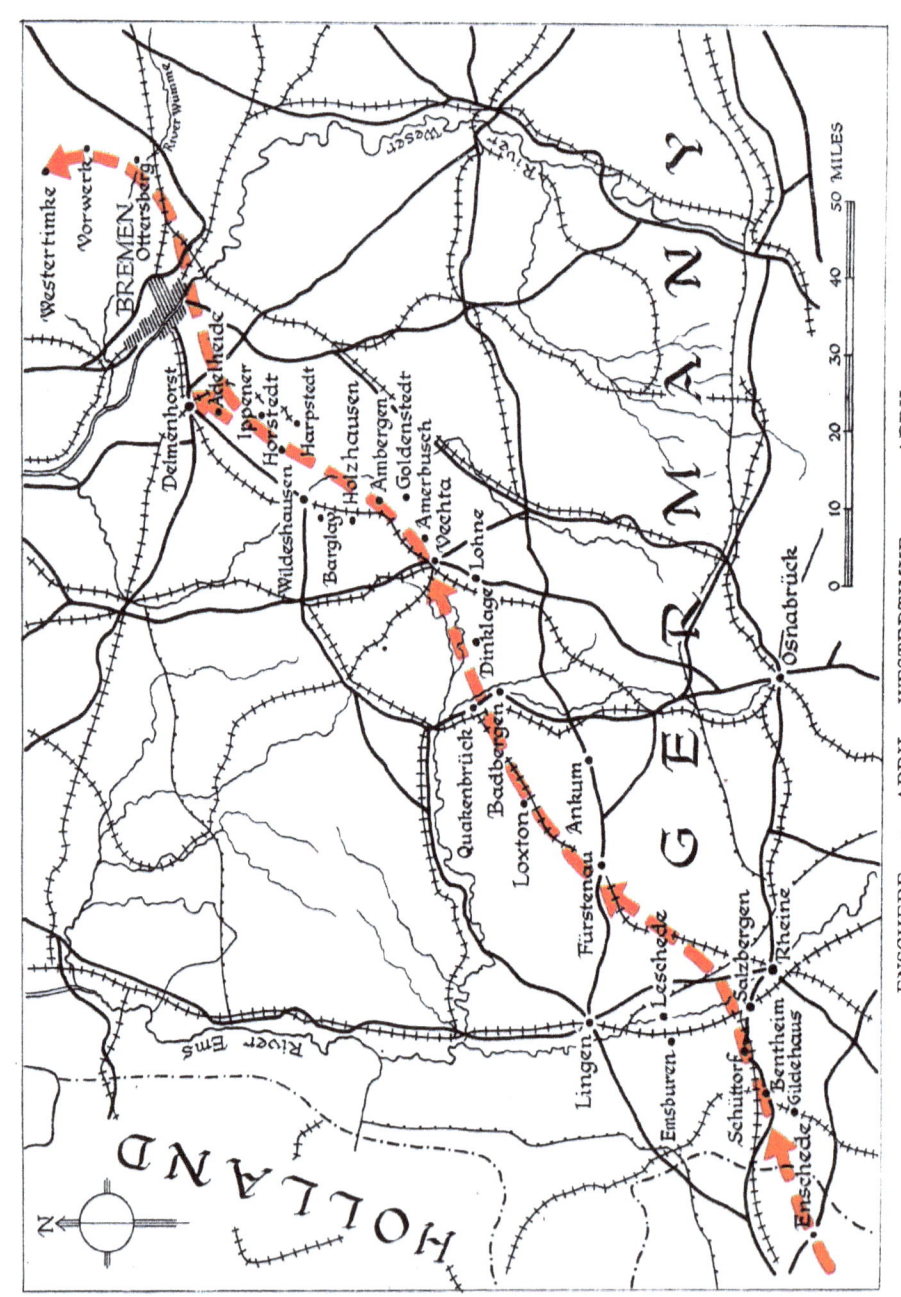

ENSCHEDE, 5TH APRIL. WESTERTIMKE, 27TH APRIL 1945

THE LAST LAP

flank. On the 27th the 7th Argylls captured Stuckenborstel, the 1st Black Watch Ottersberg, Otterstedt and Vorwerk, and the move was completed by the 7th Black Watch coming up that same evening and making contact with the Guards Armoured Division at Westertimke.

On the night of 20th-21st April, 152 Brigade had advanced on Ganderkese, which they found being defended by a considerable body of the enemy. The 2nd Seaforth were ordered to reduce the place, and went in with heavy artillery support and a half-squadron of Crocodiles, the flames from which set the whole village ablaze. That put an end to the really brave and fanatical resistance put up by the very young German paratroops in the village. The 152 Brigade moved to Selsingen on the last day of the month, and were making preparations to attack Bremervörde. The 153 Brigade continued up to the 28th holding the line near Delmenhorst, when they moved forward to Horstedt and Stafel.

The month ended on a note of sadness, for the C.R.A., Brigadier Jerry Shiel, was killed by a mine on the 29th. No gunner was ever more popular with the infantry than that very brave man. If ever a soldier had an "eye for country" it was Jerry Shiel. His friend, Tony Thicknesse of the 126th Field Regiment, was killed with another formation. Few Divisions could have had two more efficient and thrusting gunners.

It is appropriate to pay tribute here to the splendid work which was always done by the Divisional Artillery. While it is true to say that it is the infantry who ultimately have to win every battle, there was not a single infantryman in the Division who would not have admitted that, without the excellent support which the Divisional Artillery gave at all times, few battles could ever have been won and certainly none without far heavier casualties than were ever suffered. During the Division's training at home, General Wimberley, on looking back again to the lessons learned while he served with the 1914-18 Division, constantly emphasised the extreme importance of good infantry and artillery co-operation. How well that co-operation had worked out in practice! All the infantry demands from the gunners (and they were often very heavy) were invariably met, if it was humanly possible to do so, and the Divisional Artillery enjoyed the complete confidence of the rest of the Division. Meticulous care was always taken, first by Brigadier Elliot and later by Brigadier Shiel, in the preparation of the fire plans for all operations, barrages, and concentrations to help the infantry to get on to their objectives, and then (and this was always of the greatest importance) very carefully prearranged defensive fire tasks to help the infantry to ward off the enemy counter-attacks that so often occurred at a critical period in a battle. The putting of all these elaborate fire plans into operation demanded the concentrated efforts of the whole Divisional Artillery—from the C.R.A. and his Staff down to the Headquarters of the Field Regiments, to the batteries and troops, and to the individual gunners who actually fired the shells at the right time and on to the right places. Gunners have a much closer contact in battle than many people realise, and in the Highland Division the Battery Commanders and the F.O.O.s became an integral part of the battalions with which they operated. These gunner officers and their wireless operators and other specialists went into every battle with the infantry, and the closest possible liaison existed. Without that liaison this History would have told a very different story.

CHAPTER XV.

THE TOWEL COMES IN

"*Saoraidh e mi bho mo Namhaid is treasa, agus uathasan tha toirt fuath dhomh.*"
("He shall deliver me from my strongest enemy, and from them which hate me.")
Psalm xviii. 17.

"And the land rested from war."
Joshua xi. 23.

On the morning of May Day, 1945, the Highland Division lay on the east bank of the River Oste, on the other side of which stood the town of Bremervörde, where, everyone hoped, would be fought "that last great battle in the West." For the faces of the 51st were now turned westward towards the ports of Bremerhaven and Wesermünde, the ultimate objectives. General MacMillan ordered 152 Brigade to lead off the attack on that first May night, and a strange business it was, this last battle, when contrasted with the conflict at Alamein. The river in front of Bremervörde ran in a double channel, and so far the two bridges crossing that double channel were not hopelessly destroyed. The 2nd Seaforth (Lt.-Col. Dunn) sent out a patrol, who crossed the bridge over the eastern channel, walked about on the other side, and came back with the information that they had not even been challenged. There was about one hundred yards between the channels. It had been proposed that the Sutherland Battalion should cross to the attack in Buffaloes, but with this fresh information it was decided to send the Royal Engineers to repair the nearer bridge on this night of 1st-2nd May.

The Engineers carried out their work unmolested, and in the early hours of the morning the A.V.R.E. advanced to the second channel and dropped a bridge across it. Over went two companies of the 78th, and, while the Bosche artillery proved a menace, such Bosche infantry as they met were just waiting to be taken prisoners. Then the 5th Seaforth (Lt.-Col. Sym) passed through into the town, reached the far edge, where in turn the Camerons (Lt.-Col. Lang) took the lead in

Kangaroos, and by nightfall were far west of Bremervörde. The A.V.R.E. bridge came in for considerable attention from a self-propelled gun, and all battalions had a certain number of casualties.

Word came back from the 5th Camerons that the village of Orel was strongly held by units of the 15th Panzer Grenadier Division, and the 1st Gordons (Lt.-Col. Grant-Peterkin) were ordered to attack that village. They were to have been supported by Crocodiles, but a traffic jam took place and the Gordons went in alone. They cleared up Orel, and " B " Company, advancing on the next village, Barchel, were heavily counter-attacked from the front and on both flanks. The attack was beaten off, but, when it was learned from prisoners that Barchel was held by two battalions of Panzer Grenadiers, who still seemed to be fighting bravely, the Gordons were withdrawn into Orel, whence a full-scale attack supported by tanks and artillery was arranged for the following day. In the morning, however, it was discovered that the Panzers were no longer there. Some Gordon transport fell into the enemy's hands but was freed when the Battalion reached Bremerhaven.

The 5/7th Gordons (Lt.-Col. Irvine) moved through Bremervörde to Ebersdorf, and had to fight for every building along the road. They were met on approaching Ebersdorf with heavy small-arms, mortar and self-propelled gunfire. But the Gordons attacked the village from all sides, and in the morning only two enemy self-propelled guns, supported by infantry, were firing. They were so placed that they could neither advance nor withdraw, and the Gordon self-propelled gun commander, Lieutenant Cuthbertson, got his artillery in position and left both the enemy guns " flaming wrecks." The Gordons then went on to Waterbeck. The 5th Black Watch (Lt.-Col. Bradford) had been responsible for the village of Hipstedt, which they had taken with little opposition.

At first light on 3rd May 154 Brigade received orders to advance through 153. The 7th Argylls (Lt.-Col. MacKinnon) travelled in Kangaroos as far as Meckelstedt, where they debussed, and advanced on foot towards their objective, Lintig. On the afternoon of the 4th two German Red Cross men arrived in their lines from Bederkesa, requesting that we should cease shelling that village, since it contained a very large hospital full of wounded. But the Germans kept shelling for some time afterwards. The 7th Black Watch (Lt.-Col. Innes) passed through the 5/7th Gordons at Abersdorf, captured Grossenham without opposition, along with a complete company of the Regiment Lubeck, and then pushed on to Meckelstedt. At the same time the 1st Black Watch (Lt.-Col. Hopwood) had moved into Grossenham.

And that is how the Division lay on the morning of 4th May, when a patrol of Derbyshire Yeomanry, moving down the road towards Ringstedt, were met by a dozen Germans who gave themselves up. One of them was a Major, and he was asked to surrender the village. He said that was beyond his powers, since " any surrender would have to be done at Divisional level." He was sent back with instructions to contact his Division, and a reply was brought back that a British officer be sent to their headquarters to negotiate. This over-arrogant request was treated as it deserved.

A Major from the German Divisional Artillery Headquarters then arrived with much the same proposals. He was also firmly dealt with. Finally Brigadier Oliver arranged that, if the Germans would send a properly qualified staff officer to the Headquarters of 154 Brigade, a staff officer from that Brigade would be sent to the German Divisional Headquarters to explain the unconditional surrender terms. Oliver arranged for a local truce while negotiations were taking place. We now know that the German formation was the 15th Panzer Grenadier Division, and some time later a captain appeared from their headquarters. He was taken to the Headquarters of the 7th Argylls, where Brigadier Oliver informed him of the terms of unconditional surrender. The German captain said that the terms as they stood would be unacceptable to his Divisional Commander, whose views he explained. The gist of them is given in the 51st Highland Division Intelligence Summary No. 349 of 7th May 1945, as follows :—

" The 15th Panzer Grenadier Division, though considerably weakened, was still a reasonably equipped and well-disciplined fighting formation which would sell its life dearly and was still a force to be reckoned with. Though fully aware of the major war situation and of our local strength, his Commander pointed out that if the 15th Panzer Grenadier Division continued to oppose our advance the struggle would be severe and would cost both sides heavy losses. Since this could in no way alter the ultimate outcome of the war, he was anxious to avoid this unnecessary bloodshed, but in return he considered that for several reasons he was entitled to request certain exceptions to be made in the terms of surrender. The reasons were largely based on the well-worn German theme of military honour and sentiment in warfare which had so often been the mainstay of German negotiators on the wrong side of the table, but is conspicuously absent when the boot is on the other foot. He stated that even the British wireless admitted that the 15th Panzer Grenadier Division was the only field formation still fighting as such on German soil, and secondly he drew attention to what he called the long and honourable association in warfare between the 15th Panzer Grenadier Division and the 51st Highland Division. The German's claim to an 'honourable association in warfare' between his Division and the 51st was founded on the fact that the 15th Panzer Grenadier Division was a resuscitated formation of the Afrika Korps. The original 15th Panzer Grenadier Division was a leading Division of that Afrika Korps, and had on many occasions been opposed to the Highland Division in North Africa.

On these grounds he put forward the suggestion that his Division be allowed to surrender as a formation and that they be given an area within our territory in which to assemble for disarmament and demobilisation. He also requested that the Division be employed as a formation on police duties within Germany after the war and that the officers be permitted to retain their revolvers."

Brigadier Oliver replied that no debate could be made about the terms of surrender laid down by the Supreme Commander, and that neither of the latter requests could be considered in any way whatsoever. He consulted General MacMillan, and subsequently informed the German emissary that, provided the O.C. 15th Panzer Grenadier Division agreed to the unconditional surrender terms, it was considered a possibility that the 15th Panzer Grenadier Division's surrender as a formation into a specified area for completing their disarmament could be arranged, but that, once that disarmament had been completed, no further responsibility for their future could be undertaken.

It was decided to treat the village of Ringstedt as neutral territory while the negotiations were proceeding, and representative officers from both sides were stationed there. The Germans were given till 10 P.M. to return an answer. The Intelligence Summary continues:—

"During dinner came the first intimation, in the form of a B.B.C. announcement, of the coming surrender of all Field-Marshal Busch's troops opposing the 21st Army Group in North-West Germany. No such warning was received through the proper military channels for some time afterwards, which naturally placed the negotiators in a slightly awkward position.

Meanwhile the German Commissary had already returned to the rendezvous, where he informed our representative that the Commander 15th Panzer Grenadier Division was unable to accept the terms of unconditional surrender, but that he would like to prolong the truce until the results were known of negotiations which were believed to be taking place between Field-Marshal Montgomery and Admiral Friedburg. The Germans were, however, unaware of the announcement of the Army Group surrender, which was communi-

GERMAN COMMANDERS SURRENDER AT BREMERVÖRDE. MAY 1945

VICTORY MARCH PAST AT BREMERHAVEN. General HORROCKS TAKES THE SALUTE. 12TH MAY 1945

UNVEILING
OF
DIVISIONAL
MEMORIAL
AT
ST VALÉRY.
JUNE 1950

By courtesy of
Aberdeen Journals
Ltd.

THE TOWEL COMES IN

cated to them. In view of this they were told that the Commander 15th Panzer Grenadier Division and the Commander of Corps E.M.S. or whoever commanded the entire peninsula, together with two staff officers, would be required to present themselves at the rendezvous at 1000 hours the following day to be conducted to higher headquarters on this side to receive the orders of Commander 30th Corps. In order to permit them to lift mines or build a bridge where necessary, and to avoid unnecessary bloodshed, it was agreed that the truce would be extended to 0800 hours, when the general Cease Fire would take effect. The German officer went back to his headquarters with this message and returned at about 0100 hours to say that his Commander and the Corps Commander would present themselves at the rendezvous as ordered.

Accordingly at 1035 hours, 5th May, Lieut.-General Raspe, Commander Corps E.M.S., and Major-General Roth, Commander 15th Panzer Grenadier Division, together with a naval representative and several staff officers and clerks, arrived at this headquarters. This party was considerably in excess of the numbers ordered and the Commander 51st Highland Division stated that he would only deal with General Raspe, his Chief of Staff and one interpreter, and the remaining officers and other ranks were segregated in another room. In the presence of the Commander 51st Highland Division, Commander 154 Brigade, and certain staff officers, B.G.S. 30th Corps then transmitted to the German Corps Commander the immediate orders of the Commander 30th Corps.

General Raspe was put in command of all armed forces in the peninsula, whether or not they were under his command at the time of surrender. The surrender terms were those which were laid down for all formations by the Supreme Commander.

Generally speaking, the Germans made no difficulty and seemed thoroughly co-operative, though General Raspe made a considerable effort to obtain permission for his officers to retain their small arms to enforce his orders amongst the miscellaneous troops previously not under his command. B.G.S. 30th Corps refused this request and countered by pointing out that guards for dumps could perfectly well be armed with sticks, clubs and truncheons, &c., while, if the General had no confidence in the reaction of some of the fresh troops put under his command, the answer was to disarm his own troops last. General Raspe was so favourably impressed by the excellence of this answer that, in true German military manner, he approved it heartily and appeared quite to overlook any inconvenience it might cause him. Shortly after this the meeting broke up and the German delegates were given three-quarters of an hour to confer among themselves as to how our requirements were going to be carried out. A few harsh orders were given and a bevy of staff officers, clerks, and interpreters went into a huddle while the General regaled himself with a cigar in the doorway and gave the photographers another chance.

At the end of this period the room was again cleared for our Commanders and staffs to return. The German Chief of Staff then raised the minimum of sensible questions, which were duly answered, instructions were given for the meeting later in the day between Commander 30th Corps and General Raspe, and the meeting broke up.

Thus was settled in a most fitting manner a score dating from 23rd October 1942, when the 51st Highland Division first participated in the struggle against the Deutsche Afrika Korps, and the old 15th Panzer Division which finally surrendered in Tunisia in May 1943. It is indeed satisfying that in May 1945 its successor should meet a similar fate at the hands of the 30th Corps and ourselves."

It was fitting that, in a Division which prided itself on being Territorial, the Brigadier of 154 Brigade, at the completion of the war, should have been a Territorial, James Oliver of Arbroath. Oliver had fought with the Division in every battle since Alamein, and in a remarkable manner had escaped being seriously wounded. A born soldier and a born commander, had Oliver decided to make the Army his whole career, he would have certainly gone far. It can be said without fear of contradiction that the debt, which not only 154 Brigade but the whole 51st, owed to Brigadier Oliver for the great reputation they acquired was no small one.

And so dawned the 8th day of May 1945—V.E. Day.

On that morning, almost five years after St Valéry, was the Highland Division's warfare accomplished. In this second European conflict it numbered its casualties at over 9000.[1] How many of the enemy it had killed and wounded can never be known, but from the time it had landed on the Normandy beaches alone it had made prisoner 408 officers and 23,541 other ranks. It could now rest on its laurels and listen to congratulatory messages from the Supreme Commander, from Field-Marshal Montgomery, and from His Majesty the King.

Before May was out, General MacMillan, who had so successfully led the Division to its final victory, was ordered to the War Office as Assistant Chief of the Imperial General Staff, and was succeeded in the command of the 51st by Brigadier Cassels (Seaforth) from 152 Brigade. MacMillan combined efficiency with a high sense of duty and a great charm of manner, and the Highlanders had been fortunate in their Commander in their last battles. General MacMillan added to his many honours when later, in his own right, he was acknowledged Chief of his Clan.

[1] For casualties in Africa and Sicily, see pp. 99 and 134.

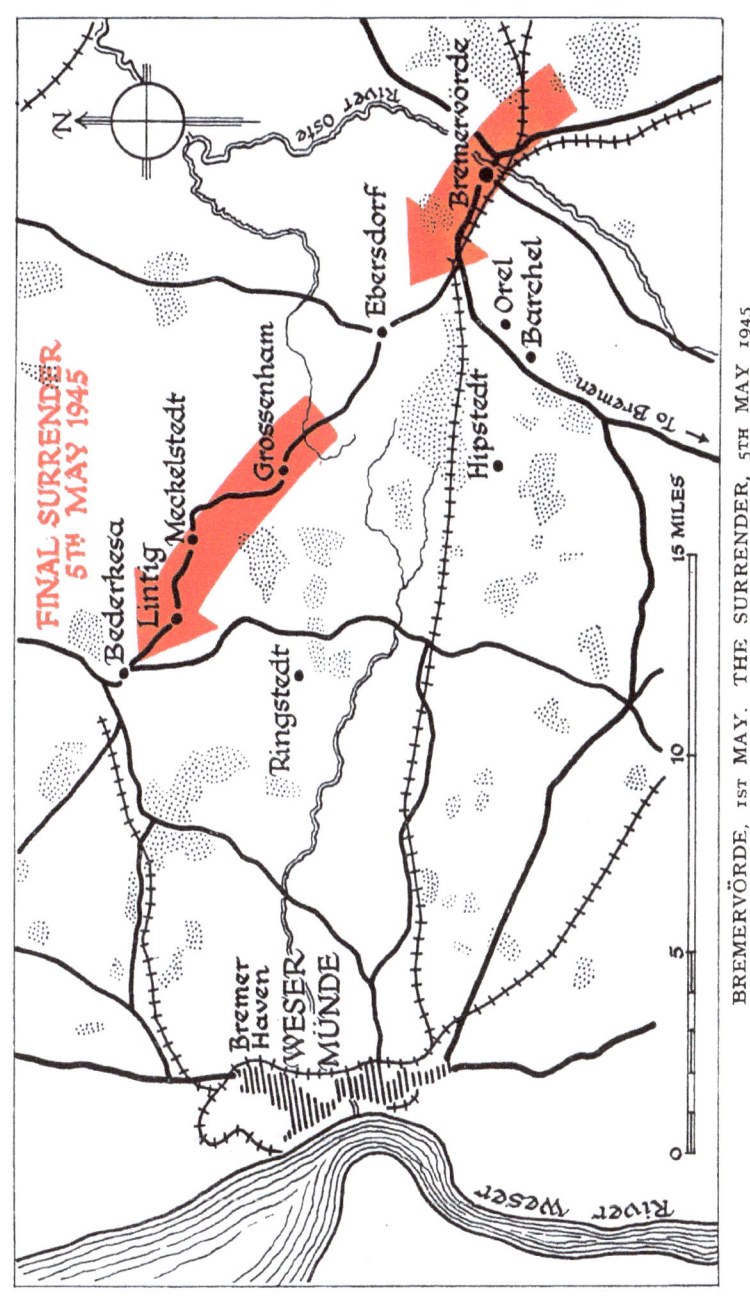

BREMERVÖRDE, 1ST MAY. THE SURRENDER, 5TH MAY 1945

Three months later, in August, the Highland Division became part of the Army of the Rhine—and in December 1946 came the sad news from the War Office that the 51st Highland Division had ceased to exist as a separate formation. It had apparently been decided that Scotland was now to have in the post-war Army only one Infantry Division—the 51st/52nd (Scottish), an amalgamation of the Highland and Lowland Divisions. General Sir Neil Ritchie, G.O.C. Scottish Command, and General Wimberley as Director of Infantry in the War Office, had done all they could for the retention of these two historic Divisions in Scotland, the 51st as an Infantry Division and the 52nd as an Armoured Division. But the Army Council had made their decision, and that—for a short time—was that. (As had indeed been pointed out, the amalgamation which seemed feasible on paper did not work in Scotland, and the 51st started again as a separate Division in 1948.)

So we leave the Highland Division now as they take part in their Victory March at Bremerhaven on 12th May 1945, when Lieut.-General B. G. Horrocks, C.B., D.S.O., M.C., Commander 30th Corps, took the Salute.

The Guards of Honour were from the United States Naval and Military Forces in Bremerhaven, and the Black Watch (Royal Highland Regiment) under Major P. S. Douglas, M.C., who had now recovered from the serious wounds sustained by him during the previous year and had returned as Second-in-Command of the 42nd.[1]

On parade were the Massed Pipes and Drums of the 51st Highland Division, comprising bands from the Black Watch (Royal Highland Regiment), the Seaforth Highlanders (Ross-shire Buffs, the Duke of Albany's), the Gordon Highlanders, the Queen's Own Cameron Highlanders, the Argyll and Sutherland Highlanders (Princess Louise's), The Scottish Horse, and the Royal Corps of Signals.

And so now instead of another last Order of Battle, we can append the first Order of Peace—the Bremerhaven Victory Parade Order of March—so far as the Highland Division were concerned.

[1] Douglas went to Korea with the 42nd in 1952.

BREMERHAVEN VICTORY PARADE. MAY 1945

ORDER OF MARCH

Major-General G. H. A. MacMillan, C.B., C.B.E., D.S.O., M.C.,
late The Argyll and Sutherland Highlanders (Princess Louise's)

COMMANDER, 51ST HIGHLAND DIVISION

Lieutenant-Colonel N. D. Leslie,
The Queen's Own Cameron Highlanders

G.S.O.1

Lieutenant-Colonel J. G. B. Gray,
The Gordon Highlanders

A.A. and Q.M.G.

MARCHING TROOPS

HEADQUARTERS, 51ST HIGHLAND DIVISION
and
51ST HIGHLAND DIVISIONAL SIGNALS

under

Major R. J. Henderson, D.S.O., M.B.E., Royal Signals
Captain I. M. Waters, The Gordon Highlanders

2ND DERBYSHIRE YEOMANRY (Royal Armoured Corps
51ST HIGHLAND DIVISIONAL RECONNAISSANCE CORPS

under

Major A. F. C. Langly Smith, M.C.

152ND HIGHLAND BRIGADE

Brigadier A. J. H. CASSELS, C.B.E., D.S.O.,
The Seaforth Highlanders (Ross-shire Buffs, The Duke of Albany's)
Commander

HEADQUARTERS, 152ND HIGHLAND BRIGADE

under

Major J. A. F. WATT, The Seaforth Highlanders

D.A.A. and Q.M.G.

2ND BATTALION, THE SEAFORTH HIGHLANDERS (Ross-shire Buffs, The Duke of Albany's)

under

Lieutenant-Colonel G. W. DUNN, D.S.O., M.C. (The Black Watch)

5TH BATTALION, THE SEAFORTH HIGHLANDERS (Ross-shire Buffs, The Duke of Albany's)

under

Lieutenant-Colonel J. M. SYM, D.S.O.

5TH BATTALION, THE QUEEN'S OWN CAMERONS

under

Lieutenant-Colonel D. B. LANG, D.S.O., M.C.

153RD HIGHLAND BRIGADE
Brigadier J. R. SINCLAIR, D.S.O., The Gordon Highlanders
Commander

HEADQUARTERS, 153RD HIGHLAND BRIGADE
under
Major L. W. MILLAR, M.C., The Gordon Highlanders
D.A.A. and Q.M.C.

5TH BATTALION, THE BLACK WATCH (Royal Highland Regiment)
under
Lieutenant-Colonel B. C. BRADFORD, D.S.O., M.B.E., M.C.

1ST BATTALION, THE GORDON HIGHLANDERS
under
Lieutenant-Colonel J. A. GRANT-PETERKIN, D.S.O.
(Cameron Highlanders)

5/7TH BATTALION, THE GORDON HIGHLANDERS
under
Lieutenant-Colonel C. F. IRVINE, M.C.

154TH HIGHLAND BRIGADE
Brigadier J. A. OLIVER, C.B.E., D.S.O., T.D.,
The Black Watch (Royal Highland Regiment)
Commander

HEADQUARTERS, 154TH HIGHLAND BRIGADE
under
Major D. PUNTON, The Black Watch (Royal Highland Regiment)
Brigade Major

51ST HIGHLAND DIVISION

1ST BATTALION, THE BLACK WATCH (Royal Highland Regiment)
under
Lieutenant-Colonel J. A. HOPWOOD, D.S.O.

7TH BATTALION, THE BLACK WATCH (Royal Highland Regiment)
under
Lieutenant-Colonel B. A. INNES

7TH BATTALION, THE ARGYLL AND SUTHERLAND HIGHLANDERS
(Princess Louise's)
under
Lieutenant-Colonel A. MACKINNON, D.S.O., M.C.

1/7TH BATTALION, THE MIDDLESEX REGIMENT
(Duke of Cambridge's Own)
under
Lieutenant-Colonel D. G. PARKER

ROYAL ENGINEERS OF THE 51ST HIGHLAND DIVISION

274TH FIELD COMPANY, ROYAL ENGINEERS
275TH FIELD COMPANY, ROYAL ENGINEERS
276TH FIELD COMPANY, ROYAL ENGINEERS
239TH FIELD PARK COMPANY, ROYAL ENGINEERS
16TH BRIDGING PLATOON, ROYAL ENGINEERS
under
Lieutenant-Colonel R. H. WALKER, R.E.
Commander, Royal Engineers, 51st Highland Division

ROYAL ARMY SERVICE CORPS OF THE 51ST HIGHLAND DIVISION

458TH (DIVISIONAL TROOPS) COMPANY, ROYAL ARMY SERVICE CORPS
525TH (INFANTRY BRIGADE) COMPANY, ROYAL ARMY SERVICE CORPS
526TH (INFANTRY BRIGADE) COMPANY, ROYAL ARMY SERVICE CORPS
527TH (INFANTRY BRIGADE) COMPANY, ROYAL ARMY SERVICE CORPS

under

Captain W. E. WRIGHT, R.A.S.C.

ROYAL ARMY MEDICAL CORPS OF THE 51ST HIGHLAND DIVISION

174TH FIELD AMBULANCE
175TH FIELD AMBULANCE
176TH FIELD AMBULANCE

under

Lieutenant-Colonel G. H. C. HOPE, M.C., R.A.M.C.

ROYAL ARMY ORDNANCE CORPS OF THE 51ST HIGHLAND DIVISION

ASSISTANT DIRECTOR ORDNANCE SERVICES STAFF
51ST HIGHLAND DIVISION ORDNANCE FIELD PARK
302ND MOBILE LAUNDRY AND BATH UNIT
152ND INFANTRY BRIGADE WORKSHOP STORES SECTION
153RD INFANTRY BRIGADE WORKSHOP STORES SECTION
154TH INFANTRY BRIGADE WORKSHOP STORES SECTION

under

Captain H. E. DAVIS, R.A.O.C.

ROYAL ELECTRICAL AND MECHANICAL ENGINEERS OF THE 51ST HIGHLAND DIVISION

152ND INFANTRY BRIGADE WORKSHOPS
153RD INFANTRY BRIGADE WORKSHOPS
154TH INFANTRY BRIGADE WORKSHOPS
under
Major D. M. MACLEAN, R.E.M.E.

ROYAL ARTILLERY OF THE 51ST HIGHLAND DIVISION

126TH FIELD REGIMENT, ROYAL ARTILLERY
under
Major W. A. HAMILTON, M.C., R.A.

127TH FIELD REGIMENT, ROYAL ARTILLERY
under
Major G. H. WAGSTAFFE, M.C., R.A.

128TH FIELD REGIMENT, ROYAL ARTILLERY
under
Major J. T. LAING, M.C., R.A.

79TH MEDIUM REGIMENT, ROYAL ARTILLERY (The Scottish Horse)
(attached)
under
Major E. R. COX, T.D., R.A.

61ST ANTI-TANK REGIMENT, ROYAL ARTILLERY
under
Major G. D. SCRUPLE, R.A.

40TH LIGHT ANTI-AIRCRAFT REGIMENT, ROYAL ARTILLERY
under
Major R. VETCH, M.C., R.A.

And, as at the beginning of this, his story, so at this, its end, the infantryman of the 51st salutes his good companions in all those other units which, with his own, made up that brotherhood known as the Highland Division—the reconnaissance yeoman in his armoured car fearlessly searching out the enemy wherever he might be found; the signaller coolly laying and keeping in repair those very life-lines of communication under the continual menace of the foe; the machine-gunner, a valued comrade at his shoulder in every action; the sapper ever in the valley of the shadow of unseen death, clearing the hidden enemies from his path and making a way for him across desert and ditch, flood and field; the man who, through a rain of shot and shell, brought him his food and water; the man who in the tortured fields of battle bound up his wounds; the man who kept his vehicles in good repair; and, last but not least, the gunner who put down a guard of shell around him, who blasted the enemy in front of him, who smashed the tank that strove to crush him, and the aeroplane that aimed to bomb him. They were the friends he had, and, " their adoption tried," he did indeed " grapple them to his soul with hoops of steel."

Eric Linklater has pointed out how " to the Highland Territorials who composed the 51st Division in the earlier German War, a strange thing happened: regimental loyalty . . . was to a large extent replaced by their greater pride in the Division. . . . Its quality was acknowledged, not only by English commanders and French allies, but by the enemy, while in Scotland its powers became an accepted legend." This phenomenon was repeated in the 1939-45 War. The Division again won for itself a reputation as a great fighting force, and again its soldiers, when asked to what formation they belonged, would answer first and foremost, not the name of their regiment or corps, but simply "The Highland Division." *Esprit de corps* had again become *esprit de* Division.

Neil Munro wrote of the 51st in 1917-18 that "from every war some unit of command—a regiment or a brigade—comes through with popular laurels, a name for ever after to be illustrious. In this greatest of wars that glory went to a whole division, and that a Scottish one, composed entirely of Highland territorials." A difficult reputation to sustain! The 51st of the Second World War had a great tradition to remember and uphold. In this short history an attempt has been made to tell how it succeeded in that most difficult task, and the opinion of those best qualified to judge is printed at the beginning of this volume. Time will give the final verdict, but it can be claimed that the story of the Highland Division, throughout the two Great Wars at the beginning of the Twentieth Century, is a saga that will be told as long as the tartan is worn by Scottish men, as long as the pipes sound among the hills, in the glens, in the burgh-towns and in the cities of Scotland.

CHAPTER XVI.

THE AULD ALLIANCE

> "*An sith araon luidhidh mi, agus caidlidh mi.*"
> ("I will lay me down in peace, and take my rest.")
> Psalm iv. 9.

> "Write the vision, and make it plain upon tables, that he may run that readeth it."
> Habakkuk ii. 2.

ON the high east cliff of St Valéry-en-Caux, the Falaise d'Amont, stands a massive pillar of Scots granite, the latest milestone on the long road that the 51st Highland Division travelled in the days that are gone. The first milestone on that road stands at Beaumont-Hamel, the second on a Sicilian hill by Sferro, this third at St Valéry. The road disappears into the mist which hides the days to come, but whithersoever it leads and whenever the hour strikes, the Highland Division of Scotland will march forward along it without fear and without question. On the opposite cliff, the Falaise d'Aval, is a pillar of stone from the Vosges Mountains near Luneville in Lorraine, which tells of that French Second Light Cavalry Division which fought alongside the 51st in the sorrow-shrouded days of June 1940.

Ten years later, on 10th June 1950, the anniversary of the day of sorrow and surrender, a summer sun shone brightly on the sparkling waters of the Channel, on the great beeches of the Bois d'Etennamare, on the little valley sweet with orchards in which lies St Valéry (in one of which orchards is the military cemetery, a resting-place of the Highland Division's dead), and finally on the new road laid in the devastated harbour area of St Valéry. Beside that road a platform had been erected. M. Henri Cherfils, the Maire, welcomed his town's guests there. Among them was a Scottish military delegation headed by Major-General Douglas Wimberley, and including Major-General Robert Keith Arbuthnott, Major-General Colin Muir Barber, Major-General Sir Kenneth Gray Buchanan, Brigadier C. P. R. Johnston, Brigadier J. A. Oliver, and Captain R. F. Elkins, Royal Navy, who was the Liaison Officer to the Division at St Valéry in 1940. The Lord Provosts of Aberdeen, Dundee, Perth and Elgin were there, with the Provosts of Stirling and Inverness, and the Secretary of State for Scotland. The Marquis and Marchioness of Huntly were also guests, as were Mrs Rennie, widow of Major-General T. G. Rennie, and Captain G. B. Fortune, son of the late Major-General Fortune. To represent France were present M. René Massigli, French Ambassador in London, and many French Generals and Admirals. The Guard of Honour was commanded by Major A. F. Hendry, 7th Argylls. On that memorable morning Monsignor Martin, Catholic Primate of Normandy, with Highland Division Protestant (both Presbyterian and Episcopalian) ministers assisting him, conducted a memorial service over the graves of the men who are buried in the Cemetery of St Valéry, the granite-pillared gateway to which (a gift from the people of North-East Scotland to the Valériquais) was unveiled by the Marchioness of Huntly.

In the afternoon from that platform by the harbour, which was surrounded by Scots Highlanders and French Cavalry with Naval Commando units, General Wimberley gave an address in which he spoke of the centuries-old comradeship-in-arms of Scot and Frenchman. He said :—

"Now, if our dead were here to speak to us to-day, many of them would tell us of all the kindnesses paid them by the people of France—kindnesses when they were wounded, or as fugitives, or perhaps merely generously offered in the way of food to those hungry on the march, ay, and for much more than kindnesses ; indeed of the very grave risks so often willingly run by Frenchmen and Frenchwomen on their behalf.

Some would no doubt speak, too, of our comrades-in-arms, the great-hearted French Cavalrymen who died fighting near here, close to St Valéry. It is for that reason that we Scots have expressed here, on this monument, in the Gaelic tongue of our Highland forbears, the same sentiment that was assuredly uppermost in our thoughts in 1924, when we were honoured by the presence of that very great Marshal of France—Foch—who then unveiled for us our Beaumont-Hamel Memorial, and so it is from that Memorial that we have again repeated the same words in Gaelic on that granite block up there on the cliff, the words that read—'Friends are good in the day of battle.'

We, in Scotland, know full well that in putting up this Memorial in Normandy we have delivered it into the hands of true friends and allies ; we know that you will care for it and respect it, just as you will do your own ; and so to the Glory of God, and to the brave men who fought and died for Britain and her Commonwealth, and for our own dear land of Scotland, this Memorial will now be unveiled."

As General Poidenot replied, many a thought went to another memorial, the 1914-18 Monument to the 15th (Scottish) Division at Buzancy, which unites that Division with the 17th French Division in the words :—

"Ici fleurira toujours le glorieux chardon d'Ecosse parmi les roses de France."

Then the pipers of the Black Watch played "The Flowers of the Forest," and when the Lament had died away, the Union Jack was withdrawn and, as the bugles sang out "The Last Post" and then "The Reveille," the pillar from the quarry near Balmoral was revealed glittering in the sunlight, and under the famous "H.D." sign the words were there for all to see : "In proud and grateful memory of all ranks of the 51st Highland Division who gave their lives during the War 1939-45." On the column in the ancient Gaelic tongue of the Clans and Highland regiments is the phrase "Là a' bhlàir 's math na càirdean" (Friends are good in the day of battle) as a kind of a wave of the hand to the French pillar on the opposite cliff. On the back of the monolith is another Highland Division sign and below it is the following inscription in French :—

A LA MEMOIRE
DE SES GLORIEUX ENFANTS
OFFICIERS, SOUS-OFFICIERS ET SOLDATS
DE LA 51e DIVISION
L'ECOSSE
A ELEVE CE MONUMENT
SUR LE SOL
DE SON ANTIQUE ALLIE
1939-45.

The base of the monolith is surrounded by paving-stones which are coloured and laid in such a way as to outline a St Andrew's Cross.

The townsfolk also had their great hour, for the French Secretary of State for War, M. André Maroselli, handed over a Croix de Guerre to St Valéry, represented on this occasion by M. Roger Andrieux, who had lost his parents and five brothers and sisters in the 1940 shelling of that town.

On the Sunday morning, following the dedication of the cliff pillar, a service was held beside it. Again the sun is shining and lights up the sombre tartan kilts of the Black Watch, the Argyll and Sutherland Battalion, picks out the yellow stripe of the Gordons, and the white of the Seaforth, and makes the Cameron kilts redder still—those famous tartans of the Highland regiments which the sons of Scotland have worn in the van of countless battles down two hundred years of British history. The Scots Provosts and others laid wreaths at the foot of the pillar, and the Rev. Ironside Simpson, a Senior Chaplain of the Division, the Rev. A. Drummond Duff, who served in both wars, and the Rev. Canon Lake of the Episcopal Church of Scotland, took part in the service, while General Arbuthnott (Black Watch), the present Commander of the 51st, read the lesson. Later another service was held in the church at St Veules. It was conducted by the Abbé Beonard, who had been wounded in the 1940 attack on that village.

Next day, on the local sports ground, representative Pipes and Drums of the Highland Division played " Retreat." Another day for the soldier was over. And for many there came marching back to take their ease in the bivouacs of memory the men who, like their fathers before them, had done their duty at the price of all that they had to give in the strange silence of the Maginot woods, in the weary fields from the Somme to the Bresle, in the great spaces of African desert and Tripolitanian hills, in Sicilian orange-groves, in the Triangle, and by the ways that led back across the Seine to St Valéry, in the water-logged fields of Geertruidenberg, in the Ardennes and the Reichswald Forest, on both banks of the Rhine, and that memory goes forward into memory with all the other memories, for the old men who with Ulysses cry :—

> " Though much is taken, much abides ; and tho'
> We are not now that strength which in old days
> Moved earth and heaven ; that which we are, we are ;
> One equal temper of heroic hearts
> Made weak by time and fate, but strong in will
> To strive, to seek, to find and not to yield."

Or the young men who with Ecclesiasticus reverently say :—

" Let us now praise famous men, and our fathers that begat us. . . . All these were honoured in their generations, and were the glory of their times. There be of them that have left a name behind them, that their praises might be reported. . . . Their bodies are buried in peace, but their name liveth for evermore."

51ST HIGHLAND DIVISION—BATTLE CASUALTIES

N.W. EUROPE

FROM D DAY, 6TH JUNE 1944, TO 5TH MAY 1945

Unit	Killed Offrs.	Killed O.R.s	Wounded Offrs.	Wounded O.R.s	Missing Offrs.	Missing O.R.s	Total Offrs.	Total O.R.s
H.Q. 51 Div.	1	2	2	4	..	..	3	6
Postal Unit	..	..	..	1	..	..	..	1
2 Derby Yeo.	1	38	28	162	1	31	30	231
H.Q. R.A.	1	..	..	4	..	..	1	4
126 Fd. Regt.	5	18	15	67	..	..	20	85
127 Fd. Regt.	4	28	8	96	2	9	14	133
128 Fd. Regt.	..	7	15	70	..	..	15	77
61 A.-Tk. Regt.	3	21	15	126	6	..	18	153
40 L.A.A. Regt.	1	16	7	61	..	2	8	79
C.M.O.	..	..	1	1	..	..	1	1
H.Q. R.E.	1	..	2	1	..	..	3	1
239 Fd. Pk. Coy.	..	1	..	19	..	1	..	21
274 Fd. Coy.	4	10	7	65	..	1	11	76
275 Fd. Coy.	..	7	4	28	..	2	4	37
276 Fd. Coy.	1	12	4	47	..	4	5	63
16 Br. Pl.	..	..	..	3	..	..	..	3
Div. Sigs.	3	12	4	48	..	5	7	65
H.Q. 152 Bde.	3	3	13	12	..	1	16	16
2 Seaforth	10	125	31	612	..	64	41	801
5 Seaforth	7	118	34	484	1	14	42	636
5 Camerons	17	176	59	882	1	16	77	1074
H.Q. 153 Bde.	1	1	4	11	..	..	5	12
5 Black Watch	19	206	52	880	3	100	74	1186
1 Gordons	17	172	55	691	4	115	76	978
5/7 Gordons	6	106	32	595	3	61	41	762
H.Q. 154 Bde.	..	..	3	4	..	..	3	4
1 Black Watch	11	122	36	534	3	44	48	700
7 Black Watch	12	143	48	581	..	21	60	745
7 A. & S.H.	11	160	47	595	2	45	60	800
1/7 Middlesex	3	35	20	185	..	7	23	227
525 Coy. R.A.S.C.	..	1	1	5	..	..	1	6
526 Coy. R.A.S.C.	1	..	..	1	..	..	1	1
527 Coy. R.A.S.C.	..	1	1	5	..	..	1	6
458 Coy. R.A.S.C.	..	2	..	3	..	1	..	6
174 Fd. Amb.	..	4	2	21	..	3	2	28
175 Fd. Amb.	..	5	..	6	..	..	..	11
176 Fd. Amb.	..	4	..	14	..	2	..	20
6 Fds.	..	..	1	7	..	..	1	7
152 Bde. W/Shops	..	1	..	..	..	..	..	1
153 Bde. W/Shops	..	..	1	2	..	..	1	2
Pro. Coy.	..	2	..	2	..	..	..	4
Div. O.F.P.	..	..	..	..	..	2	..	2
Totals	143	1559	552	6935	20	557	707	9051

APPENDIX

THE 51ST HIGHLAND DIVISION
ORDER OF BATTLE AT THE OPENING OF AND BATTLE OF ALAMEIN

G.O.C.	Major-General D. N. Wimberley (Camerons)
G.S.O.1	Lt.-Col. R. Urquhart (H.L.I.)
A.A. & Q.M.G.	Lt.-Col. J. A. Colam (R.A.)
152 Highland Brigade	Brigadier G. Murray (Seaforth)
2nd Seaforth	Lt.-Col. K. McKessack
5th Seaforth	Lt.-Col. J. E. Stirling
5th Camerons	Lt.-Col. R. D. M. C. Miers
153 Highland Brigade	Brigadier D. A. H. Graham (Cameronians)
1st Gordons	Lt.-Col. H. Murray (Camerons)
5th Black Watch	Lt.-Col. T. G. Rennie
5/7th Gordons	Lt.-Col. H. W. B. Saunders
154 Highland Brigade	Brigadier H. W. Houldsworth (Seaforth)
1st Black Watch	Lt.-Col. W. N. Roper-Caldbeck
7th Black Watch	Lt.-Col. J. A. Oliver
7th Argylls	Lt.-Col. Lorne M. Campbell
1/7th Middlesex Regiment (Machine Gunners)	Lt.-Col. J. W. A. Stephenson
The Royal Artillery, C.R.A.	Brigadier G. M. Elliot
The Royal Artillery, 126 Field Regiment	Lt.-Col. H. J. A. Thicknesse
The Royal Artillery, 127 Field Regiment	Lt.-Col. H. M. Perry
The Royal Artillery, 128 Field Regiment	Lt.-Col. W. A. Shiel
40 Light A.A. Regiment	Lt.-Col. R. A. L. Fraser-Mackenzie
61st Anti-Tank Regiment	Lt.-Col. J. H. B. Evatt
The Royal Engineers, C.R.E.	Lt.-Col. H. W. Giblin
The Royal Engineers, 239 Field Park Coy.	Captain R. S. Maitland
The Royal Engineers, 274 Field Coy.	Major S. B. Russell
The Royal Engineers, 275 Field Coy.	Major H. L. Lloyd
The Royal Engineers, 296 Field Coy.	Major John Lamb
The Royal Corps of Signals	Lt.-Col. C. P. S. Denholm Young
The Royal Army Medical Corps	Colonel R. W. Galloway
174 Field Ambulance	Lt.-Col. A. M. Campbell
175 Field Ambulance	Lt.-Col. R. M. J. Gordon
176 Field Ambulance	Lt.-Col. C. H. Kerr
The Royal Army Service Corps	Lt.-Col. H. H. Bruton
Recce Regiment	Lt.-Col. E. H. Grant (A. & S.H.)
Divisional Workshops, R.E.M.E.	Lt.-Col. G. S. McKellar
A.P.M. of Provost	Major A. A. Ferguson (Camerons)
R.A.O.C.	Lt.-Col. G. E. G. Malet
Senior Chaplain	Rev. Jock Elder (Church of Scotland)

INDEX

A

Persons and Units

Afrika Korps, 38, 79.
Aitken, Major K., 163.
Aitkenhead, Sergeant, 142.
Alexander, Sergeant, 116.
Alexander, General, 51, 73, 74, 75, 77, 78, 96.
Allen, Lieutenant M., 42.
Ambler, Sam, 165.
American Air Force, 166, 169.
American 22nd Assault Squadron, 228.
Anderson, Major, 190.
Andrews, Lt.-Colonel, 216.
Arbuthnott, General, 269, 272.
Argyll and Sutherland Highlanders—
   1st Battalion, 121, 195.
   2nd Battalion, 184, 195.
   7th Battalion, 7, 9, 12, 13, 17, 33, 40, 41, 47, 50, 60, 64, 79, 83, 86, 103, 104, 105, 113, 115, 116, 117, 121, 124, 126, 127, 141, 144, 154, 156, 159, 160, 168, 178, 180, 181, 188, 190, 192, 197, 202, 209, 214, 220, 224, 226, 233, 236, 242, 247, 251, 254, 255, 270.
   8th Battalion, 7, 12, 13.
Ark Force, 13, 15.
Arkwright, Brigadier, 118.
Armies—
   British—
     1st Army, 75, 77, 96, 97.
     2nd Army, 138, 184, 191, 192, 204, 213.
     8th Army, 30 *et seq.*
   Canadian—
     1st Army, 152, 153, 180, 184, 213, 214.
     2nd Army, 202.
   U.S.A.—
     1st Army, 138, 205.
     3rd Army, 210.
     7th Army, 102, 108, 121.
     9th Army, 205, 206, 214.
Arnim, General von, 75.

Place Names

Abbeville, 10, 17.
Aberlour, 25.
Abu Suivera, 58.
Adjedabya, 54, 55, 57.
Adrano, 121, 122, 126, 127.
Agheila, 54, 56.
Agira, 121.
Akarit, 56, 85, 86, 87, 94, 95.
Alamein, 17 *et seq.*
Alam el Halfa, 30.
Alençon, 152.
Aldershot, 25.
Algeria, 97, 100, 101.
Amfreville, 144.
Ancourt, 12.
Angelico Farm, 122, 123.
Anholt, 241.
Antwerp, 6, 184, 186, 205.
Ardennes, 204, 205, 212.
Argentan, 152.
Arnhem, 200, 201.
Arques, 12, 13.
Asper, 221.
Asperden, 221.
Astrang River, 241.
Augusta, 108.
Avola, 107, 108.

B

Persons and Units

Baillie, Captain H. M., 117.
Bain, Corporal, 90.
Bake, Trooper, 169.
Baker-Baker, Major, 116.
"Balmorals" Concert Party, 24, 72, 73, 131.
Barber, Major-General, 245.
Barker, Sergeant F., 72, 81, 131.

INDEX

Barlow, Major, 77.
Battle Casualties—
  October 1942–May 1943, 99.
  Sicilian Campaign, 134.
  N.W. Europe, 273, 274.
Bauld, Sergeant, 40.
Beacham, Lance-Corporal, 45.
Beales, Captain D., 219.
Bird, Lieutenant, 106.
Black Watch, The—
  1st Battalion, 6, 7, 10, 12, 13, 14, 17, 19, 33, 42, 47, 52, 58, 63, 64, 67, 69, 71, 79, 86, 88, 91, 94, 103, 104, 106, 112, 113, 115, 116, 117, 124, 125, 126, 127, 141, 151, 157, 159, 168, 178, 180, 186, 188, 197, 201, 208, 209, 215, 219, 220, 224, 226, 235, 242, 247, 248, 255.
  4th Battalion, 7, 13.
  5th Battalion, 33, 39, 43, 45, 47, 62, 66, 83, 85, 90, 107, 112, 118, 119, 127, 128, 138, 139, 141, 142, 143, 145, 147, 159, 161, 162, 163, 164, 165, 187, 189, 192, 196, 200, 201, 208, 209, 210, 216, 217, 219, 223, 224, 226, 230, 236, 237, 238, 240, 247, 254.
  6th Battalion, 6.
  7th Battalion, 23, 27, 33, 41, 47, 60, 63, 64, 67, 68, 71, 86, 88, 89, 91, 94, 103, 105, 106, 113, 115, 116, 117, 121, 124, 125, 126, 127, 136, 144, 145, 147, 148, 154, 157, 159, 160, 166, 168, 178, 180, 188, 189, 190, 197, 201, 202, 209, 214, 215, 219, 220, 224, 233, 236, 242, 247, 248, 249, 251, 254.
Blair, Lt.-Colonel N., 104, 106, 116, 126.
Blair, Major N., 26.
Border Regiment, 12.
Borthwick, Alastair, 35, 210, 241.
Boyle, Major R., 235.
Bradford, Lt.-Colonel W., 160, 163, 164, 208, 216, 236, 254.
Bremerhaven Victory Parade—
  Detail of, 260 *et seq.*
Bridges, Private D. M., 89, 90.
Brigades—
  Armoured—
    2nd, 46, 47.
    4th, 141.
    22nd, 57, 62, 67.
    23rd, 66, 67, 83, 93, 108, 110, 113, 118.
    33rd, 153, 154, 155, 157, 169, 187, 192, 207.
    Guards, 226.
    New Zealand, 48.
  Infantry—
    " A," 12, 13, 15.
    4th Special Service, 180.

    5th Guards, 247.
    5th Indian, 51.
    8th, 248.
    9th, 247.
    9th Canadian, 231, 236.
    11th Parachute, 201.
    13th, 104, 121, 128.
    13th Parachute, 202.
    27th, 242.
    44th, 200, 228.
    46th, 184.
    151st, 47, 49.
    152nd, 7, 10, 12, 19, 29, 33, 47, 48, 49, 50, 58, 61, 63, 77, 86, 88, 90, 92, 104, 107, 108, 111, 113, 121, 122, 127, 128, 135, 136, 137, 138, 140, 142, 143, 148, 154, 158, 165, 173, 174, 175, 176, 177, 184, 187, 189, 191, 195, 196, 199, 201, 202, 204, 210, 215, 218, 219, 221, 223, 225, 226, 231, 240, 241, 242, 248, 249, 251, 253, 258.
    153rd, 7, 10, 12, 29, 33, 35, 43, 58, 61, 62, 67, 77, 79, 85, 86, 92, 104, 107, 111, 112, 113, 118, 121, 126, 127, 128, 138, 139, 141, 143, 145, 148, 154, 158, 161, 163, 164, 174, 175, 176, 178, 183, 184, 187, 188, 189, 191, 192, 195, 196, 197, 202, 208, 209, 210, 216, 219, 223, 224, 231, 236, 240, 242, 245, 247, 249, 251, 254.
    154th, 7, 10, 12, 13, 29, 33, 35, 42, 50, 58, 61, 62, 63, 64, 77, 79, 86, 88, 92, 103, 104, 105, 107, 112, 113, 115, 121, 122, 124, 126, 127, 135, 136, 138, 141, 144, 153, 154, 158, 159, 162, 166, 172, 175, 176, 178, 180, 181, 182, 183, 187, 188, 189, 191, 195, 196, 197, 201, 202, 208, 209, 214, 215, 216, 218, 219, 220, 224, 226, 227, 231, 233, 239, 241, 242, 244, 246, 249, 254, 255, 257, 258.
    158th, 183, 184.
    201st Guards, 56, 79, 83, 85.
    231st Malta, 102, 104, 106, 107, 112, 121.
    Czech, 181.
    Royal Netherlands, 183.
Bright, Lieutenant F. E., 111.
Briley, Sergeant, 161.
Brody, Lance-Corporal, 111.
Brooke, General A., 29, 74, 228, 232.
Buffs, The, 12.
Bullen-Smith, Major-General C., 129, 135, 137.
Burney, Brigadier G. T., 7.
Busch, Field-Marshal, 256.

INDEX

Place Names

Baarlo, 197, 199.
Banchory, 25.
Barchel, 254.
Bardia, 54, 55.
Bastogne, 205, 206.
"Battle of the Hills," 64, 68.
Beauchamps, 12.
Beaulieu, 209.
Belfort, 5.
"Ben, The," 41.
Ben Gardane, 77.
Benghazi, 54, 55, 56, 57.
Bergues, 180.
Best, 184.
Bethune, 12.
  River, 12, 13.
Beveland, 184.
Biancavilla, 127, 128, 129.
Bienen, 231, 236.
Blangy, 12.
Boeckelt, 225, 226.
Bois de Bavent, 144.
Bosville, 14.
Bougie, 97.
"Boxes," 31.
Boxtel, 187.
Boyenhof, 226.
Bray-Dunes Plage, 180.
Bremervörde, 251, 253, 254.
Bresle River, 10, 17.
Breville, 141, 142, 144.
Brussels, 205.
Buccheri, 107, 111, 112.
Bucrat, 56, 57, 61, 62, 67, 68.

C

Persons and Units

Cairns, Major H. W., 148.
Calin, Sergeant D., 200.
Cameron, Captain D. H., 200.
Cameron, Captain C. A., 42.
Cameron, Captain I. C., 9, 51.
Cameron Highlanders of Canada, 202, 217.
Cameron Highlanders of Ottawa, 202.
Cameron Highlanders, Queen's Own—
  4th Battalion, 7, 10, 14, 173, 174.
  5th Battalion, 33, 41, 42, 50, 63, 67, 82, 86, 88, 91 104, 107, 108, 110, 119, 122, 124, 140, 142, 143, 148, 158, 165, 166, 173, 177, 184, 187, 189, 190, 191, 196, 199, 201, 202, 210, 215, 216, 218, 220, 221, 225, 240, 241, 242, 248, 249, 253, 254.
Cameronians, The, 184.
Campbell, Lt.-Colonel L., 33, 40, 87, 104, 121.
Campbell, Pipe-Corporal, 42.
Campbell, Major I., 180.
Canadian Seaforth Highlanders, 128.
Cape, Captain Rev. R. E., 144.
Cape Town Highlanders, 41.
Carr, Lt.-Colonel R., 225.
Carruth, Lieutenant J., 52.
Carter, Lieutenant, 169.
Cassels, Brigadier A. J. H., 136, 161, 215, 240, 248, 258.
Cassels, General, 136.
Cathcart, Lt.-Colonel C., 41, 144, 154, 157, 214, 224, 233, 247.
Chavasse, Lieutenant, 57, 69.
Chisholm, Piper J., 173.
Churchill, Rt. Hon. W. S., 15, 29, 73, 228, 232, 244.
Cochrane, Major, 77, 86.
Cochrane, Lt.-Colonel J., 243.
Colam, Lt.-Colonel J. A., 27, 101.
Colquhoun, Lieutenant D., 227.
Cormack, Private J., 109.
Corps—
  1st, 137, 138, 148, 176.
  2nd Canadian, 153, 155, 214.
  8th, 148.
  10th, 102.
  12th, 152, 186, 191, 230, 231.
  13th, 32, 102, 103, 108, 121.
  17th, 19
  30th, 32, 46, 56, 61, 96, 102, 117, 121, 126, 127, 137, 138, 152, 202, 204, 205, 214, 231, 246, 257, 258.
Corps of Military Police, 2.
Cox, Lieutenant, 190.
Cox, Driver C., 125.
Cracroft, Lt.-Colonel R., 154.
Crerar, General, 170, 228, 245.
Crowhurst, Private P., 111.
Cumming-Bruce, Major the Hon., 147, 158, 160, 163, 164, 165, 200, 228.
Cunningham, General Sir A., 19.
Cuthbertson, Lieutenant, 254.

Place Names

Cabourg, 138.
Caen, 138, 140, 143, 145, 148, 152, 155.
Cailleville, 174.
Cairo, 29.
Caltigirone, 112.
Cap Bon, 96.
Cap de la Heve, 178.

Cape Town, 26.
Capo Passero, 106.
Capuzzo, 54.
Carentan, 138, 152.
Casanuova, 108.
Cassel, 180.
Cassibile, 108.
Castleverde, 67.
Catania, 108, 113, 115, 120, 128, 133.
Catenanuova, 122.
Caumont, 152.
Celles, 205.
Centuripe, 122, 126.
Champlon Cross-roads, 210.
Chebir Wadi, 61.
Cheffar Wadi, 93.
Cherbourg, 15, 152, 175.
Churgia, 63.
Cocola, 126.
Colombelles, 145.
Contentin Peninsula, 138.
Corradini, 64, 69.
Cramesnil, 154.
Crispe, 63, 72.
Cuyjx, 200, 202.
Cyrenaica, 54, 56.

D

Persons and Units

Davey, Lieutenant A., 43.
Davey, Major I., 33, 42.
Davidson, Major J. H., 89.
Dawson, Lieutenant H., 110.
Dawson, Captain, 173.
Dean, Corporal, 123.
Dempsey, General M., 192, 243.
Derbyshire Yeomanry, 136, 160, 169, 173, 184, 186, 208, 248, 249, 255.
Dickson, Private E., 111.
Divisions—
  Airborne—
    6th, 138, 141, 144.
    82nd U.S., 215.
    101st U.S., 200.
  Armoured—
    1st, 33.
    7th, 54, 56, 58, 60, 61, 74, 77, 79, 80, 97, 165, 186, 187, 189, 190, 225.
    7th U.S., 194.
    10th, 51.
    33rd, 186.
    Guards, 242, 247, 248, 249.
    Polish, 158, 159, 160.

Infantry—
  1st Canadian, 102, 108, 112, 121.
  1st South African, 32, 40, 47.
  2nd Canadian, 214.
  2nd New Zealand, 27, 32, 40, 41, 47, 54, 56, 61, 74, 77, 80, 85, 96.
  3rd, 135, 138, 140, 150, 231, 241, 247, 248, 249.
  3rd Canadian, 138, 214.
  3rd U.S., 127.
  4th Indian, 51, 56, 80, 82, 85, 86, 96.
  5th, 104, 121, 128.
  9th Australian, 27, 31, 32, 48, 51.
  9th Scottish, 19.
  15th Scottish, 129, 135, 184, 186, 187, 194, 195, 200, 214, 217, 228, 231, 243.
  43rd, 214, 220, 231, 242, 249.
  46th, 19.
  49th, 176, 178, 201, 240.
  50th, 56, 79, 82, 83, 85, 96, 103, 107, 121, 138.
  52nd Lowland, 136, 208, 214, 227, 231, 260.
  53rd Welsh, 183, 184, 186, 187, 190, 191, 194, 200, 214, 217, 224, 249.
  56th, 97.
  78th, 121, 126, 127.
Dodds, Bombardier, 52.
Donaldson, Lieutenant I., 190.
Douglas, Major P. S., 125, 168, 260.
Du Boulay, Major, 44, 187.
Dunlop, Sergeant, 45.
Dunlop, Lt.-Colonel, 104, 121, 126.
Dunn, Major G., 163, 216, 219, 223, 230, 240, 253.

Place Names

Daba Aerodrome, 46.
Demouville, 142, 143, 148.
Dieppe, 12, 173.
Dinant, 205.
Dingwall, 25.
Dittaino River, 113, 115, 117, 118, 121, 122, 123.
Dives River, 161, 162.
Djidjelli, 97, 100, 101, 107.
Dommel River, 187.
Douvres, 139, 140, 141, 144.
Drunen, 191.
Duclair, 172.
Dunkirk, 180, 181.
Durban, 26.

INDEX

E

Persons and Units

East, Captain, 43.
East Lancashire Regiment, 162.
East Riding Yeomanry, 154, 166, 195.
East Yorkshire Regiment, 83, 107, 248.
Eden, Brigadier H. C. H., 7.
Edward, Private J., 119.
Eisenhower, General, 75, 102, 136.
Elliot, Brigadier G., 37, 251.
Elliot, Captain J., 126.
Evans, Lieutenant, 241.
Evatt, Lt.-Colonel J. H. B., 38.

Place Names

East Anglia, 137.
Ebersdorf, 254.
Ecajeul, 162, 164.
"Edinburgh Castle," 64.
Eindhoven, 182, 184, 191, 194.
Elbœuf, 173.
Elgin, 25.
Empel, 192, 242.
Enfidaville, 86, 96.
Enschede, 245, 246, 247.
Envermeu, 12.
Escoville, 143.
Esserden, 231, 236, 240.
Etain, 10.
Etna, 121, 128.
Eu, 12.
Eysden, 230.

F

Persons and Units

Faiers, Sergeant, 143.
Fausset-Farquhar, Lt.-Colonel, 45, 93, 103, 106.
Fergusson, Colonel Bernard, 17, 71.
Ferguson, Major A., 54.
Fife and Forfar Yeomanry, 220, 224, 227.
Filardi, Major B., 140.
Fisher, Sergeant, 124.
Forbes, Lance-Corporal, 124.
Forfar, Captain, 163.
Forster, Lt.-Colonel D., 154, 157.
Forsyth, Corporal, 127.
Fortune, Lieutenant G. B., 64, 270.
Fortune, Major-General V. M., 4, 7, 12, 13, 14, 15, 16, 17, 171, 174, 175, 270.
Fraser, Lieutenant, 45.
Fraser-Mackenzie, Lt.-Colonel, 38.
Free French Troops, 94, 96.
Freyberg, Lt.-General, 48, 49, 80, 92.
Friedburg, Admiral, 256.

Place Names

Falaise, 138, 152, 155, 172.
Favières, 165.
Fécamp, 13.
Fleri, 128.
Floridia, 107.
Fontana Muralato River, 122.
Fontaine-la-Mallet, 177.
Francofonte, 107, 108, 109, 110, 111, 112.
Franleu, 17.

G

Persons and Units

Gall, Lieutenant, 52.
Gardiner, Captain, 241.
German Troops—
  Armies—
    1st, 229.
    5th (Panzer), 205, 229.
    6th (Panzer), 205.
    7th, 205, 229.
    15th, 229.
    Parachute, 229.
  Corps—
    E.M.S., 257, 258.
  Divisions—
    15th Panzer, 77.
    15th Panzer Grenadier, 254, 255, 256, 257, 258.
    21st Panzer Armoured, 83.
    90th Light, 27, 56, 63, 77, 91, 97, 142.
    164th, 77.
  Regiments—
    2nd Parachute, 109.
    6th Infantry, 16.
    7th Infantry, 16.
    25th Panzer, 16.
    1055th Infantry, 158.
  Battalions—
    8th M.G., 16.
    37th Pioneer, 16.
Gibson, 2nd Lieutenant, 81.
Gillies, Lieutenant, 41.
Gilmour, Major, 89.

Glasgow Highlanders, 184.
Gordon, C.S.M., 191.
Gordon Highlanders—
   1st Battalion, 7, 10, 12, 14, 19, 43, 47, 62, 67, 68, 73, 81, 83, 93, 94, 103, 104, 106, 107, 112, 119, 127, 128, 138, 141, 142, 145, 147, 158, 159, 161, 164, 165, 178, 187, 189, 192, 195, 196, 200, 201, 208, 210, 216, 217, 219, 223, 224, 236, 237, 239, 241, 247, 249, 254.
   2nd Battalion, 184.
   5th Battalion, 7, 14.
   6th Battalion, 7, 14.
   5/7th Battalion, 33, 46, 47, 62, 67, 77, 80, 83, 107, 112, 119, 127, 128, 138, 141, 142, 159, 160, 161, 162, 163, 164, 173, 178, 187, 188, 189, 192, 196, 197, 200, 201, 208, 209, 214, 215, 223, 224, 236, 247, 249, 254.
Gort, Lord, 104.
Gort Force, 8.
Graham, Brigadier D., 27, 33, 92, 97, 104, 138.
Graham, Lance-Sergeant J., 123.
Graham, Private J., 123.
Grant, Captain J., 113, 115, 164.
Grant, Colonel, 33.
Grant-Peterkin, Lt.-Colonel J. A., 200, 208, 216, 221, 228, 236, 238, 254.
Gray, Major J., 101.
Green Howards, The, 82.
Grigg, Sir James, 100.

Place Names

Gabes Gap, 80, 85, 94.
Gamanches, 12.
Garcelles, 154, 159.
Garci Mountain, 96.
Garibaldi Valley, 55.
Gazelle, 148.
Geertruidenberg, 184, 186, 189, 190, 192.
Gela, Gulf of, 102, 108.
Genima Wadi, 64.
Gennep, 216, 217, 219, 223.
Gerbini, 115, 117, 118, 121, 129, 132.
Ghedahia, 55.
Ghyvelde, 180.
Givet, 205.
Goch, 220, 221, 223, 224, 225, 227.
Gorna Lunga River, 111, 113.
Grafenthals, 221, 228.
Groenwoud, 191.
Groin, 240, 241.
Guzzarano, 127.

H

Persons and Units

Haig, Field-Marshal Sir D., 3.
"Hammerforce," 66, 67.
Harding, General J., 56.
Hardy, Lieutenant, 46.
"Harper's Duds," 3.
Haugh, Brigadier D. H., 136.
Hay, Major J. M., 43, 44, 107.
Henderson, Lieutenant R., 235.
Henderson, Major, 243.
Hendry, Major A. F., 270.
Henry, Lieutenant, 122.
Hewan, Sergeant, 227.
Highland Light Infantry of Canada, 231, 235, 236.
Highland Reconnaissance Regiment, 136.
Hightens, Private S., 50.
Hitler, 205, 245, 246.
Hogg, Captain, 220.
Home, Captain, 163.
Hopwood, Lt.-Colonel J., 126, 144, 154, 168, 188, 199, 208, 215, 219, 220, 231.
Horne, Lt.-Colonel R. D., 66, 89, 107.
Horrocks, Lt.-General B. G., 202, 227, 231, 239, 260.
Houldsworth, Brigadier H., 33, 50, 51, 60.
Houldsworth, Captain, 60.
Hunter, Sergeant C., 68.
Hussars, The 11th, 67.
Hutchison, Major B., 124, 125.
Hyland, Private J., 119.

Place Names

Haarsteeg, 191, 192.
Halder, 188.
Halfaya Pass, 54.
Halsche River, 187, 188.
Hamma, El, 85.
Hammam, El, 31.
Hekkens, 217, 218, 219, 220, 221.
Helmond, 186.
Heronvillette, 142, 144.
Hervost, 221, 223.
Heyhuijzen, 195.
Hodister, 208.
Hollands Hof, 241.
Homs, 21, 55, 57, 63, 64, 69.
Honnepel, 231, 233.
Hooge, 189.
"Horseshoe," 79.
Horst, 189.
Hotton, 205, 207.

INDEX

Houffalize, 207.
Hubermont, 210.

I

Persons

Imrie, Lt.-Colonel H. Blair, 162, 163.
Innes, Lt.-Colonel B., 247, 254.
Irvine, Lt.-Colonel C., 46, 208, 214, 223, 236, 254.

Place Names

Iazzovechio Farm, 122.
" Island, The," 190, 191, 200, 201, 202.
Isselburg, 241, 245.
Issel River, 241.

J

Persons

Jackson, Lieutenant, 46.
Jamieson, Captain, 161.
Jardyne, Captain, 46.
Jarvis, Private, 157.
Jeffrey, Sergeant J., 69.
Johnston, Corporal J., 69.
Johnstone, Captain D., 42.
Jolly, Lt.-Colonel A., 154.
Jones, Sergeant C., 69.

No Place Names

K

Persons and Units

Kensington Regiment, 8, 13.
Keogh, Captain, 43.
Kemlo, Sergeant A., 81.
Kermack, Captain D., 233.
Kerr, Colonel, 243.
Kerr, Private J., 201.
King George VI., H.M., 101, 102, 258.
Kippenberger, Brigadier, 39, 41, 73.
Kyle, Captain, 224.

Place Names

Kendel River, 217, 225, 226.
Kessel, 217, 220.
Khatatba, 29.
Klein Esserden, 231, 235, 236.
Ksibia, 79.

L

Persons and Units

Lake, Lance-Corporal, 40.
Landing Craft, Types of, 103.
Lang, Lt.-Colonel D. B., 148, 166, 173, 187, 199, 210, 215, 240, 253.
Le Clerc, General, 96.
Le Mesurier, Lieutenant J. R., 218.
Lee, Major A. W., 240.
Leese, General O., 23, 32, 56, 58, 66, 74, 83, 95, 126, 129.
Leslie, Lt.-Colonel N. D., 122, 240.
Levack, Lt.-Colonel D. P., 7.
Lindsay, Major M., 136, 208, 216, 217, 238.
Linklater, Eric, 5, 18, 267.
Lorrbond, Major T. R., 157.
Lothians and Border Horse, 7, 12, 14, 175, 227.
Low, Lance-Corporal, 118.
Lowe, Major K. A., 215.

Place Names

La Bû-sur-Rouvres, 162, 166.
La Chausée, 12.
La Forge Vallée, 165.
Laroche, 207, 208, 209, 210, 212.
Le Godet, 168.
Le Havre, 4, 5, 12, 13, 15, 160, 171, 172, 173, 175, 176, 178, 179.
Le Mans, 152.
Le Tréport, 12.
Lek River, 200, 201.
Lentini, 110.
Leonforte, 121.
Leptis Magna, 63.
Lezarde River, 176.
Liège, 205, 206, 207, 212.
Lille, 7.
Lillebourne, 13.
Linguaglossa, 128.
Lisieux, 159, 162, 164, 165, 166, 172.
Longueval, 143, 144, 145, 147.

Loon op Zand, 189.
Lorquichon, 158.
Louvain, 205.

M

Persons and Units

Macalister, Lt.-Colonel R., 121.
Macbeath, Lance-Corporal D., 50.
Macbride, Lance-Corporal, 242.
MacDonald, Lance-Corporal A., 173.
Macdonald, Lance-Corporal W., 100.
Macdougall, Major J. L., 40, 87, 116.
MacIntosh, Lieutenant J., 111.
Macintosh-Walker, Major R., 17.
MacKay, Sergeant H., 50.
MacKay, Captain, 174.
Mackenzie Ian, 90.
Mackenzie, Sergeant, 90.
Mackenzie, Sergeant A., 143.
MacKessack, Lt.-Colonel K., 33, 46.
MacKinnon, Lt.-Colonel A., 188, 192, 215, 224, 233, 254.
MacKinnon, Private, 111.
MacLean, Piper J., 173.
Macleod, Captain A. M., 122.
MacMillan, Brigadier G. H., 103, 109, 122, 135, 240, 245, 256, 258.
MacNab, Major A. L., 177.
MacRae, C.S.M., 91.
MacRae, Sergeant A., 173.
Macrae, Captain D., 50.
MacRae, Lieutenant F. A., 50.
Maplesden, Corporal, 110.
Masefield, Dr John, 19.
Mathieson, Lt.-Colonel R., 104, 105, 116, 117.
McAllister, Lieutenant, 157.
McAndrew, Lieutenant, 77.
McClew, Sergeant, 218.
McCulloch, Private G., 43.
McGarry, C.S.M., 144.
McGowan, Corporal, 45.
McGrigor, Admiral, 102.
McHardy, Captain, 89.
McIntyre, Private D., 39.
McLauchlan, Private J., 123.
McLean, Sergeant, 110.
McLean, Piper, 196.
McNair, Captain, 238.
McNeil, Piper R., 173.
McNeill, Captain, 44.
McPhail, Lance-Corporal, 144.
Meiklejohn, Lt.-Colonel J., 40, 144, 154, 168.
Melville, Major, 70, 200.

Middlesex Regiment, 35, 47, 62, 66, 67, 79, 86, 91, 103, 110, 122, 123, 126, 143, 159, 184, 233, 235.
Miers, Lt.-Colonel R., 50, 63, 91, 104.
Miller, Captain L. W., 63.
Milligan, Captain R., 144.
Milne, Captain D. W., 177.
Milton, Sergeant, 81.
Mitchell, Lieutenant, 159.
Mitchell, Corporal, 90.
Molteno, Major I., 221.
Moncrieffe, Private, 159.
Monro, Lt.-Colonel A., 122, 142.
Montgomery, General B., 20, 23 *et seq.*
Morshead, General, 31.
Munro, Major R. M., 200.
Murray, Lt.-Colonel T. P. E., 7, 33.
Murray, Brigadier G., 33, 49, 50, 63, 66, 100, 103, 118.
Murray, Brigadier H., 43, 44, 104, 105, 112, 136, 138, 139, 160.
Murray, Captain G., 158.

Place Names

Maas (Meuse) River, 6, 184, 186, 187, 189, 190, 191, 192, 193, 194, 195, 200, 202, 205, 207, 213, 230.
Maestricht, 205, 206.
Maginot Line, 5 *et seq.*
Mahares, 93.
Malta, 103, 104.
Mauny, 172, 173.
" Marble Arch," 60.
Marche, 205, 207, 210.
Mareth, 56, 71, 75, 77, 78, 80, 81, 94.
Marolles, 168.
Martuba, 54, 56.
Massa Parlata, 126.
Matmata Range, 75, 80.
Matratin Wadi, 55, 60.
Medinine, 56, 77, 80, 113.
Melah Wadi, 80.
Mena, 29.
Mersa Brega, 56, 58, 60, 69.
Messina, 102, 121, 127.
Metz, 8.
Mierchamps, 210.
Milo, 128.
Mira Wadi, 61.
Mirbat-Kamli Cross-roads, 46.
Misurata, 57, 62, 63.
Miteirya Ridge, 41.
Mittelburg, 240.
Monaci River, 113.
Monaster, 96.

INDEX

Monchaux, 12.
Montevilliers, 176.
Montgeon Forest, 176.

Maps

Abbeville and St Valéry, 1940, 11.
Port Tewfik–El Alamein, 28.
Battle of Alamein — Night, 23rd-24th October 1942, 34.
Operations, December 1942-23rd January 1943, 59.
Operations, Homs-Wadi Genima, January 1943, 65.
Operations, February-May 1943, 76.
Battle of Wadi Akarit, 6th April 1943, 84.
Campaign in Sicily, 10th July-20th August 1943, 114.
Normandy, D Day, and St Sylvain, 9th August 1944, 146.
La Bû-sur-Rouvres, Lisieux, August 1944, 167.
Wilhelmina Canal, Vught, Geertruidenberg, 185.
Nederweert, Baarlo, November 1944, 198.
The Island, 28th November-19th December 1944, 203.
The Ardennes, January 1945, 211.
The Reichswald, February 1945, 222.
The Rhine Crossing, 23rd March 1945, 234.
Enschede, Westertimke, April 1945, 250.
Bremervörde, 1st May. The Final Surrender, 5th May 1945, 259.

N

Persons and Units

Napier, Major, 81.
Nichols, Lt.-Colonel, 243.
Nicol, Private D., 124, 125.
Nicoll, Lt.-Colonel D., 168, 192.
Niven, Corporal J., 45.
Noble, Major C. A., 110, 148.
Northamptonshire Yeomanry, 153, 154, 157, 168, 178, 209, 230, 242.
Nova Scotia Highlanders, 236.

Place Names

Nab, El, 66, 69.
Namur, 207.
Nederweert, 195, 199.
Neufchâtel, 10, 13.
Niers River, 216, 217, 219, 220, 225.
Nieuwkuijk, 191, 192.
Nijmegen, 182, 183, 186, 194, 200, 201, 202, 205, 213, 230.
Nisramont, 210.
Norder Canal, 195, 196.
Noto, 102, 105, 107, 108.

O

Persons and Units

Oliver, Brigadier J., 33, 88, 105, 116, 121, 126, 136, 154, 178, 180, 181, 182, 183, 199, 214, 218, 233, 240, 242, 249, 255, 256, 258.
Orr-Ewing, 2nd Lieutenant A., 9.
Oxfordshire and Buckinghamshire Light Infantry, 158.

Place Names

Olland, 187, 188.
Onder, 197.
Orel, 254.
Orne River, 138, 141, 143, 144, 145.
Ornemouth, 138.
Ortho, 209.
Oste River, 253.
Oues-Ca Wadi, 61.
Ourthe River, 207, 208.

P

Persons

Palmer, R.S.M., 163.
Parker, Major A. N., 177, 187.
Paterson, Corporal N., 111.
Paton, Major, 44.
Patton, General, 75.
Playfair, "Bunny," 72.
Pooley, Major K. W., 119, 120.

Place Names

Pachino, 102, 105, 106, 107.
Palagonia, 113.
Palazzolo, 103, 105, 106, 107.
Paris, 138, 172.
Paterno, 122, 129.

Pegasus Bridge, 140, 141.
Percy, 162.
Pietraperciata, 126.
Pisano, 128.
Point 112, 89, 90.
Point 198, 88, 89, 90.
Point 224, 122, 123.
Portopalo Bay, 103, 106.
Portsmouth, 138.
Poussy, 158.

Q

No Persons and Units

Place Names

Quassassin, 27.
Quattara Depression, 30.

R

Persons and Units

Rae, Lieutenant B., 45.
Rainer, Major P. W., 93.
Raspe, Lt.-General, 257, 258.
Reconnaissance Regiment, 33, 52, 209, 248.
Redican, Private, 162.
Reilly, Signalman, 243.
Rennie, Colonel Lloyd, 26, 33.
Rennie, Major-General T. G., 14, 17, 61, 104, 116, 122, 126, 127, 135, 136, 138, 150, 151, 154, 170, 174, 176, 190, 202, 207, 218, 230, 239, 245.
Renny, Lt.-Colonel G. D., 173, 178, 187, 196, 208.
Reynolds, Gunner G., 69.
Reynolds-Payne, Lieutenant, 81.
Richards, Brigadier, 66.
Rifle Brigade, The, 58.
Ritchie, Lieutenant, 46.
Ritchie, Lt.-General N. M., 19, 20, 24, 186, 231, 260.
Robertson, 2nd Lieutenant, 46.
Rollo, Major T. L., 233.
Rommel, General, 15, 16, 29, 30, 53, 56, 75, 78, 80.
Roper-Caldbeck, Lt.-Colonel, 33, 88, 104.
Ross, Major G., 101.
Roth, Major-General, 257.

Routledge, Major J. S., 117.
Royal Air Force, 57, 61, 70, 80, 94, 96, 98, 169, 182, 237.
Royal Army Medical Corps, 2, 52.
  152nd Field Ambulance, 7.
  153rd Field Ambulance, 7.
  154th Field Ambulance, 7, 13.
  174th Field Ambulance, 103.
  175th Field Ambulance, 125.
  176th Field Ambulance, 103, 239.
Royal Army Ordnance Corps, 2, 8.
Royal Army Service Corps, 2, 8, 70, 183.
Royal Artillery, 2, 119, 157, 251.
  Anti-Tank Regiments—
    51st, 7, 13.
    61st, 66.
    241st (Battery), 86.
    243rd (Battery), 184.
  Field Regiments—
    17th, 7, 13.
    23rd, 7.
    75th, 7, 13.
    76th, 7.
    77th, 7.
    97th, 8.
    126th, 61, 64, 125, 251.
    127th (Highland), 69, 77.
    128th, 52, 123.
    456th (Battery), 103.
    492nd (Highland Battery), 199.
  Horse Artillery—
    1st, 8.
    11th, 103.
  Medium Regiments—
    51st, 8.
  Mountain Battery—
    454th, 238.
  Scottish Horse, 125.
Royal Botha Regiment, 40.
Royal Corps of Signals, 2.
  51st Divisional Signals Company, 7, 52.
R.E.M.E., 2.
Royal Engineers, 38, 45, 71, 86, 139, 145, 225, 226.
  26th Field Company, 7.
  213th Field Company, 8.
  236th Field Company, 7.
  237th Field Company, 7, 13.
  239th Field Park Company, 7, 13, 120.
  244th Field Company, 103.
  274th Field Company, 52, 69, 169.
  275th Field Company, 103, 111, 169.
Royal Marines, 121.
Royal Navy, 98, 100, 105, 141.
Royal Norfolk Regiment, 8, 14.
Royal Northumberland Fusiliers, 8.
Royal Scots Fusiliers, 8, 12, 13.

Royal Sussex Regiment, 45, 248.
Royal Tank Regiments—
  40th, 62, 64, 67, 86.
  46th, 117.
  50th, 33, 50, 103, 118.
  107th, 227.
  144th, 153, 154, 157.
  148th, 153, 154.
Royal Ulster Rifles, 247.
Rundsted, General Von, 212.
Russell, Major D., 41, 178.

Place Names

Raamsdonk, 190.
Ragil Depression, 30.
Ragusa, 108.
Ramacca, 113.
Ranville, 141, 142, 144.
Rees, 231, 236, 237, 238, 239, 240.
Reggio, 127.
Reichswald Forest, 213, 214, 215, 216, 217, 218, 219, 220, 227.
Rhine, River, 202, 213, 229 *et seq.*
Ringstedt, 256.
Robertmesnil, 158, 159.
Roermond, 191, 194, 230.
Ronchamps, 210.
Rosalini, 107.
Rouen, 173.
Roumana Ridge, 85, 86, 87, 88, 91.
Roupage, 209.

S

Persons and Units

Samwell, Major P., 209.
Sands, Private C., 143.
Saunders, Lt.-Colonel H. W. B., 33, 45, 46, 47.
Scott, Captain, 124, 125.
Scott, Brigadier H., 153.
Scottish Horse, 228.
Seaforth Highlanders—
  2nd Battalion, 7, 10, 19, 33, 46, 47, 50, 63, 64, 66, 67, 69, 86, 88, 89, 91, 107, 109, 110, 122, 128, 142, 148, 158, 187, 189, 191, 195, 196, 210, 216, 218, 221, 224, 226, 230, 231, 240, 241, 248, 251, 253.
  4th Battalion, 7, 10, 14, 17.
  5th Battalion, 33, 42, 50, 60, 63, 66, 67, 82, 85, 86, 88, 89, 91, 107, 108, 109, 122, 123, 128, 140, 142, 143, 147, 148, 158, 165, 166, 173, 177, 184, 186, 187, 189, 191, 196, 200, 210, 216, 218, 221, 226, 240, 242, 248, 253.
  6th Battalion, 7, 128.
Serocold, Lt.-Colonel P., 169, 248.
Sharp, Captain, 46.
Sherwood Foresters, 12.
Shiel, Brigadier J., 123, 158, 183, 251.
Simon, Viscount, 104.
Simonds, Lt.-General G., 153, 245.
Simpson, General, 206.
Sinclair, Brigadier R., 160, 216, 228, 236, 247.
Skivington, Captain, 44.
Sleeth, Lance-Corporal H., 47.
Smail, Lt.-Colonel H. M., 7.
Small, Major S., 226.
Smith, Sergeant, 40.
Smith, Private J., 41.
Smith, Private, 90.
Smith, Sergeant A., 111.
Smith, Corporal, 118.
Smith, Sapper K. H., 120.
Smith, Private, 219.
Sorel-Cameron, Lt.-Colonel, 104, 107, 110.
South Lancashire Regiment, 248.
Staffordshire Yeomanry, 232, 248.
Stanley-Clarke, Brigadier A. C. L., 7, 13.
Stephenson, Lt.-Colonel, 35, 47.
Stephenson, Sergeant, 45.
Stenton, Private W., 119.
Stevenson, Lt.-Colonel, 147.
Stevenson, Sergeant, 168.
Stewart, Brigadier H. W. V., 7.
Stewart, Private G., 80, 81.
Stewart, Captain, 239.
Stirling, Lt.-Colonel, 33, 35, 61, 63, 64, 104.
Stuart, Lieutenant, 45.
Sudan Defence Force, 62, 63.
Sugden, Lt. Colonel, 71, 77, 225.
Supercharge Force, 42.
Swinburn, Lt.-Colonel, 7.
Sym, Lt.-Colonel J. M., 216, 240, 242, 253.

Place Names

Saar, 6.
Sallenelles, 144.
Salso River, 129.
Schijndel, 187, 188, 192.
Scordia, 110, 113.
Secqueville, 154, 159.

Seine River, 15, 172.
Sfax, 77, 80, 85, 86, 93, 94, 101.
Sferro, 118, 119, 120, 121, 125, 126, 129, 130.
s'Hertogenbosch, 187, 188, 190, 191, 192, 200, 202.
Sicily, 96 *et seq*.
Siebengewald, 226.
Siegfried Line, 6, 172, 214, 218, 227.
Simeto River, 113, 115, 122, 123, 126.
Siracusa, 102, 108.
Snout, The, 96.
Soliers, 159.
Sollum, 54, 55.
Sousse, 77, 80, 86, 94, 96, 101, 103, 121.
Southampton, 15.
Speldrop, 231, 235.
Spezia, Mount, 126, 127.
Stalag 383, 18.
St Aignan, 154, 157.
St Honorine, 142, 143, 144, 147.
St Julien, 164, 166, 168.
St Lo, 152.
St Maclou, 161.
St Oedenrode, 181, 182, 186, 187.
St Piérre-le-Viger, 13.
St Piérre, 162, 166.
St Sylvain, 159, 161.
St Valéry-en-Caux, 5, 10, 13, 14, 15, 16, 17, 170, 171, 172, 173, 174, 175, 176, 269.
St Valéry-sur-Somme, 10.
St Vith, 206.
Strada di Palermo, 123.

T

Persons

Taylor, Major P., 197, 215, 219.
Taylor, Lance-Corporal R., 106.
Tedder, Air Chief Marshal Lord, 97.
Thicknesse, Lt.-Colonel T., 61, 251.
Thoma, General Von, 49.
Thomas, Captain V., 110.
Thompson, Corporal, 90.
Thomson, Captain, 43.
Thomson, Private A., 109.
Thomson, Major A. J., 224.
Thomson, Lt.-Colonel C., 90, 107, 112, 118, 119, 138, 139, 140, 142, 160.
Thornton, Major J., 161.
Tilly, Captain D., 199.
Todd, Major A., 221.
Travena, Private J., 116, 117.
Tweedie Lieutenant, 239.

Place Names

Takrouna Village, 96.
Tamet, 62.
Tarhuna, 57.
Tel el Aqqaqir, 40, 50.
Thomashof, 224.
Tilburg, 184, 187.
Tilly-la-Campagne, 158.
Tobruk, 54, 56.
Touffreville, 141.
" Triangle, The," 141, 144, 147, 148.
Tripoli, 36, 55, 56, 61, 67, 70, 72, 77, 102.
Troarn, 143, 148.
Tunis, 80, 94, 95, 96, 97.
Turcisi, Mount, 122.

U

Persons

Urquhart, Colonel R., 27, 102, 104.

Place Names

Uitwaterings (Zig) Canal, 199, 200.

V

Persons

Van Rockel, Lieutenant, 225.
Viney, Lieutenant, 189.

Place Names

Valetta, 104, 105.
Varempage, 209.
Varenne River, 12, 13.
Varennes, 10.
Venlo, 191, 194, 200.
Veules-les-Roses, 14, 173, 174.
Viccini, 103, 112.
Vie River, 162, 164, 165, 166.
Vlijmen, 191.
Vught, 188, 189, 190.

INDEX

W

Persons and Units

Waddell, Lieutenant, 118.
Wade's Highland Companies, 2.
Walford, Lt.-Colonel, 82, 107, 109, 123, 140, 147, 165, 173, 187, 216.
Walsh, Brigadier, 95.
Watkins, Lieutenant O. H., 165.
Watt, Sergeant, 162.
Wedderburn, Captain (Rev.) D., 120.
Wedon, Sergeant, 111.
Welch Regiment, 186, 199.
Williamson, Lieutenant, 43.
Williamson, Lt.-Colonel T. C., 154.
Williamson, Captain W. O., 181.
Willock, Corporal 90.
Wilmot, Chester, 196.
Wilmot, Sir A., 32.
Wilson, Sergeant, 81.
Wimberley, General D. N., 19-133, 136, 269, 270.
Wingate-Gray, Captain W., 117, 181.
Wrampling, Lieutenant, 123.
Wright, Corporal, 233.

Place Names

Waal River, 200, 201.
Waalwijk, 190.
Walcheren, 180, 184.
Waspik, 189, 192.
Weert, 191, 194.
Wessem Canal, 195, 196.
Wijbosch, 187.
Wilhelmina Canal, 182, 184.
Wormhoudt, 180.

Y

Persons

Young, Lt.-Colonel D., 152.
Young, Desmond, 15.

No Place Names

Z

No Persons and Units

Place Names

Zafferrana, 129.
Zaret, 79.
Zeelst, 182, 183.
Zelen, 200.
Zemzen Wadi, 61.
Zenadi Wadi, 64.
Zessar Wadi, 80, 81.
Zeuss Wadi, 80, 81, 82.
Zigzaou Wadi, 71, 79, 80, 82, 83.
Zliten Valley, 55, 63.
Zuidwilhelms Canal, 187, 188

SECOND WORLD WAR
BRITISH DIVISIONAL HISTORIES

All Written Shortly After The Cessation Of Hostilities

Authoritative and scholarly they are essential to any serious study of the Second World War

THE FOURTH DIVISION 1939 to 1945

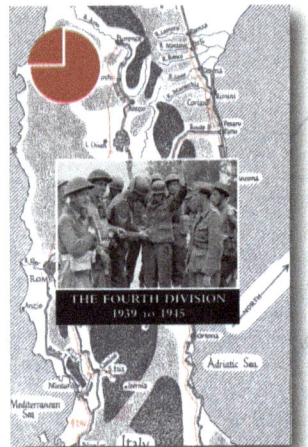

The British Fourth Division was engaged in World War Two from beginning to end. It was part of the BEF in 1939, left France from Dunkirk in 1940, moved to Tunisia and fought throughout the campaign in Africa. It then moved to Italy fighting all the way up the Italian mainland to Forli and Faenza before being sent off to Greece to aid the civil power during the Greek Civil War. It was an honourable division which through the fortunes of war did not take part in the great adventure in Normandy, being thereby consigned to the relative background in the military history of the Second World War. Such divisions are unjustly given less attention than those which were chosen for Overlord, but their histories are none the less of great importance. This history is one of those narratives. The book is illustrated with a number of photographs and a good set of maps.

SB 9781474536646

HB 9781474536943

THE FIFTH BRITISH DIVISION 1939-1945

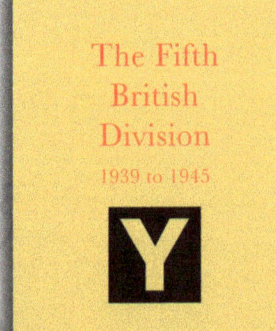

The story of the Fifth British Division 1939-1945 begins with the division in the BEF in France in 1940 which it joined from reserve division status. It returned to the UK and underwent training before taking part in the Madagascar operation. Then it went to India and Persia before moving to the Middle East Theatre in 1943 where it took part in the conquest of Sicily before moving into Italy. It fought through much of the Italian Campaign before finishing the war in Lubeck, having made the final move to France and then Germany shortly before the end of the war.

SB 9781783316083

HB 9781783316649

TAURUS PURSUANT
A HISTORY OF 11TH ARMOURED DIVISION

11th Armoured Division is widely recognised as one of the best British armoured divisions in the Second World War, earning its spurs in all of the most famous actions of the North West European campaign and commanded by the desert legend Pip Roberts. Originally printed in occupied Germany soon after WW2 had finished, this is an excellent Divisional History, with good, clear colour maps and a well written narrative. A Roll of Honour by regiment (Name, Date and Place) completes this fine history.

SB 9781783315611
HB 9781783316663

43RD WESSEX DIVISION AT WAR 1944-1945

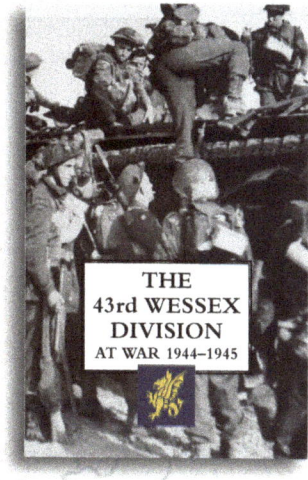

This is the story of the 43rd Division from its arrival in France during Operation Overlord in June 1944 through to the end of the war with Germany. It relates how the division fought and where, and is illustrated with 21 maps. The division was engaged on the River Odon, and at Hill 112, then in the Seine crossing, the attempted relief at Arnhem, at Groesbeek, in Operation Blackcock and the advance to Goch and Xanten. It also took part in the Battle of the Rhineland and in Operations Plunder and Varsity and made its final move to capture Bremen in 1945. A very readable and an important Divisional History.

SB 9781783316076
HB 9781783316571

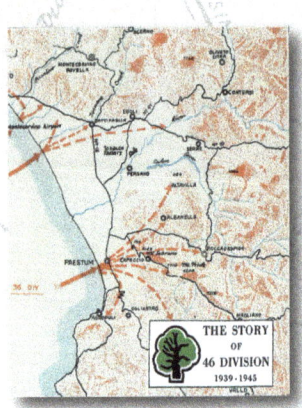

THE STORY OF 46 DIVISION, 1939-1945

Although not one of the D-Day Divisions, like many other formations, it was fundamental to the success of the broad plans for the direction of the war. The fighting in North Africa and Italy is detailed. Good photos, coloured maps, rolls of commands, staff, awards, and an Order of Battle complete this very good contemporary Infantry Divisional that is scarce in its original 1948 printing.

SB 9781783316335
HB 9781783316564

THE PATH OF THE 50TH

THE STORY OF THE 50TH (NORTHUMBERLAND) DIVISION IN THE SECOND WORLD WAR 1939-1945

This is a very valuable history of the 50th (Northumberland) Division in the Second World War. The division fought in France, North Africa, Sicily, and took part in the D-Day landings, finally ending the war in Holland. illustrated with photographs and maps.

SB 9781783316090
HB 9781783316632

THE HISTORY OF THE 51ST HIGHLAND DIVISION 1939-1945

The 51st Highland Division fought and lost in France in 1940, was reborn, and fought and won in the North African desert, Sicily and finally in North Western Europe from D-Day to the end of the war. As a division the men earned the respect of friend and foe alike, and this is their story. Amply illustrated with 36 photographs, 18 maps and battle plans (many coloured) that help the reader to follow the course of the conflict. A good index (persons, units and place names) and a statistical battle casualties list complete this good WW2 Divisional History.

SB 9781474536660
HB 9781474536950

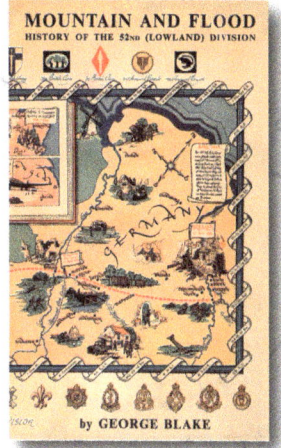

MOUNTAIN AND FLOOD
THE HISTORY OF 52ND (LOWLAND) DIVISION

The 52nd Lowland Division was one of very few "special" divisions of infantry, in that it was trained for mountain warfare, although it spent much time after D-Day locked in battle on the flat lands of the North European coastal plain. This history of the division starts before the war in England, and goes on to describe operations in France in 1940. For four years they then trained and waited, before forming part of 21st Army group, and fighting the Germans in France, Holland and Germany. As with all good divisional histories, it is the story of men in battle that counts, and this volume is no exception.

SB 9781783316069
HB 9781783316588

THE STORY OF THE 79TH ARMOURED DIVISION OCTOBER 1942 - JUNE 1945

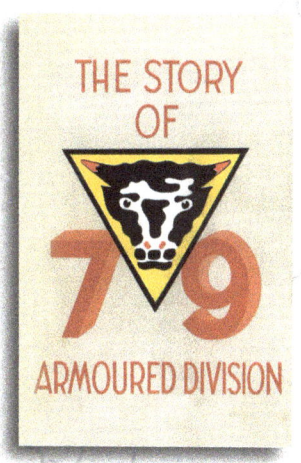

A magnificent and fully illustrated official history of Britain's 79th Armoured Division - the specialised unit which developed and operated 'Hobart's Funnies', the adapted tanks which carried out a range of tasks on D-Day and after ranging from mine clearance to bridge laying. Follows the unit from its formation to victory in Europe.

SB 9781783310395
HB 9781783316731

www.naval-military-press.com

The Naval & Military Press offer specialist books and ground breaking CD-ROMs for the serious student of conflict. Our hand picked range of books covers the whole spectrum of military history with titles on uniforms, battles, official and regimental histories, specialist works containing medal rolls and casualties lists as well as titles for genealogists, medal collectors and researchers.

The innovative approach we have to military bookselling and our commitment to publishing have made us Britain's leading independent military bookseller.

www.naval-military-press.com

www.ingramcontent.com/pod-product-compliance
Lightning Source LLC
Chambersburg PA
CBHW061123010526
44114CB00029B/2995